OMA's Kunsthal in Rotterdam
Rem Koolhaas and the New Europe

OMA's Kunsthal in Rotterdam
Rem Koolhaas and the New Europe

Tibor Pataky

PARK BOOKS

Contents

7   **Acknowledgments**

        Plates 1.1–1.18
        Kunsthal, Legnani/Cappelletti 2017

37   **Introduction**

        Plates 2.1–2.8
        Rotterdam's Dijkzigt Area

61   **1—Doom and Gloom**
        OMA in the 1980s

        Plates 3.1–3.6
        OMA/Rem Koolhaas, Museumpark Rotterdam

97   **2—The Better Half of Architecture**
        OMA's Museumpark

        Plates 4.1–4.12
        OMA/Rem Koolhaas, Kunsthal I and NAi, 1988

145   **3—An Overdue Crisis**
        Kunsthal I, the NAi, and Deconstructivist Architecture

        Plates 5.1–5.8
        OMA/Rem Koolhaas, Kunsthal II, November/December 1988

197   **4—Squaring the Circle**
        Kunsthal II: The Scheme of December 1988

        Plates 6.1–6.14
        OMA/Rem Koolhaas, Kunsthal, January/February 1989

245   **5—Modernism Obsolete**
        A New Approach for a New Europe

        Plates 7.1–7.14
        OMA/Rem Koolhaas, Kunsthal, April 19, 1990

293   **6—Fragmentations**
        The Development of the Design 1989–92

        Plates 8.1–8.18
        OMA/Rem Koolhaas, Kunsthal, the construction site and completed building

377   **7—Excess Is Always a Bearer of Consciousness**
        The Building of October 1992

        Plates 9.1–9.14
        Kunsthal, new drawings

417   **Appendix**

Acknowledgments

In retrospect, four individuals have been pivotal in determining my approach to architectural history: Bernardo Secchi, who stirred my interest in the history and theory of architecture through his lectures at Università Iuav di Venezia; architects Lorenzo Giuliani and Christian Hönger, who introduced me to the art of building at their offices in Zurich; and Markus Peter, who introduced me to writing about construction. While I was his assistant at ETH Zurich it was his research that taught me to look at construction as a "battleground of architectural theory" rather than as a craft.

I owe deep thanks to Christophe Van Gerrewey for his generosity, persistent support, criticism, and trust in supervising the doctoral thesis upon which this book is based. I am similarly grateful to Roberto Gargiani, Martino Stierli, and Pier Vittorio Aureli for their comments and advice. Thanks also to student assistants Romain Barth and Alice Biber for their commitment to drawings of the Kunsthal. Further, I would like to thank Fuminori Hoshino for sharing his recollections and thoughts in a series of particularly intense and enriching conversations. Thanks to Rem Koolhaas (also for his generous support), Petra Blaisse, Toni Adam, Gregor Mescherowsky, Koos Hage, Wim van Krimpen, Kees Christiaanse, Mike Guyer, Oliver Lütjens, Christine Enzmann Giuliani, and Job Floris. I am indebted to each of them for the valuable clues, insights, and ideas that emerged from our conversations and correspondence.

I thank the Swiss National Science Foundation for funding the research and for supporting this book with a grant. Furthermore, I am thankful for the financial support of the Lab of Architecture, Criticism, History, and Theory at EPFL Lausanne. Special thanks go to the staff at Het Nieuwe Instituut, Stadsarchief Rotterdam, and to Annemarie Nigten of Kunsthal Rotterdam for granting access to the latter. Thanks also to the staff at the Stadsontwikkeling department in Rotterdam, the OMA Archives in Rotterdam, Arup's London archives, Inside Outside in Amsterdam, the architecture collection of the Centre Pompidou in Paris, and the library at EPFL.

Three more people have contributed to this book in ways that are as significant as they are different: Thomas Padmanabhan during numerous conversations filled with curiosity and astute comments; Michelangelo Sabatino as a mentor of strategic choices; and of course my wife Barbara for the thousand acts of kindness that only a daily companion can provide.

P 1.1   The building along Westzeedijk.

P 1.2 South facade.

P 1.3 Detail of the portico.

P 1.4   Detail of the portico and east facade.

P 1.5   East facade.

P 1.6   Detail of the north facade.

P 1.7   West facade and Blue Plaza.

P 1.8 Hellingstraat. (→ next page, left)
P 1.9 The original main entrance along Hellingstraat. (→ next page, right)

P 1.10 Entrance hall and auditorium.

P 1.11 Auditorium and restaurant seen from the balcony next to the original main entrance.

P 1.12 Hall 1. (right)

P 1.13 Hall 2. (← previous page, left)
P 1.14 Hall 2. Detail of the ceiling. (← previous page, right)
P 1.15 Hall 2. Passage to the eastern exhibition halls.

P 1.16 Left: stepped ramp ascending to the roof. Right: auditorium.

P 1.17 Roof garden. Background: buildings along Westzeedijk.

P 1.18 Restaurant. Ceiling: light sculpture by Günther Förg.

Introduction

... it is tempting to see a connection between the modernization of Paris put through by Napoleon III and his henchmen—in particular by his prefect of the Seine, Baron Haussmann—and the new painting of the time.

T. J. Clark

If Manet's paintings reflect societal transformations in the Paris of the second half of the nineteenth century, the Kunsthal in Rotterdam by OMA/Rem Koolhaas is a building with similar qualities. It reflects socioeconomic and political transformations of epochal proportions: the transition from the Cold War to globalization, from Western post-1968 defeatism to the "end of history," from the welfare state and a split Europe to neoliberalism and the European Union. It considers the state of architecture in the late 1980s, questioning postmodernism as much as deconstructivism and the emulation of modernist masters. The Kunsthal foreshadows the new: the era of the "iconic" and the "diagram" along with a profound transformation in production at OMA during the 1990s. This book seeks to present the exceptional wealth and creativity of the design's response to its sociopolitical and architectural context.

Rem Koolhaas—cofounder of the Office for Metropolitan Architecture (OMA)—has always been a keen observer of his time, responding quickly to what he perceives, often with far-reaching consequences for his work. In the course of the 1970s, 1980s, and early 1990s he would rail against rationalism, contextualism, postmodern and deconstructivist architecture, Dutch structuralism, and the movements advocating the reconstruction of the European city. He would side with the dynamics of modernization, American popular culture, hedonism, and European integration, asking his peers to draw the ideological consequences of the "disappearance of socialism" five months after the events of November 1989. The Kunsthal, planned and built between 1987 and 1992, reflects the context of its origin essentially through the lens of this responsiveness. It is this kind of refraction that underlies the architecture as an "image" of the transition from the EEC to a united Europe, from the "long 1970s" to the neoliberal turn of the 1990s, and from the old to the new OMA.

In *OMA's Kunsthal* I tell the entwined stories of the arts center's genesis and the reconfiguration of Koolhaas' oppositions, concerns, and fascinations, which led to a radical revision of his approach to architecture and urbanism at the turn of the 1990s. The narrative combines a sweeping look at the broader historical context with a close study of the project itself: its origins, the client, the brief, and how it developed. For this it draws on two types of sources: on the one hand, the pertinent literature—on postmodernism at large, European integration, the architecture and architectural debates of the 1980s, Rem Koolhaas, and the work of OMA—and, on the other hand, a vast number of archival documents on the Kunsthal project that are to this day largely unexploited, along with a series of interviews I conducted with several protagonists involved in the project both at OMA and externally. On this basis I will reconstruct in some detail the inner logic of the design and its development from the first sketches through to the completed building. Separate chapters address OMA's Museumpark (1987–93) and its competition entry for the Netherlands Architecture Institute, known as NAi (1988). All three projects were designed parallel to each other for the same site, with the Kunsthal and the NAi— eventually built by Jo Coenen—located at opposite ends of the park.[1] As will be seen, the final scheme for the Kunsthal (Kunsthal II) relates to Museumpark, the NAi, and a first project for the Kunsthal (Kunsthal I) much like a synthesis in a chain of dialectical progression. Illustrations—images of the surviving sketches, drawings, and working models— will help to reveal the wealth of ideas the architects produced along this route. Contemporary photographs and a new, research-based set of drawings (→ P 9.1–9.14) allow us to reimagine the building as it was when completed in 1992. Photographs by Delfino Sisto Legnani and Marco Cappelletti show the building after it had been renovated, likewise by OMA, in 2013–14.

The voice of the project

In 2002, Joan Ockman identified Rem Koolhaas as "undoubtedly the prepotent intellectual force in the architectural world and the most visionary architectural thinker to emerge from the disenchanted generation of '68."[2] Her assessment bespeaks the fact that Koolhaas has often been seen as an intellectual, a thinker, a theorist, and an author rather than as an architect who builds things. Over the past five decades, his writings, talks, and the interviews he has given have grown into a scattered body of literature that occasionally is referred to collectively as Koolhaas' theory, discourse, or thinking. Explications of OMA's approach to architecture and urbanism, specific projects along with comments on Koolhaas' writings, and their relation to his work, are an integral part of this discourse. Its impact on the reception of OMA's architecture can hardly be overestimated—and this applies both to architectural criticism and scholarly literature. Much of what has been written about the work of OMA tends to anchor its interpretations in Koolhaas' own writings and statements, keywords, phraseology, and ideas. Koolhaas' advocacy of program at the expense of form is one example, and it is of particular importance for this book.[3] Koolhaas' often-avowed ambition to strive for an architecture that is all program and no form has often been anticipated as an accomplished feat by critics and scholars alike, including the suggestion that the term "form" be abandoned altogether. In 2004, Robert Somol proposed "shape" as a counterterm, referring to then recent projects such as the CCTV Headquarters in Beijing and the Casa da Musica in Porto.[4] In his recent monograph *Projekt ohne Form* (Project Without Form) on OMA's competitions in 1989, Holger Schurk explores Koolhaas' methodical eschewal of formal concerns during the design process.[5] Sanford Kwinter does not reject the term form as such, but describes it as a side effect of programming that he calls "the geometrization of the event." "All of Koolhaas' recent work," Kwinter wrote in 1992, "is evolved—rather than designed—within the hypermodern 'event-space' of complex, sensitive, dynamical indeterminacy and change."[6] Forms, he explains, "follow and fill the wake of concrete yet unpredeterminable events."[7] Similarly, Hubert Damisch suggested a pragmatist disregard for "aesthetics" when writing in 1987 about OMA's Netherlands Dance Theater in The Hague: "If this is a collage it was in no way produced with a concern for aesthetics: it was made in order to use financial and volumetric allowances in the most economical way possible."[8] In 1996, Jeffrey Kipnis discerned in the buildings' use (its "event-structure")—as opposed to its "aesthetics"—the primary concern of Koolhaas' latest work, observing an "acceleration away from Architecture towards pure

1   Since 2013, Coenen's building has accommodated Het Nieuwe Instituut (HNI), which resulted from a fusion between the NAi and the former institutes for design and e-culture.
2   Joan Ockman, "The ¥€$ Man: Can Rem Koolhaas Make Consumerism Safe for Intellectuals?" in *Architecture*, 2 (2002), p. 78.
3   For instance, when stating in 1985: "Duiker is about form and form doesn't interest me." Mil De Kooning, "De economie van de verbeelding," in *Vlees & Beton*, 4 (1985), n.p. (author's translation).
4   Robert E. Somol, "12 Reasons to Get Back into Shape," in *Content*, eds. AMOMA/Rem Koolhaas et al., Cologne: Taschen, 2004, pp. 86–87. Somol's notion of shape builds on the essay "Notes Around the Doppler Effect and Other Moods of Modernism," which he co-authored with Sarah Whiting. It proposes replacing architecture's critical dimension with a "projective" quality that offers "alternative (not necessarily oppositional) scenarios." Robert E. Somol and Sarah Whiting, "Notes Around the Doppler Effect and Other Moods of Modernism," in *Perspecta*, 33 (2002), p. 75. In the 2004 text, Somol characterizes shape as being not only more accessible than form (opposing its graphic quality to the "rhetorical excess of form") but also more flexible, not least with regard to the requirements of the market ("shape has been commoditized"), while also taking recourse to a number of themes from Koolhaas' manifesto on "Bigness," such as the large scale and the incongruence between the interior and exterior. On Somol's argument of shape versus form, see Pier Vittorio Aureli, "Who Is Afraid of the Form-Object," in *Log*, 3 (Fall 2004), pp. 29–36.
5   Holger Schurk, *Projekt ohne Form: OMA, Rem Koolhaas und das Laboratorium von 1989*, Leipzig: Spector Books, 2020. As Schurk points out, the book's title and argument denotes "an uncommonly abstract type of architectural project which is still in the fluid state of the design process, prior to its realization as a building." Ibid., p. 8 (author's translation).
6   Sanford Kwinter, "Urbanism After Innocence: Four Projects: The Reinvention of Geometry," in *Assemblage*, 18 (1992), p. 84. Kwinter refers to OMA's masterplans for Melun-Sénart (1987), La Defense (1991), Yokohama (1992), and Euralille (1989–94).
7   Ibid., p. 85.
8   Hubert Damisch, "Cadavre exquis: Théâtre nationale de danse, La Haye," in *Architecture Mouvement Continuité*, 18 (1987), pp. 21–22.

organization."[9] With respect to OMA's scheme for the Tate Gallery in London, he explains: "It is a work of urban infrastructure whose core strategy is organization, whose techniques belong to engineering, and whose fundamental measure is not aesthetic quality, but performance over time at maximum use."[10]

I have devised this book as a reversal of the above tendency. Focusing on a single work of architecture, I will privilege the "voice of the project" over that of the author, and I will scrutinize its form, albeit form in the widest sense: not looked at in formalist isolation, but form as a means to articulate ideas and, on this basis, to relate to the changing world of which it is a part. Key to my argument are the following: formal analogies between the architecture—of the Kunsthal as much as of OMA's work at large—and its broader context of origin; the imagery and metaphors conveyed by form; the cause it implies; the vision it conjures up of the building's future use; and its critical as well as its utopian quality. It is essentially through form in this sense, I will argue, that the Kunsthal reflects its context of origin: not mechanically, "informed by its time," but creatively, and demonstrably, as the architect's conscious response. Establishing, eschewing, or obscuring formal analogies between OMA's designs and the givens of the present moment was essential for Koolhaas in intellectualizing his designs and defining his stance as an architect, especially during the 1970s and 1980s.[11]

Sources

The amount of available archival material on the Kunsthal is immense. Along with the evidence of the existing building it is treated as a primary source. The material comes from all the main parties involved in the planning process and comprises models, sketches, technical drawings, presentation drawings, plans of the structure and the building services, photographs, correspondence, minutes, reports, costs estimates, and time schedules, among other things. Since 1994, the vast majority of the models, sketches, drawings, and papers have been held by what used to be known as NAi and is now Het Nieuwe Instituut (HNI) in Rotterdam. Between 1994 and 1995, the institute's then interim director Hein van Haaren initiated the purchase of the dossier on the Kunsthal and five more projects in order to assist OMA at a point when it was experiencing severe financial difficulties.[12] Other important sources were Rotterdam's municipal archives (Stadsarchief Rotterdam) and the city's department for urban development (Stadsontwikkeling Rotterdam), which hold documents that the planning team submitted to the municipality from 1989 onwards, as well as the archives of OMA in Rotterdam and Ove Arup in London. The HNI in Rotterdam has also been the main source on Museumpark and OMA's competition entry for the NAi. Additional sources on the park were Rotterdam's municipal archives, the archives of landscape architect Petra Blaisse, and the architectural collection of the Centre Pompidou in Paris.

Structure and method

The narrative follows a broadly chronological order. Seven chapters reconstruct the genesis of the project from its origins in 1986–87 to the opening of the Kunsthal in October 1992. In each chapter, I will single out either a different stage of this process or a specific aspect of the historical backdrop, and explore if and how the architects responded to the circumstances. This often requires the volatile dynamics of the political events, the architectural debate, Koolhaas' agenda, the demands of the client, and the development of the design to be studied year by year. As an author, architect, and spokesman for OMA, Koolhaas seems to have reacted first and foremost to the present. Accordingly, much attention is devoted to the literature of the period when the project was first devised: to what Koolhaas wrote and said, to what was written about him and his work, to contemporary architectural debates, and to the museums built and discussed at the time. Regardless of their undeniable significance, later comments will be treated with caution because the intricate fabric of Koolhaas' architectural oeuvre, theoretical agenda, and conversational commentary has been subject to permanent reinterpretation—not least by Koolhaas himself. If, for example, Koolhaas patiently accepts being labeled a postmodernist in 2011,[13] or is willing to discuss the proportions of his buildings in 2018,[14] his comments appear more instructive with respect to their historical

---

9   Jeffrey Kipnis, "Recent Koolhaas," in *El Croquis*, 79 (1996), p. 34. Kipnis refers to OMA's competition entries for the Jussieu Libraries (1992), the extension of the Tate Gallery in London (1994–95), and the opera houses in Miami (1994) and Cardiff (1994). He understands "event-structure" as the "social activities and chance events, desirable or not, that an architectural setting stages or conditions. These include, but are not limited to the expressed activities of the program." Ibid., p. 30.
10 Ibid., p. 34.
11 In this, my approach is more akin to the "inclusive" criticism suggested by Michael Hays in "Critical Architecture: Between Culture and Form," in *Perspecta*, 21 (1984), and by Aureli in "Who Is Afraid of the Form-Object?" than to the above proposition by Somol and Whiting.
12 Sergio M. Figueiredo, *The NAi Effect: Creating Architecture Culture*, Rotterdam: NAi010, 2016, pp. 267–68.
13 Charles Jencks, "Radical Post-Modernism and Content," in *Architectural Design*, 5 (2011), pp. 32–45.
14 Guillaume Houzé and François Quintin, "Composer les mures de son espace," in *9 Plâtre: Lafayette Anticipations—fondation d'entreprise Galeries Lafayette: un bâtiment de OMA/Rem Koolhaas*, eds. Guillaume Houzé et al., Paris: Lafayette Anticipations, 2018, pp. 24–25.

distance from the 1980s and 1990s than to the ideas he did advocate at the time. OMA's oeuvre as a whole is marked by a series of divergent approaches and results, and the views that Koolhaas expressed about architecture over the past five decades do anything but add up to a single coherent agenda. No more than ten years separate his functionalist manifesto "Our 'New Sobriety'" from the professed need "to break with the vocabulary of modernism."[15]

As a general rule, I have taken any oral statement or text about the genesis of the Kunsthal, Museumpark, and NAi into account, albeit as clues of a secondary order. The "final say" is given to the building completed in 1992; to the models, drawings, and sketches; to the facts recorded in the minutes; and to the evidence of faxes and letters. Plausibility vis-à-vis these primary facts is the test to which any claim is put. This goes, too, for the interviews conducted and correspondence exchanged in the course of my research with protagonists who had been involved in the Kunsthal, Museumpark, and NAi projects. The recollections of former team members certainly were an important source of suggestions, hints, and insights. Oral testimony of people's own personal experience seems valuable in itself, considering how little is known about OMA's working practices, and about how Koolhaas worked—as an architect—during the first two decades of the firm's existence. Nonetheless, I have treated the information obtained as an indication of a hypothetical value rather than as actual evidence.

Conservation of matter

What has been observed with respect to OMA's oeuvre as a whole—the recurrence of themes, motifs, and concepts over multiple projects—seems to hold true too for the different stages of a single project. In the case of the Kunsthal, "borrowings" from other OMA projects and buildings are frequent, especially during the first two years. Over time, however, the design "created" its own stock of concepts and ideas. What is peculiar is how the project absorbs all of them, and how it accumulates, transforms, and juxtaposes them. Mostly, the ideas are plain and straightforward at their inception, but then gradually change to the point of becoming arcane, if not undecipherable. It is probably the privilege of reconstructing the design's development to make these ideas and concepts legible. It allows us to trace, step by step, the introduction, metamorphoses, journeys, spread, and superimposition of concepts, ideas, motifs, and themes like the layers of an MRI screening the concealed parts of a body.

Distinction

In 1985, Patrice Goulet asked Koolhaas: "To think differently, is this, for your part, the result of reflection?" Koolhaas replied: "No, it's a veritable instinct. That is completely unconscious."[16] On other occasions Koolhaas tends to reject similar observations with apparent unease. In 1998, when Jean-François Chevrier was looking back at OMA's architectural and urban agenda of the 1970s and 1980s, Koolhaas interrupted him, objecting: "You are defining a coherence that is in danger of reducing my entire career to a single, uniform formula of contradiction—anti-Archigram, anti-Rowe, anti-Jencks, anti-Palermo. But I see my career from my own point of view, and I think it is not [as] simple as that."[17] Certainly, it would be wrong to explain Koolhaas' work solely by the dynamics of opposition. His oeuvre appears to be informed at least as much by genuine fascination that is largely independent from circumstance, as, for example, is the case with Leonidov, Mies, Le Corbusier, and surrealism.

If Koolhaas does react at all, his responses seem to fall into one of two different categories. Either he contradicts, openly and fiercely, aiming at solitary opposition; or, with no less noise, he yields willingly while claiming to suffuse his surrender with the seeds of a subtle subversion. This has been often observed—for example when comparing him to a "silent dynamiter"—and it has been implied by Koolhaas himself when likening the architect to a surfer who employs the most dangerous waves for his art.[18] The two attitudes are probably seldom mentioned on the same occasion because they relate to entirely disparate spheres. The first regards his peers, while the second concerns powers outside the realm of architecture which are,

---

15 Paul Vermeulen, "Metropolitane architectuur: Projekt-Koolhaas voor Zeebrugge," in *De Standaard* (April 28–29, 1990) (author's translation).

16 Patrice Goulet, "La deuxième chance de l'architecture moderne …," in *L'Architecture d'Aujourd'hui*, 238 (1985), p. 4 (author's translation). There are numerous statements of similar content. In an interview with Léa-Catherine Szacka, Koolhaas comments on OMA's contribution to the Venice Biennale in 1980: "The text, together with our non-facade, was a way of asserting difference." Léa-Catherine Szacka, "Translucent oppositions: OMA's proposal for the 1980 Venice Architecture Biennale," in *OASE*, 94 (2015), https://www.oasejournal.nl/en/Issues/94/TranslucentOppositions (accessed July 1, 2022).

17 The interview was published only in 2005. Jean-François Chevrier, "Changing Dimensions," in *L'Architecture d'Aujourd'hui*, 361 (2005), p. 102. In 2003, Frances Hsu asked: "Why do you think that most of the things that you do or that you're telling me of seem to be against something else? You have this tendency …" Koolhaas replied: 'I don't think it [sic] a tendency to do things against [something], its [sic] more an instinct to consider that perhaps certain things which are rejected might actually contain important potentials. It's more about a kind of automatisms of judgement." Frances Hsu, "The Ends of Modernism: Structuralism and Surrealism in the Work of Rem Koolhaas," PhD diss., ETH, 2003, p. 171.

18 Jean-Louis Cohen, "The Rational Rebel, or the Urban Agenda of OMA," in *OMA–Rem Koolhaas*, ed. Jacques Lucan, New York: Princeton Architectural Press, 1991, p. 9.

seemingly, beyond its reach. Even if instinctive and spontaneous in each particular case, the urge for opposition against some sort of mainstream—such as postmodern and deconstructivist architecture, or, more recently, the city as the ultimate urban consensus—appears to be a potent constant in Koolhaas' work and thinking, driven by some sort of Bourdieuian desire for distinction.[19] This holds particularly true for the Kunsthal and for the way in which Koolhaas revised OMA's agenda at the turn of the 1990s. As a major driving force of Koolhaas' reactivity, I consider these dynamics of opposition (which I will try to reenact) to be critically important in understanding both of them.

Authorship

Koolhaas has repeatedly argued that the question of authorship is pointless in the case of OMA, given that each project fuses a variety of ideas which may stem from anybody involved in the development of the design. In a 2004 interview, he uses the Kunsthal as an example of this: "The moment in the design of the Kunsthal at which two slopes start to intersect came after an endless struggle. Imagine that another collaborator of the office has brought the design to the point that enables me to put a step forward: I will never claim that it was me who came up with this particular step."[20] In statements like these, Koolhaas reduces the notion of authorship to the accumulative, indeed collective, process of contributing ideas to choose from. The ideal of collective creativity that seems to underlie Koolhaas' persistent rejection of individual authorship—apparently rooted in the art movements of the 1960s and endowed with egalitarian overtones—eclipses the other, no less significant components of any design work: defining the tasks and topics to start from, judging whether or not a proposition is good, to be pursued further, or dismissed; taking decisions. For the Kunsthal, it appears that this role was reserved for Koolhaas alone, and that the actual steering of the design process needs to be accredited to him.[21] This is indicated by the account of former team members along with numerous drawings and faxes marked with either "ok Rem" or "Rem's no."[22]

On the use of some recurring terms

I will make ample use of the terms "fragmentation," "postmodern architecture," and "deconstructivist architecture." Not the terms themselves but the phenomena they denote are central for my argument.

As a general rule I will use them in the rather generic manner in which they were used by Koolhaas at the time, in order to understand how Koolhaas turned his notion of postmodern and deconstructivist architecture into a means to oppose them. While rarely naming any architect or building in particular, Koolhaas' writings, talks, and statements—which I will quote and discuss in detail—do indicate the exhibitions, publications, ideas, and architects he had in mind.[23] Among them are seminal events like Charles Jencks' book *The Language of Post-Modern Architecture*, Rowe and Koetter's *Collage City*, the Venice Biennale's *Presence of the Past* in 1980, the MoMA exhibition *Deconstructivist Architecture* in 1988, and the corollary publications and debates in the architectural press.[24] To the extent that the wish for distinction was a major motive for rejecting both -isms, their more apparent and recognizable features must have been decisive to his thinking rather than a specific definition of the term. Much of the work of Stirling, Moore, Hollein, Johnson, Graves, Stern, Portoghesi, and Rossi in the 1970s and 1980s is likely to be part of what Koolhaas had in mind when referring to postmodernist architecture. The same applies to the work of Hadid, Tschumi, Eisenman, Coop Himmelb(l)au, Libeskind, and Morphosis in the 1980s and 1990s, in conjunction with Koolhaas' use of the term deconstructivist. More recent reevaluations of postmodernist

19 There is, of course, a significant difference to Pierre Bourdieu's notion of "distinction" as explicated in his synonymous 1979 book: Bourdieu refers to a hierarchy of social classes and strata, not to the individual wishing to distinguish themselves among their peers, as I do in the case of Koolhaas. And yet the very urge to distinguish oneself vis-à-vis a specific group of people appears vital, both for the dynamics I am referring to and for Bourdieu's theory of distinction.

20 Camiel van Winkel and Bart Verschaffel, "'Ik ben verblufft over de rechten die het artiestieke zich aanmeet.' Vraaggresprek met Rem Koolhaas," in *de Witte Raaf* (May/June 2004), p. 5 (author's translation).

21 In an article from 1997/98, former collaborators Philipp Oswalt and Matthias Hollwich wrote: "Settling a solution, or to put it more precisely, filtering out a solution from the pool of ideas, takes place very late; the alternatives are developed in parallel over a longer period. [...] Rem himself takes the decision, very often asking other people their opinion, sometimes initiating debates. In this process, apprentices and visitors just as much as the project leaders are drawn in." Philipp Oswalt and Matthias Hollwich, "OMA at work," in *Archis*, 5 (1997/98), p. 21.

22 Colenbrander and Bosman wrote in 1995: "OMA operates according to a flat organizational model, with a single orchestrator (Koolhaas) and no middle echelons." *Reference OMA: The Sublime Start of an Architectural Generation*, eds. Bernard Colenbrander and Jos Bosman, Rotterdam: NAi Publishers, 1995, p. 15.

23 Koolhaas' use and understanding of the term appears akin to the notion described by Mary McLeod in 1989: "The first, and still the most common, understanding of the term [postmodern architecture] refers to the tendency that rejects the formal and social constituents of the modern movement and embraces a broader formal language, which is frequently figurative and historically eclectic. [...] While advocates of postmodern architecture have often agreed more about what they reject than what they endorse, certain themes have been constantly explored: historical styles, regionalism, decoration, urban contextualism and morphologies, among others." Mary McLeod, "Architecture and Politics in the Reagan Era: From Postmodernism to Deconstructivism," in *Architecture Theory Since 1968*, ed. K. Michael Hays, Cambridge, Massachusetts: The MIT Press, 2000, p. 680. The essay was first published in 1989.

24 Charles Jencks, *The Language of Post-Modern Architecture*, London: Academy Editions, 1977; Colin Rowe and Fred Koetter, *Collage City*, Cambridge, Massachusetts: The MIT Press, 1978.

architecture—by Reinhold Martin (*Utopia's Ghost*), Emmanuel Petit (*Irony*), and Glenn Adamson and Jane Pavitt (*Postmodernism: Style and Subversion 1970–1990*)—have been valuable sources for my research, above all with respect to those characteristics that OMA's work in the 1980s *shares* with it, while also providing additional clues about the relation between postmodern architecture and fragmentation.[25]

As for the latter term—"fragmentation"—I will use it metaphorically rather than in the literal sense, denoting the parts of a whole that is either incomplete or lost. When talking about fragmentation I am referring to an "aesthetic motif" of the kind that Mary McLeod once proposed with respect to deconstructivist architecture, explaining that "we use the word when designs look 'fragmented,' not because they are literally broken."[26] Formal heterogeneity, multiple diverse shapes, grids, constructions, materials, colors, and connotations are the hallmarks of what I understand by the term. I stress this issue because I consider fragmentation along with its metaphorical charge—and implicitly the relationship between part and whole—indispensable for an understanding of OMA's 1980s architecture and the Kunsthal in particular. The discussion of these issues will focus on the projects and their context of origin, while barely touching upon the theory connected to the notion of the term "fragment" and more global arguments like the relation between the fragment and modernity.

The meanings of the fragment as explicated by Linda Nochlin in her lecture *The Body in Pieces* are contrary: the fragment expresses either nostalgia for a lost whole and the past it stands for, or commitment for a utopia to come; either the whole from which the fragment is taken is being mourned, or it was deliberately destroyed so as to make way for the new. But even the methodical fragmentation of everything—as Nochlin points out with regard to impressionist painting—might accompany the "will toward totalization" and suggest a new whole.[27] At the Kunsthal each of these options appears to play a role in one way or another.

With good reason, the formal fragmentation of OMA's early work has been compared to collage and montage in art and film.[28] There are obvious parallels between form and technique on the one hand and artistic production in the respective fields on the other, and in this book I will use analogies of this kind as a point of reference. The terms "collage" and "montage" will refer to the example of well-known works of art rather than to definitions provided by art and film theory. The distinction between collage/photomontage and filmic montage is evident: whereas the first two unfold in space, the third unfolds in time;

whereas collage and photomontage are largely composed of fragments, the single frames of filmic montage tend to be complete entities in themselves, even if some show collages or montages. When applied to architecture, the comparison with collage and photomontage implies looking at the building—or distinct parts of it like a facade or space—in its totality, in a manner that is analogous to the contemplation of a picture, whereas the comparison with filmic montage puts the accent on the sequential experience of the spectator in motion. Collage and photomontage, in turn, are primarily distinguished from one another by the difference in the material used. In *Montage and the Metropolis*, Martino Stierli writes: "collages draw their force from the inclusion of objects or object fragments from outside the confines of art; montages, on the other hand, use generally photographic representations of objects or images rather than the objects themselves. [...] Collage is symptomatic of a crisis of representation, directly representing fragments of reality rather than re-presenting them, whereas montage is the affirmation of the work of art in the age of technological reproducibility."[29] Both techniques were significant for OMA's architectural production in the 1980s, also as a means of representation. Interiors were rendered as a Miesian combination of perspective drawing and photographic cutouts, while elevations were built as full-fledged collages. Both techniques did resonate with OMA's architectural approach of this period. The design of the Kunsthal, however, appears more closely related to collage than to (photo-)montage. Its architecture doubtless possesses figurative qualities, but they do not compare to those of a montage as understood by Stierli. Like most architecture, the Kunsthal confronts the observer with artifacts that do not necessarily represent something they are not, and certainly not in the easily accessible manner of a photograph.

25 Reinhold Martin, *Utopia's Ghost: Architecture and Postmodernism, Again*, Minneapolis: University of Minnesota Press, 2010; Glenn Adamson and Jane Pavitt, *Postmodernism: Style and Subversion 1970–1990*, London: V&A Publishing, 2011.

26 Mary McLeod, "'Order in the Details,' 'Tumult in the Whole'? Composition and Fragmentation in Le Corbusier's Architecture," in *Fragments: Architecture and the Unfinished. Essays Presented to Robin Middleton*, eds. Barry Bergdoll and Werner Oechslin, London: Thames & Hudson, 2006, pp. 291, 316.

27 Linda Nochlin, *The Body in Pieces: The Fragment as a Metaphor of Modernity*, London: Thames & Hudson, 2001, p. 53. The lecture was held and first published in 1994.

28 See for instance Martino Stierli, *Montage and the Metropolis: Architecture, Modernity, and the Representation of Space*, New Haven: Yale University Press, 2018, pp. 228–67; Cynthia Davidson, "Koolhaas and the Kunsthal: History Lesions," in *ANY*, 21 (1997), pp. 36–41; Aarati Kanekar, "Space of Montage: Movement, Assemblage, and Appropriation in Koolhaas' Kunsthal," in *Architecture's Pretext: Spaces of Translation*, London: Routledge, 2015, pp. 134–54; Mathieu Berteloot and Véronique Patteeuw, "OMA's Collages," in *OASE*, 94 (2015), special issue on "OMA: The First Decade," pp. 66–74; Wilfried Wang, "Drawing Together the Different Perspectives of the Seattle Central Library," in *Take One Building*, eds. Ruth Conroy Dalton and Christoph Hölscher, pp. 207–08.

29 Stierli, *Montage and the Metropolis*, p. 18.

Right consciousness

Some time before I committed to writing a book on the Kunsthal, I was struck by the idea that Koolhaas' Kunsthal in Rotterdam, perhaps more than any other building of the late twentieth century, exemplifies in architecture what Adorno called "right consciousness" in art. In Adorno's *Aesthetic Theory*, right consciousness figures as the actual yardstick against which art is to be judged.[30] The term bespeaks its origins in Marxist thought, with right consciousness being used as a counterterm for the "false consciousness" of unenlightened ideology. But Adorno's notion of contemporary art did not aim to illustrate Marxist ideas. Kafka and Beckett, not Brecht, are being proposed as the models of contemporary literature. In "Trying to Understand *Endgame*" Adorno introduces Beckett as a polymath writer who *does* reflect upon the consequences of capitalist alienation and the abyss of Auschwitz, while using the "most advanced artistic means" of his own discipline so as to absorb what is expressed while changing it through form.[31] For Adorno, right consciousness in art is as much about art itself as about the world as it is. It demands a correspondence between artistic means and the state of affairs in human history. In times of social change, the claim for societal truth implies the artistic imperative of innovation. Highly perceptive in both realms, right consciousness in art eschews "everything now impossible": forms that are no longer adequate or have lost their edge through repetition, the cliché. *Dégoût*, Adorno explains, is a major productive force of Beckett's work. I have conceived of this study independently of Adorno's theory of art; overlaps with Adorno's ideas were neither intended nor considered. But today, the Kunsthal still strikes me as a building that does epitomize the aforementioned notion of right consciousness in architecture. The Kunsthal as architecture—the physical construct as a bearer of meaning—seems to abound with a similar kind of *dégoût*, an avant-garde sense of newness, a historical awareness of societal conditions, a sensitivity for the relation between these conditions and form. Disclosing one by one the different layers of "consciousness" that are latent in the Kunsthal, it appears in retrospect, is the idea underpinning this book.

---

30 Theodor W. Adorno, *Ästhetische Theorie*, Frankfurt am Main: Suhrkamp, 2000, first published in 1970.

31 Theodor W. Adorno, "Versuch, das Endspiel zu Verstehen," in *Adorno: Noten zur Literatur*, Frankfurt am Main: Suhrkamp, 2003, pp. 281–321. Written in 1958 and first published in 1961.

P 2.1 Aerial photograph of the Dijkzigt area, 1937.

P 2.2 Dijkzigt Park, May 14, 1940. Rotterdammers taking refuge after the German bombardment. To the right is Museum Boijmans Van Beuningen.

P 2.3   Rochussenstraat in the 1980s. Left: Unilever Building by F. Mertens (1930–31). Right: apartment blocks along Rochussenstraat (1930s).

P 2.4 Mathenesserlaan (renamed Museumpark) in the 1980s.
Left: Museum Boijmans Van Beuningen by A. J. van der Steur (1928–35).

P 2.5　Dijkzigtpark in the 1980s. Museum Boijmans van Beuningen by A. J. van der Steur (1928–35).

P 2.6 Jongkindstraat in the 1980s. Left: Boevé House (1931–33) by Brinkman & Van der Vlugt. Right: Villa Merkes by Jan van Teeffelen (1932–34).

P 2.7　Westzeedijk in the 1980s. Medical faculty of Rotterdam's Erasmus University by OD 205 (1965–68).

P 2.8   Westzeedijk in the 1980s vis-à-vis the future Kunsthal.
Right: apartment block by F.L. Lourijssen (1928).

Doom and Gloom

OMA in the 1980s

In the year 2525, if man is still alive …

Zager and Evans, 1969

Rem Koolhaas first positioned himself against postmodernism in 1977, which was the very year that Charles Jencks published *The Language of Post-Modern Architecture*. In his "Story of the Pool," featured in the May issue of *Architectural Design*, Koolhaas caricatured the emerging anti-modern climate among his American peers. Anticipating an imaginary critique of his project for a floating swimming pool, he recounted: "The New Yorkers were all against Modernism now. The pool was so bland, so rectilinear, so boring; there were no historical allusions; there was no theatricality."[1] The manifestly postmodern New York architects of Koolhaas' story, which is set in 1976, produce "flaccid country mansions," "academic pornography of [...] trite geometries," and a "spectacle of [...] irrelevant sophistication."[2] In a 1979 article, Koolhaas criticized "the Rationalists in Europe and the Post-Modernists in America" for their "misguided 'historicism'" and withdrawal from modern architecture's ambition to transform society. "The best minds in modern architecture," he wrote, "are ready to abandon the claims staked out in the 1920s for an activist profession with a capability, and indeed a responsibility, for redesigning the human environment. The new architects are determined to pose the issues of architecture in traditional terms once more. Doric columns, pediments, moldings, piazzas—all are making their prodigal return."[3] Despite these attacks OMA was invited to participate in the 1980 Venice Biennale entitled The *Presence of the Past*, which was curated by Paolo Portoghesi with Robert Stern, Charles Jencks, and Vincent Scully as members of the advisory commission. Kenneth Frampton withdrew from the board three months before the opening of the show, fearing that the Biennale would "represent the triumph of postmodernism;"[4] apparently it was on his initiative that OMA was invited. Koolhaas wrote the countermanifesto "Our New Sobriety" for the catalog, outlining the oppositional stance OMA was to take vis-à-vis the thrust of the exhibition. Postmodern and rationalist architecture, Koolhaas implied, was obsessed by form, uncritical, servile to the past, and dismissive of modernism, inhibited from adapting to the present by its historicist and typological doctrines.[5] Conversely, OMA would preserve and revise the modernist tradition of programmatic imagination, be concerned with content as opposed to form, embrace the dynamics of societal transformation, and give shape

1 Rem Koolhaas, "The Story of the Pool," in *Architectural Design*, 5 (1977), p. 356.
2 Ibid.
3 Rem Koolhaas, "The Future's Past," in *The Wilson Quarterly*, 3.1 (1979), p. 140.
4 Léa-Catherine Szacka, "Criticism From Within: Kenneth Frampton and the Retreat from Postmodernism," in *OASE*, 97 (2016), p. 113.
5 Rem Koolhaas and Elia Zenghelis, "Our 'New Sobriety,'" in *The Presence of the Past: La Biennale di Venezia 1980*, ed. Paolo Portoghesi, London: Academy Editions, 1980, pp. 214, 216.

to a "culture based on the givens of density, technology and definitive social instability."[6] Looking back, Koolhaas explained in 2015: "It was the Europeanization of postmodernism. I lived in New York in the 1970s, so I was there when American postmodernism was born and when the arguments for it were being developed. I had an intimate overview of all the authors and how they interacted. I was alert to what postmodernism implied and I was horrified when I realized that it had reached Europe. That is probably why I tried to show a strong opposition to it. Taking part in the 1980 Venice Architecture Biennale was the occasion to make my opposition manifest."[7]

Apart from Koolhaas' polemic, this opposition was voiced through the facade OMA designed for the Strada Novissima, a "street" of facades built in the Corderia of Venice's former Arsenale by Cinnecittà technicians. Whereas the facades of Charles Moore, Robert Stern, Michael Graves, Venturi & Scott Brown, Paolo Portoghesi, Léon Krier, Hans Hollein, and others were dense with the emblems of classicist and historicist architecture, Koolhaas' consisted of a blank undulating canvas, pierced by a pole to which a sign bearing the neon lettering "OMA" was attached. The amorphous shape of the canvas and the cutout framing the lettering implies formlessness, while the bright red color of the sign and the slanted pole imply some kinship to the Russian avant-gardes of the 1920s and their ambition to "program" society. The kinship is underscored by OMA's projects on show—the extension of the Dutch parliament in The Hague (1978) and the renovation of the prison in Arnhem (1978–80)—which employ references to the Soviet vanguard and modernism at large. Taken together, OMA's contributions to the Biennale in Venice consolidated two antagonisms that lay at the heart of Koolhaas' opposition to postmodern architecture and would continue to do so throughout the 1980s: on the one hand, there was a modernist frame of reference versus one that was premodern, while on the other there was the program and near absence of form versus formalism.[8]

The message was heard. In 1982, Belgian critic and theoretician Geert Bekaert observed: "The great monument to Koolhaas' war of attrition with architectural form was unveiled at the Venice Architecture Biennale […], where he was placed amidst an anti-modernist mob."[9] Recognizing the connection Koolhaas established between OMA's work and the "claims of the Modern Movement, which presented its architecture not as a formalistic game but as a social necessity," Bekaert inferred: "This places him in a comfortable polemical position with regard to the many forms of so-called postmodernism, which still suffer from avant-gardism and desperately try to make the foundation of their identity. Koolhaas' identity is perfectly secure; his *différence* is unmistakable."[10] Thirty-five years later, Stefano de Martino, who had been Koolhaas' collaborator at the time, recalled: "The Biennale confirmed that we were on the right track. To know that we were in a minority was exhilarating. We upset a lot of people. Everyone else fell into a camp […]."[11]

Before the bifurcation

During the 1970s and 1980s, the relation between OMA's work and postmodern and rationalist architecture was much more intricate than Koolhaas' writings and interviews from the same period suggest. In 1975, Léon Krier organized the exhibition *Rational Architecture* in London and then functioned as the "organizational hand" behind the 1978 book of the same name.[12] In the latter, OMA's Egg of Columbus Center project (1973) and its plans for Roosevelt Island (1975) in New York are shown alongside works by Aldo Rossi, Giorgio Grassi, Massimo Scolari, Bernard Huet, Oswald Mathias Ungers, James Stirling, and the Krier brothers, many of whom had also participated in the Venice Biennale. More importantly, the inclusion of the two projects was not based on a complete misreading of OMA's intentions. Shown in the section on housing, they figured as examples of projects that "tend to overcome their limiting technical programs (which are the result of zoning)."[13] Like Koolhaas, Léon Krier was an advocate of collectivity, and like Koolhaas, he saw the integration of "all forms of urban life" as an urban quality.[14]

6   Ibid.
7   Léa-Catherine Szacka, "Translucent Oppositions: OMA's Proposal for the 1980 Venice Architecture Biennale," in *OASE*, 94 (2015), https://www.oasejournal.nl/en/Issues/94/TranslucentOppositions (accessed October 23, 2019).
8   In the 1980s, Koolhaas continued to reject ideas associated with postmodernism, such as irony in architecture, an exclusively mimetic understanding of contextual relations, the reduction of the morphological and typological repertoire to premodern models, incomprehensibility, a misguided insistence on coherence, and the abandonment of the modernist tradition of social engagement. Statements of this kind are to be found, for instance, in Hans van Dijk, "Rem Koolhaas interview," in *wonen-TA/BK*, 11 (1978), pp. 17–20; Rem Koolhaas, "Urban Intervention: Dutch Parliament Extension, The Hague," in *International Architect*, 1 (1980), pp. 47–50; Franco Raggi, "Edonista-puritano," in *Modo*, 58 (1983), pp. 26–28; Patrice Goulet, "La deuxième chance de l'architecture moderne… Entretien avec Rem Koolhaas," in *L'Architecture d'Aujourd'hui*, 238 (1985), pp. 2–9.
9   Geert Bekaert, "The Odyssey of an Enlightened Entrepreneur: Rem Koolhaas," in *Rooted in the Real: Writings on Architecture by Geert Bekaert*, ed. Christophe Van Gerrewey, Ghent: Ghent University, 2011, p. 293. First published in Dutch in 1982 under the title "De Odyssee van een verlicht ondernemer: Rem Koolhaas."
10 Ibid., pp. 280–81.
11 Szacka, 'Translucent Oppositions', n. p.
12 Harry Francis Mallgrave and David Goodman, *An Introduction to Architectural Theory: 1968 to the Present*, Chichester: Wiley-Blackwell, 2011, p. 61.
13 Léon Krier, "The Reconstruction of the City," in *Rational Architecture: The Reconstruction of the European City*, Brussels: Archives d'Architecture Moderne, 1978, p. 99.
14 Ibid., p. 42.

OMA's work, like that of Krier, counteracted the disentanglement of functions that was so characteristic of early modernism. Asked about OMA's project for Roosevelt Island and the "supposed 'antimodernist' stance associated with both rationalism and early postmodernism," George Baird answered in 2001: "I think the Roosevelt Island competition entry has to be seen as an integral part of the critique [of modernism] you mention. Surprising as it may seem from the end of the millennium, the 1970s production of OMA/Koolhaas participated in the developing critique of modernism at the same time that it revived certain strong modernist themes [...]. One of the consequences of the bifurcation referred to above has been the laying down of a sharp ideological demarcation line, and most activist architects have difficulty in resisting the strong pressure to declare allegiance to one faction or another. But the fact of the matter is that this line did not yet exist in the 1970s."[15]

Drawing was our work

After all, postmodernists and rationalists belonged to an architectural scene that Koolhaas himself was part of. In Jencks' "evolutionary tree" of postmodern architecture, Koolhaas featured in the Historicism branch alongside the Venturi school, Stern, and the Grays.[16] Many architects of the Strada Novissima had their drawings sold by the same gallerists, published essays in the same journals, and presented their work at the same conferences as Koolhaas. OMA by then was renowned for the beauty and refinement of its renderings, and Koolhaas had made a name for himself as the author of *Delirious New York*.[17] Altogether, the work produced by OMA between its founding in 1975 and the first half of the 1980s widely coincided with what commonly figured in contemporaneous reviews as "paper architecture." The phrase is indicative not only of the absence of built work, but also of an architectural production that essentially relies on drawings in the widest sense. In a 2009 lecture, Elia Zenghelis (1937–), cofounder of OMA, explained: "We had become known because of our drawings and nothing else. We had not built anything. So we very heavily relied on drawing and drawing technique, and how to communicate through drawings. [...] Drawing, for us, that was our work."

In the 1970s and 1980s, the architectural drawing gained the status of an autonomous architectural object, a development that had been propelled by the simultaneous rise of architectural publications and the emergence of private galleries selling architectural drawings, either exclusively or on a regular basis.[18] OMA's drawings were shown at Max Protetch in New York (1978–), Aedes in Berlin (1980–), and Van Rooy in Amsterdam (1980–90), along with work by Rossi, Grassi, Ungers, Venturi, Graves, Stern, John Hejduk, Frank Gehry, the Krier brothers, Josef Paul Kleihues, Bernard Tschumi, Coop Himmelb(l)au, Zaha Hadid, Peter Eisenman, Daniel Libeskind, and Arata Isozaki. In a parallel step, institutions like the Canadian Center for Architecture in Montreal (CCA), the Deutsches Architekturmuseum in Frankfurt (DAM), and the Getty Center in Los Angeles began to purchase, collect, and exhibit contemporary architectural drawings. Quoting gallerist Max Protetch, Kauffman suggests that at some point the new market created a dynamic of its own: "As time progressed […] Protetch found that architects began 'speaking like artists and insisting on doing a show,' by which Protetch meant that they began to prepare works specifically for display, of their productions as gallery pieces rather than as evidence of their critical practices. 'It was every one, right from Graves through Isozaki, Zaha, and Rem.'"[19]

An astonishingly homogeneous milieu

In 1981, an adapted version of the Strada Novissima was shown to the public in the Chapelle de la Salpetière in Paris—omitting a number of "unorthodox" contributions, among them those by Venturi and Koolhaas. When Stanislaus von Moos was invited to comment on the exhibition at a corollary conference, he questioned the seemingly irreconcilable opposition of modern and postmodern architecture, observing that both sides belonged to "an astonishingly homogeneous milieu." It was "one of 'theoretician' architects, members of the architectural haute couture, based at universities and manifesting themselves through a number of international magazines considered 'avant-garde.' Seen from the outside, not only does Rossi resemble Venturi and Stirling resemble Van Eyck; seen from the outside, Charles

15 Ann Marie Brennan, Nahum Goodenow, and Brendan D. Moran, "OMA, 'Neo-Modern,' and Modernity," *Perspecta*, 32 (2001), p. 33. In Heinrich Klotz's 1984 monograph *Moderne und Postmoderne*, the author dedicated a section to Rem Koolhaas in the chapter on rationalist architecture in northern Europe, presenting OMA's projects for the prison in Arnhem, Boompjes in Rotterdam (1980), and Kochstrasse/Friedrichstrasse in Berlin (1980) alongside work from the 1970s. Heinrich Klotz, *Moderne und Postmoderne: Architektur der Gegenwart 1960–1980*, Braunschweig and Wiesbaden: Vieweg & Sohn, 1985, pp. 311–12.

16 Charles Jencks, *The Language of Post-Modern Architecture*, London: Academy Editions, 1978, p. 80.

17 Rem Koolhaas, *Delirious New York: A Retroactive Manifesto for Manhattan*, New York: The Monacelli Press, 1994; first published by Oxford University Press, New York in 1978.

18 On this subject, see Jordan Kauffman, *Drawing on Architecture: The Object of Lines, 1970–1990*, Cambridge, Massachusetts: The MIT Press, 2018.

19 Ibid., p. 238.

Jencks, Bruno Zevi, Léon Krier, Manfredo Tafuri, Paul Chemetov, Claude Schnaidt, is essentially the same thing. They are 'theorists' whose activities assure the functioning of architecture as an intellectual affair."[20] It was the very milieu in which Koolhaas sought to distinguish, position, and assert himself as an architect, author, and intellectual. Although von Moos proffered Koolhaas as a counterexample to the narrowmindedness of postmodernist orthodoxy, the above sociological profile applied to his protégé as well.

In 1981, OMA had literally built nothing, and it would take another four years for its first interior to materialize.[21] Koolhaas was well connected with academic institutions. He had been a visiting fellow at the Institute for Architecture and Urban Studies (IAUS) in New York until 1979, and since the mid-1970s he had occasionally taught at Delft University and the Architectural Association (AA) School of Architecture in London.[22] The dissemination of his ideas and theoretical projects and those designs that did not materialize was largely owed to publications in leading intellectually sophisticated architecture magazines such as *Oppositions, Lotus, Casabella, Architectural Design, L'Architecture d'Aujourd'hui*, and *Archithese*. Koolhaas' last project as a student of the AA School of Architecture, "Exodus, or The Voluntary Prisoners of Architecture" (1972–73), was just as unlikely to be implemented as were the speculative projects by Archigram, Superstudio, and Archizoom. In retrospect, Koolhaas labeled *Delirious New York* along with the projects shown in the book's fictional conclusion as "aggressively realistic."[23] But it is obvious that none of these projects, whether designed by himself or other members of OMA, were seriously designed as structures that were to be built. Rather, the book's polemic confrontation between unfulfilled European utopias and realized American dreams prepared some ideological ground for the commitment to building, which would become important for Koolhaas at a later stage.

Back in the 1970s and 1980s, although many of Koolhaas' peers taught in architecture schools, they built either little or nothing, especially those with whom he worked most closely, such as Oswald M. Ungers, Peter Eisenman, Bernard Tschumi, Zaha Hadid, Léon Krier, and Daniel Libeskind. Tschumi taught at the AA in London and IAUS in New York. The first stage of La Villette park in Paris, completed in 1988, was his debut as an architect. Hadid, a former student of Koolhaas and Zenghelis who became an associate for a brief period, taught at the AA between 1980 and 1987, succeeding her teachers as the director of Diploma Unit 9.[24] A couple of minor works aside, her first buildings were the IBA housing project in Berlin (1986–93) and the Vitra fire

F 1.1

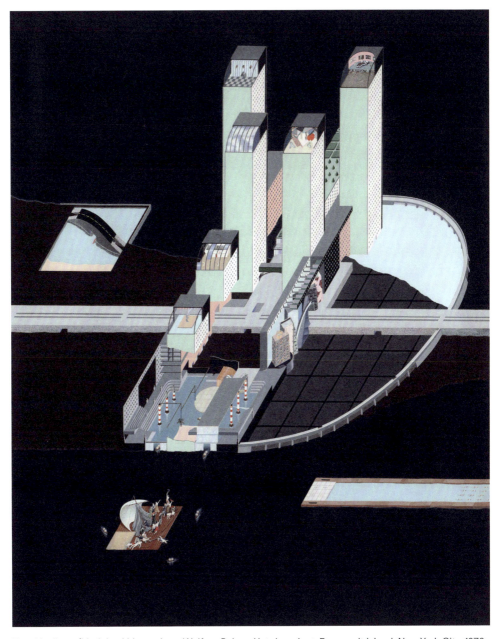

Rem Koolhaas/Madelon Vriesendorp, Welfare Palace Hotel, project. Roosevelt Island, New York City, 1976.

20 Stanislaus von Moos, "Les refuses du post-modernisme," in *Techniques & Architecture*, 339 (1981), p. 104 (author's translation).
21 The interior of the Lintas Offices in Amsterdam (1984–85) was the first project OMA was able to implement.
22 Jacques Lucan, ed., *OMA–Rem Koolhaas*, Princeton Architectural Press: New York, 1991, p. 168.
23 Rem Koolhaas, "Sixteen Years of OMA," *A+U*, 217 (1988), p. 17.
24 *El Croquis*, 52 (1995), p. 5. Hadid commented on her relationship with OMA: "I was their student for two years and I was their partner for six months. [...] My relation with OMA is more fundamental than working with them. There is almost a non-visible dialogue between us, we remain very close friends, Rem and I, we talk a lot." Richard Levene and Fernando Márquez Cecilia, "Interview with Zaha Hadid," in *El Croquis*, 52 (1995), p. 10.

station in Weil am Rhein (1990–93). Léon Krier taught at the AA, temporarily parallel to Koolhaas, Tschumi, and Libeskind. Libeskind, who had been a research assistant at IAUS and started teaching at the AA parallel to Koolhaas, was the director of the Cranbrook Academy of Art in Michigan from 1978 to 1985, and a senior scholar at the Getty Foundation from 1986 to 1989.[25] The Jewish Museum in Berlin (1989–99) was his first commission to materialize. His Micromegas of 1979 are as aloof from the realm of building as the Roma Interrotta projects for Rome (1978), Rossi's Città analoga (1976), and Tschumi's Manhattan Transcripts (1978). Libeskind's Chamber Works of 1983 provoked Robin Evans to speculate sarcastically about a possible disappearance of the edifice: "The building can be discarded as an unfortunate aftermath, and all the values that are worth keeping can be held in the drawing."[26] Koolhaas' Welfare Palace Hotel of 1976 is a buildable project and yet not devised for implementation (→ F 1.1). The corollary text reads like a pessimist allegory of Western decadence. The stage of the theater and nightclub/restaurant is carved out of a sinking ship. "Guests can sit, eat and watch performances on the terraces along the water or they may board life-boats—luxuriously equipped with velvet benches and marble table-tops [...]. Outside the Hotel [...] floats a gigantic reproduction of Géricault's *Raft of the Medusa*"—that is, a painting commemorating acts of cannibalism committed by members of the enlightened world.[27]

Doom and gloom

Von Moos' 1981 talk addressed the fact that the architects' withdrawal from the realm of building went hand in hand with their withdrawal from social commitment. "The discussion on the so-called post-modern architecture," von Moos told his audience in Paris, "regards above all 'paper' architecture and journalism. It allows critiques, editors and architects to compensate the lack of direct contact with the shaping of the environment through the intention (or illusion) to act as interpreters of the major problems of the age."[28] Postmodern architecture was not concerned with social needs.

Following Bernard Huet's "Small Manifesto" in 1978, von Moos suggested that contemporary architecture be measured by the standards of Walter Benjamin's 1934 essay "The Author as Producer."[29] According to Benjamin the decisive question to be asked was: Did the author simply supply the capitalist system of production, regardless of his (or her) views, however revolutionary they might be? Or was this author able to transform this system and, ultimately, society? The former was true in the case of postmodern architecture, von Moos implied. For Manfredo Tafuri, the lack of transformative capacities extended to contemporary architecture as a whole, regardless of whether or not it was built: "There is no hope for architecture to influence structures or relations of production," he categorically stated in his 1976 essay "The Ashes of Jefferson."[30] According to Tafuri, the example of Jefferson—the architect-politician who shapes society through building—belonged to a past that had been lost. In the essay, Tafuri refers to the architectural avant-garde of the United States, namely Venturi, Eisenman, Meier, Graves, Stern, Moore, and Hejduk; in 1974's "L'architecture dans le boudoir" he draws similar conclusions about their European colleagues, including Stirling, Rossi, Scolari, Hollein, Léon Krier, and Koolhaas, likewise with reference to Benjamin's "The Author as Producer."

It was, however, not only the architects and their critics who lost faith in their ability to transform society. In the 1970s, Western societies were pervaded by a climate of disillusionment and defeatism. Disconcerting experiences like the war in Vietnam and the atomic threat of the Cold War challenged long held beliefs in modernization and technological progress as carriers of prosperity that would change society for the better. Especially for the political Left—defined by the Civil Rights Movement in America and the antiauthoritarian movements in Europe—the end of the 1960s turned into a disaster. In 1968, hopes for societal and political reform saw a broad violent backlash through events such as the Soviet invasion in Prague, the assassination of Martin Luther King in Memphis, and the shooting of Rudi Dutschke in Berlin.

The violent suppression of political activism on both sides of the Atlantic was soon to be followed by economic anxieties. Western countries and the United States in particular began to realize that the seemingly infinite growth in the wake of World War II had come to a halt. In 1970, the US economy grew only 0.5 percent, while growth was slowing down in West Germany (2.6 percent) and booming in Japan

25 Daniel Libeskind, *Daniel Libeskind: Counterdesign*, New York: Rizzoli, 1992, p. 139.
26 Robin Evans, "In Front of Lines That Leave Nothing Behind," in *Architecture Theory Since 1968*, ed. K. Michael Hays, Cambridge, Massachusetts: The MIT Press, 2000, p. 488.
27 Rem Koolhaas, "Welfare Palace Hotel," in *Architectural Design*, 5 (1977), p. 345.
28 Von Moos, "Les refuses du post-modernisme," p. 104 (author's translation).
29 Bernard Huet, "Small Manifesto," in *Rational Architecture: The Reconstruction of the European City*, Léon Krier et al., Brussels: Editions des Archives d'Architecture Moderne, 1978, p. 54.
30 Manfredo Tafuri, "The Ashes of Jefferson," in *The Sphere and the Labyrinth: Avant-Gardes and Architecture from Piranesi to the 1970s*, Cambridge, Massachusetts: MIT Press, 1990, p. 293. The essay was first published in 1976 in *L'Architecture d'Aujourd'hui*.

Terry Gilliam, *Brazil*, 1985, film still. Jonathan Pryce getting out of a Messerschmitt Kabinenroller, a microcar produced during the booming years of the postwar period.

(10.7 percent).³¹ Alarmed by these developments and the rise of the competing economies in Asia and Europe, the Nixon government took a step that would fundamentally destabilize the global economy in the long term: "In 1971 the US government acted to defend its own economic interest. By abruptly suspending the fixed rate of exchanging dollars for gold, it in effect devaluated the US dollar against other currencies, helping American exporters and domestic business. It thereby deliberately destroyed the Bretton Woods system, in which most other currencies had been pegged to the dollar at a fixed exchange rate."³² Both in the United States and in western Europe, the 1970s were marked by "stagflation" (the stagnation of markets and inflation) and unemployment: "Economic growth was sluggish and inflation higher than it had been for three decades, reaching 13 percent toward the end of the decade. The Ford Administration's critics started using the term 'stagflation', symbolizing all that was wrong with the US economy. Although almost all major economies experienced the same combination of low growth and high inflation during the 1970s, critics of the US Administration presented it as if it were a particular US phenomenon, and a telltale sign of Washington's weakness vis-à-vis other countries. In reality, stagflation was the product of free floating currencies, globalization of capital and investment, increasing raw material prizes, and, over time, increasing international competition. Gradually, these developments would actually help the US economy to recover faster than many others. But seen from the mid-seventies all seemed to be doom and gloom."[33]

In 1972, the report *Limits to Growth* commissioned by the Club of Rome was published, predicting a worldwide collapse of economies within a hundred years either "because of nonrenewable resource depletion," or due to environmental pollution, unless industrial growth could be significantly slowed down.[34] As if to prove the vulnerability of Western economies, they were hit by the two oil crises of 1973 and 1979. Fears of all sorts converged in dystopian fiction. Films like *Soylent Green* (1973) by Richard Fleischer, *Mad Max* by George Miller (1979), and Ridley Scott's *Blade Runner* (1982) bespeak a notion of the future that stands in sharp contrast to the optimism of the postwar era, common prosperity, and the welfare state. In *Soylent Green*, the immiserated masses of an overpopulated world are sustained by industrialized cannibalism. In *Blade Runner*, artificial intelligence kills humans for the sake of its own survival, and AI also runs amok in *Westworld* by Michael Crichton (1973) and *Terminator* by James Cameron (1984); in Terry Gilliam's *Brazil* (1985), the blessings of technology are caricatured as monstrous, reframing the enthusiasms of the "long boom" (→ F 1.2).

Go back to practice

At a 1982 architecture conference in Charlottesville, Léon Krier warned his colleagues who could not resist the temptation of profit-driven large-scale commissions: "To you I say, you will burn in hell for what you are doing, because it is wrong and you know it is wrong!"[35] (→ F 1.3). The prophecy was preceded by Philip Johnson and John Burgee's presentation of the 180,000-square-meter "International Palace" in Boston. The project, located in what used to be a low-rise neighborhood, included two 180-meter-high office towers. Johnson brushed aside the criticism of his colleagues, retorting: "I am a whore and I am paid very well for building high-rise buildings."[36]

31 Odd Arne Westad, *The Cold War: A World History*, London: Allan Lane, 2018, p. 396.
32 Ibid.
33 Ibid., p. 487.
34 Donella H. Meadows et al., *The Limits to Growth: A Report of the Club of Rome's Project on the Predicament of Mankind*, New York: Universe Books, 1972, pp. 125, 127.
35 Jaquelin Robertson, ed., *The Charlottesville Tapes*, New York: Rizzoli, 1985, p. 22.
36 Ibid., p. 19.

F 1.3

The conference in Charlottesville, 1982.

Johnson was by no means the only participant to present projects for large developments. Jaquelin Robertson, one of the organizers of the event, shared Krier's position to some extent, lamenting the architect's recent surrender to private sector forces: "Interestingly, the once-hated developer has become our hero, and we have followed him as uncritically as any emperor, king, or bishop of the past, to the point where we architects find ourselves assisting in the privatization of the public realm and helping to turn our cities into a series of 'high-amenity,' isolated enclaves, competing commercial islands in a vast urban neglect."[37] Although Robertson was referring to architects in the United States and Japan, and, implicitly, to large-scale projects, he suspected that Europe was also not immune to its temptations: "Ironically, it seems that when Europeans do get the 'big chance' they become, overnight, equally American—i.e. equally commercial."[38] Obviously Robertson was thinking here of Oswald Mathias Ungers' 60,000-

square-meter office tower for Frankfurt's trade fair site, which he was the first to review, comparing the project to a "cigar-cutter or guillotine."[39] Philip Johnson, startled, commented: "This could be in Kansas City," insinuating that the project had undesirable American qualities, and he reminded Ungers with wistful nostalgia of his first house, which had been "small' and "full of fantasy."[40] When Léon Krier moralizingly dismissed the project as kitsch, Ungers replied: "I spent ten years theorizing, and many people profited from that. [...] But you know what? I decided to go back to practice, get my fingers dirty, and work with those big developers. And I wish you would do the same. Then we can talk again. But at this level we can't."[41]

Many projects were harshly criticized, especially the large ones such as Henry Cobb's 175,000-square-meter Fountain Place in Dallas, and a 90,000-square-meter project for San Antonio by Michael Graves. Nonetheless, despite the criticism raised by Krier, Robertson, and others, the event illustrates that even within the circles of the American and European avant-gardes, the era of "paper architecture" was drawing to a close. Koolhaas was among the participants at the conference. His colleagues' comments on OMA's then still unconstructed project for the Netherlands Dance Theater—one of two unbuilt versions in Scheveningen—bespeak the shift in mood. For Rafael Moneo, ultimately, everything depended on the "proof" of the built work, and Robert Stern added: "This tends to be a problem of drawn architecture: the actual building is not nearly so captivating."[42] Moneo was neither the first nor the last to wonder how OMA might translate its drawings into actual construction. In a 1985 interview, Patrice Goulet also queried how the abstract quality of OMA's renderings could be translated into built architecture. Koolhaas answered somewhat uncomfortably: "The problem right now is that our projects are not built yet and that they lend themselves to all sorts of speculations."[43]

Harrison or Skidmore

At the end of the 1970s, Koolhaas moved back to Europe with the intention of establishing a practice that would be focused on construction. In 1980, he set up OMA's headquarters in Rotterdam, abandoning the AA School of Architecture in London in 1980–81.[44] According to Kees Christiaanse, the decision was preceded by the prospect of three

---

37 Robertson, "Introduction: Setting the Scene," in *The Charlottesville Tapes*, p. 9.
38 Ibid., p. 9.
39 Ibid., p. 67.
40 Ibid.
41 Ibid., p. 73.
42 Ibid., p. 186.
43 Goulet, "La deuxième chance," p. 8 (author's translation).
44 Roberto Gargiani, *Rem Koolhaas/OMA: The Construction of Merveilles*, Lausanne: EPFL/PPUR, 2008, p. 90.

commissions: the projects for Boompjes in Rotterdam (1980), the prison in Arnhem (1980), and IJplein in Amsterdam (1981–88).[45] Christiaanse, who had trained as an architect at Delft's University of Technology, joined OMA Rotterdam at its very inception and became a partner in 1983 after the tragic death of Koolhaas' first partner Jan Voorberg.[46] During those years, collaboration became more sporadic with OMA's cofounder Elia Zenghelis, who headed the firm's London office. The Parisian schemes for Parc de la Villette (1982–83), the 1989 Universal Exhibition (1983), and Parc Citroën-Cevennes (1985) were the last OMA projects in which Zenghelis was involved. Elia Zenghelis would still occasionally be listed as a partner in the following years—alongside his wife Zoe and Koolhaas' wife Vriesendorp—and the Checkpoint Charlie project in Berlin (1981–90) would be completed only five years later under his aegis.[47] But the actual collaboration with Koolhaas apparently ended in 1985.[48]

Around that time, the Rotterdam office moved from its premises in Scheepmakerskade to the top floor of Boompjes 55, a nondescript modernist office building from the 1960s overlooking the River Maas in Rotterdam's old harbor district. Meanwhile, the first projects were being implemented. OMA's police station in Almere and the interior of the Lintas offices in Amsterdam were completed in 1985, and by 1986 they had been joined by a virtually unknown apartment block in Frederiksstraat, facing the Dutch capital's Vondelpark.[49] Together with two apartment blocks in Groningen (1983–88), a development for mixed use at Veerplein in Vlaardingen (1986–89), and the Byzantium in Amsterdam (1985–91), these three projects belong to a group of structures that received little if any attention by the architectural press. And apparently they were not meant to. A comic strip in *S, M, L, XL* aside, none of them is included in the monographic publications OMA curated of its own work.[50] Kees Christiaanse commented in 2020: "There were very important projects, and there were projects that were, say, more dirty realism projects, which for OMA at that time were also a kind of introduction into the art of building. […] Dutch building culture is extremely sober. So we really had to get used to making housing in the Netherlands. Specifically, for commercial clients."[51]

Many of the commissions, it seems, had been solicited by Christiaanse, and Koolhaas was not always interested in the projects or lost interest when changes were imposed that he considered unacceptable.[52] Referring to the development at Veerplein, Christiaanse explains: "This commission was also [like the Byzantium] a competition, and the client was Blauwhoed woningen, which at the time was a very commercial developer in the Netherlands, making mountains of row houses and so on. And we won the competition, and the competition design was quite interesting, I must say. But then during the elaboration [...] the most qualitative aspects of that project were not wanted by the client, and consequently the project was changed, and it became extremely banal. I think we finished it because we made some money on it, but we immediately forgot about the project after it was realized."[53]

F 1.4

OMA/Rem Koolhaas, Netherlands Dance Theater, The Hague, 1981–87.

45 Interview with the author, April 14, 2020. Unlike the IJplein project, OMA's proposals for Boompjes and Arnhem Prison did not materialize.
46 Interview with the author, April 14, 2020. Both are listed as partners in a 1988 exhibition catalog: *Office for Metropolitan Architecture*, ed. Carolina de Backer, Antwerp: deSingel, 1988, p. 6. Christiaanse explains: "When OMA got the projects for Boompjes, Arnhem Prison, and IJplein, Koolhaas asked Voorberg to become his office partner. I and several other students joined the office in 1980 as free-lance staff." Email to the author, January 24, 2023.
47 In a 1988 exhibition catalog, Elia Zenghelis is listed as a partner, while his wife and Vriesendorp are mentioned as collaborators. De Backer, *Office for Metropolitan Architecture*, p. 6.
48 In a 2009 lecture, Elia Zenghelis recalls having left OMA in 1985. Elia Zenghelis, "The 1970s and the Beginning of OMA," lecture at the Berlage Institute held on November 24, 2009: https://vimeo.com/377509180 (accessed August 4, 2022). The date has been confirmed by Zoe Zenghelis. Asked in 2014 when Elia Zenghelis stopped working with OMA, she replied: "When he met Elena. She was working with the office, and she's Elia's wife now. She got Elia to help her with her thesis in 1985. That's when he left London." "Interview with Madelon Vriesendorp and Zoe Zenghelis," in *Clog* (2014), special issue on "Rem," p. 22.
49 The building still exists. According to their own accounts, Kees Christiaanse and Toni Adam had been in charge of the project. Interviews with the author on April 14, 2020 (Christiaanse) and September 25, 2018 (Adam).
50 The projects are not included, for instance, in Lucan, *OMA—Rem Koolhaas, El Croquis*, 53 (1992), or *El Croquis*, 79 (1996).
51 Interview with the author, April 14, 2020.
52 The assumption is based on interviews with Kees Christiaanse (April 14, 2020) and Mike Guyer (May 22, 2020). Guyer worked at OMA between 1984 and 1987.

Koolhaas explained to Janet Abrams in 1988 that he had decided to start his practice in the Netherlands for the very reason that "here, if the buildings didn't work out, I could hide them."[54] Nonetheless, the buildings at Veerplein, the police station in Almere, the Groningen towers, and the Byzantium do share some themes, ideas, and motifs with OMA's "important works" of the same period. Likewise, they betray a more than economic interest and ambition, even if the results seem to be only partly successful. When Patrice Goulet addressed the Almere police station in his interview, Koolhaas played down its importance, explaining that these "small projects […] are important […] in terms of construction skills," as if referring to an exercise—and the issue was dropped. Conversely, OMA's Netherlands Dance Theater in The Hague (1981–87) was a building that Koolhaas apparently wished to be noticed, and that was very much what did happen (→ F 1.4). As Christophe Van Gerrewey writes, the Dance Theater "featured on the cover of a roll call of international magazines: *L'Architecture d'Aujourd'hui, Architecture Moniteur Continuité, Techniques & Architecture, De Architect, Archis, Quaderns, Architectural Record, Bauwelt* and *A+U*."[55] The reviews began to appear in October. Not surprisingly, several authors mistook the theater for OMA's first building.[56] In general, the critiques were favorable, and some were enthusiastic. Many authors used Koolhaas' writings as a guideline for their own interpretation. Critics like Hans van Dijk, Hubert Damisch, and Jacques Lucan recognized in the building numerous topics from *Delirious New York*, such as "congestion" and the metropolitan condition, an architecture both "popular and ambitious," surrealism and the technique of the *cadavre exquis*. Altogether there was a tendency to treat *Delirious New York* as a straightforward manifesto rather than a retroactive one, with the consequence that the architecture was then measured by its standards. Van Dijk, for instance, came to the conclusion that the Netherlands Dance Theater was too small for OMA's metropolitan ambitions—which is instructive, above all else, with regard to the expectations stirred up by Koolhaas' writings and statements.[57]

      Some reviewers assessed OMA's building skills positively, among them Olivier Boissière in *L'Architecture d'Aujourd'hui*: "Does he [Koolhaas] know to build? One does wonder. The answer is yes!" Boissière was one of the first to understand that Koolhaas' constructive approach had little to do with detailing "in a 'Scarpa-ist' sense," instead being inspired by a "certain American architecture, a mixture of neglect and minute care."[58] But at least as many critics drew antithetical conclusions, such as Paul Groenendijk in *architectuur/bouwen*:

"Koolhaas' fascinating concepts have hitherto existed verbally and visually above all else, but they [still] deserve an adequate realization."[59] Similarly, Deborah Dietsch commented in the *Architectural Record*: "Sadly, however, the detailing at prominent junctures between the building's disparate elements [is] a nagging reminder of the 43-year-old Dutch architect's inexperience with working drawings."[60] In 1987, the magazine *Forum*—since 1959 the voice of Dutch structuralism, ridiculed by Koolhaas for its misguided "humanism"—published Madelaine Steigenga's devastating review of the police station in Almere. Steigenga insisted that architecture "does not legitimate itself until it has been built," and qualified the police station as a "debacle" and its execution as "abominable." Her conclusion, anticipated in the opening passage, reads like an irrevocable verdict: "The location is abominable, the concept is dead, the joke does not work, and the building is only photogenic when photographed at cruising height. The building is literally shaking, there are cracks in the walls. We have lost an illusion: Dutch Architecture will not be saved by O.M.A. either."[61] Steigenga instead put forward Muziekcentrum Vredensburg in Utrecht (1973–88) by Herman Hertzberger as a paradigm, and proof of the fact that the ever more difficult process of realization could be mastered and "great architectonic quality" still be achieved.

Koolhaas' competence as a practicing architect and his willingness to engage with the art of construction would be discussed and questioned for almost another decade. At that time, with four projects built—and six more either under construction or in preparation—such criticism stood in peculiar contrast to the actual commitment of the office and the daily efforts of a team comprising more than thirty architects. "[I]n the intimacy of my own ideas," Koolhaas confessed to Olivier Bossière and Dominique Lyon in 1986, "I have dedicated the next five years to become as professional as Harrison or Skidmore. That is my only true ambition."[62]

53 Interview with the author, April 14, 2020.
54 Janet Abrams, "Delirious Visions," *Blueprint*, 44 (February 1988), p. 32.
55 Christophe Van Gerrewey, "Goodbye Paper," in *AA-Files*, 74 (2017), p. 99.
56 See for instance Janny Rodermond, "Nederlands Danstheater: Een uitermate utilitair gebouw," in *De Architect* (October 1987), p. 77. Umberto Barbieri, "Teatro di Danza, L'Aia," in *Domus*, 689 (1987), p. 47.
57 Hans van Dijk, "Ambitie op zoek naar een "kritische massa," in *Archis*, 4 (1988), p. 36.
58 Olivier Boissière, "La Haye, Le Théâtre de la danse," in *L'Architecture d'Aujourd'hui*, 257 (1988), p. 33 (author's translation).
59 Paul Groenendijk, "Muziek en dans aan het Spui," in *architectuur/bouwen*, 3 (1987), p. 56 (author's translation).
60 Deborah K. Dietsch, "First Position: Dance Theater in The Hague," in *Architectural Record*, 4 (April 1988), p. 73.
61 Madelaine Steigenga, "Not Without a Scratch: Police Station Almere," in *Forum*, 2 (1987), p. 2.
62 Olivier Bossière and Dominique Lyon, "Entretien avec Rem Koolhaas," in *Cahiers du CCI*, 1 (1986), p. 84.

OMA in 1987

In 1987, the year Koolhaas was commissioned to design the Kunsthal, OMA lacked neither work nor the opportunity to actually build their commissions. According to the statistics in *S, M, L, XL*, at that point OMA was a medium-sized office with about thirty-five members of staff, the number increasing steadily until it had reached around sixty-seven in 1992.[63] By 1987, Dutch architect Ron Steiner had joined Koolhaas and Christiaanse as an associate, and the firm was involved in more than a dozen projects comprising competitions, studies, and buildings, which together are likely to have required a workforce of more than thirty people. There were the competitions for the Scientopia science park in Rotterdam, the Biocenter in Frankfurt, and the masterplan for Melun-Sénart in France, the renovation of the Bijlmermeer area in Amsterdam (1986–87), the Eusebius Tower in Arnhem, and De Vendel, an office park in Veenendaal near Utrecht.[64] The bus terminal at Rotterdam's central station (1985–87) opened in April, followed by the Netherlands Dance Theater in The Hague in September.[65] The IJplein buildings in Amsterdam—comprising two apartment blocks with shops and a community center, along with a primary school and a sports hall—were only completed in 1988 (→ F 1.5), along with Patio Villa in Rotterdam (1984–88), and the apartment blocks in Groningen in 1988. Three more projects were either under construction or soon to be constructed: the 13,000-square-meter development for mixed use on Veerplein in Vlaardingen (1986–89), the 15,000-square-meter Byzantium complex in Amsterdam (1985–91), likewise for mixed use, and Villa dall'Ava in Paris (1984–91).[66]

In one way or another, all these designs followed the path indicated at the Venice Biennale in 1980; in other words they were devised in opposition to the remainder of the Strada Novissima, stressing antagonisms, such as modern versus premodern, program versus form, utility versus meaning, facade versus non-facade (→ F 1.6). IJplein in Amsterdam, the Netherlands Dance Theater in The Hague, and the competition entry for Parc de la Villette in Paris lend themselves to illustrating the three recurrent design strategies: first, close approximations to either early or postwar modernism (IJplein); second, collages of multiple modernist references (the Netherlands Dance Theater); third, parklike projects of programmed, essentially unbuilt surfaces (Parc de la Villette) (→ F 1.7). It was from the "loose ends" of these strategies and projects that the designs for the Kunsthal, Museumpark, and the Netherlands Architecture Institute (NAi) were developed.

F 1.5

OMA/Rem Koolhaas, IJplein, Amsterdam, 1981–88.

OMA's IJplein buildings are a particularly bold "remake" of 1920s and 1930s modernism. The exterior of the apartment block on pillars with ribbon windows and access balconies recalls the work of Brinkman & Van der Vlugt and Willem van Tijen, but also Moisey Ginzburg's Narkomfin building in Moscow, given the emphasis on "collective" space and facilities—notably, the open promenade and community center on the first floor and the continuous "street in the air" of the attic. The Netherlands Dance Theater—most of which was demolished in 2015–16—was far more diverse in terms of references, shapes, and materials. The foyer was painted red, blue, yellow, black, and white, evoking the color palette of De Stijl. The exterior combined a number of features: walls in black brick and white tapered pilasters, reminiscent of a nondescript modernist building of the 1950s; two more modern-looking stories in corrugated aluminum that give the impression of being a later addition; a golden cone, reminiscent of Ivan Leonidov's project for the Narkomtiazhprom building in Moscow; a volume in gray plaster

63   Rem Koolhaas and Bruce Mau, S, M, L, XL, New York: The Monacelli Press, 1995, with opening endsheets. The figures vary significantly depending on the source.
64   The De Vendel study is one of at least a dozen literally unknown projects that OMA was involved in during the 1980s. Dossiers of several such projects are held by the HNI. Like the apartment blocks in Groningen and the House in Holten (1992–95), De Vendel was commissioned by the developer Geerlings. The project did not materialize.
65   Tomaso and Brigitta Zanoni et al., eds., Office for Metropolitan Architecture: Arbeiten 1972–1988, exhibition catalog, Basel: Architekturmuseum Basel, 1988, n.p.
66   OMA's building at Checkpoint Charlie in Berlin (1981–90) had been under construction since 1987, and was developed by OMA London with Elia Zenghelis as the partner in charge.

Strada Novissima, Venice Architecture Biennale, 1980. The facades by Paolo Portoghesi and OMA are center and right.

OMA/Rem Koolhaas, Parc de la Villette, Paris, 1982–83. Model of the park's central section.

with a concave roof, reminiscent of Wallace Harrison's UN headquarters in New York; and an undulating black roof and rear in corrugated metal, reminiscent of a warehouse. Each volumetric fragment indicated a different function in a manner similar to functionalist designs of the 1920s, such as the Van Nelle factory in Rotterdam by Brinkman & Van der Vlugt or the constructivist schemes of the Vesnin brothers. But whereas the facades of these buildings are unified by a homogeneous white skin, the parts of the Netherlands Dance Theater scarcely seem to belong to the same building. Anyone unfamiliar with the design might have taken the building for a piecemeal construction by multiple architects or even for multiple buildings instead of one. Rather than an actual design, OMA presented the entry for Parc de la Villette (1982–83) as a diagram of functions and their organization in space. Given the scheme's exclusive focus on program, the opposition to postmodern architecture as criticized by Koolhaas—that is, obsessed with form at the expense of programmatic issues—was complete.

No other country

In his 1990 book *The Condition of Postmodernity*, economic geographer David Harvey wrote: "The sharp recession of 1973, exacerbated by the oil shock, evidently shook the capitalist world out of the suffocating torpor of 'stagflation' [...] and set in motion a whole set of processes that undermined the Fordist compromise. The 1970s and 1980s have consequently been a troubled period of economic restructuring and social political readjustment. In the social space created by all this flux and uncertainty, a series of novel experiments in the realms of industrial organization as well as in political and social life have begun to take shape. These experiments may represent the early stirrings of the passage to an entirely new regime of accumulation, coupled with a quite different system of political and social regulation."[67] Even though Harvey's investigation did embrace a global perspective, its actual focus—notably in terms of the "new regime's" impact on society—is on the developments of the 1970s and 1980s in the US. The Dutch economy, too, was seriously affected by the two oil crises in 1973 and 1979, the decline of its manufacturing industries (coal mining, textiles, clothing, footwear, leather, shipbuilding) since the mid-1960s,[68] changing conditions for international competition and inflation, coupled with an aging population and longer life expectancy, which all entailed a decade

---

67 David Harvey, *The Condition of Postmodernity*, Oxford: Blackwell Publishing, 2015, p. 145. First published in 1990.

68 Jelle Visser and Anton Hemerijck, *"A Dutch Miracle": Job Growth, Welfare Reform and Corporatism in the Netherlands*, Amsterdam: Amsterdam University Press, 1997, p. 121.

of high unemployment, early retirement, and an increasing national debt due to the inequality between governmental expenditure and income.[69] But the Netherlands—which by that time had transformed into an exemplary welfare state—continued to guard its citizens against the pressures of the labor market's persisting crisis. In 1986, Peter Flora wrote about the Netherlands in a comparative study on European welfare states: "In no other West European country has the welfare state expanded to such an extent after World War II."[70]

Towards the mid-1980s, the Dutch economy began to recover from deep recession, and jobs slowly but steadily started to grow.[71] The "major overhaul of social security" happened in the early 1990s.[72] In the second half of the decade, the "Dutch job miracle" drew international attention, with the unemployment rate having dropped from almost 14 percent in 1983 to only 6 percent in 1997, albeit at the price of increasing part-time work, low pay, and earnings inequality, on the one hand, and few career prospects, high long-time unemployment, and gender inequality on the other.[73] In the building sector, the government remained strongly committed to the provision of social housing until 1994. During the 1970s and 1980s, more than 60,000 units were produced in peak years, and the annual total seldom fell below 30,000.[74] At the same time, policymakers continued to actively develop the country's cultural institutions. The Kunsthal originates from this earlier period and has its roots in the Dutch welfare state, prior to its revision and partial dismantling during the 1990s. As will be seen, the project was first and foremost the brainchild of government representatives, and the same holds true for Museumpark and the NAi.[75] The projects for the Kunsthal and Museumpark were initiated, funded, and largely devised by Rotterdam's municipality. The founding of the Architecture Institute and the construction of its premises in Rotterdam was realized under the combined tutelage of the ministries of culture (WVC) and housing (VROM).[76]

A pretty strong policy

In her monograph *Imagine a Metropolis*, Patricia van Ulzen describes the 1980s as a decade marked by a particularly fruitful and initiative cultural policy operated by Rotterdam's municipality.[77] The implementation of Museumpark, the NAi, and the Kunsthal were among the foremost achievements of this period. Landscape architect H. E. (Riek) Bakker (1944–), the head of Rotterdam's department for urban development between 1986 and 1991, was a major driving force behind these

F 1.8

OMA/Rem Koolhaas, Patio Villa, Rotterdam, 1984–88.

projects, along with Joop Linthorst (1948–2021), who was a member of the Dutch Labor Party (PvdA) and alderman of Rotterdam's city council between 1981 and 1994.[78] Linthorst in particular has been described as a critical protagonist within the municipal administration "who has worked wonders for the urban-cultural climate in Rotterdam."[79] Linthorst himself recalled in 2004: "You can't say it all happened in the

69 Ibid., pp. 9, 12.
70 Peter Flora, Introduction to *Growth to Limits: The Western European Welfare States Since World War II*, vol. 2, Berlin: Walter de Gruyter, 1986, p. XIX. In a 1997 study, Jelle Visser and Anton Hemerijck quote from a 1982 article in *The Economist*: "Foreign observers ridiculed the Dutch, in particular with respect to 'keeping more than a million people supported by the welfare state', as 'cloudy and lacking in realism'. The expression Dutch disease made its appearance in economics textbooks as an example of expensive unsustainable public welfare policies.'" Visser and Hemerijck, "*A Dutch Miracle*," p. 9.
71 Ibid., p. 26.
72 Ibid., p. 16. On this issue, see also ibid., pp. 117–51. On the impact of the Wassenaar Agreement from 1982, see ibid., p. 101 and Mara A. Yerkes, *Transforming the Dutch Welfare State*, Bristol: The Policy Press, 2011, pp. 10–11.
73 Visser and Hemerijck, "*A Dutch Miracle*," pp. 11, 23–44.
74 Marja Elsinga and Frank Wassenberg, "Social Housing in the Netherlands," in *Social Housing in Europe*, eds. Kathleen Scanlon and Christine Whitehead et al., Chichester: John Wiley & Sons, 2014, pp. 29–30. The Dutch government ended its subsidy program for social housing with the "grossing and balancing operation" of 1995. By comparison, about 10,000 units per year were produced between 2000 and 2010. Ibid., pp. 28–30.
75 On the intricate origins of the foundation and the building of the NAi, see Sergio M. Figueiredo, *The NAi Effect: Creating Architecture Culture*, Rotterdam: NAi010, 2016.
76 Ibid., pp. 188–99, 214–17, 220.
77 Patricia van Ulzen, *Imagine a Metropolis: Rotterdam's Creative Class 1970–2000*, Rotterdam: 010 Publishers, 2007.
78 Geert van Asbeck and Tom-Jan Meus, "Ex-wethouder steunt Peper," in *NRC Handelsblad* (January 27, 2000). The left-leaning Labor party had governed Rotterdam since the end of World War II.
79 Van Ulzen, *Imagine a Metropolis*, p. 39.

mid '80s, but if you look back you have to conclude that for Rotterdam a number of fairly crucial milestones were reached or thresholds crossed somewhere around that time. [...] For the council too it was a time when we pursued a pretty strong policy, and saw it implemented."[80]

The friendship between Koolhaas and Linthorst is an open secret. Perhaps they became friends while Koolhaas designed and built his private house, Patio Villa in Rotterdam, which was commissioned in 1984 and completed in 1988 (→ F 1.8). In *S, M, L, XL*, the chapter on Patio Villa is subtitled "House for Two Friends."[81] Linthorst's name does not appear in the correspondence that preceded the commission for the Kunsthal. But considering that he was a member of the board comprising Rotterdam's mayor and aldermen who were responsible for awarding the Kunsthal commission, it appears rather likely that he supported if not propelled the notion that Koolhaas be entrusted with the project.

Agreements made

The commission for the Kunsthal seems to trace back to a 1986 accord between Koolhaas and Rotterdam's municipality. On Monday, February 9, 1987, OMA received a letter from J. Laan, the city's alderman for traffic and transport: "Dear Mr. Koolhaas, with reference to your conversation between the mayor [Bram Peper] and myself on December 3, 1986 and a conversation that I had with you on January 15, I hereby report the following as [written] confirmation of the agreements made: It is [currently] being established that some private projects which concerned you as an architect will not be realized. This applies among other things to the office building for Mackenzie Hill/Muon at Churchillplein. The municipality was not formally involved as a party in that respective case, and it was stated that you cannot make any claims towards the municipality for non-compensation of the commission as a consequence of the planning being discontinued. We agreed that it is neither in your interest nor that of Rotterdam's municipality to continue this discussion, and thus we have drawn a clear line under the 'past.' In order to underscore our appreciation of your engagement we announced to you that the board of mayor and aldermen[82] intend to appoint you as the architect of the arts center which will be set up by the municipality in Museumpark, a plot of land for which the director of the department for urban development has drafted a basis plan."[83] In addition to OMA's project for Churchillplein (1984), Laan probably had two further "private projects" in mind, if not more: the towers OMA proposed in 1980 for Rotterdam's Boompjes Boulevard, and a lesser-known 1985 study commissioned for the harbor area, which included a spherical information center called De Bol that would likewise be located on Boompjes Boulevard.

Obviously, Koolhaas was not ignorant of the state of affairs at Rotterdam's municipality. On the previous Friday—the same day Laan posted his letter—Koolhaas had already sent a twofold offer to the local authorities. The first offer included an overview (*oriëntatie*) of comparable institutions, such as arts centers and museums, as well as a proposal for the program and a draft of the Kunsthal; the second was for an urban investigation of the area where the Kunsthal ought to be located.[84] On June 15, OMA received an answer from the director of the department for urban development, Riek Bakker. Apart from the urban investigation, Bakker ordered what OMA had offered, asking for the results of the study to be delivered within three months.[85] In a letter to OMA of June 24, Bakker confirmed an additional commission: an urban study on Museumpark that would take new requirements into account, such as the integration of an architectural institute and a "house of art" (*kunsthuis*).[86]

---

80 Ibid., p. 103.
81 Koolhaas and Mau, *S, M, L, XL*, p. 65.
82 "College B&W" [college van Burgemeester en wethouders].
83 J. Laan (Ruimtelijke Ordening, Verkeer en Vervoer), letter to Rem Koolhaas, February 6, 1987 (author's translation). OMAR 3267, 4509.
84 Rem Koolhaas, "Offerte Kunsthal," February 6, 1987. OMAR 3267.
85 Ibid.
86 Riek Bakker, letter to Rem Koolhaas, June 24, 1987. OMAR 3267.

P 3.1　Model of Museumpark by Yves Brunier. Front center: model of Kunsthal I.

P 3.2 Orchard. Painted photograph by Yves Brunier.
P 3.3 Podium. Collage by Yves Brunier. (→ next page)

P 3.4 Romantic Garden. Painted photograph by Yves Brunier. Left: the glass bridge. Right: pond.

Romantic Garden. Painted photograph by Yves Brunier. View of the pond.

P 3.6 Romantic Garden. Painted photograph by Yves Brunier. View of the open-air theater.

The Better Half of Architecture

OMA's Museumpark

2

All in all it's just another brick in the wall.

Pink Floyd, 1979

The projects for the Kunsthal and Museumpark emerged from a series of municipal initiatives launched in the second half of the 1980s. In 1986, Rotterdam's alderman for the arts, Joop Linthorst, commissioned a strategic paper on the concept for the Kunsthal, and in the same year the city's department for urban development worked out an initial scheme for Museumpark. For OMA these were the givens to start from, constituting a conceptual framework that would prove formative for both projects in one way or another. Rather than being isolated endeavors, the municipal projects for Museumpark and the Kunsthal were parts of a comprehensive plan to further the development of downtown Rotterdam, namely the Inner City Plan ("Binnenstadplan") dating from 1985. Koos Hage—a representative of Rotterdam's department for urban development who would accompany the entire planning process of the arts center and the park—described the plan as "the final scenario for the last round in the city's reconstruction," referring to the destruction of large parts of the city during World War II.[1] After a German air raid on May 14, 1940, the center of Rotterdam had burned for four days straight. Although few buildings survived within the *brandgrens*, or fire boundary, most parts of Rotterdam beyond this point remained completely undamaged. Reconstruction started after the end of the war along the lines of the "basic plan" devised by Cornelis van Traa (1899–1970) in 1946 (→ F 2.1). Van Traa's plan was conceived in general accordance with CIAM principles, including functional segregation, a drastic reduction in density, and broad streets securing efficient traffic circulation.[2] By and large, the plan was implemented in the following decades and continued to be effective in the 1980s.[3] It has been repeatedly observed that this longevity was owed to the plan's strategic flexibility, granting a relatively large degree of liberty to architects and urban planners alike.[4] It was precisely this flexibility, however, that fostered the extreme heterogeneity of Rotterdam's townscape. In the 1980s, the city's fragmented appearance was generally perceived as a shortcoming. According to Dutch critic Donald Lambert, the Inner City Plan for Rotterdam that was devised in 1985 to supplement Van Traa's 1946 plan[5] was meant to amend this lack of

---

1 Koos Hage, "Westersingel in Historic Perspective," in *Beelden in de Stad/Sculpture in the City*, eds. Richard Artschwager et al., Utrecht: Veen/Reflex, 1988, p. 30.
2 Ibid., p. 27.
3 Donald Lambert, "Het mogelijkheden en de beperkingen van een stedelijk plan: Het nieuwe Binnenstadplan voor Rotterdam," in *Wonen-TA/BK*, 10 (1985), p. 10.
4 "Thanks to its flexibility, the Basic Plan enjoyed an exceptionally long life as a juridical foundation and it is even still valid today," commented Frank Kauffmann. "Towards a 'modern' city center," in *Het Nieuwe Bouwen in Rotterdam 1920–1960*, eds. Wim A. L. Beeren et al., Delft: Delft University Press, 1982, p. 82.
5 Van Traa's basic plan remained effective even after the Inner City Plan had been issued in 1985. See Lambert, "Het mogelijkheden en de beperkingen van een stedelijk plan," p. 10.

Cornelis van Traa, basic plan for the inner city of Rotterdam, 1946. Bottom left: the Dijkzigt area, flanked on the right by Westersingel leading northwards to the main train station.

coherence: "The fragmentation so typical for Rotterdam in the seventies and at the beginning of the eighties has been reinforced by the attitude of the municipal service, which is mainly concerned with architecture. Some five years ago, when it became clear that reconstruction had not produced positive results, people began to look for remedies. At the beginning of 1985, a new overall plan for this city center was presented for the first time."[6]

Witteveen's plan

The Inner City Plan distinguished three focal areas, among them the so-called "Park Triangle," bordering the western margin of Rotterdam's inner city and the River Maas to the south.[7] The creation of Museumpark along with the construction of the Kunsthal and the NAi were envisaged as the key interventions within this area. Both the project for Museumpark and the concept of the Park Triangle as a whole took recourse to an urban expansion plan by Willem Gerrit Witteveen (1891–1979) that dates back to 1926 (→ F 2.2).[8] The centerpiece of the expansion plan was a property of 56 hectares—pastureland for the most part—that the city had purchased in 1924.[9] Witteveen, then head of the expansion and construction section at Rotterdam's public works department, proposed leaving most of the land unbuilt and transforming it into a public park. The name chosen for both the plan and the park was Dijkzigt, reflecting the proximity of Westzeedijk, a dike delimiting the area to the south. The park's triangular perimeter made it possible to connect three green spaces that had been designed in the 1850s by Jan David Zocher and his son Louis Paul: Het Park next to the River Maas, the Westersingel, and the Zoological Garden.[10] To the north, the tip of Dijkzigt Park joined Westersingel, a broad boulevard with a green space and a canal, or *singel*, in its middle. In the 1920s, the boulevard led to the zoological garden some 500 meters further north close to the present-day main train station. To the south, Dijkzigt Park widened up to meet the northern edge of Het Park, thus providing one continuous green space between the zoo to the north and the River Maas to the south. Between the two parks, however, there was—and still is—the Westzeedijk embankment, which protects the city from flooding.

Only the eastern and western margins of the Dijkzigt neighborhood were assigned for construction. The new street blocks were conceived as a seamless extension of the existing city fabric. A bird's-eye view of Witteveen's scheme shows the new streets and buildings as a variation on the perimeter block development of the surrounding area, which was built for the most part in the late nineteenth century. His plan—Berlagian in many respects—was approved by the city council in 1927 and partly implemented in the years that preceded the war.[11] As an aerial photograph from 1937 shows, the park essentially materialized in accordance with Witteveen's proposition (→ P 2.1).[12] The perimeter of Dijkzigt Park was slightly modified, but the funnel-shaped green space did link Westersingel with Het Park. Witteveen stipulated that the former Villa Hoboken (1850)—dubbed "Dijkzigt"—and the English landscape garden surrounding it should be incorporated into the scheme. The buildings constructed at the margins of the park similarly followed Witteveen's ideas in principle, and comprised several apartment blocks along Rochussenstraat, Mathenesserlaan, and

6 Donald Lambert, "Rotterdam, recoller les fragments," in *L'Architecture d'Aujourd'hui*, 257 (1988), pp. 38–39.
7 The other two areas were the "Center District" between Westersingel and Coolsingel and the "Water City" between Leuvehaven and Oudehaven.
8 Noor Mens, *W. G. Witteveen en Rotterdam*, Rotterdam: Uitgeverij 010, 2007, p. 34.
9 The Dijkzigt area is often referred to as the "land of Hoboken," as it had previously been owned by the Hobokens, a Rotterdam family of shipbuilders.
10 Hage, "Westersingel in Historic Perspective," pp. 22–24.
11 Mens, *W.G. Witteveen en Rotterdam*, pp. 70, 77.
12 Joris Molenaar, *Brinkman & Van der Vlugt Architects*, Rotterdam: nai010 publishers, 2012, p. 194.

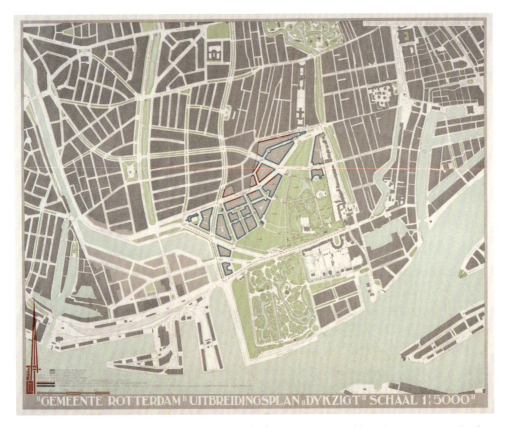

Willem Gerrit Witteveen, expansion plan for Dykzigt [sic], Rotterdam, 1926. Along the eastern margin of the park is Westersingel, leading northwards to the zoological garden.

Nieuwe Binnenweg, complementing the Oude Westen district to the north; Museum Boijmans Van Beuningen (1928–35) by Adrianus van der Steur directly adjacent to the eastern edge of the park; the Unilever Offices (1930–31) by H. F. Mertens to the west; the Erasmiaans grammar school (1935–36), similarly by Van der Steur; and the GEB tower (1927–31) by Van der Steur, J. Poot, and Witteveen himself.[13] Even the design of the exteriors was subject to the control of Witteveen's municipal department: "The various perimeter blocks along Rochussenstraat, Mathenesserlaan, Binnenweg and other connecting streets were finished in the early thirties and subsequently. In compliance with official guidelines, the appearance of the blocks was strictly regulated. [...] All the buildings were brick; some of them had saddle roofs. The architecture of the blocks had a luxurious, modern air. By contemporary standards and in accordance with the Department for Town Planning, the resulting townscape was exceptionally harmonious" (→ P 2.3–2.5).[14]

The apparent "misfit" were four villas to which two more were added in the 1950s (→ P 2.6). These two-story houses surrounded by small private gardens signified a clear rupture with the closed street fronts and scale of virtually all other buildings in the area. The villas were built vis-à-vis Museum Boijmans Van Beuningen, and more or less at the same time (1928–35). Three of them were designed by exponents of the Nieuwe Bouwen movement: Boevé House (1931–33) and Sonneveld House (1929–33) by Brinkman & Van der Vlugt; and Kraayeveld House (1938–39) by G. Baas and L. Stokla. The large fenestrations, undercut volumes, and white finish of the exterior exacerbated the contrast to the stout-looking red brick facades of the neighboring buildings.

Unlike the center of Rotterdam, the area surrounding the former Dijkzigt Park was not destroyed during the war. The *brandgrens* passed some 500 meters further east, meandering half-way between Westersingel and Coolsingel. Photographs taken in the afternoon of May 14, 1940 show a large crowd on Hobokenplein, just north of Museum Boijmans Van Beuningen, watching the burning city in the background (→ P 2.2). After the war, most new buildings in this area followed in one way or another the path indicated by Witteveen in the 1920s. Examples are the Greek Orthodox church by Taen and Nix (1947–57), the first extension of Museum Boijmans Van Beuningen by A. Bodon (1963–72), and the C-shaped blocks by P. P. Hammel (1975–77) along Nieuwe Binnenweg; even Ernst Groosman's modernist thirteen-story apartment block at Westzeedijk (1949–58) is clad in exposed red brickwork.

Once more

The Park Triangle area, as defined by the 1985 Inner City Plan, largely coincided with the perimeter of Witteveen's expansion plan dating back to 1926. Once more, a sequence of green spaces—Westersingel, the future Museumpark, and Het Park—constituted the plan's actual centerpiece. And once more, the plan aimed to strengthen the bonds between Rotterdam's inner city and the River Maas (→ F 2.3). In November 1986, the city's department for urban development, Stadsontwikkeling Rotterdam, held a workshop entitled "Museumpark." The results were synthesized in an A3 booklet comprising sixteen pages.[15] The booklet explicitly refers to the "Witteveen plan" as a source of inspiration.[16] Like Witteveen's Dijkzigt Park, Museumpark was devised as a link between Westersingel to the north and Het Park to

13 Elli Adriaansz, "A Modern Villa Park in the City: Its History: The History of the Land van Hoboken," Wiederhall, 20 (2001), p. 13.
14 Ibid.
15 Stadsontwikkeling Rotterdam, "Museumpark: Uitkomst atelier November 1986." OMAR 1497.
16 Ibid., p. 5.

the south (→ F 2.4–2.5). Its surface, however, was reduced from 56 hectares to a narrow corridor of about six. To the east, the area was flanked by Museum Boijmans Van Beuningen and Jonkindgstraat; to the west, it bordered the vast hospital complex of Erasmus University's medical faculty (1965–68), which had been designed by OD 205.

Another major difference with respect to Dijkzigt Park was a pronounced shift from nature to "culture." In a deliberate contrast to the more remote and "quiet" Het Park, the department for urban development envisaged Museumpark as "a platform for the exchange of ideas."[17] A straight promenade, dubbed the "Axis of Development," would link Rochussenstraat at the park's northern margin with Maasboulevard and the dike to the south.[18] The 1986 scheme proposed locating two new buildings alongside the promenade: the Architecture Institute adjacent to Museum Boijmans Van Beuningen and the Kunsthal bordering Westzeedijk and Maasboulevard at its crown. Together with the future natural history museum—to be housed in Villa Dijkzigt—the three museums were intended to augment the cultural facilities in the area, notably the neighboring Museum Boijmans Van Beuningen. The Axis of Development was meant to hinge at the "culture axis" to the north—i.e. the art galleries and congress centers that were aligned along Westersingel, along with Rotterdamse Kunststichting, which was accommodated in the reconstruction of J. P. P. Oud's Café de Unie. An open space for temporary public events called the "Manifestation Field" was to be located on what used to be Hobokenplein and is now the site of the present HNI.[19] To provide the requisite facilities for Rotterdam's theater and music festival, Teatro Fantastico would become an integral part of the brief for Museumpark. But the Manifestation Field was also intended to have a commemorative function: recalling the fact that many Rotterdammers took refuge in the northern section of Dijkzigt Park during the fire caused by the German bombardment in May 1940.[20]

Support for the moderns

In 1987, OMA produced at least two studies of the Kunsthal and Museumpark, both based on the municipal project from the previous year. German architect Gregor Mescherowsky, who had graduated from Berlin's Technische Universität and joined the office in the same year, was the project manager in charge.[21] The first study, entitled "Kunsthal Rotterdam: Preliminary Town Planning Study," dates from May 1987 and covers the area of the Park Triangle as a whole, stressing

F 2.3

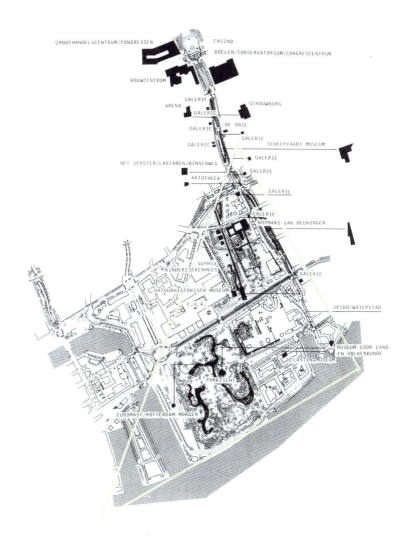

The plan of Park Triangle and Westersingel produced by Stadsontwikkeling Rotterdam in 1986. The Park Triangle—marked in yellow—is bisected by Westzeedijk boulevard. The Dijkzigt area and Westersingel or "culture axis" are located above Westzeedijk, while Het Park and the River Maas are below it.

17 Ibid., p. 4.
18 Ibid., p. 5.
19 Ibid., pp. 5–6. OMAR 1497. On the ideas for the Manifestation Field proposed by the department for urban development in 1987, see Koos Hage, "Manifestatieterrein," September 29, 1987; and Stadsontwikkeling Rotterdam, Center District, "Manifestatieterrein in Rotterdam," November 2, 1987. OMAR 4492.
20 J. W. Vader, letter to "Plangroep Museumpark," September 3, 1987. OMAR 3267. The municipality initially planned to inaugurate the Manifestation Field on the fiftieth anniversary of the event in May 1990.
21 Emails to the author by Mescherowsky dated October 22 and December 19, 2018. Mescherowsky is also listed among team members of the Kunsthal (I) and Museumpark in *S, M, L, XL*, Rem Koolhaas and Bruce Mau, New York: The Monacelli Press, 1995, pp. 1275, 1277.

F 2.4

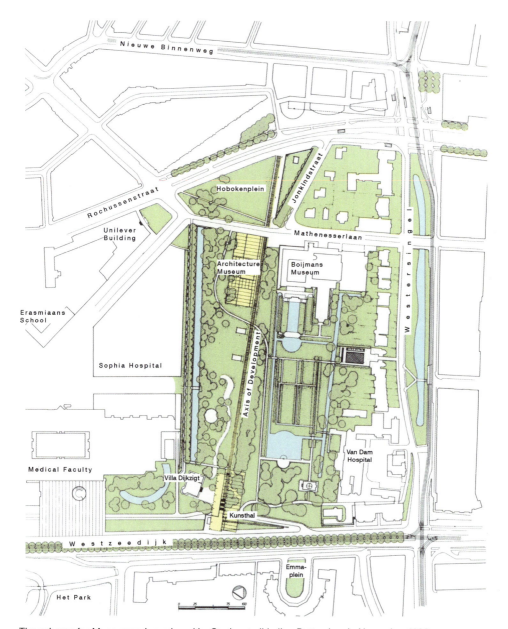

The scheme for Museumpark produced by Stadsontwikkeling Rotterdam in November 1986. Names of streets and buildings have been added by the author.

the morphological incoherence of the surroundings (→ F 2.6).[22] In *S, M, L, XL*, Koolhaas would characterize Museumpark as a "leftover rectangle [...] between four different conditions."[23] This notion of the essential incoherence of the surroundings was the point of departure for all the designs that OMA produced for this site. Two constructions doubtless contributed to this notion. To the south, the dike had been broadened and its level raised in 1974.[24] With four lanes of

F 2.5

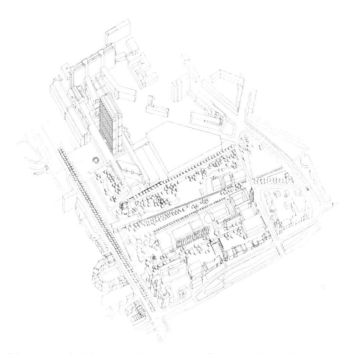

Axonometric view of the scheme for Museumpark produced by Stadsontwikkeling Rotterdam in November 1986.

traffic split by a tramway running in both directions, Westzeedijk became more of a physical barrier than ever before, not only between the two parks but also between Museumpark and the nineteenth-century street blocks on Emmaplein and in the adjacent docklands district. To the west, the medical faculty designed by OD 205 introduced an entirely new sense of scale to the center of the Dijkzigt area, along with a new, self-contained type of building (→ P 2.7). It has more affinity with a 1960s megastructure than with the traditional European city. The first 15 meters above the ground—critical for any urbanism in the tradition of Sitte and Berlage—are nothing but an indeterminate and constantly transforming footing, from which the tower arises as the only distinct shape. Its facade of white enameled aluminum sandwich panels, designed by Jean Prouvé, displays the virtues of technological innovation and industrial prefabrication, underscoring the alien character of the complex with regard to its built environment. In the park and along the dike the presence of the tower is inescapable, given its extent and its height of 114 meters.

22 OMA, "Kunsthal Rotterdam: Preliminary Town Planning Study," May 18, 1987. OMAR 1553. OMA seems to have anticipated the municipality's commission for the study. Bakker assigned OMA an "'extra' commission for a further study of Museumpark" only one month later. Riek Bakker, letter to OMA, June 24, 1987. OMAR 3267.

23 Rem Koolhaas, "New Rotterdam," in Koolhaas, Mau, S, M, L, XL, p. 405.

24 Hage, "Westersingel in historic perspective," p. 29.

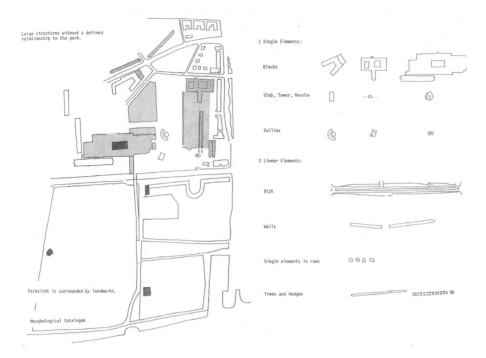

OMA/Rem Koolhaas, "Kunsthal Rotterdam: Preliminary Town Planning Study," May 18, 1987.
A "morphological catalogue" of the park and its surroundings.

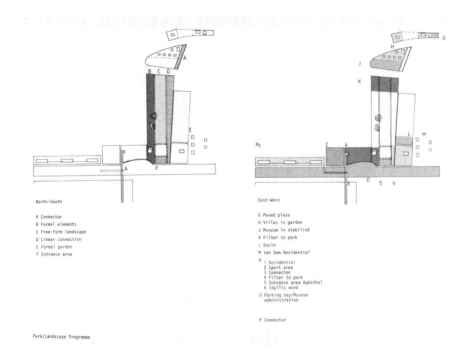

OMA/Rem Koolhaas, "Kunsthal Rotterdam: Preliminary Town Planning Study," May 18, 1987.
Elements of the park and additional buildings proposed for the surroundings.

Even if the presence of the medical faculty was lethal for any aspiration to develop the Dijkzigt area as a homogeneous whole, the conclusions to be drawn from this were less obvious. Beyond the hospital precinct, the townscape in the 1980s was still dominated by perimeter blocks, continuous street fronts and rooflines, and the use of exposed brickwork, with most buildings dating from the late nineteenth century and the interwar years. Apart from Museum Boijmans Van Beuningen, the Unilever offices, and the Erasmiaans grammar school, this also applies to the apartment blocks along Rochussenstraat and, along Maasboulevard, to F. L. Lourijssen's residential "hotel" (1928) and the adjacent neo-renaissance buildings on Emmaplein (→ P 2.8).[25] In the Oude Westen neighborhood, where a large urban renewal project was ongoing and would continue until the early 1990s, most new buildings complied with this "consensus" in one way or another.[26]

OMA's study of May 1987 prepared the ground for an entirely different proposition, recommending that a series of complementary buildings be added at the margins of the site: five villas and a small residential tower along Rochussenstraat, three residential blocks in front of the medical faculty, and three more as well as two lower buildings containing luxury apartments on the site of Van Dam Hospital, which had been designed by Brinkman & Van den Broek (1931–38) but was now scheduled for demolition (→ F 2.7). All the residential blocks were conceived as slabs with vertical, towerlike proportions. OMA's proposals were evidently intended to counterbalance the dominance of the "street block urbanism" in this area by reinforcing morphologies which were obvious exceptions at the time, such as Groosman's thirteen-story apartment block, the tower of Erasmus University, and the six modernist villas vis-à-vis Museum Boijmans Van Beuningen.

La Villette grammar

OMA's scheme for Museumpark, which was included in the study, fully embraced the municipality's ambition to link Westersingel to Het Park and the River Maas, while proposing that the positions of the Manifestation Field and the NAi be switched. In the 1986 municipal project, the NAi was located next to Museum Boijmans Van Beuningen and the

---

25 Despite numerous exceptions, an average height of 12 to 14 meters prevailed. OMA's files include a copy of a plan listing the heights of all the surrounding buildings, apparently provided by Rotterdam's department for urban development: "Globale hoogtenmaten omliggende bebouwing." OMAR 1452.

26 Hans van Dijk, "De gezelligheids-revolutie: 1965–1985," in *Vijftig jaar Wederopbouw Rotterdam: Een Geschiedenis van toekomstvisies*, ed. Martin Arts, Rotterdam: Uitgeverij 010, 2005, pp. 161–92. See also Pim Vermeulen and Fred de Riuter et al., *Stadsvernieuwing Rotterdam 1974–1984*, Rotterdam: 010 Publishers, 1985, pp. 214–21.

Manifestation Field on Hobokenplein. In OMA's scheme, the Manifestation Field is located next to Museum Boijmans Van Beuningen, while Hobokenplein is split in two halves, with the five villas and the tower to the north and the NAi to the south. Ultimately, the switch would prevent the Architecture Institute from dividing the already scarce open space into two parts, allowing the park to extend right to Mathenesserlaan (now renamed "Museumpark"), the street south of Hobokenplein.

In an obvious analogy to OMA's project for Parc de la Villette, the scheme for the Rotterdam park was organized in a series of superimposed "layers." One layer divides the surface into three strips running north to south: one with "formal elements," one conceived as a "free form landscape," and one serving as a "linear connection" leading to the Kunsthal and Maasboulevard. On a second layer, the terrain is divided into three bands running east to west: a "filter" to the park along Rochussenstraat, and another one along Maasboulevard; both filters are defined by a stabilized surface and trees distributed on a grid. The area between them, called the "Synthetic and Natural Garden," complements the existing park in the fashion of an English landscape garden and features a superimposed continuous grid of "service poles," providing "electrical and water services for special events." On a third layer, six kiosks are distributed at strategic points around the park's circulation system. The Kunsthal, situated next to Villa Dijkzigt, is "set back from the dijk into the park, where it creates four different landscapes on each of its sides."[27] Both the square shape of the footprint and its (approximate) dimensions correspond to the Kunsthal as it was eventually built. A couple of—clumsy—sketches show the building as a floating horizontal slab.[28]

At a meeting with the municipality in September 1987, Koolhaas presented a slightly modified scheme which was limited to the perimeter of the park but corresponded in essence to the proposal from May.[29] All in all, Koolhaas' presentation in September must have been approved by the municipal representatives. In the documentation entitled "Museumpark" issued by the department for urban development in December 1987—a revised version of the study from November 1986—the NAi was shifted to Hobokenplein and an axonometric projection showed three solitaires north of the museum, recalling the (modernist) villas suggested by the architects in both their propositions.[30]

Dijkzigt and the European city

Rather than proposing an architectural idea for the Kunsthal, OMA's study from May 1987 creates a partly fictional context for the project, distorting the actual givens. The purpose seems to have been two-fold: strengthening those traits of the Dijkzigt area which Koolhaas saw as paradigmatic for both Rotterdam and the typical European city of the late twentieth century; and, in doing so, counteracting contemporary movements for urban renewal as displayed by the IBA (International Building Exhibition) in Berlin. Koolhaas outlined his vision of the European city in a number of essays published in *L'Architecture d'Aujourd'hui* in 1985. In "The Terrifying Beauty of the Twentieth Century" he writes: "[T]he European Metropolis is like a reef on which each intention, each ambition, each solution, each question and each answer implacably run aground. But like the forms that can be discovered in the clouds it is possible to will this landscape into an amazing spectacle of invention."[31] Urban fragmentation, according to Koolhaas, was not a shortcoming, but a potential quality to be developed; and it was a genuine quality of the modern European city, largely dependent on the destruction wrought by World War II and the reconstruction it entailed. Berlin figured as the prime example: "The richness of Berlin resides in the prototypical sequence of its models: neo-classical city, early Metropolis, modernist testbed, Nazi capital, war victim, Lazarus, cold war battlefield, and so on."[32]

How the fragmented townscape of Berlin might be turned into a "spectacle of invention" had been demonstrated a decade earlier (1976–77) in Ungers' project "The City within the City." Starting from the assumption that the population of Berlin would continue to decrease, Ungers and his collaborators—Koolhaas among them—proposed shaping the process of the city's partial demolition and renaturation.[33] Selected districts were to be preserved and developed on the basis of "cognate" city models such as the Baroque plan for Karlsruhe, the Manhattan grid, and Leonidov's map for Magnitogorsk. The remainder

---

27 OMA, "Kunsthal Rotterdam: Primarily Town Planning Study," n.p.
28 Ibid.
29 OMA, "Analyse Museumpark," September 17, 1987. OMAR 1552. Koolhaas' presentation was scheduled in a program for a meeting on September 17. "Agenda vergadering Plangroep Museumpark, donderdag 17 september 1987". OMAR 3267.
30 Stadsontwikkeling Rotterdam, "Museumpark," December 1987. OMAR 4477.
31 Rem Koolhaas, "The Terrifying Beauty of the Twentieth Century," in *OMA—Rem Koolhaas*, ed. Jacques Lucan, Princeton Architectural Press: New York, 1991, p. 154. First published in French as "La splendeur terrifiante du xxe siècle," in *L'Architecture d'Aujourd'hui*, 238 (1985), p. 15.
32 Ibid.
33 Ungers lists Koolhaas as one of four contributors in total. The others were Peter Riemann, Hans Kollhoff, and Arthur Ovaska. Oswald Mathias Ungers, *Die Stadt in der Stadt*, Cologne: Studio Verlag für Architektur, 1977.

of the urban fabric would be turned into a continuous green space. Koolhaas drafted an initial manifesto-like project statement, entitled "Berlin: A Green Archipelago," which was later translated into German and profoundly reworked by Ungers for his publication.[34] The draft was leveled against initiatives for urban renewal and urban repair. "The present idea," Koolhaas wrote, "that inner-city area's [sic] can only be rehabilitated through more construction that restores a primordial state, is counterproductive and should be exorcised."[35]

Among the architects, academics, and critics demanding the preservation and reconstruction of historic urban centers, Léon Krier was a key figure whose ideas Koolhaas probably knew at first hand from the years 1975 and 1976, when they were both teaching at the AA School of Architecture in London. Krier ran a research program dedicated to the transformation of selected areas in the British capital that were characterized by postwar developments found to be spatially "wanting."[36] In 1978 he signed the declarations of Palermo and Brussels, along with figures such as Maurice Culot, Bernard Huet (the editor in chief of *L'Architecture d'Aujourd'hui*), and Pierluigi Nicolin (the editor in chief of *Lotus*). These two declarations stipulating the "reconstruction of the European city" are similar in content, and both resonate with Krier's anti-capitalist, anti-consumerist vision of returning to a pre-industrial society. The ideas and demands put forward include: reconstructing the city as a "city of stones," based on an artisanal construction culture; rejecting industrial methods of production; preserving the cultural heritage of a city's historical fabric; abolishing zoning; shaping public space exclusively according to the model of the traditional European street and square.[37]

In 1980, Koolhaas participated in the IBA competition in Berlin (1979–87). The site—around the intersection of Kochstrasse and Friedrichstrasse—was located in the Südliche Friedrichstadt area, which fell under the purview of the IBA Neubau category for newbuilds, headed by Josef Paul Kleihues. Kleihues explicitly distanced his efforts from a concept of reconstruction that "degenerates visibly into nostalgia," perhaps referring to Krier and the ideas pronounced in the declarations of Palermo and Brussels.[38] Instead he advocated the concept of a "critical reconstruction," which would take into account the diversity of historical traces and "transpose the classical idea of dialectic into the language and living conditions of the Modern Movement."[39] Nevertheless, Kleihues regarded the preservation and restoration of a Baroque ground plan and a uniform height for the facades (18 to 20 meters) as mandatory (→ F 2.8).[40] Koolhaas' project

F 2.8

Josef Paul Kleihues, masterplan for Südliche Friedrichstadt/Südlicher Tiergarten. Neubau section of the IBA, Berlin, 1984.

34 The typescript is published in *Die Stadt in der Stadt. Berlin: ein grünes Archipel*, eds. Florian Hertweck and Sébastian Marot, Zurich: Lars Müller Publishers, 2013, pp. 11–23. Also published in English as *The City in the City– Berlin: A Green Archipelago*.
35 Rem Koolhaas, "Berlin a Green Archipelago," in *Die Stadt in der Stadt*, Hertweck and Marot, p. 13.
36 Léon Krier, "Research and Projects in London," in *A+U*, 11 (1977), pp. 105–33.
37 André Barey, *Déclaration de Bruxelles*, Brussels: Archives d'Architecture Moderne, 1980, pp. 18, 20–21.
38 Josef Paul Kleihues and Heinrich Klotz, *Internationale Bauausstellung Berlin 1987: Beispiele einer neuen Architektur*, Stuttgart: Klett-Cotta, 1986, p. 128.
39 Josef Paul Kleihues, "Southern Friedrichstadt Area: Rudiments of History. Place of Contradictions. Critical Reconstruction," in *A+U*, 5 (1987), pp. 146, 148.
40 Lore Ditzen, "Josef Paul Kleihues interviewed by Lore Ditzen," in *The Architectural Review*, 9 (1984), p. 42.

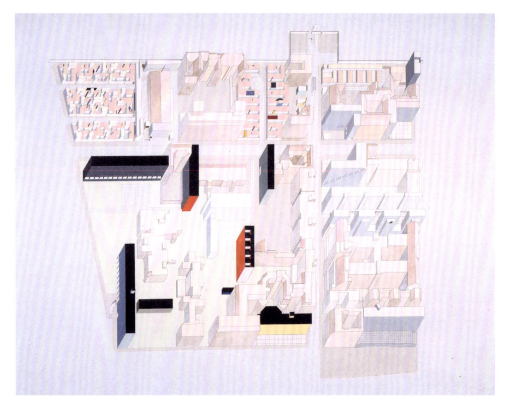

OMA/Rem Koolhaas, competition entry for Kochstrasse/Lützowstrasse, IBA Berlin, 1980.

for Kochstrasse/Friedrichstrasse was a polemic against Kleihues' concept of Critical Reconstruction, "the recent *rediscovery* of the street as the core element of all urbanism," and a restoration of its eighteenth-century grid that would "try as much as possible to hide most of the post-war buildings."[41] OMA proposed modernist typologies: a series of vertical "slabs," rendered in primary colors; and—with reference to "Mies, Hilbersheimer, Häring"—courtyard houses of one to two stories adding up to a number of "mat buildings" (→ F 2.9). Both building types—the courtyard house and the vertical slabs—would fill the gaps between the existing buildings. But instead of restoring the integrity of the block and creating a continuous street front, the new buildings perpetuate the fragmentation and heterogeneity of the street block.

      Koolhaas' experiences in Berlin largely informed his urbanist agenda in subsequent years. In the 1985 essay "Imagining Nothingness," Koolhaas envisaged the concept of the City Archipelago as a "blueprint for a theory of the European metropolis" that could be applied elsewhere as well.[42] That was particularly true for Rotterdam. As Koolhaas pointed out in "The Terrifying Beauty of the Twentieth Century," both cities had been epicenters of the modern movement, both had suffered extreme destruction during the war, and this destruction was still visible both in the guise of large urban wastelands and in the kaleidoscopic mix of divergent architectural and urbanist approaches to their reconstruction.

Even here

Koolhaas also saw parallels regarding the recent development of the two cities. "Now, today," he stated in 1985, "both are caught in the grips of intense revisionism."[43] In Rotterdam, the modernist principles of the city's reconstruction had been abandoned as public opinion turned against such beliefs in the mid-1960s.[44] Koolhaas explained: "During the '50s the new Rotterdam became a paradigm: a CIAM city of slabs that were tied together by a Team X-like 'connective tissue' by Bakema, the [Lijnbaan]. In the '60s and '70s, the emblematic architecture was discredited: on the periphery of the center, on the other side of the railway track, a second, revisionist architecture was started—an assembly of buildings by Piet Blom (a small forest of his tree houses), Bakema and others. The new reconstruction was the absolute opposite of the '50s effort: where they were sober, ordered and logical, the new city was chaotic and obsessively humanist."[45] Regardless of the respective architectural or urbanist approach, Koolhaas was also critical of the fact that the remaining large unbuilt areas within Rotterdam's center were assigned for construction. Born in Rotterdam in 1944, he had lived with his parents close to the destroyed inner city until at least the age of six.[46] In 1950, reconstruction had only just started, and the larger part of the center would have been devoid of buildings. In 1985, he lamented that "this openness came under attack; plans were made for [Rotterdam's] densification or intensification, for the realization, even here, of the 'compact city.'"[47] By this time, the municipality had begun to develop a broad boulevard called Weena between the main train

41   OMA, *OMA: Projects 1978–1981*, London: Architectural Association, 1981, p. 33.
42   Rem Koolhaas, "Imagining Nothingness," in *OMA–Rem Koolhaas*, Lucan, p. 157. First published in French as "Imaginer le néant" in *L'Architecture d'Aujourd'hui*, 238 (1985), p. 38.
43   Koolhaas, "The Terrifying Beauty," p. 154.
44   See Hans van Dijk, "De gezelligheids-revolutie: 1965–1985," p. 171.
45   OMA, *OMA: Projects 1978–1981*, p. 39. The criticism refers to the (Dutch) structuralist tendencies of a large development at the junction of Binnenrotte (a former railway line), the old harbor, and a broad boulevard called Blaak. The complex by Blom, of which the popular "cube houses" are only one part, was completed in 1984, while the public library by Van den Broek & Bakema dates from 1983.
46   According to his own account, Koolhaas was six years old when the family moved to Indonesia. Patrice Goulet, "La deuxième chance de l'architecture moderne …," in *L'Architecture d'Aujourd'hui*, 238 (1985), p. 2. The biography in Lucan's monograph from 1990 states that the family lived in Indonesia between 1952 and 1956. Lucan, *OMA–Rem Koolhaas*, p. 168.
47   Koolhaas, "The Terrifying Beauty," p. 154. In this specific passage Koolhaas refers to the 1970s, but the essay as a whole deals with the situation at the time it was written, i.e. in 1985.

station and Hofplein, with vast areas of unbuilt surface on either side. According to Donald Lambert, the city's purpose was to remedy "the image of a soulless Rotterdam [...] by clearing away at least a million square meters of surface area, mainly in the form of offices on Weena."[48]

A project of urban renewal (*stadsvernieuwing*), not dissimilar to the IBA projects in Berlin, materialized in Rotterdam's Oude Westen district, which is adjacent to the Dijkzigt area and just across Rochussentraat. Supervised by architect P. P. Hammel, the project was propelled by a local activist group which had formed in the early 1970s. Van Dijk describes it as the most important of several urban renewal initiatives in Rotterdam from this period, which had been broadly supported by the Social Democrat city council since 1974.[49] The initiative led to the replacement of several existing buildings by new ones, most of them reproducing the typology of the perimeter block.[50] To the south, Oude Westen borders the Dijkzigt area, which, according to OMA's studies in 1987, was set to contain the main elements of the European city as envisaged by Koolhaas at the time: the clash of traditionalist and modernist fragments, scales, and morphologies as well as the "void" in the guise of a park.

Metropolitanism

If the Office for Metropolitan Architecture had to provide a substitute for utopia, it was its vision of metropolitan culture, advertised as the "culture of congestion." Ever since 1978, OMA's metropolitanism drew on the model of the mythical past of Manhattan, as described by Koolhaas in *Delirious New York*. He famously summed up the metropolitan promise in the chapter on the Downtown Athletic Club, a high-rise of thirty-eight floors by Starret & Van Vleck that had been built in Manhattan at the end of the 1920s. From the broad range of functions specified in a set of plans from that period, Koolhaas inferred that the club housed a "fantastic juxtaposition of activities" with surrealist qualities.[51] Koolhaas' description culminates in the imaginary scene of naked men "[e]ating oysters with boxing gloves," inspired by a floorplan showing a locker room with an oyster bar next to a space assigned for boxing and wrestling. Moreover, the club, as pictured by Koolhaas, was a realm of "the Synthetic." Its artificial character is exemplified by an indoor golf course, "the transplantation of an 'English' landscape of hills and valleys," and, even more so, by the sardonic proposition that the club was an "incubator for adults, an instrument that permits the members to [transform] themselves into new beings [...] according to their individual designs."[52] What was it that Koolhaas' club—and, by way of extension, the metropolis and its skyscrapers—had to offer? An experience enriched by manmade magic, surreal encounters, a loss of control, the transgression of conventions, or, to use Koolhaas' own words: the exploitation of the "full potential of the apparatus of modernity," "perpetual programmatic instability," "subversiveness," and an "unforeseeable and unstable combination of simultaneous activities."[53] Despite its embrace of advanced technology, Koolhaas' metropolitanism did not promise progress in the service of a better world, to be sure. Rather it was about something like the reenchantment of a disenchanted world.

Architecture, according to Koolhaas, could chiefly contribute to this end by employing technology for its own purposes and through the spatial organization of its program. With respect to the latter, Koolhaas championed the floorplan as the ultimate instrument for plotting human activities and the way they interact.[54] This plotting and the possibility of interaction, however, was limited to each single floor because, as Koolhaas argued, the "deliberate disconnection between the stories"—or "vertical schism," as he called the spatial isolation of individual floors—was the very condition that enabled the skyscraper to harbor such a broad range of ever-changing uses.[55] With regard to the desired metropolitan qualities, the role of the physical partition is contradictory: on the one hand, it fosters the activities' freedom, "instability," and diversification; on the other, it forecloses their interaction and prevents their diversity from being experienced. For the Boompjes project in Rotterdam (1980–81), and again for the competition entry for the City Hall in The Hague (1986), OMA proposed literal adoptions of the Manhattan skyscraper. The American atrium cut into the interior of the latter was apparently intended to mitigate the contradiction, but could not resolve it.[56]

48 Lambert, "Rotterdam, recoller les fragments," p. 39.
49 Van Dijk, 'De gezelligheids-revolutie', pp. 176–90. Van Dijk mentions that the initiatives attracted international attention: "Especially from Germany (Berlin, Kreuzberg) experts came to study the 'Rotterdam model.'" Ibid., p. 168.
50 Paul Groenendijk and Piet Vollaard, *Guide to Modern Architecture in Rotterdam*, Rotterdam: 010 Publishers, 2001, p. 26. See also Vermeulen and De Riuter, *Stadsvernieuwing Rotterdam*, pp. 218–20.
51 Rem Koolhaas, *Delirious New York: A Retroactive Manifesto for Manhattan*, New York: The Monacelli Press, 1994, p. 157. First published in 1978.
52 Ibid., pp. 157–58.
53 Ibid., pp. 85, 87, 158.
54 Ibid., p. 157.
55 Ibid., pp. 105–07. According to Koolhaas, the floors' spatial isolation results from two idiosyncrasies of the skyscraper that are ultimately both consequences of its size: the elevator replacing the stairs as a spatial means of vertical circulation (the "schism"); and the relative autonomy of the facade, freed from the obligation to represent the way the interior is used (the "lobotomy"). Koolhaas, *Delirious New York*, pp. 100, 105–06.
56 In a 1985 interview, Koolhaas himself calls the floors of the skyscraper an "obstacle" (*belemmering*). Mil De Kooning, "De economie van de verbeelding," in *Vlees & Beton*, 4 (1985), n.p.

Programmed surface

Koolhaas' 1971 study on the Berlin Wall was already about the paradoxical quality of the Wall in creating and limiting freedom at the same time. According to his own account, he experienced the Berlin Wall as a revelation about the essence of architecture. In "Field Trip," his 1993 essay on the AA study, he wrote: "It was as if I had come eye to eye with architecture's true nature."[57] Part of the Wall's nature, and implicitly of walls in general, was the irresolvable conflict between its desired and undesired qualities. On the one hand, the Wall made (West) Berlin "free."[58] On the other, the "Berlin Wall was a very graphic demonstration of the power of architecture and some of its unpleasant consequences."[59] In the same essay Koolhaas insinuates that his reserve with regard to architectural form was inspired by his encounter with the Berlin Wall: "its impact," he wrote, "was entirely independent of its appearance. [...] I would never again believe in form as the primary vessel of meaning."[60]

In this context, OMA's competition entry for Parc de la Villette (1982–83) had been a major discovery. The scheme had shown that it was possible to translate the skyscraper's "fantastic juxtaposition of activities" into a new kind of project that was essentially all floor. The surface of the park was divided into some forty parallel bands of various programs in direct analogy to the stacked floors of a high-rise (→ F 2.10). Given the absence of physical partitions between adjacent bands, neighboring activities were at liberty to mix, and a passerby

F 2.10

OMA/Rem Koolhaas, Parc de la Villette, Paris, 1982–83. Detail of the model.

would have been able to experience the entire spectacle of constantly changing settings and pursuits. The ambition, with respect to the promiscuity of the program's different parts as a source of instability, was to "orchestrate on a metropolitan field the most dynamic coexistence of x, y, z activities and to generate through their mutual interference a chain reaction of new, unprecedented events."[61] That was something architecture would hardly be able to offer, given the reliance of most buildings on walls, and on floors acting as "walls." In as much as metropolitan culture relied on the freedom to participate, whether actively or passively, the park was the "better skyscraper."

After Parc de la Villette, OMA designed several more parks and other projects for large open spaces: the competitions for the 1989 Universal Exposition (1983) and Parc Citroën-Cevennes (1985) in Paris, the long-term study "Nederland Nu als Ontwerp" (Netherlands Now as a Project, 1986), the Scientopia science park in Rotterdam (1987), the urban renovation project for Bijlmermeer in Amsterdam (1986–87), and the masterplan for Melun-Sénart (1987). "Parks," Koolhaas explained in 1986, "seem to us an appropriate means to reconquer a sort of enthusiasm for architecture."[62] It is one of several statements from this period that bespeak a certain frustration with the profession at large, while suggesting that Koolhaas considered the park, or programmed surface, to be the "better half" of architecture, purified from its downside of inhibiting walls. These reservations scarcely lessened his urge to build. OMA completed at least nine buildings in the second half of the 1980s as well as participating in a dozen architectural competitions and commissioned studies; it is also worth recalling that 1986 was the same year—indeed it was in the very same interview—that Koolhaas declared "his only true ambition" was to become "as professional as Harrison or Skidmore."[63]

It appears instead that OMA pursued two concurring but ultimately related notions of architecture parallel to each other. If the programmed surface constituted the essence of the "park," its architectural counterpart was the floor. In 1980, at the Venice Biennale, he had advocated an architecture that "establishes on the 'floor' (i.e. the surface of the earth) patterns of human activity in unprecedented juxtaposition."[64] The "park" was but an extreme case of programmed

---

57 Rem Koolhaas, "A Field Trip," in *S, M, L, XL*, Koolhaas and Mau, p. 225.
58 Ibid., p. 219.
59 Ibid., p. 226.
60 Ibid., p. 227.
61 OMA, "Parc de la Villette," in *OMA—Rem Koolhaas*, Lucan, p. 86.
62 Olivier Bossière and Dominique Lyon, "Entretien avec Rem Koolhaas," in *Cahiers du CCI*, 1 (1986), p. 84.
63 Ibid.
64 Rem Koolhaas and Elia Zenghelis, "Our 'New Sobriety,'" in *Architecture 1980: The Presence of the Past–Venice Biennale*, ed. Paolo Portoghesi, New York: Rizzoli, 1980, p. 214.

surface: a purified architecture capable of creating metropolitan qualities without depending on its other, antagonistic half epitomized by the wall. It comes as no surprise, therefore, that Koolhaas advertised the "park" chiefly as a resort to freedom. In 1985, when the last large unbuilt areas of Rotterdam's center were about to be developed, he lamented: "They were blind to the mysterious qualities of the alleged void, first of all its unlimited freedom." In these no man's lands "everything was possible and not a single social trope suppressed by architecture."[65] The prospective "chain reaction of new, unpredicted events" that Parc de la Villette offered was aimed at similar acts of unplanned appropriation, as if to undo the operation of planning itself.

Program only?

In a 1985 interview, Koolhaas recalled his Floating Pool project (1977) as the epitome of what he wanted to achieve in architecture: "a project that was pure program and hardly form at all."[66] In an essay from the same year, he claimed that the program for OMA's entry for Parc de la Villette "could not be expressed in form."[67] When Mil De Kooning—skeptical about this issue despite his general high esteem of OMA's work—asked him bluntly: "To what extent is that obsessive attention to program not really an act?" Koolhaas was insistent, explaining "that architecture enables activities more through its organization than through its physical appearance."[68] He continued: "It's precisely that total disconnect between program and form which is so interesting. That's what you have in La Villette too: it could easily also be a concentration camp."[69] Koolhaas was apparently referring to the idea of "programmatic instability." But the claim is ambiguous, and lends itself to conclusions that run diametrically counter to the priority of the program advocated by Koolhaas. For if the program truly is ephemeral, does form not result as the primary task of architecture? And why care for the program at all, if the aim from the outset is to lose control over it? For the author of *Delirious New York,* as much as for the designer of Parc de la Villette, the answer to the latter question was: to set in motion the process of destabilization, with programmatic instability being understood as a quality and idiosyncrasy of the metropolis.

The "disconnect between program and form" is also implied by OMA's strategic combination of "architectural specificity with programmatic indeterminacy"—a formula often quoted and expanded to include OMA's architectural approach as a whole.[70] But regardless of the later use of a building or park, the program does seem essential as a point of departure and reference for the design. Certainly, the project for Parc de la Villette remained a concept. And yet OMA's assertion that "its program could not be expressed in form" appears to be contested by the drawings, models, and renderings produced for the competition. Françoise Choay, who had been a member of the jury, would recall that "among the 471 anonymous entries, the one—and only one—that immediately attracted the eye, puzzled and stimulated the mind by its strangeness and the questions it raised" was that submitted by OMA.[71]

The first and only

To this day, Museumpark is OMA's first and only park to have materialized. In a sketch that appears to be from April 1988, Koolhaas imagined the whole of Museumpark as "a La Villette like [sic] band to connect the 2 museums."[72] OMA seems to have resumed the work on the project only in summer 1988. A plan dating from June 8 combined the ideas found in the two studies of May and September 1987 (→ F 2.11). The park is divided into three bands running north to south, with the Axis of Development running diagonally through them as a straight promenade that would connect the future NAi, located next to Rochussenstraat, the Kunsthal, and Maasboulevard.[73] In terms of "activities," the brief for Museumpark was to provide the facilities for public events—chiefly the Teatro Fantastico—and an open-air theater for 300 to 400 people, including backstage areas, storage, restrooms, a ticket booth, and the requisite utilities.[74] The Teatro Fantastico, for its part, was an annual festival held for the first time in 1987 in the area adjacent to Museum Boijmans Van Beuningen. Like the Kunsthal, the event was supposed to attract a broad public. In addition to theatrical performances and concerts, the program included acrobatics, a dance club, restaurants and cafés, with most events taking place in tents. The

65 Koolhaas, "The Terrifying Beauty," p. 154.
66 Goulet, "La deuxième chance," p. 4 (author's translation).
67 Rem Koolhaas, "Eloge du terrain vague," in *L'Architecture d'Aujourd'hui*, 238 (1985), p. 46. Translation after Koolhaas, "New York/La Villette," in *OMA—Rem Koolhaas*, Lucan, p. 161.
68 De Kooning, "De economie van de verbeelding," n. p. Translation after De Kooning, "The Economics of Imagination," in *OMA/Rem Koolhaas: A Critical Reader*, ed. Christophe Van Gerrewey, Basel: Birkhäuser, 2019, p. 114.
69 Ibid.
70 OMA, "Parc de la Villette," p. 86.
71 Françoise Choay, "Critique," in *Princeton Journal: Landscape*, vol. 2 (1985), p. 211.
72 Cf. https://oma.eu/projects/kunsthal (accessed March 30, 2018). The date suggested on the website (1989) appears highly unlikely. The organization of the park essentially corresponds to the study of May 1987, whereas the curved annex to the dike—an idea that does not occur in any of the later versions—corresponds closely to the cover sketch of the booklet "Kunsthal Hoboken: Concept Plan," presented on April 28, 1988. OMAR 4134.
73 OMA, "Museumpark: Inrichtingsmogelykheden [sic] Kunsthal," June 8, 1988. OMAR 4475.
74 "Museumpark programma van eisen," June 19, 1988. No author specified. Probably incomplete. OMAR 4485.

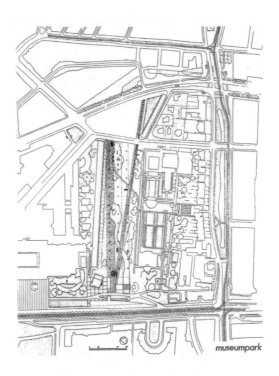

OMA/Rem Koolhaas, Museumpark, Rotterdam, June 1988.

festival was an instant success, attracting 50,000 visitors in 1987 and 60,000 in 1988. It was run by the Teatro Fantastico foundation,[75] whose board consisted mainly of representatives of Rotterdam theaters, including the directors of the Luxor Theater and the Schouwbourg.

An architect of parks

Later that year, the Museumpark project was radically redesigned by Yves Brunier, who had been working at OMA in 1986 and 1987 on projects such as the masterplan for Melun-Sénart, the urban renovation project for Bijlmermeer, Amsterdam, and the parklike Scientopia science center in Rotterdam. Brunier had trained as an architect but chose to become a landscape architect instead, a decision that seems to have been at least partly influenced by Koolhaas.[76] As a convert from an "architect of walls" to an "architect of programmed surfaces" he is likely to have personified the "better half" of architecture for Koolhaas more than anybody else. Brunier died of AIDS in 1991, two years before the park was completed. As the illness worsened, Petra Blaisse was increasingly involved in implementing the project, and after Brunier's death she remained in charge of the project. In a commemorative text from that year, Blaisse describes her role as that of an executor of Brunier's ideas: "He asked me if I would finish it for him. I said I would. And despite all the restrictions and new problems one encounters years after a design and a budget is delivered, I can only hope that we came as near to Yves' visions as possible."[77] The collaboration between OMA and Blaisse began in the late 1980s. Her projects included designing the golden curtain for the Netherlands Dance Theater in The Hague (1987) and curating the OMA exhibition *The First Decade* at Museum Boijmans Van Beuningen (1989), and she would also have some influence on the interior design of the Kunsthal.

A cavalcade of complementary spaces

Brunier seems to have begun work on Museumpark in September 1988.[78] By this time, the idea to organize the park in three parallel bands running north to south between the NAi and the Kunsthal seems to have been abandoned. Instead, its surface was divided into four roughly square sections, each extending over the whole width of the park (→ F 2.12). Even after the change, the design remained faithful to a number of seminal ideas from the Parc de la Villette scheme. First of all, Museumpark was not conceived as "of one piece" but as a sequence of sections, with each a distinct perimeter and character of its own, while being connected and crossed by a central promenade (the Axis of Development). Unlike the earlier versions, the sketches from autumn 1988 onwards show the facilities for cultural activities concentrated in two places: a large central platform for cultural events that would later be called the podium, apparently in correspondence to the Manifestation Field envisaged by the municipality; and an existing open-air theater from the 1930s that was located in the garden of Villa Dijkzigt.[79] At this point it must have become apparent that the largest portion of the park would be about landscaping rather than "programming." At the same time, the change from bands to squares implied a shift from a simultaneous perception of space to one that was sequential. Three equally sized bands, as proposed in June, would have had

75 Stichting Teatro Fantastico, "Teatro Fantastico voor de derde keer in Rotterdam," April 1989. OMAR 4457.
76 Odile Fillion, "A conversation with Koolhaas," in *Yves Brunier: Landscape Architect*, ed. Michel Jacques, Basel: Birkhäuser, 1996, p. 89.
77 Petra Blaisse, "A Personal Impression," in *Yves Brunier*, Jacques, p. 22.
78 While the site plan of the Kunsthal's preliminary design of September 7, 1988 shows no visible trace of Brunier's redesign, the revised site plan for the Kunsthal of October 7 coincides precisely with an early scheme by Brunier for the park. OMAR 1746, 1747, 4352.
79 The open-air theater was constructed through a job creation scheme during the economic crisis that preceded World War II. Egbert, J. Hoogenberk, *Het Idee van de Hollandse Stad. Stedebouw in de Nederland met de interantionale voorgeschiedenis*, Delft: University Press, 1980, p. 134.

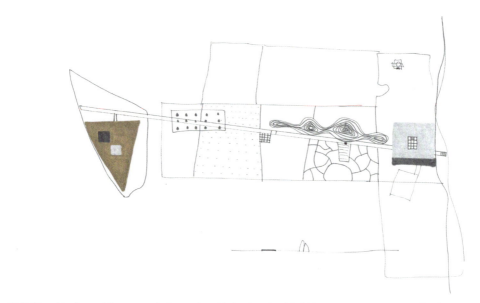

OMA/Rem Koolhaas, Museumpark, Rotterdam. Early sketch with OMA's scheme for the NAi (left) and Kunsthal I (right).

a depth of about 43 meters (50 meters in Parc de la Villette), while Museumpark as a whole measured roughly 440 by 120 meters. The adjacent sections would always have remained in sight. By contrast, the division into four parts allowed each section to have a depth of about 100 meters. Passersby following the main path would have sufficient time to immerse themselves in each of the sections as if striding through the rooms of an enfilade. In a 1989 project statement, Brunier explained: "The idea of differing and even extreme sensations blended into a walk thru [sic] a park that has taken form in a sequence, a cavalcade of complementary spaces."[80]

  A plan colored with pastels (→ F 2.13) and a working model by Brunier (→ P 3.1), apparently dating from the beginning of October 1988, anticipate the main features of the park's final design.[81] At this stage, the scheme consisted of three strongly contrasting sections. The area adjacent to Museum Boijmans Van Beuningen and facing the NAi, later called the "orchard," was envisaged as the actual entrance to the park. Brunier explained that the planting and the colors chosen for the scheme would create a "welcoming feeling."[82] The plan shows apple trees arranged on a diagonal grid next to the large existing poplars, while suggesting whitish sand and gravel for the ground. The latter would eventually be covered with white sea shells and the bark of the trees would be whitewashed, as indicated by the white circles around the trunks in Brunier's plan.[83]

To the south, the white, densely planted orchard borders the podium, its black, bare counterpart. Apart from a few cutouts for "confetti-patches of vegetation,"[84] its entire surface would be covered with asphalt. Raised about a meter above the level of its surroundings, the platform covers polluted sand that was excavated from the Museumpark site. Brunier's plan shows a black asphalted ramp with street markings that would enable the podium to be accessed from the orchard, along with a metal grandstand for open-air events and festivals like the Teatro Fantastico. The only "patches of color" are the

F 2.13

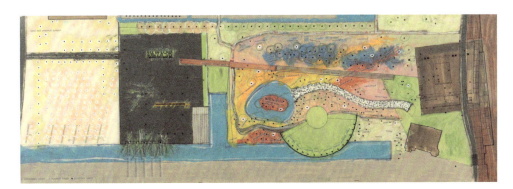

OMA/Rem Koolhaas, Museumpark, Rotterdam. Drawing with pastels by Yves Brunier.

black bamboo, the yellow osiers in two separate planters, and a row of weeping sequoias along the canal.[85] The emptiness of the envisioned space is striking. More than any other section of the park, the podium—especially at this early stage—appears cognate to the urban "void" advocated by Koolhaas in his essays of the 1980s.

A second ramp in red descends from the podium to the adjacent garden of Villa Dijkzigt, which was later called the "Romantic Garden." Comprising a preexisting pond and grove of large mature trees, it extends as far as the Kunsthal, the villa, and the embankment of the dike. The contrast with the orchard and the podium is pronounced. After the non-colors white and black, and after the rigor of a grid, a blank surface, and straight lines, both the plan and the model suggest a sea of color—in fact, different kinds of bright colors—

80 Yves Brunier, "Museum Park Rotterdam," in L'Architecture d'Aujourd'hui, 262 (1989), p. 102.
81 The model and the plan are based on the first project for the Kunsthal (I). The colored plan uses a floorplan for the Kunsthal scheme dating from October 7, 1988. OMAR 4352, 4459, 1744.
82 Brunier, "Museumpark Rotterdam," p. 102.
83 Petra Blaisse in an interview with the author, September 24, 2018.
84 Brunier, "Museumpark Rotterdam," p. 102.
85 The plan contains detailed specifications for the planting. OMAR 4352.

arranged in a free flow of curved confluent shapes. In the model, the colors are even used for the "trees" as Q-tips painted in red, yellow, and blue. A "glass bridge" that spans most of the Romantic Garden appears in some earlier sketches, too. Apparently, the initial idea was that it would span an artificial "river" connecting the pond with the Kunsthal. Several sketches present variations on this theme. Site plans of the Kunsthal from June and September 1988 show a meandering stream starting from the covered open space below the main hall.[86] By October, however, that idea had been abandoned. Instead of a proper water course, Brunier proposed a curvilinear path of white stones further to the east that was no longer crossed by the bridge.[87] However, the bridge spanning the Romantic Garden was kept, as were the pond and the old trees. As Petra Blaisse explained: "You fly over the garden. You have distance from the garden. You see it as a painting."[88]

Otherworldly

In addition to the model and the colored drawing, Brunier produced a plan in the form of a collage (→ F 2.14), probably at the turn of the year. This would go on to be widely published, supplemented by a series of painted and partly collaged photographs of the existing park (→ P 3.2–3.6).[89] Unlike the earlier version, the revised plan defines the area around the Kunsthal and Villa Dijkzigt as a fourth section of the park. A decision was apparently made to preserve that part of the garden more or less as it was. With its even lawn and scattered large mature trees, it corresponds to the common image of a park, providing a stark contrast to the orchard, the podium, and—albeit more subtly—the Romantic Garden. The glass bridge crossing the latter descends onto "Blue Plaza," that is, the forecourt and passage between the Kunsthal and Villa Dijkzigt which is paved with dark-blueish scoria bricks.

The painted and collaged photographs are "snapshots" of an imaginary visit to Museumpark and perhaps more suggestive than the implemented version has ever been. A picture of the orchard shows a winter scene in white with dark, green treetops and a dazzling sky behind. The horizon is cut off by a "mirrored wall," which serves also as a parapet for the podium at its other side. The uneven surface of the reflecting wall would not actually "duplicate" the orchard, but it would lend the space a more self-contained character, and, as Koolhaas explains in S, M, L, XL, reinforce the impact of brightness and over-exposure.[90]

F 2.14

OMA/Rem Koolhaas, Museumpark, Rotterdam, February 1989. Collage by Yves Brunier.

Most "snapshots" visualize the Romantic Garden. As in the colored plan from October, the ground is flooded with a "wave of color."[91] A planting scheme of February 1989 specifies flowers and shrubs in red, orange, pink, blue, and yellow, arranged in a patchwork of curvilinear shapes.[92] The impact of Brunier's pictures is effusive and otherworldly. At the foot of the tall shadowy trees, the continuous carpet of bright colors seems rather out of place, like fields of flowers sweeping through a forest. White dots on dark trunks indicate flowering creepers. Captured from an oblique angle, the open-air theater looks like a single large vortex in green. Brunier initially suggested reusing the existing 1930s structure, which was shaped like a Greek theater with wooden benches on a semi-circular slope.[93] Perhaps the idea was to complement the artificial embankment of the seating with a construction similar to the open-air pavilions by Frank Gehry. Images of Gehry's

86 OMA, "Kunsthal Rotterdam, Situatie" September 7, 1988. OMAR 1747. OMA, "Museumpark: Inrichtingsmogelykheden [sic] Kunsthal," June 8, 1988. OMAR 4475.
87 OMAR 4352.
88 Interview with the author, September 24, 2018.
89 OMAR 4460, 4462. The floorplan representing the Kunsthal at one end of the park dates from December 14, 1988, indicating that the plan of the park was either produced or modified after this date.
90 Koolhaas, "New Rotterdam," p. 421.
91 Brunier, "Museumpark Rotterdam," p. 103.
92 "Museumpark Rotterdam: Plattegrond: deel II&IV," February 20, 1989. OMAR 4358.
93 For a site plan and photos showing the park and the open-air theater in the mid-1980s, see *Learning from Rotterdam: Investigating the Process of Urban Park Design*, M. J. Vroom and J. H. A. Meeus, London: Mansell Publishing Limited, 1990, pp. 68–87.

World Expo amphitheater in New Orleans (1982), his Performing Arts Pavilion in Concord (1975–77), and 420 Rodeo Drive in Bel Air (1965) were among the material collected by OMA's team working on the Kunsthal and Museumpark.

Super-Nature

Ever since Parc de la Villette, OMA's parks had been conceived as urban spaces in analogy to the skyscraper: not only in terms of programming, but also with respect to their relation to nature. Rather than a representation of "pristine nature," the greenery at Parc de la Villette and Parc Citroën-Cevennes recalls a catalog of planting. Françoise Choay wrote about Parc de la Villette: "Greenery […] is treated not only as a building material but almost mechanically: it symbolizes artificiality as it is made part of the general evolving system."[94] The same can be said about the orchard and the composition of linear planting on the podium. Like the golf course of the Downtown Athletic Club, the grid of apple trees, the curtain of weeping sequoias, and the block of black bamboo were displayed as manmade "Super-Nature."[95] When the Romantic Garden was complete, large rocks, made of blue glass to resemble fragments of glacier, were glued to the "river" of stones. The ground below the bridge was fitted out with illuminations that would shine through its glazed floor at night. The trees, too, were equipped with lights. Blaisse recalls: "He [Brunier] had planned in the existing trees to have lamps at night of different colors. So it could either be completely blue, or completely red, or completely yellow, and we hung lamps with cables going up the stems of the trees."[96]

A podium of streets

In early 1989, OMA worked out the design of Museumpark in detail (→ F 2.15). Over the subsequent twelve months the drawings were modified, complemented, and refined. On the basis of OMA's design, Rotterdam's municipal engineers produced the technical drawings for the tendering process, which was held in July 1989.[97] One major change was shifting the open-air theater from the Romantic Garden to the podium (→ F 2.16).[98] In the final, implemented version of Museumpark, the theater served as the main entrance to the podium. A rectangular section was cut out from its northern edge, with the stepped rows of the seating descending towards the orchard as the "scenery" at the back of the stage. The motif of the street—Brunier's colored plan had suggested white street markings on black asphalt—became the actual guiding theme of the entire podium as planned by Brunier and Blaisse in 1990.[99] Its surface—measuring 100 by 75 meters—was organized on the basis of a square 5-meter grid. Prefab concrete elements that were 0.5 meters wide served as coverings for concealed gutters, dividing the asphalt along the north–south axis into ten strips, each 9.50 meters in width. Photographs of a model that were published in a 1993 issue of *Archis* show that the color of the elements was meant to alternate between black and white strips. Five white lines would make the podium look like a surface composed of parallel streets. Occasional "dashed lines" in stainless steel and zebra crossings in white would reinforce that impact. Road markings, zebra crossings, a giant piano, a split open-air chess board, fragments of a floorplan, and other undecipherable markings suggest activity and occupation in various ways. At a technical level, the podium offered the facilities and utilities for theatrical spectacles, festivals like the Teatro Fantastico, and other events. The podium—all floor and no walls—was a programmed

F 2.15

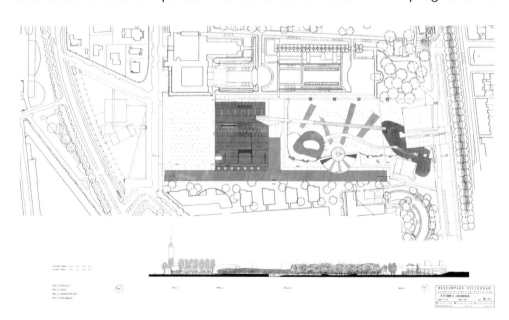

OMA/Rem Koolhaas, Museumpark, Rotterdam, February 1989. Overall plan and section. The drawing still shows the open-air theater projecting out into the canal.

94 Choay, "Critique," pp. 213–14.
95 Koolhaas, *Delirious New York*, p. 157.
96 Interview with the author, September 24, 2018.
97 The tendering process took place between July 2 and 12. The drawings were produced by Ingenieursbureau utiliteits- en waterbouw (IUW) and Ingenieursbureau groen (IG) between April and June 1990, and are now held by the archives of Stadsarchief Rotterdam and Stadsontwikkeling Rotterdam.
98 The theater's semicircular embankment projected too far into the canal at the western margin of the park.
99 IG, "Techn. Plan Podium Profielen etc.," May 21, 1990. Archives Stadsontwikkeling Rotterdam. See also OMA, "Plattegrond deel I & II," February 22, 1990. OMAR 4362.

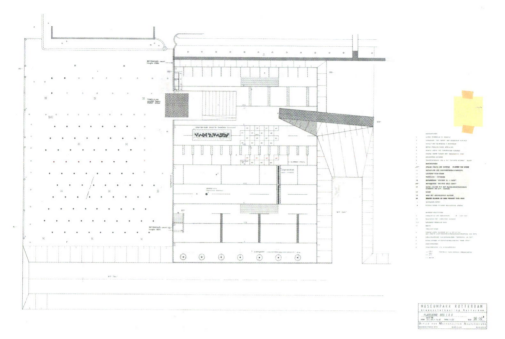

OMA/Rem Koolhaas, Museumpark, Rotterdam, February 1989. Orchard and podium. The podium already includes the seating for the open-air theater (upper section, left).

surface in the literal sense. But like OMA's scheme for Parc de la Villette, the podium anticipated its use as an image. Even the destabilization of the prospective program for Parc de la Villette seems to be implied by the interfering markings and interspersed planting, methodically overriding the rigid order of the parallel strips.

An effort of the imagination

Museumpark was officially inaugurated after a considerable delay on September 4, 1993, which was almost a year after the Kunsthal.[100] Meanwhile the public had begun to dismantle parts of the Romantic Garden. All 500 blue glass rocks, which had been glued to the rocks of the "river," disappeared in the first two months after the opening.[101] The scoria bricks of the Blue Plaza similarly began to disappear, as did the colored floodlights affixed to the trees and under the glass bridge, including the cables.[102] The Romantic Garden became a victim not only of its fragility but also, in part, of its success. According to Koos Hage, the blue rocks were popular "souvenirs," and one would occasionally come across them at people's homes.[103] The podium was replaced and the northern end of the canal was turned into a garage driveway when architect Paul de Ruiter constructed a subterranean parking facility in the ground below (2003–13). A new mirror wall was mounted—this time pierced with holes, for safety reasons.[104] The orchard had to cede its place to the Depot of Museum Boijmans Van Beuningen designed by MVRDV (2014–21). To visualize and ultimately judge the park's original state, however ephemeral, requires a major effort of the imagination.[105]

100 "Museumpark notitie tbv bespreking 11 okt 93." The minutes also mention the podium as the main cause for the delay. Inside Outside studio, Petra Blaisse. According to Blaisse, the polluted sand needed more time to settle down than expected. Interview with the author, September 24, 2018.

101 Canis Zijlmans, "Museumpark is nog lang niet af," in *Rotterdams Dagblad* (September 5, 1994).

102 Anja Guinée, "De spanning tussen kunst en openbaarhed in het Museumpark," in *Blauwe kamer*, 5 (1993), p. 21.

103 Koos Hage. Interview with the author, July 28, 2020.

104 Petra Blaisse. Interview with the author, September 24, 2018.

105 Ibid.

P 4.1   Kunsthal I, October 7, 1988. Site plan.

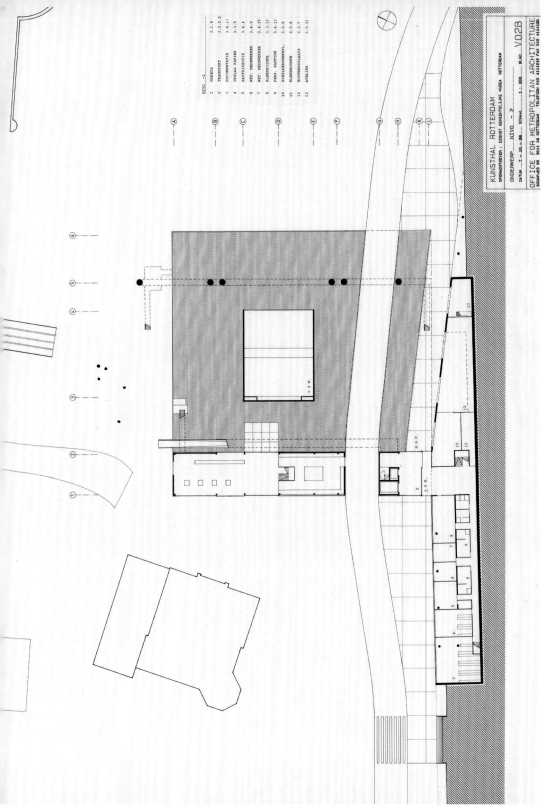

P 4.2 Kunsthal I, October 7, 1988. Park level.

P 4.3 Kunsthal I, October 7, 1988. Dike level.

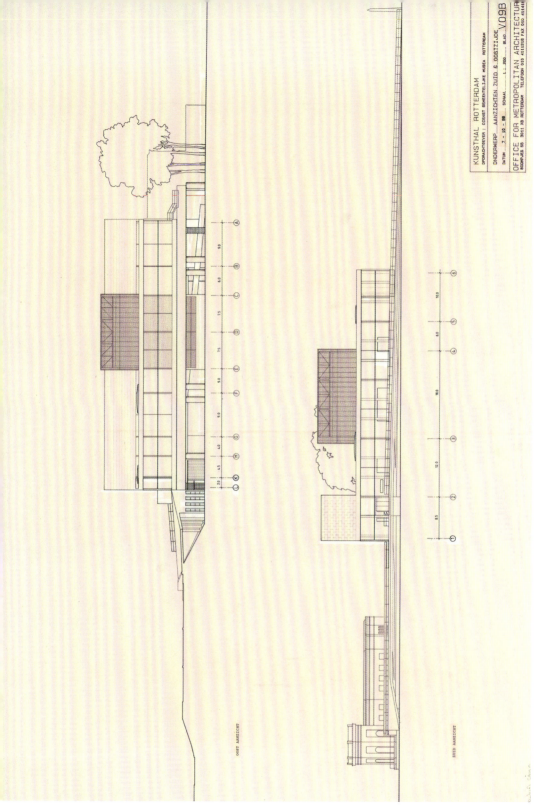

P 4.4 Kunsthal I, October 7, 1988. East and south elevation.

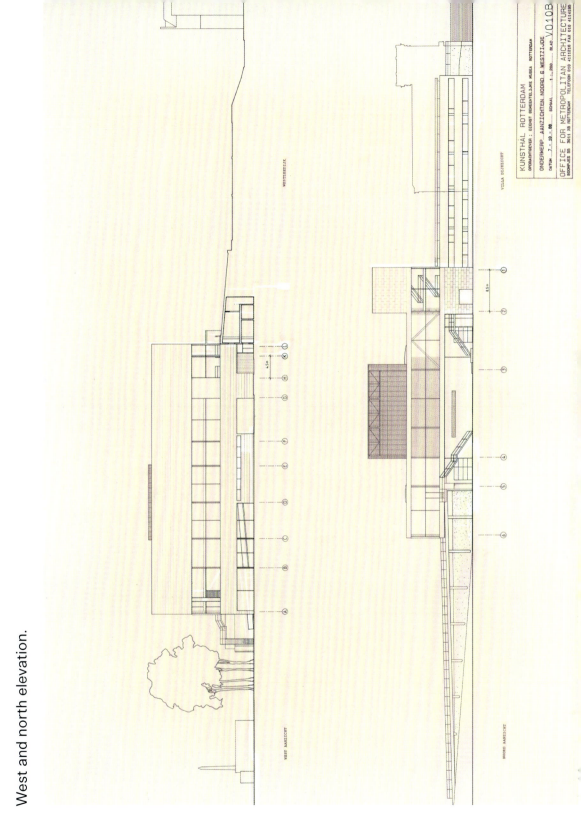

P 4.5 West and north elevation.

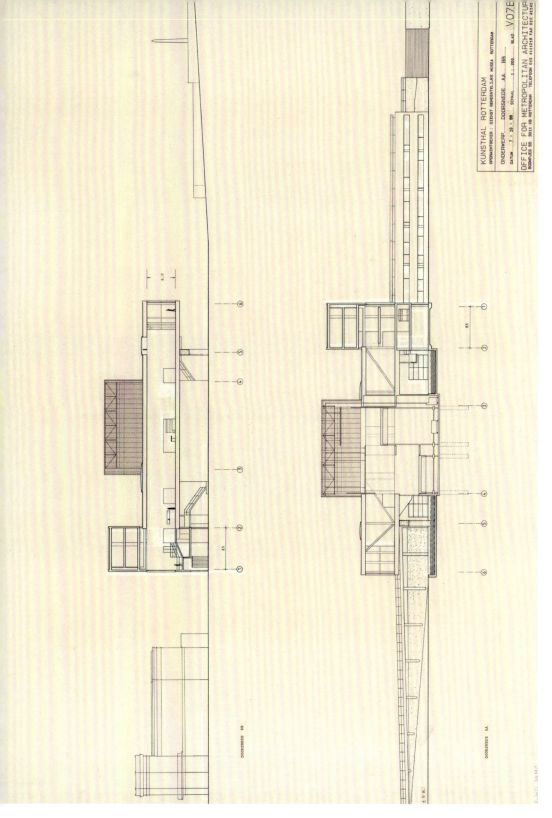

P 4.6 Kunsthal I, October 7, 1988. Main building. Cross sections (east to west).

P 4.7 Robot.

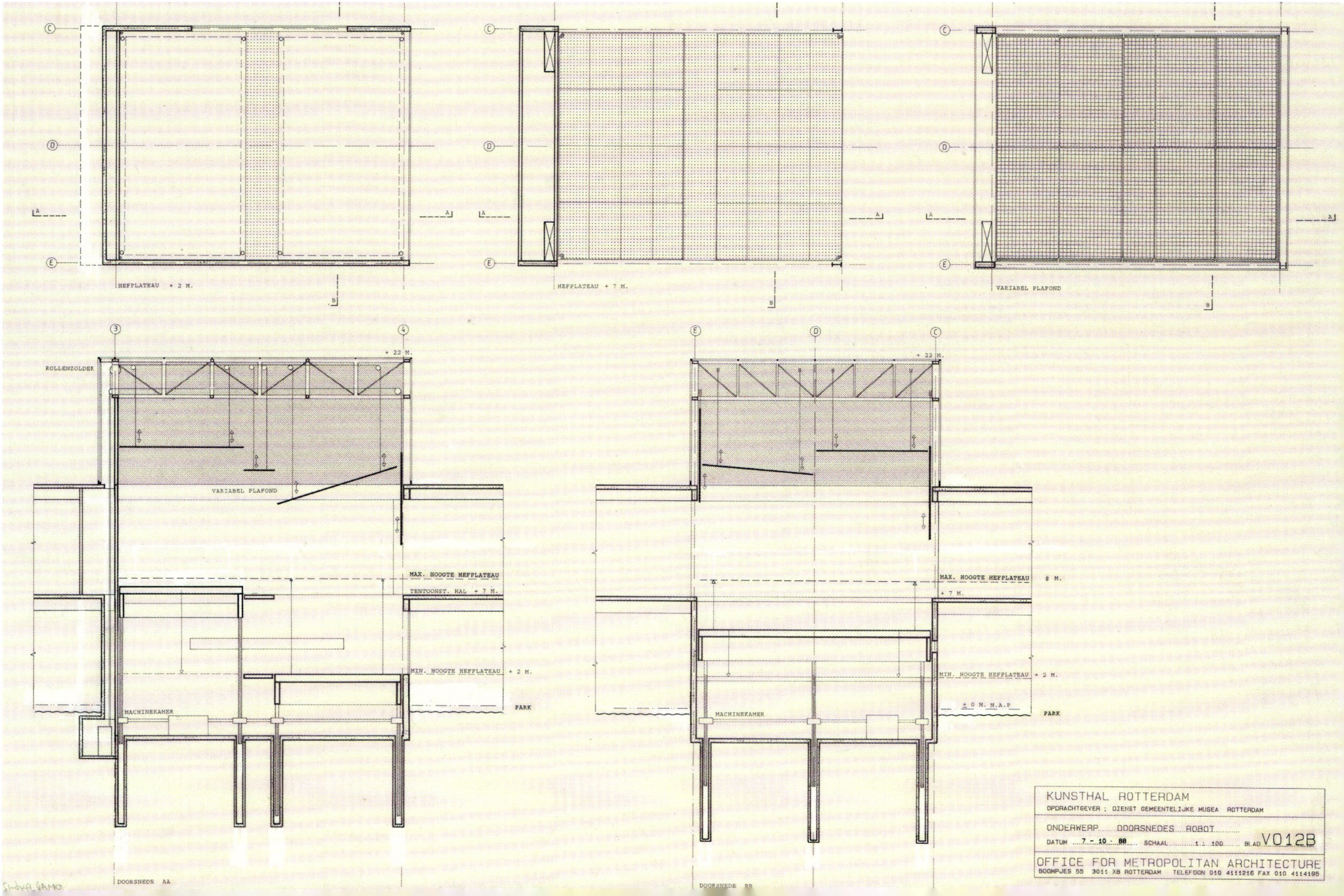
HEFPLATEAU + 2 M.
HEFPLATEAU + 7 M.
VARIABEL PLAFOND
ROLLENZOLDER
+ 22 M.
VARIABEL PLAFOND
MAX. HOOGTE HEFPLATEAU
TENTOONST. HAL + 7 M.
MIN. HOOGTE HEFPLATEAU + 2 M.
MACHINEKAMER
PARK
DOORSNEDE AA
MAX. HOOGTE HEFPLATEAU 8 M.
+ 7 M.
MIN. HOOGTE HEFPLATEAU + 2 M.
± 0 M. N.A.P
PARK
MACHINEKAMER
DOORSNEDE BB
KUNSTHAL ROTTERDAM
OPDRACHTGEVER : DIENST GEMEENTELIJKE MUSEA ROTTERDAM
ONDERWERP DOORSNEDES ROBOT
DATUM 7 - 10 - 88 SCHAAL 1 : 100 BLAD V012B
OFFICE FOR METROPOLITAN ARCHITECTURE
BOOMPJES 55 3011 XB ROTTERDAM TELEFOON 010 4111216 FAX 010 4114195

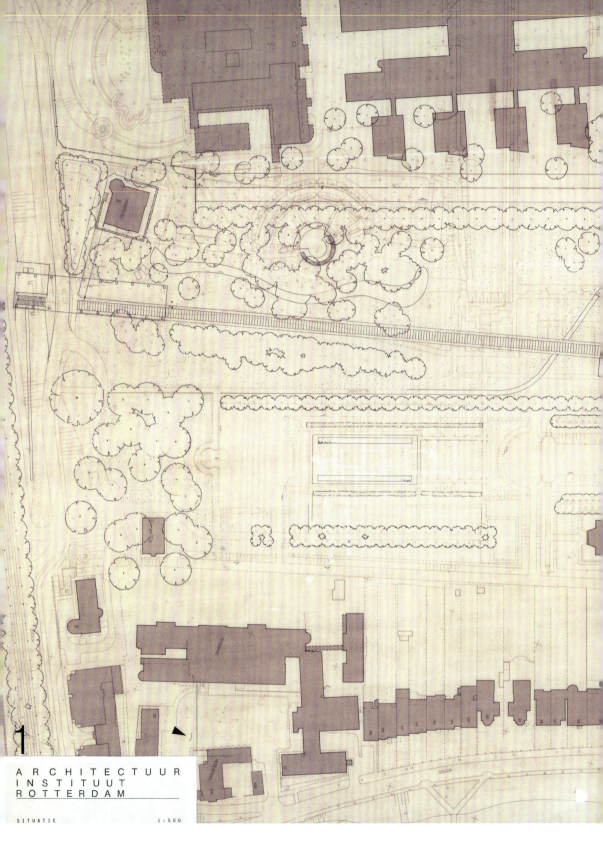

P 4.8   Competition entry for the NAi, June 1988. Site plan.

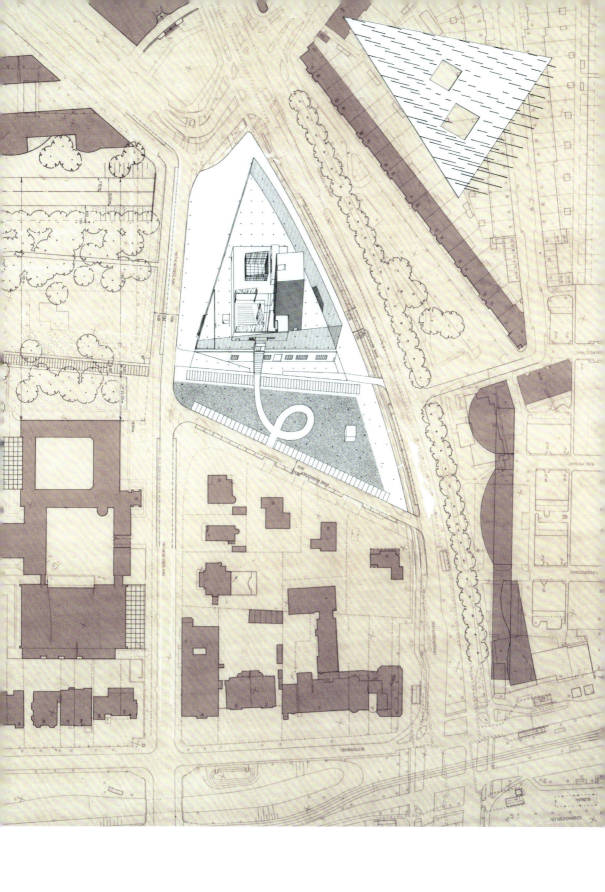

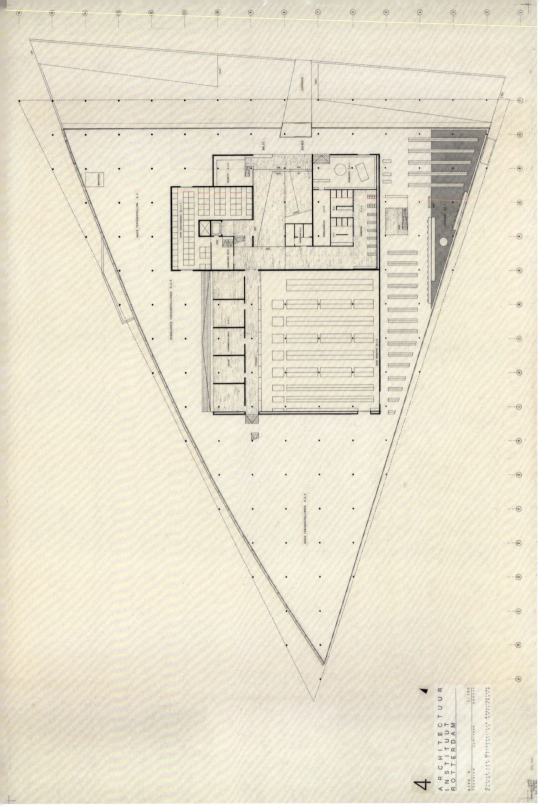

P 4.9 Competition entry for the NAi, June 1988. Street level.

P 4.10   Level 1. The auditorium is located in the lower right-hand corner of the podium.

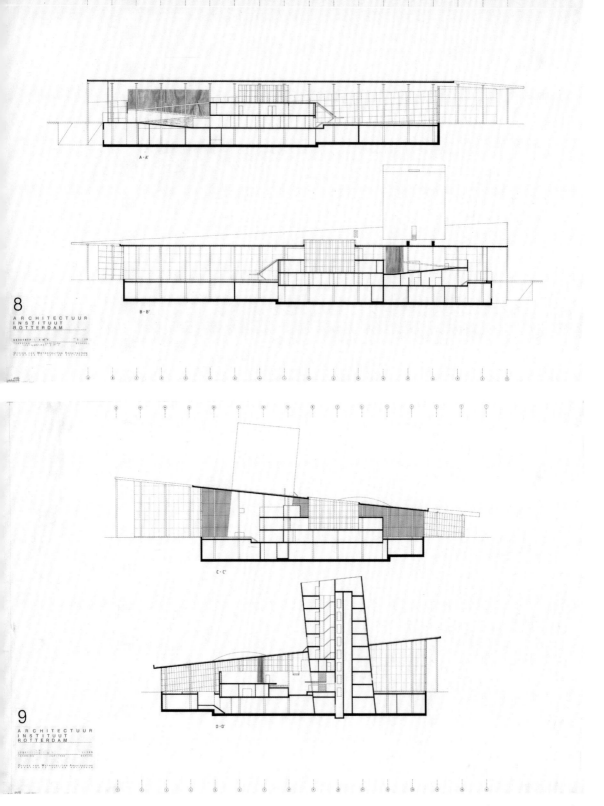

P 4.11 Competition entry for the NAi, June 1988. Cross sections (east to west).
P 4.12 Cross sections (north to south).

An Overdue Crisis

Kunsthal I, the NAi, and Deconstructivist Architecture

3

Maybe that perverseness has something to do with me becoming a chameleon in reverse—if everybody is thinking one thing I have to think the opposite.

Rem Koolhaas, 1980

In February 1986, Joop Linthorst, Rotterdam's alderman for the arts, wrote to the Dutch minister of welfare, health, and culture: "It is conspicuous that large-scale exhibitions of modern art or classical art or other museum collections are rare in our country, and if they do occur it is difficult to accommodate them in existing museums. The buildings are usually not prepared for that; permanent exhibitions have to be removed for longer periods of time, the museum's organization is temporarily disrupted, the institutions are not designed to assume large financial risks."[1] In his letter, Linthorst recommended Rotterdam as a suitable environment for a national arts center, able to house large temporary exhibitions. Linthorst also commissioned an investigation into the prospective "National Exhibition Hall" which was concluded in December of the same year. The report, authored by Charles E. van Blommestein and Janine A. Verstegen, was based on talks with institutions that might be involved in any future collaboration, such as various Dutch museums, the initiators of the architecture museum, and the Rijksdienst Beeldende Kunst (the Dutch national service for fine arts).[2] Additional information was obtained from comparable foreign institutions, namely the Royal Academy and the Whitechapel Art Gallery in London. Obviously, the investigation was coordinated with the department for urban development and the recent plans for the Dijkzigt area. In their report, Van Blommestein and Verstegen explicitly refer to the Museumpark project as things stood in November 1986.

      The Kunsthal was intended to house temporary exhibitions only. Like many *Kunsthallen* (arts centers) in German-speaking countries it would not have a collection of its own. Van Blommestein and Verstegen suggested that the Kunsthal should host large exhibitions, including the kind of traveling exhibitions produced in other countries that were then shown at art venues such as the Royal Academy in London, Grand Palais in Paris, Paleis voor Schone Kunsten in Brussels, Kunsthalle Düsseldorf, and Palazzo dell' Arte in Milan. Little indicates that they were thinking of the "intense, dynamic experience" that Dutch critics Bart Lootsma and Jan de Graaf described as characteristic for arts centers in their 1993 review of the Kunsthal. Lootsma and De Graaf were referring to art exhibitions and related events of the 1960s and 1970s that took place in museums rather than arts centers, namely in the Stedelijk Museum in Amsterdam, and Van Abbemuseum

---

1   Quoted in C.E. van Blommestein and J.A. Verstegen, "Onderzoek naar de behoefte aan een Nationale Tentoonstellingshal" (Investigation on behalf of a national arts center), Rotterdam, December 30, 1986, p. 4 (author's translation). Linthorst's letter dates from February 6. OMAR 1488.

2   Ibid.

in Eindhoven, under the direction of Willem Sandberg (1945–63) and Jean Leering (1964–73) respectively: They were "installations that literally transformed entire galleries into dynamic labyrinths. The viewer's experience took priority—among artists who poured their energy into organizing happenings and performances that could only be experienced by participating in person."[3]

The Kunsthal envisaged by Van Blommestein and Verstegen followed a more pragmatist approach of economic sustainability. Considerations about attendance figures and blockbusters were at the core of their report. Lootsma and De Graaf saw a "'new hard-line leftist' approach" in this concern for economics. The Kunsthal as imagined by Rotterdam's municipality, they suggest, was supposed to emulate "larger institutions, such as the Martin Gropius Bau in Berlin, Städtische Kunsthalle in Düsseldorf, Schirnhalle in Frankfurt, the Triennale buildings in Milan, Palazzo Grassi in Venice, and the recent Kunsthalle in Bonn designed by Gustav Peichl. These arts centers excel at putting together large-scale exhibitions, 'blockbusters' on a famous artist, for example, by assembling pieces from various collections around the world for the first time [...]. These are one-off but extremely expensive exhibitions that stand or fall on mass attendance."[4]

Proletarian entertainment

In March 1988, the Kunsthal's building committee met for the first time. Five representatives of various municipal services participated in the gathering along with Rem Koolhaas and alderman Joop Linthorst, who would chair the committee until the construction phase.[5] In part, the meeting served to summarize the situation at the time. The client was the city of Rotterdam, with the municipal museum service and the human resources and finance service as the contracting authorities (represented by J. Bronder), and Rotterdam's public works department in charge of project management.[6] The investment program of the department for urban development provided a budget of 20 million guilders, and Rotterdam's city council had discussed the possibility of opening the building in 1990. The future director of the Kunsthal was yet to be nominated. The main subject of the meeting was the schedule of requirements, drafted by the municipal project coordinator Hein Reedijk.[7] Reedijk, a former curator of the Van Abbemuseum in Eindhoven, belonged to the arts department which was chaired by Linthorst. His brief envisaged a total floor surface of 5,625 square meters, comprising eight exhibition halls of different sizes, a central patio connecting the building with the park, a bar, and a large lobby that might also be used for events such as openings, receptions, and readings.

Asked to comment on Reedijk's brief, Koolhaas used the occasion for a generic statement on recent museum design. "He [Koolhaas]," the minutes record, "has studied comparable institutions in Europe. The 1960s warranted very flexible buildings, with the Beaubourg being an obvious example. As a reaction to that, recent examples such as Mönchengladbach, Stuttgart, and Frankfurt emphasize a monumentality that leaves little room for change." Koolhaas was apparently referring to Hollein's Abteiberg Museum (1972–82), Stirling's Staatsgalerie (1977–84), Ungers' Architecture Museum (1979–84), and perhaps Hollein's project for the MMK contemporary art museum in Frankfurt (1983–91). For the Kunsthal he suggested a combination of the two approaches by dint of a flexible element in an otherwise stable building. As for the program drafted by Reedijk, Koolhaas recommended three major modifications: Firstly, in order to allow for "necessary multiformity," i.e. more flexibility—obviously referring to the eight separate exhibition halls specified in the brief. Secondly, to take more "proletarian pleasures" into account—in contrast to the municipal program, which leaned towards high culture. Thirdly, to consider other uses that would complement exhibitions, such as opening a restaurant, hosting conferences, and other "'Palais de festival' activities."

Despite these criticisms, there was some common ground between the municipality's stress on high attendance figures and blockbusters and Koolhaas' wish to open up the spectrum of activities beyond art exhibitions and address a broader public. According to Koolhaas, it was Linthorst himself who introduced the term *Palais de Festival*, envisioning the Kunsthal as a venue for both art and popular events.[8] This embrace of popular culture was fully in line with the OMA agenda, which advocated—as Koolhaas put it in *Delirious New York*—an architecture "at once ambitious *and* popular."[9] Ultimately, of course, the cultural agenda and activities that would take place in the Kunsthal were beyond the reach of the architects, and strongly dependent on municipal politics, the director of the Kunsthal, and the visitors' fancy.

3 Bart Lootsma and Jan de Graaf, "In dienst van de ervaring: KunstHAL van OMA in Rotterdam," in *De Architect*, 1 (1993), p. 22.
4 Ibid.
5 "Nieuwbouw Kunsthal/Bouwcommissie," March 17, 1988. OMAR 1517 (author's translation). The subsequent information and quotations concerning this meeting draw on the same source.
6 The Dienst Gemeentelijke Musea (DGM), Dienst Personeel and Financiën (DPF), and Gemeentewerke (GW). Ibid.
7 H. Reedijk, "Programma van eisen Kunsthal Hoboken: definitief concept." January 1988. OMAR 1437.
8 Conversation with the author over Zoom, February 8, 2023.
9 Rem Koolhaas, *Delirious New York: A Retroactive Manifesto for Manhattan*, New York: The Monacelli Press, 1994, p. 10.

When Koolhaas mentioned the Kunsthal in an interview six years after its opening, there was a note of disappointment in his comment: "[…] for instance, the current use of the Kunsthal really is a very limited version of what was originally intended. The Kunsthal was actually planned as a multifunctional building in which a whole series of different events would be organized."[10] The statement indicates the customary limits of the architect's influence on the program and use of their projects, and, by the same token, it shows the limits of an approach focused on programming. To be sure, the architect organizes the program in space. But even under conditions as favorable as those for the Kunsthal, the architect is unlikely to define its constituents, not to mention the building's actual use. Koolhaas has somewhat obscured these limits in his writings and statements. When referring to a "program," he rarely distinguishes between the functions specified by the program and their spatial organization, or between those functions and the way the building is eventually used. The respective roles of planner, client, and user are thus blurred, implicitly subsuming the competencies of the latter two under those of the architect. In *Delirious New York*, Koolhaas pictures the planning process of the Rockefeller Center as a joint venture between client, developer, and architect, with no distinct limits to their respective competences, i.e. with the potential influence of the architect on everything. In the chapter on the Downtown Athletic Club, an original section and floorplans figure as evidence of activity. The "oyster bar" on the ninth floor *does* service an adjacent locker room, complete with "boxing/wrestling" and "showers."[11] But when planned by the architects in the late 1920s, perhaps at the client's instigation, it was nothing but an assumption that the men in the locker room would frequent the bar. Whether they ever did or not was not the concern of a book that was intended to be a blueprint for an "ideal state."[12]

I love building museums

The picture that Koolhaas drew of recent museum design at the March meeting of the building committee was not inaccurate. The flexible museum of the 1950s and 1960s, providing "neutral" gallery space with temporary partitions, was widely considered to be dated. At the New York symposium "Art Against the Wall: Building the New Museum" in December 1985, Philip Johnson stated: "That modern architecture thing—with movable partitions—is gone. We're over that, over, over. We're back to where Schinkel put us. Let's stay there."[13] In a 1986 monograph that focused on both American and European museums,

Josep Montaner and Jordi Oliveras observed that Mies' idea of a continuous flexible space "does not work to house a traditional art museum, which needs walls, and to some extent enclosures with defined spaces, to create the repose and containment necessary to concentrate on the works of art."[14] Similarly, in a publication from the same year based on a symposium about contemporary museum architecture in Eindhoven, Dutch architect and theorist Cornelis van de Ven asserted that "the revival of the classic museum type in western Europe has become a fact."[15] Also the return to monumentality was virtually beyond dispute. At the aforementioned New York symposium, Johnson identified the museum as the new public monument par excellence, and one that could happily satisfy a resurging desire for monumentality.[16] Montaner and Oliveras were referring to recent work by Stirling, Meier, Moneo, Venturi, Pei, Aulenti, Hollein, and others when they observed: "the monumental emphasis is achieved essentially in two ways. On the one hand, clear typological references are used. And on the other, the public and monumental character of the museum is expressed by resuscitating the idea of monumental spaces from historic examples like the portico or the circular interior of Schinkel's Altes Museum in Berlin."[17] The enfilade, the lantern, and the stone-clad wall were further recurring features of premodern monumentality.

Among theorists, the criticism that had been expressed about museums in the past was not entirely forgotten. Authors like Hubert Damisch, Van de Ven, and Geert Bekaert were well aware of Adorno's skepticism and Valéry's rejection of the museum/mausoleum as a deadly place for art.[18] Like Damisch, Bekaert addressed the Foucaultian ambiguity of the museum's didactic mission: "Like prisons, hospitals, schools, the museum is an institution of regulation that assigns art its right place, teaches it its right place. Innocent it is not."[19] Damisch wrote in 1982: "Certainly today we are especially aware of the ideological functions fulfilled by an institution which is merely one cog [...] in the overall mechanism of the state."[20] However, the eminent social,

10   Anna Klingmann, "Architektur als kollektiver Erlebnisraum," in *Tain*, 5 (1998), p. 52 (author's translation). A longer version of this quotation can be found in Chapter 6.
11   Koolhaas, *Delirious New York*, p. 154.
12   Ibid., p. 11.
13   Suzanne Stephens, ed., *Building the New Museum*, New York: The Architectural League, 1986, p. 28.
14   Josep Maria Montaner and Jordi Oliveras, *The Museums of the Last Generation*, London: Academy Editions/ New York: St. Martin's Press, 1986, pp. 14–15.
15   Cornelis van de Ven, "Het museumgebouw, planning en ontwerp," in *Museumarchitectuur*, eds. Cornelis van de Ven and Bob Martens, Rotterdam: 010 Publishers, 1989, p. 39.
16   Stephens, *Building the New Museum*, p. 28.
17   Montaner and Oliveras, *The Museums of the Last Generation*, p. 24.
18   Van de Ven, "Het museumgebouw," pp. 18–19.
19   Geert Bekaert, "Een gebouw waar de kunst haar intrek kan nemen: Overpeinzingen over museum en museumarchitectuur," in *Archis*, 1 (1987), p. 14 (author's translation).
20   Hubert Damisch, "The Museum Device: Notes on Institutional Changes," in *Lotus International*, 35 (1982), p. 7.

political and, ultimately cultural significance of the museum was beyond dispute. Joseph Rykwert noted in 1989: "Museums are the nearest thing we have to the temple in our time. They are now quasi—, if not wholly, religious institutions."[21]

If there was something akin to a supreme architectural discipline in 1980s architecture, it is likely to have been the museum. In a 1987 issue of *Lotus International* about museums, Pierluigi Nicolin stated: "The new museums, built above all in Germany and the United States (but also in France, Britain, Spain, and even in Italy) are now influencing architectural thinking to the point where these intriguing buildings are taken as paradigms of the contemporary powers of imitation. [...] In many ways these new museum buildings draw on the finest available resources and put into effect some of the most widely debated architectural ideas, such as how to approach the problem of construction work in historic contexts, the fit design of a monumental building for our age, experiments with architectural language, the use of quotations, assimilation to the context."[22] Towards the end of the decade, most of the leading figures on the international architectural scene—such as Meier, Gehry, Stirling, Foster, Piano, Scarpa, Rossi, Moneo, Hollein, Ungers, and Isozaki—had built at least one museum or were on their way to doing so. Apart from being a matter of prestige, museums provided ample scope in terms of design. In comparison with other building types there were fewer norms and legal regulations, while the program allowed considerable leeway for interpretation. "The museum as a building type," Van de Ven wrote in 1989, "does not have any clear regulations, norms for its design, or prescriptions regarding its content and program, which definitely exist for conventional, more functional building types such as hospitals, auditoria, theaters, sports halls, offices etc."[23] Richard Meier raved: "I love building museums, because they offer the greatest range of spatial possibilities. It's a chance to create accents, relationships, breathing space for works of art."[24]

OMA's first

In April 1988, OMA seems to have delivered the overview (*oriëntatie*) of arts centers and museums that had been commissioned by Riek Bakker in June 1987.[25] Although the focus of OMA's study was on programming, the material compiled therein indicated little interest in arts centers specifically, which ran counter to what the municipality had requested.[26] Van Blommestein and Verstegen in their report, and

F 3.1

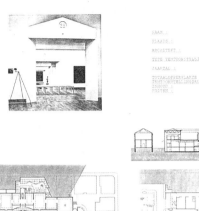
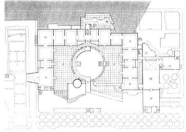
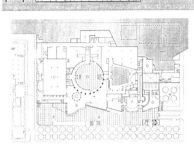

OMA/Rem Koolhaas, documentation on museums, April 27, 1988. Fact sheet on the Staatsgalerie in Stuttgart by James Stirling.

F 3.2

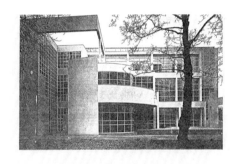

OMA/Rem Koolhaas, documentation on museums, April 27, 1988. Fact sheet on the Museum für Kunsthandwerk in Frankfurt by Richard Meier.

21 Joseph Rykwert, "The Cult of the Museum: From the Treasure House to the Temple," in *AV*, 18 (1989), p. 83.

22 Pierluigi Nicolin, "New Museums," in *Lotus International*, 55 (1987), p. 5.

23 Van de Ven, "Het museumgebouw," p. 12.

24 Galloway, "The New German Museums," in *Art in America* (July 1985), p. 83.

25 "Verslag van de 2e Bouwcommissie Nieuwbouw Kunsthal," April 28, 1988. OMAR 1517.

26 OMA, "Kunsthal Hoboken: Documentatie Musea," April 27, 1998. OMAR 3339.

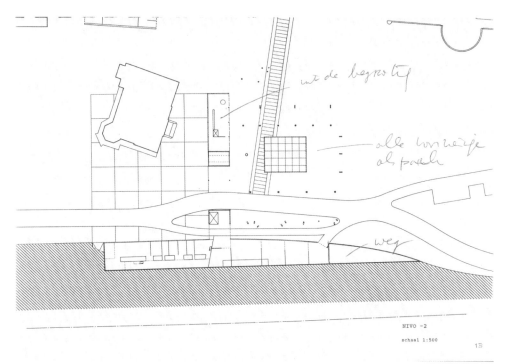

OMA/Rem Koolhaas, Kunsthal I, April 27, 1988. Park level. The annex is incorporated into the dike (hatching). The diagonal represents the southern end of the Axis of Development, meeting the service road running east to west.

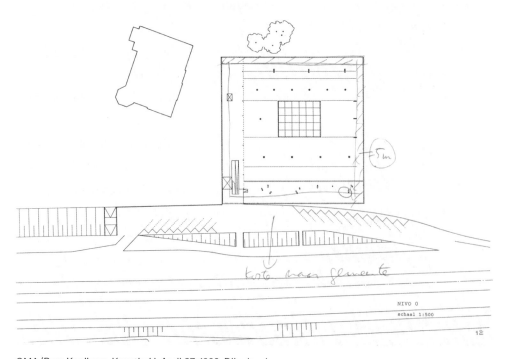

OMA/Rem Koolhaas, Kunsthal I, April 27, 1988. Dike level.

Reedijk in his brief, listed a total of thirteen examples that were either arts centers or provided exhibition halls for temporary exhibitions.[27] Yet out of the eighteen examples documented by OMA, only two qualified as genuine arts centers: the Schirnhalle in Frankfurt and Josef Paul Kleihues' 1988 competition entry for the Kunsthalle in Bonn. Most of these examples were world-famous museum designs from the second half of the twentieth century: Mies van der Rohe's Neue Nationalgalerie in Berlin; Le Corbusier's Tokyo Museum and Museum of Unlimited Growth; Kahn's Yale University Art Gallery and Kimbell Art Museum in Fort Worth, the Centre Pompidou, both its original state by Piano and Rogers and the modification by Gae Aulenti; Hollein's Museum Abteiberg; Foster's Sainsbury Centre in Norwich; Stirling's Staatsgalerie and expansion of the Tate Gallery in London (→ F 3.1); Meier's Museum für Kunsthandwerk (Museum of Applied Arts) in Frankfurt (→ F 3.2); Isozaki's Museum of Contemporary Art in Los Angeles; Piano's Menil Collection in Houston; Adrien Fainsilber's Science Centre in Parc de la Villette, and Gae Aulenti's Musée d'Orsay.[28] In terms of program, size, and budget, few examples lent themselves as models for the Kunsthal. First and foremost, OMA's documentation was an overview of museum design over the past five decades, and an ideal way of illustrating the observations Koolhaas had made to the building committee. Despite Koolhaas' efforts to leave behind the programmatic agenda of the traditional museum, he apparently envisioned the Kunsthal—and wished it to be seen—against this backdrop.

Radio City Music Hall

In all likelihood, Koolhaas presented OMA's overview of museums at a meeting of the building committee in April 1988 together with a first draft for the Kunsthal, outlined in an A3 booklet complete with sketches and plans.[29] As in OMA's study of September 1987, the Kunsthal is located at the southern end of the promenade—the Axis of Development—that connected the NAi with the Kunsthal. The project consisted of three parts: an elevated exhibition hall with a square footprint, "clamped" into a vertical slab, and a slender volume with subsidiary functions conceived as an extension of the dike (→ F 3.3–3.5). The exhibition hall had been moved closer to the embankment than its

---

27 Van Blommestein and Verstegen, "Nationale Tentoonstellingshal." OMAR 1488. H. Reedijk, letter to J. Linthorst, J. Bronder, W. Crouwel, and P. Noorman, August 24, 1987. OMAR 3267.

28 OMA, "Kunsthal Hoboken: Documentatie Musea."

29 "Verslag van de 2e Bouwcommissie Nieuwbouw Kunsthal," April 28, 1988. OMAR 1517. OMA, "Kunsthal Hoboken: Concept Plan," April 27, 1988. OMAR 4139. OMA, "Kunsthal Hoboken: Documentatie musea," April 27, 1988. OMAR 3339.

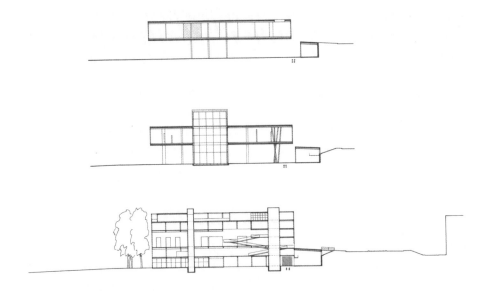

OMA/Rem Koolhaas, Kunsthal I, April 27, 1988. Cross sections (north to south) of the floating main volume, showing the Robot, the vertical slab, and the annex merging with the embankment of the dike.

original position in the 1987 study. The intention was obviously to permit direct access from Maasboulevard to the Kunsthal, while locating the building "inside" the park. The promenade, somewhat marooned, concludes in the open space under the main building, cut off by a service road that takes ambulances to the adjacent hospital. A staircase at the far end of the plaza between Villa Dijkzigt and the Kunsthal leads up to Maasboulevard.

In plan, the main building is a square measuring 60 by 60 meters (→ F 3.4). The flat floating volume contains the exhibition hall—a large double-story gallery, sandwiched between two horizontal planes and open to the sides. A system of movable platforms called the "Robot" is inscribed in a rectangle of 18 by 15 meters, occupying the center of the space. The drawings show the platforms as segments "cut out" from both the roof and the floor. The floor segment could be raised or lowered to the level of the park, split into two "steps" of different height, or inclined, thereby serving as a ramp, auditorium, orchestra pit, or patio. The roof segment could be raised to form a lantern or kept level with the rest of the ceiling. A series of freehand sketches illustrates a wide range of potential uses, such as art exhibitions, car shows, concerts, and theater performances. Variants of the Robot would reappear in OMA's Maison à Bordeaux (1994–98), the Lafayette Foundation in Paris (2012–18), and the Prada Foundation Theater (2008–18), where an exterior wall can be transformed into the floor and ceiling of a performance space. Conceptually, the Robot seized on the movable platforms described in *Delirious New York*, notably in the passages on Otis' elevator, the 1909 cartoon of a skyscraper with mobile floors, and the stage elevator of Radio City Music Hall.[30] All three examples are epiphanies of technical apparatus, on which the artificial world of the metropolis—in Koolhaas' understanding of the term—relies. In the Radio City Music Hall, these "miracles at the push of a button" exist to serve popular culture, and the same holds true for OMA's first project for the Kunsthal. The Robot would expand the possible range of uses from art exhibitions to "proletarian entertainment," such as concerts, or a "boxing ring or lion's den with the public around it" (→ F 3.6).[31] To a significant extent, the Robot was about the future building's use.

F 3.6

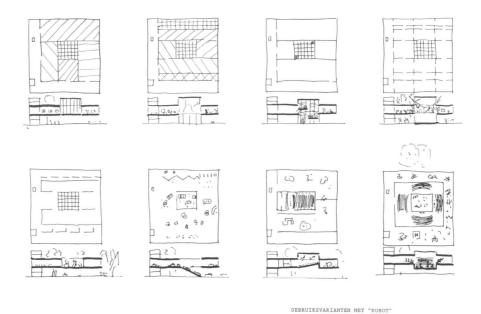

OMA/Rem Koolhaas, Kunsthal I, April 27, 1988. Illustrations showing the programmatic variety that the Robot would make possible.

30 Koolhaas, *Delirious New York*, pp. 26–27, 83, 213.

31 Quoted in Jacob Comerci, "The Robot of Kunsthal I," in *Log 36* (2016), p. 63.

Between city and nature

Complementary spaces for gastronomy, conferences, administration, storage, and building services, among other things, are accommodated in the two minor volumes. The first is a 134-meter-long and 11.5-meter-wide two-story extension of the dike; the second is a thin slab of six stories. The slab's third and fourth floors merge with the volume of the exhibition hall, whereas its first floor and second floor connect to the extension of the dike. It would be possible to access the exhibition hall from Maasboulevard via the roof of the lower structure. In the 1980s, it was nothing unusual for OMA to compose a scheme of multiple discrete or half-autonomous volumes that would connect and interlock. Often the shape and facing of the single volumes added up to ensembles of collage-like diversity. OMA's Netherlands Dance Theater in The Hague (1981–87), the Byzantium in Amsterdam (1985–91), and Villa dall'Ava in Paris (1983–91) are obvious examples. The relative autonomy of the volumes, the heterogeneity of their envelopes, and even some of the materials used recall the work of Gehry, such as his own house in Santa Monica (1977–78), "one-room buildings" like his Smith House project (1981), and the Aerospace Museum in Los Angeles (1981–84).[32]

By comparison, the Kunsthal scheme of April 1988 suggests a much more symbiotic relation between the parts and the whole, even at this stage. Both main volumes are orthogonal prisms, and at the point of intersection their fusion is complete, whereas the third volume—reduced to a single facade—is almost entirely incorporated into the dike's embankment. Only the interior of the main hall introduces elements of diversity. In plan, it is composed of seven parallel strips running east to west. Their width varies, as do the columns in terms of their shape, size, and rhythm. One row of columns resembles the irregular, needle-thin, and partly oblique supports of Villa dall'Ava (→ F 3.4–3.5). A page from Koolhaas' sketchblock indicates that the idea for the interior was related to his interpretation of the site. The sketch shows the building as a transitional space between the two opposites: "city" and "nature" (→ F 3.7). Instead of facilitating the visual connection between the two sides, a series of parallel strips and partitions running perpendicular "obstructs" it. Similarly, the columns lined up in the draft "delay" both the visitor's view and the movement from the entrance at Maasboulevard to the side overlooking the park.[33] Sketches of flat prisms with exoskeletal girders on top of the roof—reminiscent of Crown Hall at the Illinois Institute of Technology in Chicago—indicate that Koolhaas initially envisioned the main hall as some sort of "late Miesian" box.

F 3.7

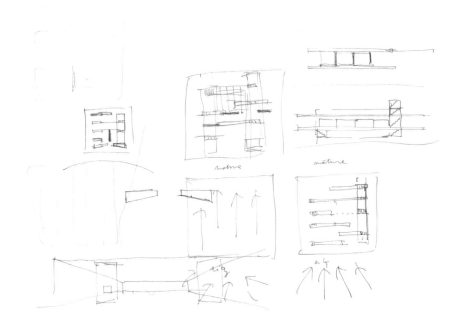

OMA/Rem Koolhaas, Kunsthal I. Sketches from Koolhaas' sketchblock on the transition from "city" to "nature."

Brussels 1958

At some point, however, another building—the Austrian pavilion at Expo 58 in Brussels—appears to have become a model for the overall composition of the volumes. Pictures of the pavilion were among the photocopies collected for the April 28 documentation on museums (→ F 3.8). The Expo pavilion, designed by Austrian architect Karl Schwanzer—better known for his BMW Museum in Munich (1972–73)—was composed of two volumes: a flat prism with a square footprint and a rectangular patio piercing its center; and a lower, slightly detached subsidiary building. The prism, containing the main exhibition hall, rested on four steel columns and was raised 6 meters above the ground. The empty space below was open on three sides. On the patio a large sphere—a constellation somewhat reminiscent of Koolhaas' Captive Globe—was arranged next to a "vertical" sculpture of wood. Apparently Koolhaas had visited Expo 58, which would have been two years after his family had returned from Indonesia. Belgian architect Paul

32 Gehry used the expression "one-room buildings" when presenting his Smith House at the "Anyone" conference in 1989. Frank O. Gehry, "Hook, Line, and Signature," in *Anyone*, ed. Cynthia Davidson, New York: Rizzoli, 1991, p. 189.

33 Sketchblock entitled "Kunsthal R'dam." OMAR 4139.

Le pavillon de l'Autriche

Quatre piliers de métal supportent, en un audacieux porte-à-faux, le plan carré du pavillon autrichien, percé d'une cour centrale.

L'entièreté de l'espace au sol, ainsi récupéré sous le pavillon, est traité en jardin et place de repos.

Des constructions basses (bureau et garderie), détachées du pavillon principal, complètent la participation.

Les murs-rideaux du pavillon, réalisés en plastique transparent, permettent le soir un éclairage total.

Karl Schwanzer, the Austrian pavilion at Expo 58 in Brussels. Photocopy from the files of the Kunsthal team.

Robbrecht, who met Koolhaas regularly while Robbrecht en Daem was planning the second extension of Museum Boijmans Van Beuningen (1999–2003), reported in a 2001 interview: "we were both incredibly 'caught' by Expo 58. Koolhaas told me: for me that was really the expression of the new."[34] In their 1993 review of the Kunsthal, Bart Lootsma and Jan de Graaf point to the fact that Rotterdam's "tradition of ambitious but temporary expos and festivals" was closely related to the Dijkzigt area and the adjacent Het Park:[35] "Rotterdam established an international reputation as a city of festivals with such public events as Rotterdam Ahoy (1950), E55 (1955), the Floriade (1960) and C70 (1970). With Ahoy, under the guidance of the architects Van den Broek and Bakema, a young generation of artists—painters, photographers, architects and sculptors—pulled out all the stops with a remarkable zeal to show the world that 'indomitable Rotterdam spirit.' It attracted one-and-a-half million visitors. E55 [the National Energy Expo] was a kaleidoscopic color chart of 'what the combined energy of the Dutch people has managed to produce in the ten years since 1945.' The three million attendees nearly derailed the city. As time went on, these expos would leave a lasting mark. The Floriade, for example, brought not only flower bulbs, but also a redesigned Park and the Euromast. C70, celebrating twenty-five years of reconstruction, joined 'man and city in festive union'; words such as 'liveability' and 'sociability' echoed on long afterward. All of these expos sported refreshingly unconventional exhibition design that cleverly combined education with fun and culture with technology. And all of them, except C70, were concentrated at The Park [Het Park] and the 'Land of Hoboken' [the Dijkzigt area], just across the Westzeedijk thoroughfare."[36]

The theater and music festival Teatro Fantastico, which was held in Museumpark, seized on this tradition, despite all the differences in terms of content and size. The Kunsthal "Robot," for its part, echoed the display of technological innovation that was so characteristic of universal exhibitions. Lootsma and De Graaf relate that rather than an "arts center," Koolhaas "prefers to call it a *'palais des festivals'* in the tradition of the world fair pavilions."[37] The apparent borrowings from Schwanzer's scheme show the importance of the idea of the expo pavilion for the architecture of OMA's first project. The implications are consequential. Embedded in "another" tradition of the site—which, in turn, is related to another building type—the project stands outside the established urbanist discourse of contextual integration. A universal exhibition tends to figure as a self-contained demonstration of national skills and achievements, with little or no consideration for its surroundings—neither of the exhibition nor of the city hosting it. This is not to say that the relationship between OMA's scheme and the environment was arbitrary, but rather that the very model of the pavilion facilitated a non-mimetic relationship with regard to the built surroundings, opposing the ideal of a homogeneous city based on a premodern urbanist repertoire. At the same time, the model of the expo pavilion seems to be a demonstration of aloofness with regard to the monumental and

---

34 Luc van de Steene, "Bouwen aan een humanere samenleving," in *De Morgen* (December 28, 2001).

35 Lootsma and De Graaf, "In Service of the Experience," in *OMA/Rem Koolhaas: A Critical Reader*, ed. Christophe Van Gerrewey, Basel: Birkhäuser, 2019, p. 282. First published as "In dienst van de ervaring" in 1993.

36 Lootsma and De Graaf, "In dienst van de ervaring: KunstHAL van OMA in Rotterdam," p. 20 (trans. d'onderkast).

37 Lootsma and De Graaf, "In Service of the Experience," p. 282.

classicist leanings of museum design in the late 1970s and 1980s. As little as OMA's scheme had been developed at this stage, it omits any claim to "cultural weight" or institutional authority. The model of the expo pavilion enabled a proposition that differed fundamentally from the contemporary museums by Hollein, Meier, Stirling, Ungers, Pei, and Isozaki. Regardless of Schwanzer's project, the expo pavilion is endowed with its own modernist genealogy of temporary lightweight constructions—such as Melnikov's timber pavilion for the 1925 International Exposition in Paris, and Le Corbusier's demountable pavilion for Nestlé in 1928—and provides a suitable contrast to (postmodern) monumentality.[38]

At second sight

Koolhaas presented downsized versions of the scheme to the building committee in June and used these as the basis for a preliminary design (*Voorlopig Ontwerp*) in September, and again in October.[39] Among other things, the footprint of the square main building was reduced to 55 by 55 meters so that it would not exceed the available budget of 20 million guilders.[40] The preliminary design includes elaborate drawings in a scale of 1 to 200, along with detailed drawings of the Robot in a scale of 1 to 100 (→ P 4.1–4.7). A project statement made in October reiterates the main ideas outlined by Koolhaas in March: "The Kunsthal is suitable for a wide range of activities. It can serve as a museum, as a commercial fair, as a conference/performance center, as a temporary car showroom. [...] Considering the persistent alternating between permanence and flexibility that characterizes recent museum architecture, the design is aiming for a duality: On the main floor—slightly off center—a 'robot' is planned: a vertical, mechanical element of 3 layers that can easily undergo a maximum number of transformations. Walls/screens can shift or disappear, the floor moves up and down, the ceiling can be adjusted, etc. The west wall of the robot is equipped with communication media, projectors, video, fax machines, etc., and functions as a 'brain.'"[41]

As in the April draft, the floorplan of the main hall was organized as a sequence of parallel strips. The lobby was located in the first strip to the south, accessible directly from Maasboulevard and separated from the exhibition hall by a 4-meter-thick "wall" containing a ticket counter, shop, and storage space, among other things. Apart from the Robot, the main hall was informed by the structural system. The idea to use different types of columns was developed further in collaboration with structural engineer Cecil Balmond, then working at the London office of the engineering group Ove Arup & Partners.[42] Balmond—the structural engineer for Stirling's Staatsgalerie in Stuttgart—had already worked with OMA on the competitions for the Morgan Bank in Amsterdam (1984–85)[43] and the town hall in The Hague (1986). The Kunsthal was the first project in the cooperation between OMA and Arup to materialize.

Instead of columns aligned in several rows, the September scheme provided a series of parallel Vierendeel trusses, the height of which coincided with the height of the main hall. With both joists covered by the floor and the ceiling respectively, the vertical members of the trusses appeared as columns. Each of the seven trusses shown in the drawings was different, and the same goes for a surviving working model in the scale of 1 to 200 (→ F 3.9).[44] The sequence of the trusses, their visual transformation in perspective, and the overall impact of their juxtaposition was the subject of numerous sketches and digital renderings, some of which were included in *S, M, L, XL*.[45] One year later, OMA's design for the ZKM media center in Karlsruhe (likewise in collaboration with Balmond) would again propose the use of Vierendeel trusses as space-containing structural members, thereby permitting clear span halls above and below. The project for Karlsruhe explores the methodical possibility to inform a building's interior by means of the "inhabited truss"—for Koolhaas probably the most significant conceptual "breakthrough" of Kunsthal I.[46] The Vierendeels of the ZKM vary from floor to floor, and within the floors often from girder to girder, exploiting the relative structural autonomy of each. Much of the suggestive quality of the model photos shown in *S, M, L, XL* depends on the presence of the project's forcibly varied structural members.

---

38   After the exhibition in 1958 the pavilion was dismantled. A modified version was rebuilt in 1964 in Vienna to house the Museum of the 20th Century, today called 21er Haus.

39   "Nieuwbouw Kunsthal/Bouwcommissie," June 9, 1988. OMAR 3356. OMA, "Kunsthal Hoboken: Concept Plan," July 6, 1988. OMAR 3340. OMA, "Kunsthal Rotterdam, Voorlopig Ontwerp," September 7, 1988. OMAR 1744. "Verslag van de 4e Bouwcommissie Nieuwbouw Kunsthal," September 7, 1988. OMAR 3267. OMA, "Kunsthal Rotterdam, October 1988," October 7, 1988. OMAR 1744.

40   The commission asked OMA to reduce the footprint at the meeting in April because of an estimated cost overrun of 8 million guilders. "Verslag van de 2e Bouwcommissie Nieuwbouw Kunsthal," April 28, 1988.

41   OMA, "Kunsthal Rotterdam," October 7, 1988. OMAR 1744 (author's translation).

42   Email to the author by OMA's former project architect, Gregor Mescherowsky, on August 27, 2019.

43   According to Koolhaas' 1993 essay "Last Apples," the collaboration with Balmond began in 1985. Rem Koolhaas, "Last Apples," in *S, M, L, XL*, Rem Koolhaas and Bruce Mau, New York: The Monacelli Press, 1995, p. 666.

44   OMAR 3267. OMAR, MAQV 940.

45   OMAR 3334. Koolhaas and Mau, *S, M, L, XL*, p. 428.

46   Koolhaas, "Last Apples," p. 671.

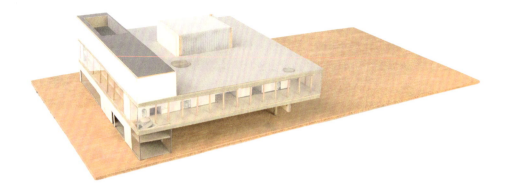

OMA/Rem Koolhaas, Kunsthal I, 1988. Scale model.

In the main hall of the Kunsthal, two distinct ideas overlap: the Miesian neutral space, and—in apparent analogy to OMA's study for the park that had been carried out in May—a Parc de la Villette-like surface composed of parallel bands that would be visually and spatially permeable. In contrast to OMA's scheme for Parc de la Villette, however, no specific function was assigned to them. An A3 booklet documenting the scheme OMA presented in October shows eleven different options for zoning that accord with the surface of the bands only in part.[47]

    The Vierendeel trusses in the main hall span 36 meters from the vertical slab with subsidiary functions to a single concrete beam resting on six *pilotis* (→ P 4.2, 4.6). From there, the trusses cantilever a further 10 meters to the edge of the eastern facade. Like the trusses themselves, the structural grid of the main hall is irregular. There are six axes running north to south and ten axes running east to west. Very few bay sizes occur more than once. Neither are they based on a common module. The spacing between the trusses varies between 4.5, 5, 6, 7.5, and 9 meters, and the facades faithfully echo the rhythm of the structural grid. The exhibition hall is enclosed by four glass walls with slender mullions, probably envisaged in steel or aluminum, like the exterior fascia of floor and ceiling. A semi-transparent box on the roof indicates the technical apparatus of the Robot. From three sides, especially towards Maasboulevard, the overall impact is "Miesian," serene, elegant. The facades disguise the complexity of the grid, structure, and interior. On the west facade, the glazed front of the exhibition hall divides the vertical slab containing the subsidiary functions into two halves. Both are clad with stone and "blind" on the top two floors. The combination of a floating volume in steel and glass with a secondary volume "in stone" that rests on the ground is another analogy to Schwanzer's 1958 pavilion. At the same time, the composition recalls Le Corbusier's villa in Garches, turning the Miesian motif into a ribbon window, topped by the "high forehead" of a windowless wall.

The exterior of the Kunsthal is completely unrelated to the brick buildings both inside the park and across the street. The closest "relative" in sight is Prouvé's tower for Erasmus University, clad with white enameled steel panels, and—according to the classification in *Collage City*—conceived not as "texture" but as an "object."[48] The date of the hospital's construction further accords with the resemblance the Kunsthal bears not only to Mies' late work but also to the numerous pavilion-like buildings following that model, including the one by Schwanzer. But all affinities are undermined by the Kunsthal's fundamental structural irregularity, contesting the repetitive rationality of construction that was so important for Prouvé. And, as if to prevent the slightest suspicion that the Kunsthal takes sides with the hospital, it is the "anachronistic" stone-clad facade that faces the ideology of technological progress embodied by the tower. Whereas Prouvé's facade emulates the look of industrial manufacturing, Kunsthal I appears to be a nod to the modernist architecture of the postwar much like buildings such as the police station in Almere, the apartment blocks in Groningen, and the bus terminal and Patio Villa in Rotterdam.

A polemic with polymorphous pleasures

In the 1980s, Koolhaas repeatedly expressed his recognition of modernist architecture from the postwar period.[49] But it appears that Koolhaas' penchant for this architecture and the relative dryness of Kunsthal I should also be viewed from the context of postmodern

47 OMA, "Kunsthal Rotterdam, October 1988," October 7, 1988. OMAR 1744.
48 Colin Rowe and Fred Koetter, *Collage City*, Cambridge, Massachusetts: The MIT Press, 1978.
49 For example, when asked in 1985 if he liked SOM's Lever House, Koolhaas answered: "Yes, and all the architecture of the 1950s and 1960s which, like Harrison's buildings, is modern without being neurotic or hysterical—this is the work of architects concerned with doing things well, who possess a skill that is now hugely lacking, and that we are now striving to acquire." (Trans. Nicola Morris). Goulet, "La deuxième chance," in *L'Architecture d'Aujourd'hui*, 238 (1985), p. 4.

architecture. Not all of OMA's production in the 1980s appears unaffected by a number of qualities commonly associated with postmodern architecture and urbanism. Irony—as Emmanuel Petit has shown—is one of them, and the interest in popular culture another.[50] Particularly those OMA projects that won most acclaim do share some common ground, however involuntarily, with the ideas advocated by Rowe and Jencks. There are obvious parallels on a formal level to the architecture and urbanism championed by the two authors as well as to the work shown by Portoghesi and Klotz.[51] Juxtaposed volumes, materials, grids, references, and the overall impact of heterogeneity, collage, and fragmentation was characteristic for the production of much of the architectural elite of the 1980s—Hollein, Stirling, Gehry, Venturi, Moore, Meier, Isozaki, Eisenman, Tschumi, Meier, and Siza, among others—even if some of these architects did not regard themselves as postmodernists or rejected postmodernist architecture altogether, as Koolhaas did. Regardless of the enormous differences between them, numerous built and unbuilt projects by these architects converge in their efforts to challenge the notion of unity. Dick Hebdige wrote: "Postmodernism may mean what Paul Virilio calls […] the 'triumph of the art of the fragment: a loss of totality, a necessary and therapeutic loss of wholeness.'"[52]

Even demonstratively sober projects like IJplein, Patio Villa, and Kunsthal I do rely on formal fragmentation, albeit in varying degrees. And yet the stress on simple forms, modernist references, and occasionally on seriality (IJplein) was meant to mark a counterposition vis-à-vis postmodernist architecture. "Needless to say the projects constitute a polemic with the polymorphous pleasures of so-called post-modern architecture": it was with these words that OMA introduced the projects for the house in Miami (1974), the Museum of Photography in Amsterdam (1975), and the "Story of the Pool" in the 1977 issue of *Architectural Design*.[53] From this and the above statements it is clear that the relatively formal rigor of those projects was—at least to some extent—an early attempt to do without this quarry of artistic expression to which formal fragmentation was essential. It was vital not only for much of the work done by Koolhaas' postmodernist peers, but also for much of OMA's work. If "asserting difference" *was* a key ambition held by Koolhaas, the polymorphous pleasures stood in his way.

A polymorphous design

In January 1988, OMA was invited to participate in the competition for the Netherlands Architecture Institute.[54] The NAi was a merger of three institutions that until then had been based in Amsterdam: the housing foundation Stichting Wonen, the Nederlands Documentatie-centrum voor de Bouwkunst (Netherlands' Documentation Centre for Architecture), and the Stichting Architectuurmuseum (Architecture Museum Foundation). As in the case of the Kunsthal, the program for the NAi was based on studying models from abroad, namely the Deutsches Architekturmuseum (DAM) in Frankfurt and the Canadian Center for Architecture (CCA) in Montreal.[55] According to a press release, a budget of 22 million guilders was reserved for the new building, and this would be supplied by the ministries of housing (VROM) and culture (WVC), which would also be responsible for the NAi's operating costs.[56] The NAi steering group, chaired by J. Jessurun of the culture ministry, supervised the competition.[57] In addition to OMA, five other teams took part: Benthem and Crouwel of Amsterdam, Jo Coenen of Eindhoven, Wim Quist of Rotterdam, Luigi Snozzi of Locarno, and Jan Hubert Henket of Boxtel, the architect of Museum Boijmans Van Beuningen's future garden pavilion (1989–91). The deadline was June 1, 1988.[58] The NAi was OMA's third project within the perimeter of Museumpark. In a 1989 interview, Mil De Kooning suggested that the "'peace' of the Kunsthal [I]" was meant to complement the "pronounced 'charge'" of the NAi; Koolhaas agreed.[59] In *S, M, L, XL*, he explained: the "Architecture Museum [NAi] is a study in weight and heaviness; the Kunsthal [I] floats above the park at the level of the dike. The core of the Architecture Museum is a solid; the center of the Kunsthal is a void."[60] Viewed in the context of OMA's previous work, the schemes also represent two of the three strategies mentioned in Chapter 1:

50 Emmanuel Petit, "Rem Koolhaas," in *Irony: Or, The Self-Critical Opacity of Postmodern Architecture*, New Haven: Yale University Press, 2013, pp. 177–211.
51 Paolo Portoghesi, ed., *The Presence of the Past: La Biennale di Venezia 1980, architectural section*, London: Academy Editions, 1980. Heinrich Klotz, *Moderne und Postmoderne: Architektur der Gegenwart 1960–1980*, Braunschweig/Wiesbaden: Vieweg & Sohn, 1985, pp. 309–14.
52 Dick Hebdige "A Report on the Western Front: Postmodernism and the 'Politics' of Style," in *Cultural Reproduction*, ed. Chris Jencks, London: Routledge, 1993, p. 80.
53 OMA, "Three Rectangular Projects," in *Architectural Design*, 5 (1977), p. 352.
54 H. Anderson (NAi steering group), letter to Rem Koolhaas, January 7, 1988. OMAR 2012.
55 Sergio M. Figueiredo, *The NAi Effect: Creating Architecture Culture*, Rotterdam: NAi010, 2016, pp. 155–99.
56 Project Architectuur Instituut, Persbericht. Undated. OMAR 2012.
57 A list of all ten of its members is enclosed in the letter. Ibid.
58 J. Jesserun (Stuurgroep Architectuurinstituut), letter to Rem Koolhaas, February 19, 1988. OMAR 2012.
59 Mil De Kooning, "OMA in Nederland: Rem Koolhaas in gesprek," in *Vlees & Beton*, 12 (1989), n. p. (author's translation).
60 Rem Koolhaas, "Kunsthal I," in *S, M, L, XL*, Koolhaas and Mau, p. 429.

one being a close approximation to modernist precedents, the other indulging in—modernist—polymorphous pleasures.

Until fall, it appears, the three projects were developed successively rather than parallel to each other: first of all—by the end of April—came the draft for Kunsthal I; second—essentially in May—was the entry for the NAi; and third, the Museumpark scheme, which was apparently resumed in summer. The teams for the NAi and the Kunsthal overlapped. The appendix of *S, M, L, XL* lists the following individuals for the NAi project: Xaveer de Geyter, Luc Reuse, Alexander Nowotny, Jeroen Thomas—in addition to Rem Koolhaas, Ron Steiner, and Gregor Mescherowsky, who were also involved in Kunsthal I.[61] The first dated sketches are from the end of April. They indicate that the visual connection between Rochussenstraat, the park, and Museum Boijmans Van Beuningen was a major concern with regard to the shape of the volume.[62] A sketch by Kees Christiaanse, dated April 26, shows a V-shaped building with a covered courtyard in the center that opens up to the villas.[63] Another sketch based on the same configuration suggests two towers on top of the northern wing (→ F 3.10).[64] The idea seems related to a series of sketches—apparently by Koolhaas—considering three options for incorporating the typology of the adjacent villas into the scheme (→ F 3.11). Option I has two "villas" on top of the roof; option II suggests filling the whole of Hobokenplein with villas, similar to OMA's studies in 1987; option III translates the volume of the villas into courtyards of corresponding dimensions. In a 2015 interview, Xaveer de Geyter recalls referring to the competition for the NAi: "In this specific case Rem got involved very late and he thought it was really not good, so there was a kind of a 'blitzkrieg' to change the whole project. We came up with the new plan in a few days. I got involved because he asked, and basically the old team was thrown out and we did it with a new team. The project changed completely."[65]

The principle of artistic contrast

A series of dated sketches indicates that the conceptual core of the design was established by the second week of May, two weeks before the deadline.[66] While the triangular footprint was retained, the relation of solid and void was inverted. Instead of having a courtyard in the center of two V-shaped wings, the whole building was reframed as a triangular hall with a rectangular solid—later called the "podium"—in its middle (→ P 4.9–4.12). The scheme responds to its urban context in unconventional ways. Two triangular segments, "subtracted" from the

F 3.10

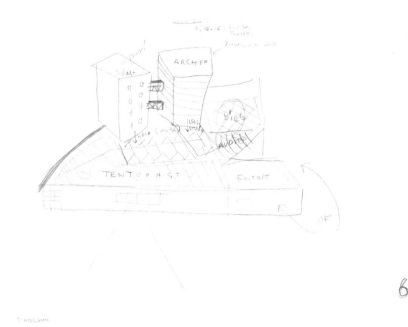

OMA/Rem Koolhaas, NAi, 1988. Sketch of the first scheme, which was abandoned.

F 3.11

OMA/Rem Koolhaas, NAi, 1988. Sketch showing the relation between the NAi and the modernist villas across Jongkindstraat.

61 Koolhaas and Mau, *S, M, L, XL*, p. 1276.
62 OMAR 2029.
63 Ibid. Christiaanse recognized the sketch during an interview with the author, April 14, 2020.
64 Undated. OMAR 2029.
65 Holger Schurk, *Projekt ohne Form: OMA, Rem Koolhaas und das Laboratorium von 1989*, Leipzig: Spector Books, 2020, pp. 90–91 (author's translation).
66 OMAR 2024, 2029.

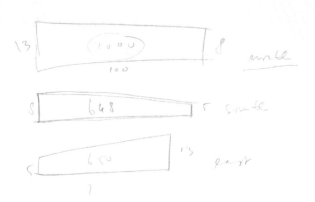

OMA/Rem Koolhaas, NAi, 1988. Sketch defining the heights of the three facades.

fan-shaped lot of Hobokenplein, were to remain unbuilt: the triangle to the south because of a major sewer,[67] while the other, along Jongkindstraat, would provide a generous spatial and visual connection between Museumpark and the more central parts of the city (→ P 4.8). The western edge of this corridor coincided with the Axis of Development that the municipality had proposed. The volume of the NAi would occupy the third and largest triangular segment of Hobokenplein. Each of its three corners differed in height: the corner pointing towards Westersingel and the inner city would more or less touch the 13-meter-tall roofline of the apartment houses north of Rochussenstraat; the western corner was raised about 8 meters above street level; and the southern corner was approximately 5 meters tall (→ F 3.12). The sequence 5-8-13 was evidently based on the golden ratio. The sloping roof descended slightly towards the west and more steeply towards the open space of the park, articulating the transition from the "vertical city" to the horizontal surface of Museumpark. It was pierced by a leaning tower echoing its slope.

It goes without saying that the contextual quality of the scheme differed radically from more established ways of relating to a given site. Huge sloping planes and leaning towers did not occur in the surroundings. Neither did most of the design's materials and colors. While most facades in the vicinity were made either of exposed brickwork or white, the tower—square in plan and without any openings—

was in black concrete. The color of the roof was gold. Two of the facades were envisaged as glass walls—tinted gray facing the park, and green on the side where the entrance was situated. The facade along Rochussenstraat was clad with translucent panels of corrugated polyester, filtering the visual disquiet of the traffic. Dismissing established recipes of "contextuality," OMA's scheme explored non-mimetic forms of relating to the environment. In this regard, the design was reminiscent of Ivan Leonidov's competition entry for the Narkomtjazhprom building. In an article from 1974, Koolhaas and Oorthuys analyzed in detail how Leonidov related to the surroundings based on the "principle of artistic contrast."[68] Like Leonidov in his explanatory note, OMA's NAi "insists" on the freedom to choose the manner in which the relationship between project and context might be established. As for the Narkomtjazhprom, the "flamboyance" of the gilded cupulas on St. Basil's cathedral is echoed by hyperboloids and the mushroom-shaped golden platforms attached to a high-rise. Similarly, what OMA seems to propose with the NAi is a metaphorical contextualization that has nothing to do with an urbanism of spatial, material, and morphological continuity. If the oblique roof "points" to Rotterdam's city and descends to the park in straightforward analogy to their respective verticality and horizontality, the tower—visually cut off by the roof and perpendicular to its slope—appears as a black counterpart to the adjacent villas. A project statement—opening an A3 booklet with corollary texts and drawings, and an "Engineering Concept Report" by Arup London—explains: "A black cube, roughly of the same dimensions as the white villas, stands at a right angle on the roof."[69]

Like a collage

The tower was intended to house the archives. Surfacing from the basement, its tilted shaft merges with the rectangular podium, harboring a depot, offices, a reading room, a cafeteria, a ticket desk, cloakrooms, and a bookshop.[70] As the booklet explains, the podium's interior was conceived in contrast to the vast open space enclosed between its exterior and the perimeter of the triangular volume. The entire exterior of the podium is clad with travertine. Adjacent to the entrance a large

67 OMA, "Architectuurinstituut Rotterdam," June 1988. Site plan. OMAR 4233.
68 Rem Koolhaas and Gerrit Oorthuys, "Ivan Leonidov's Narkomtiazhprom," in *Oppositions*, 2 (1974), p. 99.
69 OMA, "Architectuurinstituut Rotterdam," June 1988, p. 3. Ove Arup, "Engineering Concept Report. Architecture Institute, The Netherlands," May 1988. OMAR 4233. A note by Koolhaas, headed "Questions Cecil" indicates that Balmond was in charge of the structural concept. OMAR 2014. Balmond and Mirvat Bulbul are also listed as structural engineers in *S, M, L, XL*. Koolhaas and Mau, *S, M, L, XL*, p. 1276.
70 OMA, "Architectuurinstituut Rotterdam," June 1988, pp. 4–5.

rectangular area has been "excavated" from its imaginary mass. Within this cavity, a sequence of ramps leads to the top of the podium, from which a staircase on the other side leads back down to the first floor at street level. A section of the ramp system widens up to almost square proportions and can be used as an auditorium. A yellow silk curtain may be drawn around the seating. What used to be a second solid on the roof in some of the early sketches has been inverted into a square patio, supplying light to the offices and cafeteria inside the podium. The bottom of the courtyard was designed to function like a mirror, so that the visually doubled volume would equal the length of the tower.[71]

The podium divides the triangular interior into three areas of comparable size. Two of them were intended to be for exhibitions, and one for a public library. Steel columns, distributed on a square grid of 6 by 6 meters, carry the sloping roof, creating a "forest of columns" or hypostyle hall. The clue given in *S, M, L, XL*—an "old Moorish device that makes architecture out of a box"—brings to mind the Mezquita in Cordoba, with the gothic cathedral inside the mosque piercing its roof.[72] The relative intimacy created by the columns would respond to the ephemeral and fragile character of the exhibits. The corollary text explains: "The materials produced and left behind by the architect are often not intrinsically impressive. Yellowed paper, faded drawings, clumsy sketches, wrecked models."[73] The columns' diameters (20, 22, and 25 cm) and colors (black, gray, and white) vary according to the height of the sloping roof (approximately 4.5 to 13 meters). Both the use of different colors and the "needle-like" proportion of the longer columns bear some resemblance to the exterior supports of Villa dall'Ava. The proportions are also akin to Libeskind's City Edge project in 1987, and among OMA's sketches for the NAi there is one that shows a bundle of long columns, annotated "Dani Libeskind"—perhaps a reminder not to repeat what Libeskind had already done.[74] Unlike Libeskind's project, all the NAi's columns are vertical, and they end with an exposed round steel plate (shear head) where they connect to the ceiling. The plates have a constant diameter of 80 centimeters, which would supposedly both unify the space and "lessen the effect of span."[75] Despite their proportion-denying flatness, visiting architects might have been tempted to understand the shear heads as capitals; that is, as a modernist interpretation of the classical column in the Miesian tradition. Perhaps the detail was precisely about denying the purported nobility of the supports. With their flat projecting tops, the columns would have looked like giant nails, in a striking resemblance to the nails used for the model.

F 3.13

OMA/Rem Koolhaas, Competition entry for the NAi, 1988. East elevation.

Two of the collaged elevations—north and east—focus on the ensemble of the tower and podium (→ F 3.13). Its presence towards the outside is filtered to varying degrees by the facades' respective greenish or corrugated skin, each cut out in the center to offer an unimpeded glimpse into the interior. The ensemble of the tower and podium recalls a collage in its own right. The bright surface of the podium and the black volume of the tower interlock, while intersecting with the yellow silk curtain suspended from the ceiling and the glass walls of the courtyard ascending to the roof. Further complexity is added by the corrugated surface (the bar) on top of the podium, by the attached staircase, by the openings cut out from its "mass," and by the layering of the partly cut back facades. The heterogeneity is echoed, almost imperceptibly, by the assorted colors of the columns partly overlapping in the renderings.

As the model shows, the ensemble of the podium, tower, courtyard, and bar is a "collage" of multiple partly intersecting solids rather than surfaces. As such, it resembles OMA's most complex, fragmented-looking exteriors. Both the Netherlands Dance Theater and Villa dall'Ava are composed of several distinct volumes, articulated by means of their form, material, and color. As in the case of the podium,

71 Ibid., p. 5.
72 Koolhaas, "New Rotterdam," in *S, M, L, XL*, Koolhaas and Mau, p. 407.
73 OMA, "Architectuurinstituut Rotterdam," June 1988, pp. 8–9.
74 OMAR 2024.
75 OMA, "Architectuurinstituut Rotterdam," June 1988, section 2.4.1.

OMA/Rem Koolhaas, Villa dall'Ava, Paris, 1984–91.

the volumes' integrity is contested in one way or another—cut off at one side by a wall, for instance, like the stacked boxes next to the concrete slab of Villa dall'Ava (→ F 3.14). The different parts of the main facade of the Byzantium in Amsterdam—gray plaster, blue brickwork, and black metal panels—are echoed by relief-like setbacks, recalling the cardboard layers of OMA's collaged elevations.[76] As with the Netherlands Dance Theater, the impact of unity is undermined to the point that the whole may appear to be the result of a piecemeal planning and building process—one that is ultimately not dissimilar to the "contextualist" simulations of growth Koolhaas despised.[77] If some parts of the Dance Theater were reminiscent of the 1950s, there could be no doubt that the whole belonged to an entirely different era, striving for fragmentation, heterogeneity, and dissonance. Conversely, the projects approximating postwar modernism more closely were at risk of being taken for some sort of nostalgic emulation of the 1950s. In other words, in order to incorporate modernist references in an artistically productive way—which at the time was vital for all of OMA's architecture—Koolhaas relied on the techniques of collage and montage, entailing varying degrees of an overall fragmented impact.

Friendly monumentality

After the inauguration of the exhibition accompanying the NAi competition in Museum Boijmans Van Beuningen on July 8, the major Dutch architecture magazines discussed OMA's scheme with recognition, enthusiasm, even admiration.[78] The way the project reacted to the site; the feeling of openness created by the transparent and translucent facades; the "forest of columns" as a response to the character of the exhibits; the suppression of any monumentality and false pretensions: critics praised all these qualities almost unanimously. But Coenen's scheme, too, won strong approval, above all for the relation it established to the site. Hans van Dijk, for instance, feared Coenen's project might be too expensive, "because it is a wonderful design that adapts to its environment in an exciting and subtle way."[79] Similarly, Rodermond acknowledged that "landscape, city, and architecture are interwoven in a very elegant manner."[80] No doubt, Coenen's design contained explicit references to the apartment blocks and exposed brickwork of the surroundings, and its pool and pergola motif connect to the adjacent park. While Rodermond approved of the scheme's "friendly monumentality," Bekaert dismissed it as "the Versailles of Dutch architecture."[81]

The board of the Stichting Nederlands Instituut voor Architectuur en Stedenbouw (Netherlands Institute for Architecture and Urban Planning), which had been set up in August 1988, selected the winning scheme.[82] The ten members of the board gathered on September 13 and invited Quist, Koolhaas, and Coenen for a meeting on September 22.[83] On October 2, an announcement was made that Coenen had won the competition and it was his scheme that would be implemented.[84] In a comment entitled "Coenen, a surprising choice," Hans van Dijk mentioned that a cost overrun for the winning design was

---

76 On the plasticity of OMA's collaged facades, see Mathieu Berteloot, Véronique Patteeuw, "OMA's Collages," in *OASE*, 94 (2015), pp. 67–73.

77 See Rem Koolhaas, "Urban Intervention: Dutch Parliament Extension, The Hague," in *International Architect*, vol. 1 (1980), p. 48.

78 H. Andersson (project manager for Stuurgroep Architectuur Instituut), June 14, 1988. OMAR 4215.

79 Hans van Dijk, "'Zes architecture op zoek naar een opdrachtgever,' De ontwerpen voor het Nederlands Architectuurinstituut," in *Archis*, 7 (1988), p. 9.

80 Janny Rodermond, "Zes ontwerpen voor een architectuurinstituut," in *De Architect*, 7 (1988), p. 38.

81 Geert Bekaert, "A Versailles for Dutch Architecture: The Netherlands Architecture Institute by Jo Coenen," in *Rooted in the Real: Writings on Architecture by Geert Bekaert*, ed. Christophe Van Gerrewey (2011), p. 247. First published in 1993 under the title "Een Versailles voor de Nederlandse architectuur: Het Nederlands Architectuurinstituut door Jo Coenen."

82 Figueiredo, *The NAi Effect*, p. 227.

83 Letters from H. Andersson (project manager for Nederlands instituut voor architectuur en stedebouw), August 29 and September 14, 1988. OMAR 4215.

84 J.P. Baeten, "Catalogus van de collectie 'Meervoudige opdracht Nederlands Architectuurinstituut Rotterdam' 1988," p. 4. OMAR 4218.

to be expected.[85] In fact, according to cost estimates, Coenen's scheme was more expensive than OMA's.[86] The report of the assessment committee was never made public.[87] The basis on which the board took its decision is not clear.[88] Concerns regarding the feasibility of OMA's scheme might have played a role.[89] In any case, due to this failure, OMA's competition entry became a source of ideas that—once adapted and developed further—would enter, enrich, and reshape the design of Kunsthal II.

A problem of distinction

Three weeks after the deadline of the NAi competition, the exhibition *Deconstructivist Architecture* opened on June 23 at the Museum of Modern Art in New York (MoMA), curated by Philip Johnson and Mark Wigley. Rem Koolhaas was among the architects selected for the show, along with Frank Gehry, Daniel Libeskind, Peter Eisenman, Zaha Hadid, Coop Himmelb(l)au, and Bernard Tschumi (→ F 3.15–3.19). The exhibition was preceded by a symposium and an edition of *Architectural Design*, both on the topic of deconstruction in architecture, and featuring more or less the same protagonists. The symposium, held in March at the Tate Gallery in London, was opened by a recorded video interview with Jacques Derrida. Among the speakers were Wigley, Eisenman, Hadid, Tschumi, and Charles Jencks.[90] The issue of *Architectural Design*, published in April 1988, included essays by Jencks, Tschumi, and Elia Zenghelis amongst others, as well as a fourteen-page interview with Eisenman and projects of the architects to be shown at MoMA. A second symposium was held in New York after the opening of the exhibition. The panel consisted of Rosalind Krauss, Kurt Foster, Anthony Vidler, Michael Hays, Jeffrey Kipnis, and Mark Wigley, who moderated the discussion. Koolhaas participated in neither of the symposia, nor did he contribute a text to the April issue of *Architectural Design*. This silence—or absence of comment—with regard to deconstructivism would continue for more than a year, in spite of the widespread and persistent attention the subject received in architectural debates.[91]

No doubt, "asserting difference" vis-à-vis deconstructive architecture was difficult. In the case of postmodernist architecture, the antagonisms stressed—program vs. form, modern vs. premodern, and so forth—were bold enough to hide the features in common, such as the affinity to formal fragmentation and collage, which OMA's most successful designs did share with many an icon of postmodernist architecture. In the context of the projects subsumed under the label

F 3.15

Frank O. Gehry, Familian House, Santa Monica, 1978. Shown at the *Deconstructivist Architecture* exhibition, MoMA, New York, 1988. Image taken from the catalog.

F 3.16

Zaha Hadid, The Peak, Hong Kong, 1982–83. Site presentation model. Shown at the *Deconstructivist Architecture* exhibition, MoMA, New York, 1988. Image taken from the catalog.
© Zaha Hadid Foundation

85 Hans van Dijk, "Coenen, een verrassende keuze," in *Archis*, 11 (1988), p. 7.
86 Figueiredo, *The NAi Effect*, pp. 227, 229.
87 Ibid., p. 225.
88 Ibid., p. 230.
89 Ibid., p. 228.
90 Editorial, "Deconstruction at the Tate Gallery," in *Architectural Design*, 3/4 (1988), p. 7.
91 An interview in 1990 appears to have been one of the first occasions for Koolhaas to distance himself from deconstructivist architecture. See Chantal Béret, "Rem Koolhaas: La condition métropolitaine," in *Art Press*, 148 (1990), p. 19.

Peter Eisenman, Biocenter for the University of Frankfurt, Frankfurt, 1987. Shown at the *Deconstructivist Architecture* exhibition, MoMA, New York, 1988. Image taken from the catalog.

OMA/Rem Koolhaas, Boompjes apartment building, Rotterdam, 1980. Shown at the *Deconstructivist Architecture* exhibition, MoMA, New York, 1988. Image taken from the catalog.

Coop Himmelb(l)au, Skyline, Hamburg, 1985. Shown at the *Deconstructivist Architecture* exhibition, MoMA, New York, 1988. Image taken from the catalog.

of "deconstructivism," OMA's stance was less distinct. Like Koolhaas, many of the architects whose work was identified as deconstructivist were perceived (or positioned themselves) as opponents to postmodernist architecture, rejecting contextualism and classicist references, while drawing in one way or another on the tradition of the modern movement, Russian constructivism, and suprematism. The MoMA exhibition drew attention to the parallels between constructivism and deconstructivism. The first of a total of three galleries presented Russian art from the years between 1913 and 1933, including works by Casimir Malevich, El Lissitzky, Alexander Rodchenko, Vladimir Tatlin,

Aleksander Vesnin, and Yakov Chernikov.[92] The *folies* of Tschumi's Parc de la Villette, the tilted open web trusses of OMA's Boompjes project, and Hadid's project for the Peak Club in Hong Kong from 1982 were explicitly referenced to their work.

In the heartland of Koolhaasian discourse

In the essay included in the catalog, Wigley disclaims any link between "the contemporary philosophy known as 'deconstruction'" and the work shown at MoMA, explaining that the "projects can be called deconstructivist because they draw from Constructivism and yet constitute a radical deviation from it."[93] It is a well-known fact, however, that the subject of Wigley's 1987 dissertation was Jacques Derrida and deconstruction in architectural discourse.[94] That Wigley's understanding of deconstructivist architecture owed much to Derrida's "strategy of deconstruction" is obvious and had soon been noticed.[95] Like deconstruction, deconstructivist architecture would operate "from within," entering its object and appropriating its structure; like deconstruction, deconstructivist architecture would expose the intrinsic contradictions—or "imperfections"—of its object, concealed by an enforced unity. Like Derrida, Wigley insinuates analogies to psychoanalysis, suggesting that deconstructivism discloses the "unconscious" of architectural form.[96] Like deconstruction, deconstructivism, according to Wigley, did not destroy or fragment but rather distort and deform.[97] Equating regular volumes, such as the cube or cylinder, with "harmony, unity, and stability," Wigley regarded their distortion as an expression of conflict and instability. Such instability, he suggested, would challenge the traditional notion of order and unity. It is in this apolitical sense that Wigley recognizes deconstructivist architecture as "critical" and "subversive."[98] Considerations regarding the impact of architecture on society—so vital for constructivist thinking—are as absent from Wigley's introduction as from his subsequent explications of the "deconstructivist" projects. Wigley's reading of OMA's Boompjes project is essentially formalist, focusing on the design's ambiguity between slab and tower, orthogonal and diagonal shapes, modernist stability and constructivist instability. And yet when pointing to the Russian avant-gardes of the 1920s, or raising the issues of instability, subversion, the unconscious, or "the hidden potential of modernism," Wigley operated in the heartland of Koolhaas' discourse and work, while identifying all of this as common ground for a new strand in contemporary architecture.[99]

They break a building into seemingly unrelated parts

The critique of formalism recurred in the reviews published after the opening of the MoMA show. More than one critic inferred that the exhibits had been selected solely on the basis of formal likeness, while observing that the catalog also discussed the work in exclusively formal terms. Many authors dismissed the exhibition as a reductive, politically inoffensive attempt to tone down significant differences between the appearance of the work being displayed and the respective approaches behind it.[100] Many held Philip Johnson responsible for the superficial take on the architecture on show, which drained deconstructivism and constructivism of their societal implications, as Johnson (and Hitchcock) had done with modernist architecture at the *International Style* exhibition fifty-six years before.[101] But the press covered the exhibition extensively. At least fifty-five articles on the event were published between 1987 and 1989 in American magazines and journals alone.[102] The MoMA show left a lasting impact and proved to be the breakthrough moment for "decon" as a label for contemporary architecture. Unlike the curators, the architects were largely exempt from criticism: "The majority of the projects on view at the Modern," observed Herbert Muschamp, "are indeed among the most challenging of our time, worth almost any amount of hoopla."[103] In an essay from April 1988, Charles Jencks acknowledged deconstructivism as a new style that gained "widespread acceptance." According to Jencks, the "Neo-Constructivist aesthetic unites the work of Gehry with that of such designers as Rem Koolhaas, Arquitectonica, Zaha Hadid and

---

92 Simone Kraft, *Dekonstruktivismus in der Architektur? Eine Analyse der Ausstellung "Deconstructivist Architecture" im New Yorker Museum of Modern Art*, Bielefeld: Transcript, 2015, p. 50.

93 Wigley, "Deconstructivist Architecture," in *Deconstructivist Architecture*, eds. Philip Johnson and Mark Wigley, exh. cat., New York: The Museum of Modern Art, 1988, pp. 10, 16.

94 Wigley received his PhD, entitled *Jacques Derrida and Architecture: The Deconstructive Possibilities of Architectural Discourse*, at the University of Auckland in New Zealand.

95 Michael Sorkin, "Decon Job," in *The Village Voice*, 27 (1988), p. 83; Robin Evans, *The Projective Cast*, Cambridge, Massachusetts: The MIT Press, 1995, p. 89.

96 Wigley, "Deconstructivist Architecture," p. 20.

97 In his essay on Tschumi's project for Parc de la Villette, Derrida wrote: "These *folies* do not destroy." According to Derrida, the project even implies (deconstructive) affirmation. Jacques Derrida, "Point de folie— Maintenant l'architecture," in *Architecture Theory Since 1968*, Hays, p. 575. First published under the same title in 1986.

98 Wigley, "Deconstructivist Architecture," pp. 10, 11, 16.

99 Ibid., p. 19.

100 For instance, Sorkin, "Decon Job," in *The Village Voice*, 27 (July 5, 1988), pp. 81–83; Herbert Muschamp, "The Leaning Tower of Theory," in *The New Republic*, 3 (August 1988), pp. 36–40.

101 For instance, Sorkin, "Decon Job," pp. 81, 83; Muschamp, "The Leaning Tower of Theory," p. 40.

102 See the bibliography compiled by Simone Kraft, in *Dekonstruktivismus in der Architektur?*, pp. 350–354.

103 Muschamp, "The Leaning Tower of Theory," p. 36.

Bernard Tschumi into a clearly identifiable 'school.'"[104] Two months earlier, Joseph Giovannini had already announced deconstructivism as a "New School of Architects" in an article for the *New York Times*.[105] Referring not only to the firms selected for the show in New York, but also to Morphosis, Bahram Shirdel, Thomas Leeser, Michele Saee, and others, Giovannini wrote: "Known as Deconstructivists, these architects—who over the last decade have been joined by their students and the students of their students—are designing real and theoretical projects. Unlike conventional designs that strive for architectural unity, theirs look fragmented and accidental: they splinter walls, unhinge corners and shift floors like so many tectonic plates. Uninterested in the 90-degree angle and parallel lines, they break a building into seemingly unrelated parts: walls don't meet floors; door frames are distorted. The Deconstructivists have been loosely inspired by Russian Constructivism, the revolutionary art movement of the 1920s, and by Deconstructionism, a contemporary French literary movement. They eschew the classical forms and sense of balanced symmetry that typify much recent design, especially post-modernism. [...] The designers have turned what they see as the instability of our times into an architectural virtue."[106]

Giovannini's article bespeaks the extent to which some cornerstones of OMA's approach were diffused in contemporary architecture and discourse: apart from the rejection of postmodernism and the references to constructivism, the catchword and gesture of "instability" as well as formal fragmentation were about to become commonplace in what promised to become the latest architectural fashion. To be sure, when Koolhaas used the word "instability"—in *Delirious New York*, "Elegy for the Vacant Lot" (1985), or "How Modern is Dutch Architecture?" (1990)—he was not referring to a visual impact, but rather to change in terms of program, urban transformations, and cultural change in the widest sense;[107] likewise, he hardly ever used the terms "fragmentation" and "collage" during those years, perhaps *because* formal fragmentation and collage were widely considered key characteristics of postmodern architecture. But Johnson and Wigley's exhibition at the MoMA was like a spotlight cast on these and other characteristics that Koolhaas' work shared with a larger number of peers, and the "deconstructivist architecture" branding brought them into focus. Taking a look at the best-known architectural firms reveals parallels such as a preference for skewed, "distorted," or unstable-looking forms (Libeskind, Eisenman, Hadid, Gehry, Lebbeus Woods, Coop Himmelb(l)au, Domenig, Fuksas, Enric Miralles, Behnisch); ostentatiously unpretentious materials like corrugated sheathing, exposed plywood, and mesh wire (Gehry, Behnisch); borrowings from constructivism and suprematism (Tschumi, Hadid); the superimposition of diverse layers of order (Eisenman, Tschumi, Morphosis); and, finally, the absence of a unifying volume in virtually all of the work associated with deconstructivist architecture.

Tapping the unconscious

There were correspondences, too, beyond mere resemblances of form. Herbert Muschamp makes several points, including the fact that all the architects involved in the MoMA exhibition rejected the idea of their discipline being secluded in self-referential autonomy, suggesting instead an architecture rooted in and nourished by its expanded cultural context, such as theory, art, literature, and music.[108] No less important was the interest in the subversive potential of architecture, shared in one way or another by Wigley, Derrida, Tschumi, and Koolhaas. According to Derrida, deconstruction in architecture would measure itself "against institutions in their solidity [...]: political structures, layers of economic decision, the material, phantasmatic apparatuses which connect state, civil society, capital, bureaucracy, cultural power and architectural education."[109] Tschumi, and Eisenman in his own way, embraced the conception of such (post-)structuralist "resistance." Andreas Papadakis, at the time editor of *Architectural Design*, paraphrases Eisenman's explication of deconstruction given during the symposium at London's Tate Gallery in March 1988 as follows: "Deconstruction looks for the 'between'—the ugly within the beautiful, the irrational within the rational—to uncover the repressed, the real resistant."[110] Tschumi explained that his Parc de la Villette would question the idea of order, challenge the program's ideology, oppose totality, and subvert its context, while looking "at new social and historical circum-

104 Charles Jencks, "Deconstruction: The Pleasures of Absence," in *Architectural Design*, 3/4 (1988), pp. 17, 20.
105 Joseph Giovannini, "The Limit of Chaos Tempts a New School of Architects," in *The New York Times* (February 4, 1988).
106 Giovannini, "The Limit of Chaos Tempts a New School of Architects" (1988).
107 Koolhaas hardly ever commented on the image of instability that OMA's projects recurrently conveyed. But his preface to Cecil Balmond's 2002 monograph *informal* indicates that he did establish a direct relation between the image and cultural condition of instability: "[...] he [Balmond] has destabilized and even toppled a tradition of Cartesian stability [...]. Instead of solidity and certainty his structures express doubt, arbitrariness [...]. He is creating a repertoire that can engage the uncertainty and fluidity of the current moment." Rem Koolhaas, Preface, in *informal*, Cecil Balmond, Munich: Prestel, 2002, p. 9.
108 Muschamp, "The Leaning Tower of Theory," p. 38.
109 Derrida, "Point de folie–Maintenant l'architecture," p. 578.
110 Editorial, "Deconstruction at the Tate Gallery," in *Architectural Design*, 3/4 (1988), p. 7.

stances."[111] Charles Jencks, even though incredulous at any such pretensions, synthesized the rebellious gestures of deconstructivist architecture as "claims to pluralism, *différence*, 'war on totality' and defense of 'otherness.'"[112]

Koolhaas was introduced to (post-)structuralist thought by Hubert Damisch during his studies at Cornell University at the beginning of the 1970s. As Frances Hsu has shown, French critical theory had a lasting impact on his writings on architecture.[113] Perhaps one consequence of Koolhaas' leanings towards French theory was his concern for the unconscious as a source and subject of architecture. When he wrote *Delirious New York*, Koolhaas seems to have been well aware of the theory of Jacques Lacan and its connection to surrealism and Salvador Dalí in particular. The notes mention Lacan's dissertation as a "reinforcement for Dalí's theses," referring to the latter's Paranoid Critical Method (PCM).[114] Surrealist writings and art played a seminal role for Lacan, who had been friends with Breton and on close terms with Dalí.[115] His theory asserts that the unconscious creates access to the "forbidden *jouissance* which is the only valuable meaning that is offered to our life."[116] Puritan repression of unconscious desires by the architectural modern movement of the 1920s and 1930s is a subject that recurred in the thinking of Eisenman, Tschumi, Koolhaas, and Wigley. According to Koolhaas, the "possible 'hidden' dimensions of modern architecture" reside in its embrace of hedonism.[117] No less important than this, surrealist techniques for tapping the unconscious—such as the PCM and the *cadavre exquis*—played a seminal role for much of the work of Koolhaas and OMA, as Roberto Gargiani has shown in his monograph *The Construction of Merveilles*.[118] But Koolhaas' interest in the unconscious was not limited to surrealist techniques for artistic production. The imaginary scene of naked men "[e]ating oysters with boxing gloves" charges the skyscraper with the promise of a surrealist loss of control, while recalling Lautréamont's chance encounter of a sewing machine and an umbrella on a dissecting table.[119] A chance encounter is an encounter with the unconscious in a realm where rules and conventions are suspended. Ultimately, the methodical surrender to the dynamics of the large building—filling the role of the unconscious—is aimed at life itself: the metropolitan life of marvel and adventure.[120] As for the surrealists, the unconscious figures as a liberating force are capable of destabilizing the existing order's "inhibitions," even if only within the enclaves of a skyscraper or park.[121]

Johnson, Betsky, Jencks

In his 1990 book *Violated Perfection*, Aaron Betsky featured work by the architects participating at the MoMA exhibition, alongside projects by Morphosis, SITE, Lebbeus Woods, Diller Scofidio, Mecanoo, Günther Behnisch, Steven Holl, Miralles, and other contemporary architects who were mainly from the Los Angeles area.[122] Betsky discerned a common trait among these projects, namely an approach that embraces the process of modernizing and technologically transforming our environment, albeit in a critical manner: raising consciousness, unmasking the current state of technology, and "violating" the control it exerts.[123] Charles Jencks, in a monograph from the same year, coined the term "Neo-Moderns."[124] His genealogical diagram of neo-modern approaches includes most of the architects in Betsky's selection, as well as Kazuo Shinohara, SITE, and Jean Nouvel. In a table with thirty neo-modern "variables," there are characteristics such as "*différence*, 'otherness'"; "fragmented, destructive/constructive"; "disjunctive complexity, awkward dissonance"; "explosive space with tilted floors"; "indeterminate functions, flux"; "ahistorical, Neo-Constructivist"; "fracture, 'space of accidents'"; "dis-harmony, 'random noise,' layering of discontinuous systems."[125] Many of these terms have been employed in order to

---

111 Bernard Tschumi, "Parc de la Villette, Paris," in *Deconstruction: Omnibus Volume*, ed. Andreas Papadakis et al., New York: Rizzoli, 1989, pp. 176, 180–81.

112 Jencks, "Deconstruction: The Pleasures of Absence," p. 31.

113 In her dissertation, Hsu focuses on the impact of Roland Barthes and Jacques Lacan. See Frances Hsu, *The Ends of Modernism: Structuralism and Surrealism in the Work of Rem Koolhaas*, PhD diss., ETH, 2003.

114 Koolhaas, *Delirious New York*, p. 316, note 6.

115 David Macey wrote on this issue: "Lacan is not influenced by surrealism, as though it were some external factor impinging upon his subjectivity; his writing is part of the same web." In *Lacan in Contexts*, David Lacey, London, New York: Verso, 1988, p. 74.

116 Jacques Lacan, "Of Structure as an Inmixing of an Otherness," in *The Languages of Criticism and the Sciences of Man: The Structuralist Controversy*, eds. Richard Macksey and Eugenio Donato, Baltimore: The Johns Hopkins Press, p. 195.

117 OMA, "La Casa Palestra," in *AA Files*, 13 (1986), p. 8.

118 Roberto Gargiani, *Rem Koolhaas/OMA: The Construction of Merveilles*, Lausanne: EPFL/PPUR, 2008.

119 Koolhaas, *Delirious New York*, p. 155.

120 "[I]n the fantastic juxtaposition of activities, each of the Club's floors is an infinitely unpredictable intrigue that extols the complete surrender to the definite instability of the Metropolis." Ibid., p. 157.

121 Walter Benjamin saw surrealism as an ultimately revolutionary endeavor: "In all its books and projects, surrealism is concerned with harnessing the powers of intoxication for the revolution." (Trans. Nicola Morris). Walter Benjamin, "Der Sürrealismus: Die letzte Momentaufnahme der europäischen Intelligenz," in *Walter Benjamin, Ein Lesebuch*, ed. Michael Opitz, Leipzig: Suhrkamp, 1996, p. 161. First published in 1929.

122 Johnson, Preface, in *Deconstructivist Architecture*, Johnson and Wigley, p. 8. Aaron Betsky, *Violated Perfection: Architecture and Fragmentation of the Modern*, New York: Rizzoli, 1990. It seems to have been Betsky who first approached Johnson with the idea for a MoMA show about what would later be called "Deconstructivist Architecture." The title as originally envisaged had been "Violated Perfection." See Diane Ghirardo, "Diane Ghirardo's Exposé of MoMA's Deconstructivist Show," in *The Architectural Review*, 1096 (1988), p. 4.

123 Betsky, *Violated Perfection*, pp. 11–13, 15–16.

124 Charles Jencks, *The New Moderns: From Late to Neo-Modernism*, London: Academy Editions, 1990.

125 Ibid., p. 27.

describe deconstructivism, a word that, in spite of all the criticism, entered the terminology of architectural discourse and would come to distinguish a large part of contemporary architecture.

However crude and simplistic such categorizations may appear, they demonstrate that OMA's work was increasingly perceived as emblematic of a number of widespread tendencies in architecture of the late 1980s. If it is true that "asserting difference" has been critical for Koolhaas' work and thinking, the 1988 breakthrough of "decon" is likely to have caused concern. Like Giovannini, Wigley, Jencks, and Betsky, Koolhaas must have realized that there *were* parallels between his own work and what was being produced by many of his peers—chiefly on a formal level, but also in terms of references and discourse. It was not difficult to foresee that *Deconstructivist Architecture* would have a certain impact on how contemporary architecture would be perceived, discussed, and practiced in the years to come, considering that the exhibition was curated by Johnson, housed by MoMA, preceded by the 1985 collaboration between Tschumi, Eisenman, and Derrida at Parc de la Villette, and assisted by an architectural press that, despite much criticism, appeared ready to launch the next trend.[126]

Internalizing the Dance Theater

The curators of *Deconstructivist Architecture* must have contacted OMA by January 1988, as the show and Koolhaas' participation in it was announced that month in a *New York Times* interview with Philip Johnson.[127] The MoMA administration started to inform the press in March, soliciting a broad response even before the opening of the exhibition.[128] Perhaps Koolhaas reacted to the harbingers of the event, pondering its possible consequences, while working on the Kunsthal and the NAi in April and May. Viewed in this light, the scheme for Kunsthal I seems to disclaim any affiliation with deconstructivism. The restrained modernism of the exterior, reminiscent of the postwar decades, has little to do with the visionary Soviet architecture of the 1920s and 1930s. The irregularity of the Vierendeel trusses aside, the design is devoid of any characteristics that qualify as deconstructivist. The three volumes of the exterior do not feel fragmented or in conflict with each other. The perfect fusion of the vertical "slab of stone" with the horizontal "Miesian box" on three sides smooths over the seeming incompatibility of the two constructions. Rather, the scheme recalls the functionalist approaches and composite volumes of early modernism, adapting the shape and position of each part to its prospective use.

It is a different story with OMA's competition entry for the NAi. With its sloped roof, leaning tower, and fragmented interior and skin, the project displays some of the proverbial deconstructivist characteristics. In a review of the competition, critic Tom Maas promptly recognized the obliqueness of the design as a deconstructivist image of instability, concluding: "That's certainly pleasing about Koolhaas: You know that his building will be partly tilted as if the world were instable."[129] Did Koolhaas not mind, or was OMA's work more "deconstructivist" than he would admit? Various statements made by Koolhaas in subsequent years indicate that he *did* mind. Perhaps he considered the obliqueness of the roof and tower to be substantial for the design, and probably the techniques of fragmentation and collage were far too important for the architectural production of OMA to be abandoned overnight. Nonetheless, the scheme for the NAi meant a subtle shift with regard to OMA's previous work, a shift that appears as an—arguably unconscious—reaction to the deconstructivist "threat." Like the projects for the prison in Arnhem and the parliament extension in The Hague, for the Netherlands Dance Theater and Villa dall'Ava, the design for the NAi seizes on the principle of "collaged volumes." But at the NAi, most of the volumetric complexity is withdrawn to the interior, filtered in varying degrees by the facades' partly translucent and partly transparent skin. With the exception of the tower's exposed top, the exterior consists of a single triangular volume. When viewed as a design strategy, the relative volumetric simplicity points to an approach that avoids one of the distinguishing marks of deconstructivist architecture, namely the disintegration and apparent fragmentation of the exterior. Up to that point, compact volumes had been rare in OMA's work in the 1980s, especially in the more collaged designs. But the "internalized" volumetric complexity of the NAi scheme would allow OMA to continue pursuing the path of heterogeneity, fragmentation, and collage, while coming up with designs in contrast to the volumetric disintegration that was characteristic of the work of architects like Gehry, Libeskind, Tschumi, Hadid, Eisenman, Morphosis, Woods, Fuksas, Miralles, Coop Himmelb(l)au, Domenig, and Behnisch.

---

126 On this issue, see Robin Evans, *The Projective Cast*, pp. 83–89.

127 Kraft, *Dekonstruktivismus in der Architektur?*, p. 31.

128 Ibid., pp. 56–57.

129 Tom Maas, "Zes plannen voor het Architectuurinstituut," in *architectuur/bouwen*, 6/7 (1988), p. 15 (author's translation).

Meeting Nov 2, 1988

- KONST HAL.
  - 建物をdijkによせる.　(どの範囲に建設可能かGregorに聞くこと)
  - 2つのZoneが建物を横断する
    - ROAD (irregular shape)
    - STREET (regular shape)
      LAMP & ROOF
    - OPEN TO PUBLIC

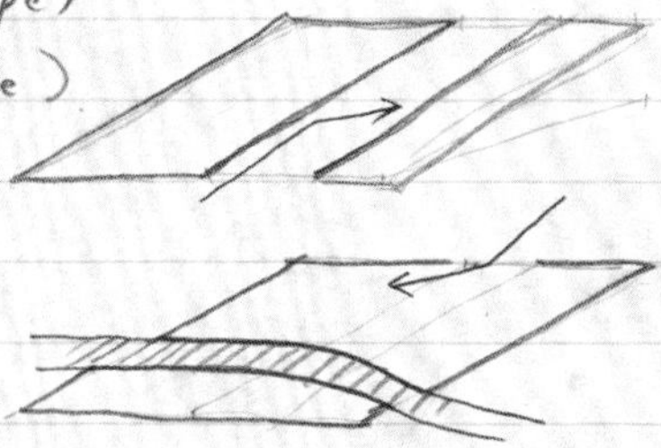

- EXHIBITION SPACE
  - GF　LAMPの下でつながる
  - 1F　LAMPの上でつながる
  - RF　Terrace + Pavillon.
- Next Meeting

- International Housing Exposition in Kashi, Fukuoka 1989.
  - 担当してくれ!
  - イソザキ事務所にtelすること.
    - 参加したい旨伝えること
    - 提案したい.
      Rem + Steven Holl + Mark Mack の3人が
      A-1, A-2, B-4, を担当する.

(Rem called Steven Holl ヤローゼ)
(lv 16th. to Japan)

P 5.1　Minutes by Fuminori Hoshino. November 2, 1988.

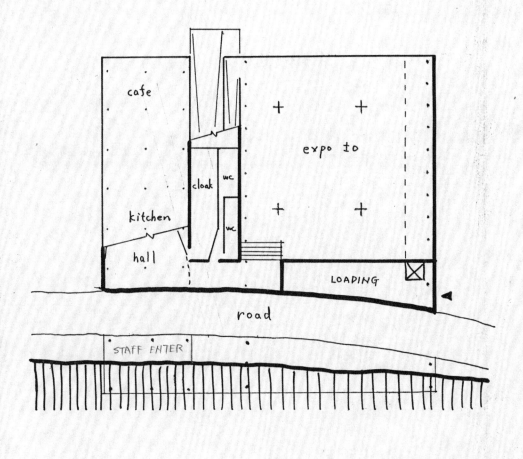

P 5.2 December 2, 1988. Park level. Right: Hall 1 ("expo +/-0").

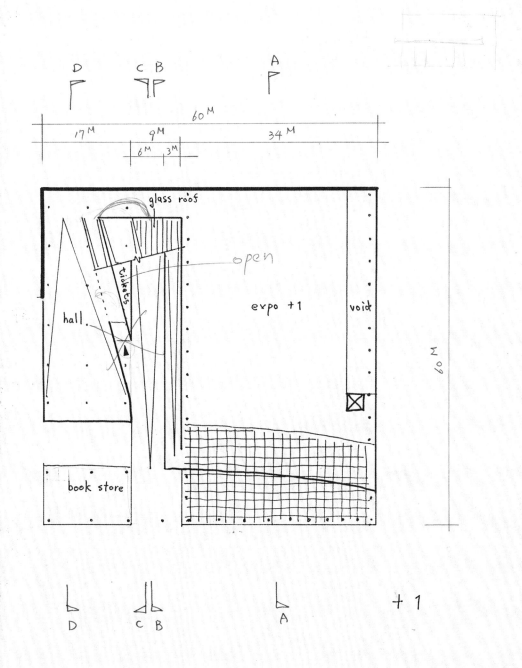

P 5.3   December 2, 1988. Dike level. Right: Hall 2 ("expo +1").

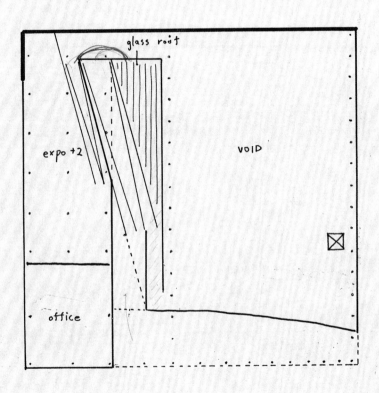

P 5.4 December 2, 1988. Third level. Hall 3 ("expo +2").

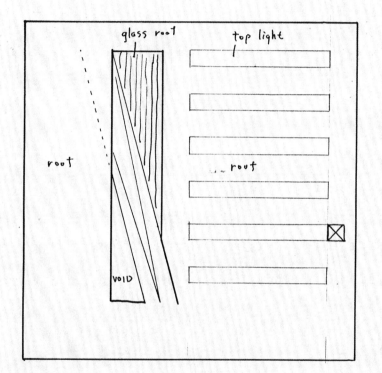

P 5.5   December 2, 1988. Roof.

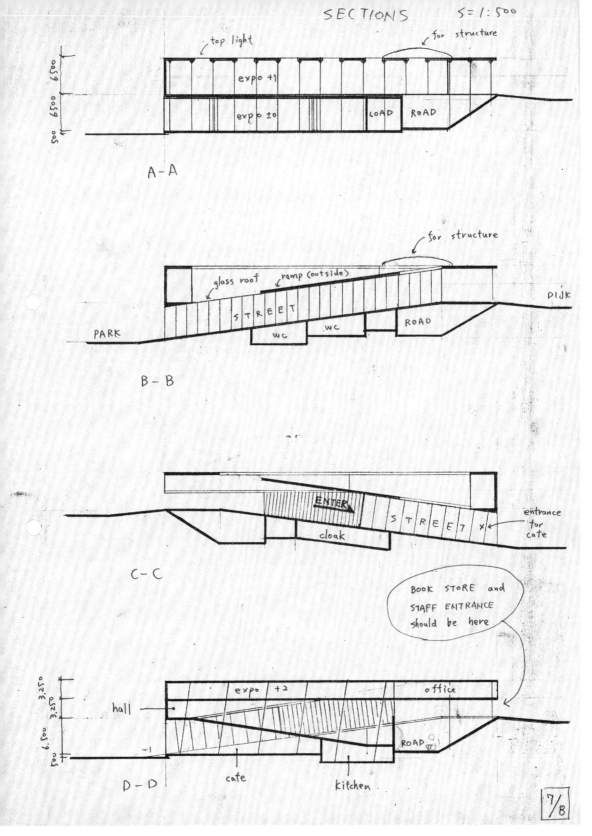

P 5.6   December 2, 1988. Cross sections (north to south). Below: the two intersecting ramps of the auditorium and Hellingstraat.

ELEVATIONS

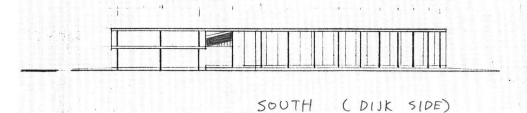

SOUTH (DIJK SIDE)

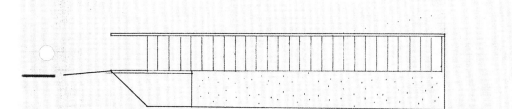

EAST

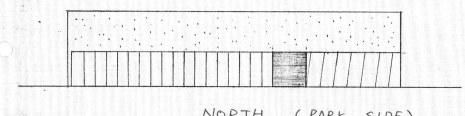

NORTH (PARK SIDE)

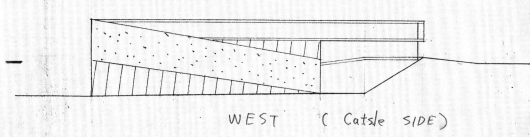

WEST (Catsle SIDE)

P 5.7   December 2, 1988. Elevations.

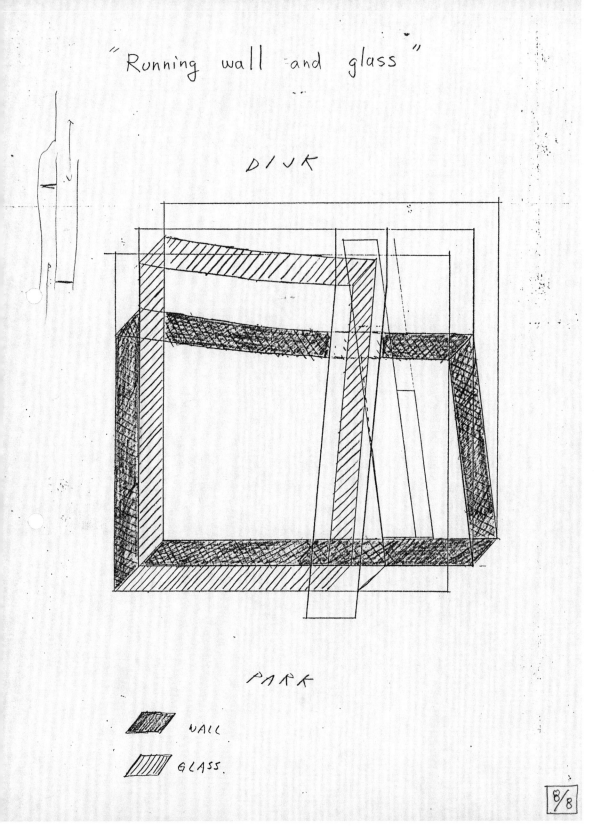

P 5.8 December 2, 1988. Axonometric view of the exterior. Left margin, turned by 90°: sketched cross section through Halls 1 and 2.

Squaring the Circle

Kunsthal II: The Scheme of December 1988

Amongst her companions moored to the bank, and all bigger than herself, she looked like a creature of higher breed—an Arab steed in a string of carthorses.

Joseph Conrad

At the meeting of the building committee on October 7, 1988, Wim van Krimpen was announced as the future interim director of the Kunsthal.[1] According to Van Krimpen, alderman Joop Linthorst had offered him the position.[2] Van Krimpen (1941–) had begun his career as an art gallerist in Amsterdam. In the 1980s he had initiated KunstRAI as the first Dutch fair for modern and contemporary art, housed in the city's RAI Exhibition and Convention Centre.[3] In 1984 he became the director of the art fair, a position he held until 1990.[4] In a 1989 interview, Van Krimpen underlined his resolution to address a broader public for economic reasons: "I saw far more visitors at foreign fairs. That should be possible here as well. The WVC [the Dutch ministry of health, welfare, and culture] has subsidized us from the beginning, but in the long run we have to become self-sufficient. That is why we have become bigger and are trying to bring together different audiences. KunstRAI must become a meeting point for everybody. That's the reason for inviting galleries that are active in other disciplines, such as design, photography, and ceramics."[5] Both the entrepreneurial spirit and the ambition to establish KunstRAi as an art fair with international scope resonated with the concept for the Kunsthal being outlined by Rotterdam's municipality. As was the case with KunstRAi, Van Krimpen's task in Rotterdam would be to establish a cultural institution of international standing that was also economically self-sufficient. Van Krimpen was to replace the municipality's representative, Hein Reedijk, in his function as project coordinator. From this moment on, the brief for the Kunsthal—in particular its organization, design, and the technical requirements of the interior—needed to be negotiated with Van Krimpen.[6]

    At the October meeting, Koolhaas presented a slightly downsized preliminary design (→ P 4.1–4.7).[7] The total floor surface of the project had been reduced once more in order to comply with the agreed cost ceiling of 25 million guilders.[8] It was, however, crucial to find out whether "the ideas of Van Krimpen correspond with those of Koolhaas," as the minutes record, obviously referring to the Kunsthal I project.[9] To this end the municipality envisaged direct talks between Koolhaas,

1. "Verslag van de 5e Bouwcommissie Nieuwbouw Kunsthal," October 7, 1988. OMAR 1517.
2. Interview with the author, July 28, 2020.
3. The acronym RAI stands for Rijwiel en Automobiel Industrie (Bicycle and Automobile Industry), the complex having been formerly used and owned by Dutch bicycle and car manufacturers.
4. Wim van der Beek et al., eds., *Art Amsterdam: 25 jaar in 50 portretten / Art Amsterdam: 25 Years in 50 Portraits*, Deventer: Thieme Art, 2009, p. 59.
5. Ibid. (author's translation).
6. Both Van Krimpen's position as the Kunsthal's interim director and the replacement of Reedijk as the project coordinator were formally confirmed when the building committee met on December 14. OMAR 3251.
7. OMA, "Kunsthal Rotterdam," October 7, 1988. OMAR 1744.
8. See Chapter 3. The cost limit was envisaged at the meeting on June 9, 1988. 5 million guilders were supposed to be funded by subsidies and sponsors.
9. "Verslag van de 5e Bouwcommissie Nieuwbouw Kunsthal," October 7, 1988.

Van Krimpen, J. Bronder of the DGM (municipal museum service), and G. Vet of the GW (public works department). A minimum delay of one month was expected, with a definitive version of the preliminary design anticipated at the beginning of November.

The end of Kunsthal I

Given Van Krimpen's managerial policy at KunstRAI, it would be natural to assume that he agreed with Koolhaas to some extent about the arts center's curatorial policy. After all, the latter's wish that the Kunsthal should host a wide range of events was cognate to Van Krimpen's initiative in opening up the Amsterdam art fair to domains beyond the realm of fine art. Likewise, Van Krimpen's ambition to address a large audience and make the art fair a "meeting point for everybody" must have intersected, to some extent, with Koolhaas' longstanding interest in popular culture. Van Krimpen, in turn, appears to have appreciated Koolhaas as an architect and OMA's Netherlands Dance Theater in The Hague in particular.[10] Nevertheless, Van Krimpen disapproved of OMA's project for Kunsthal I.[11] On November 15, he sent OMA a two-page fax with requirements and preferences, apparently as a complement to Reedijk's brief. Two of the demands were hard to reconcile with the scheme Koolhaas and his team had been developing over the previous few months: that "exhibition areas with closed walls and light entering from above" be provided, and that the peripheral columns be integrated into the exterior walls, obviously envisaging these walls as permanent surfaces for displaying exhibits.[12] In OMA's project, the facades of the exhibition area were entirely glazed, and the only "closed walls" were movable partitions.

Besides technical concerns, Van Krimpen's fax also implies criticism in terms of the design. A phrase in large letters on the first page reads: "What counts in architecture is variety of form."[13] A corollary text excerpt states: "After years of being dominated by the practically lifeless dogmas of the Moderns, architecture is gradually springing once more from imagination. There is a need for a new architecture. We can no longer tolerate these stereometric, unornamented forms, whose exterior serves no other purpose than to intimate the interior's construction."[14] Bart Lootsma and Jan de Graaf have suggested that Van Krimpen had chosen these quotes in order to express a preference for postmodern architecture, which may have been implied by the call for "variety of form" and a "new architecture" after an era of modernist domination.[15] More specifically, Van Krimpen might have (also) had

OMA's Netherlands Dance Theater in The Hague in mind. Apart from the fact that its architecture did offer "variety of form" in abundance, the building is mentioned in one of the preferences listed in the fax. The proposition for a "café-restaurant as independent 'entity' visible (see dance theatre)" refers to the golden cone next to the entrance of OMA's building in The Hague.[16]

According to Van Krimpen's own account, he expressed his disapproval of Kunsthal I at his first meeting with Linthorst and—at the invitation of the alderman—while visiting Koolhaas in his Rotterdam office.[17] Koolhaas recalls: "He hated the idea."[18] When exactly the meetings took place is not clear. Considering that Van Krimpen had been designated as the interim director of the Kunsthal by October 7, it appears likely that he and Koolhaas met soon after the gathering, if not before. Koolhaas, for his part, initiated the research for an entirely new scheme towards the end of the month, about two weeks after the committee's meeting and two weeks before receiving Van Krimpen's fax of November 15.[19] In *S, M, L, XL*, Koolhaas describes Kunsthal I as a complement to OMA's project for the NAi: "The Architecture Museum is a study in weight and heaviness; Kunsthal I floats above the park [...]. The core of the Architecture Museum is a solid; the center of Kunsthal I is a void."[20] With Jo Coenen having won the competition, Koolhaas infers, Kunsthal I became obsolete. The decision of the jury was made public on October 2. Around this time, the redesign of Museumpark was taking shape; Brunier's scheme, organized in four sections running east to west, put an end to the previously confluent relation between the Kunsthal and the park. In OMA's study of May 1987, the park's three strips running north to south are accurately aligned with the footprint of the Kunsthal, and the site plan from June 1988 still shows three strips literally "growing" out of the square main hall into the park. The fragment of Museumpark that is included in the October 7 site plan for

10 Interview with the author, July 28, 2020.
11 Koolhaas himself mentions the "future director's dislike" in *S, M, L, XL*. Rem Koolhaas, "New Rotterdam," in *S, M, L, XL*, Koolhaas and Bruce Mau, New York: The Monacelli Press, 1995, p. 429.
12 Fax from Wim van Krimpen to OMA/Rem Koolhaas. November 15, 1988. OMAR 1436. In addition to the fax, the file contains two English translations of the requirements listed.
13 Ibid. (author's translation).
14 Ibid. Quoted in Christophe Van Gerrewey, ed., *OMA/Rem Koolhaas: A Critical Reader*, Basel: Birkhäuser, 2019, p. 283.
15 Bart Lootsma and Jan de Graaf, "In dienst van de ervaring: KunstHAL van OMA in Rotterdam," in *De Architect*, 1 (1993), p. 25.
16 Fax from Wim van Krimpen to OMA/Rem Koolhaas. November 15, 1988.
17 Interview with the author, July 28, 2020. In the interview Van Krimpen mentioned concerns about the Robot, the size of the exhibition area, the pool under the building, and the functionality of the restaurant.
18 Conversation with the author over Zoom, February 8, 2023.
19 That OMA began to work on a new scheme at the end of the month is evident from notes taken by his collaborator Fuminori Hoshino on October 25 and 28, 1988, as detailed below. OMAR 1546, 1538.
20 Koolhaas, "New Rotterdam," p. 429.

the Kunsthal precisely matches Brunier's new scheme for the park, indicating that by then his proposal had been adopted (→ P 4.1).[21] But regardless of these developments, Koolhaas' enthusiasm for Kunsthal I appears to have been limited. In the 1992 issue of *El Croquis* on OMA, the project for the NAi is documented at great length, while the first project for the Kunsthal is not even mentioned; and whereas fourteen pages of *S, M, L, XL* are dedicated to the former, Kunsthal I is dealt with on two, showing nothing but a perspective rendering of the Vierendeel girders in the exhibition area. Pictures of the model, or drawings that would convey what the design actually looked like, were omitted. "It wasn't complete or clear enough as a statement," Koolhaas commented in 1989.[22]

Kunsthal II

The scheme for Kunsthal II was developed in an intense and close collaboration between Koolhaas and Japanese architect Fuminori Hoshino over a period of about four weeks in November/December 1988. Hoshino would go on to join Koolhaas as one of the two leading design architects for the Kunsthal and for Nexus Housing in Fukuoka (1988–91).[23] After graduating from the University of Tokyo, he had initially remained in Japan for another four years, planning and implementing a few small houses for two local architecture firms.[24] The job at OMA was his first employment in Europe, and the Kunsthal was the project he started with.

A few notes made by Hoshino on October 25, probably taken during his first meeting with Koolhaas, still relate to Kunsthal I. Under the heading "Problem," the notes record: "Huge space under museum is dead" and "Access from park."[25] Three days later, a concept had emerged for a building with a solid plinth and a transparent pavilion on top, a configuration somewhat reminiscent of Philip Johnson's Wiley House in New Canaan (1952–53).[26] On November 2, Hoshino received entirely new instructions which would provide the starting point for Kunsthal II.[27] His notes include an annotated sketch showing a square-shaped building with two floors (→ P 5.1). The upper floor, level with the crest of Westzeedijk, is divided by a ramp, later called Hellingstraat (Ramp Street), which would connect Museumpark with Maasboulevard. The lower floor, level with the park, is divided by the curved service road along the foot of the embankment. Hoshino's notes specify "OPEN TO PUBLIC," obviously referring to the two passages intersecting the building. The two floors and the roof terrace are listed as

F 4.1

F 4.2

F 4.3

OMA/Rem Koolhaas, Kunsthal II, November 1988. Scale models.

22 OMA, "Kunsthal Rotterdam," October 7, 1988. OMAR 1746. Scheme for the Museumpark. OMAR 4352.

22 Mil De Kooning, "OMA in Nederland: Rem Koolhaas in gesprek," in *Vlees & Beton*, 12 (1989), n.p. (author's translation).

23 In many of the reviews of the Kunsthal, Koolhaas and Hoshino are distinguished from the rest of the team as the designers in charge. The archival material held by the OMAR Archive at the Het Nieuwe Instituut (HNI) in Rotterdam indicates that Hoshino contributed massively to the design of the Kunsthal II during all stages of its genesis.

24 Fuminori Hoshino in an interview with the author, July 25, 2017. The interview is also the source of the subsequent biographical information.

25 "Kunsthal," October 25, 1988. OMAR 1546.

26 October 28, 1988. OMAR 1538.

27 "Meeting," November 2, 1988. OMAR 1517.

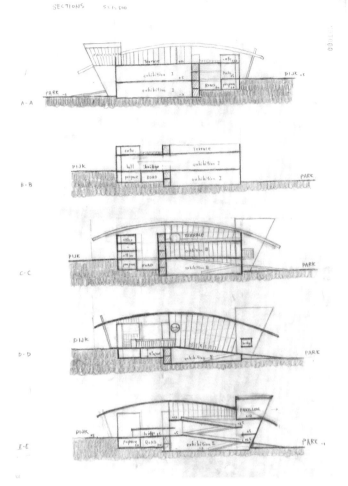

OMA/Rem Koolhaas, Kunsthal II, November 4, 1988.
Cross sections (north to south).

"EXHIBITION SPACE," and Hellingstraat provides access both from the park and the dike.[28]

    Judging from the number of surviving models and sketches, Hoshino produced at least eight different schemes over the subsequent four weeks.[29] It seems that a scale model in blue foam was also prepared for each version, as well as a set of sketched cross sections and floorplans in a scale of 1 to 500 (→ F 4.1–4.3). An A4 sheet of cross sections dated November 4 faithfully incorporates the ideas recorded two days previously: Hellingstraat connects park and dike, and the service road below that, along with two levels featuring exhibition areas and a roof terrace with a café giving access to a projecting "pavilion"; this would be cone-shaped like the bar of OMA's Netherlands Dance Theater in The Hague (→ F 4.4).[30] The entire vertical circulation is concentrated along Hellingstraat, which cuts through all three levels of the building, just like the service road along the dike. Apparently, the latter was meant to be left uncovered like a veritable street. A series of skywalks bridge the two intersecting routes so as to ensure horizontal circulation. A few sketches—probably by Koolhaas—capture ideas that recur in most variants dating from early November, as if assorting a tool kit to resolve the design: the horizontal circulation, bridging Hellingstraat at both ends; a glass wall dividing Hellingstraat into an interior and an exterior public half; the plan crossed by two intersecting routes, recalling what Koolhaas later would call "four separate squares" (→ F 4.5).[31]

On November 15, when OMA received Van Krimpen's fax containing additional requirements for the Kunsthal, Koolhaas and his team had already been working on the new scheme for two weeks. The fax probably had a significant impact on the design of the Kunsthal, prompting what in retrospect appears to be the final spatial configuration of the project. The seemingly marginal requirements list a "large café-restaurant at the square, possibly in the shape of an amphitheater, to be used additionally as an auditorium or concert hall for major events, as well as for rental to other parties, open on the square as a summer cafe."[32] "Square" apparently refers to the plaza between the

F 4.5

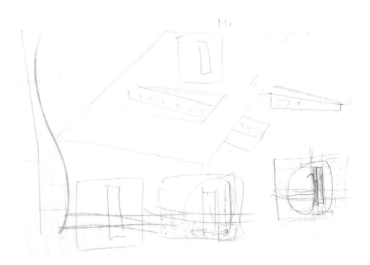

OMA/Rem Koolhaas, Kunsthal II. Probably the first half of November 1988. Principles of circulation.

28 When Koolhaas first asked Hoshino to comment on the scheme, the latter recalled suggesting an additional entrance to the Kunsthal on the side facing the park. Interview with the author, July 25, 2017.
29 Models: OMAR MAQV 502.02–08. Sketches: OMAR 1546–1548, 1567, 1692.
30 OMAR 1692.
31 OMAR 1538, 1546.

Kunsthal and Villa Dijkzigt. To meet Van Krimpen's wish, the scheme was mirrored along the north to south axis running parallel to Hellingstraat.[33] The large exhibition spaces were shifted to the east and the smaller galleries and secondary functions to the west, with the restaurant overlooking the plaza.

After the "switch," an attempt was made to use a single sloping surface as an auditorium, a restaurant, and a ramp. A series of axonometric sketches suggest variants on this idea (→ F 4.6–4.7).[34] Obviously the aim was to decentralize the circulation in order to create a fluid circuit without dead ends that would encompass all parts of the building. The second floor, level with the dike, is shown as a single square surface floating above the ground. Various ramps and stairs appear "cut out" and "bent" to the level below, emphasizing the unity of the floor. But despite the introduction of additional ramps, certain impasses could not be avoided until Hoshino integrated an auditorium into his version of the scheme that featured a sloping floor descending in the opposite direction of Hellingstraat.[35] On the basis of this idea, a plan was worked out in which the tilted floor of the auditorium, the interior section of Hellingstraat, and the two main exhibition spaces (later called Halls 1 and 2) add up to a continuous sequence, traversing the central public passage twice: once above the slope and once below. The principle of circulation—a twofold loop—was singled out in a separate sketch, showing that visitors would come full circle twice before reaching their point of departure (→ F 4.8).[36] The building was to be entered from the point where the two crossing slopes meet (→ F 4.9).[37] The point of intersection was the only option for accessing the sloping entrance hall from Hellingstraat. All entrances were meant to be concentrated along the public passageway between the park and the dike, in order to underline the urban, streetlike character of this space. The distinction between vertical and horizontal circulation became fluid, as did the allocation of functions. The sloping surface along the western facade was three things at once: an entrance hall, an auditorium, and a ramp.

There was still some uncertainty about how to end the circuit. In several variants, a sloped covering over Hellingstraat served as a second ramp to access the roof and an additional exhibition space (later called Hall 3) above the auditorium, transforming the circuit from a loop into a spiral. At some point, a decision was made to rotate the upper ramp by 15 degrees, overriding the tripartition of the scheme (→ F 4.10).[38] To the north, the ramp—later called the "Skew Ramp"—penetrated the auditorium and the restaurant below; to the south it cut into the roof on top of the two large exhibition halls. Obviously, the rotation was

F 4.6

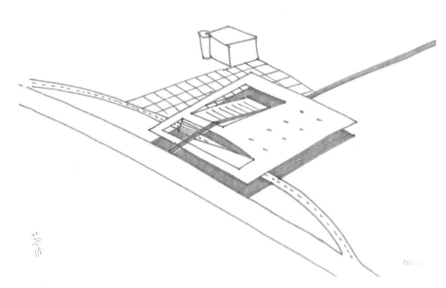

OMA/Rem Koolhaas, Kunsthal II. Variant with the large exhibition halls shifted to the east.

F 4.7

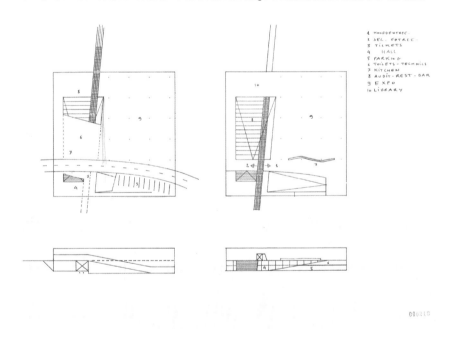

OMA/Rem Koolhaas, Kunsthal II. Variant with the large exhibition halls shifted to the east.

32 English translation of the fax from Wim van Krimpen to OMA/Rem Koolhaas. November 15, 1988.
33 Hoshino recalls the scheme having been mirrored along the north to east axis after working on the Kunsthal for a few weeks. Interview with the author, June 25, 2017.
34 OMAR 1549, 4139.
35 OMAR 1546.
36 OMAR 1538.
37 OMAR 1546, 1548, 1567.
38 OMAR 1538, 1545, 1548. A third exhibition hall was introduced to meet Van Krimpen's wish for an exhibition area of 4,000 square meters. Reedijk's brief of January 1988 stipulated an exhibition area of 2,700 square meters. OMA's scheme of October (Kunsthal I) proposed an exhibition area of 2,713 square meters.

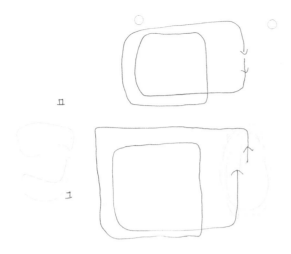

OMA/Rem Koolhaas, Kunsthal II. Sketch of the circuit. The arrows mark the main entrance while also indicating that the route would work both ways.

intended to supply Hellingstraat with daylight through the two resultant triangular openings. At the same time, the visibility of the Skew Ramp ascending to the roof is increased for visitors entering the auditorium.[39] On a formal level, the rotation binds the building's three segments together, fastening each in its position like a turned key in a lock.

On December 2, Hoshino sent a fax to structural engineer Cecil Balmond with what appears to be the first complete version of the Kunsthal's final design (→ P 5.2–5.8).[40] Visitors would enter the building from Hellingstraat, either descending from Maasboulevard or ascending from Museumpark, and find themselves on the slope of the auditorium. Turning left they would descend and, after following a corridor and a few steps, reach Hall 1, level with the park. From Hall 1 they would ascend a ramp—the interior half of Hellingstraat—to Hall 2 overlooking Maasboulevard, and visually reconnect to Hall 1 through an oblong void along the eastern facade. From a corridor at the far end of Hall 2 the visitors would either return to the auditorium or ascend the Skew Ramp to Hall 3 or, alternatively, on the exterior continuation of the ramp, to the terrace on the roof. The space to the south between Hall 2 and Maasboulevard has been left almost unbuilt: only the floor and the roof extend to the perimeter of the building. The edge of the roof is supported by a row of columns, the bays of which gradually increase from east to west. Given its position at the southern front of the building as a kind of prelude to the entrance, the open space is endowed with the essential ingredients of a portico. Secondary functions along with the restaurant fill the remainders of the prism. The southwest

F 4.9
F 4.10

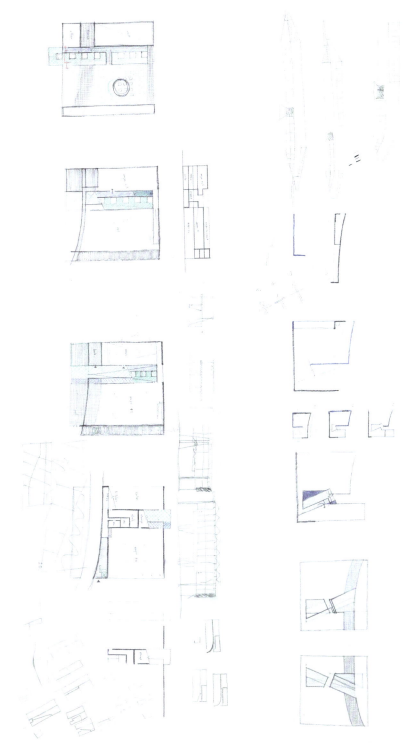

OMA/Rem Koolhaas, Kunsthal II. Floorplans and cross sections. Left: cross sections of Hall 1 with tapered columns (bottom right). Right: early version of the Skew Ramp. Top: sketches of the exterior.

39 Fuminori Hoshino in an interview with the author, July 25, 2017.

40 Fuminori Hoshino. Fax to Cecil Balmond, December 2, 1988. OMAR 1555.

corner would house an office block for the administration, with the staff entrance on the service road, as well as a bookshop overlooking the portico. The restaurant and a kitchen occupy the space under the auditorium. The toilets and the cloakroom fill the gap under Hellingstraat, while loading facilities border the service road to the east.

Hoshino remembers the December 2 scheme as a distinct breakthrough that might have earned him his position as the Kunsthal's project architect.[41] The cover note of another fax he sent to Balmond two weeks later betrays self-confidence, if not pride: "Hello. These are the sketches for a new Kunsthal. Now we are developing from these ones."[42] The scheme of December 2 undoubtedly marks a fissure. From then on, changes became more subtle in comparison to the profound, incessant metamorphosis of the project in the previous weeks.

A diagrammatic turn

According to some of the later reviews of the Kunsthal, Koolhaas explained the building's double divide as "necessitated […] by the planning regulations."[43] But it seems that the main obstacle for the circulation—namely Hellingstraat—was a self-imposed idea. There is no indication of any urban prerequisites for the park to be connected to the dike by means of a public passageway cutting through the center of the Kunsthal.[44] Neither did any of the earlier projects propose a connection of this kind: in both the municipal scheme of 1986 and OMA's Kunsthal I, the stairs ascending to the dike were located outside the building as a continuation of the plaza.[45] Much in contrast to the scheme for Kunsthal I, for which Karl Schwanzer's Austrian pavilion at Expo 58 in Brussels had served as a model, the scheme for Kunsthal II was developed from an expanding set of initially loosely connected ideas, such as the two routes crossing the building, the pavilion on the roof, the continuity of the circuit, the bisected ramp, and the transparency of the interior. Multiple new combinations of these and other ideas propelled a constant—and at times surprising—metamorphosis of the design, as is evident from the surviving working models and sketches. Apparently, the final configuration was uncertain, and this was intentional, in general accordance with what Jacques Lucan later called the principle of "non-composition."[46] The scheme of December 1988 was not composed as an assembly of forms, but rather "generated" through a design process based on concepts, or "rules," in order to bypass considerations of form as much as references to architectural precedents. Just as had been the case six years previously with

Parc de la Villette, concept became a motor of formal invention, turning form into an unpredictable and heteronomous "given." Throughout the planning process, Koolhaas and his team would be mindful about basing their design work on a concept, understood as a set of rules that could be refined and expanded whenever new design issues emerged as the project was implemented.

Early on, Koolhaas seems to have considered the spiraling circuit and the two routes dividing the "square into four parts" as the conceptual core of Kunsthal II. Several sketches capturing the idea of the circulation and the intersecting routes bear witness to that, and the covers of OMA's first booklets on the Kunsthal were adorned with sketches of this kind (→ P 4.11).[47] But other parts of the design, technically unrelated to issues of circulation, were also increasingly informed by the motifs of the circuit and the two crossing routes. An axonometric sketch concluding Hoshino's fax of December 2 shows that the elevations were conceived as a twofold loop of rectilinear strips, half "glass," half "wall" in a proportion of exactly 1 to 1, apparently in analogy to the circuit (→ P 5.8). Taken together they form a continuous ribbon wrapped twice around the building, reminiscent of a Moebius loop with two "binary" sides.[48] The axonometric view corresponds exactly to the elevations in the same fax, comprising a diagonal wall traversing the western facade along the slope of the auditorium's floor (→ P 5.7). The drawings also show the limits to the applicability of this logic: the horizontal bipartition was unsuitable for depicting the upper end of the spiral, in other words the Skew Ramp and Hall 3; the southwest corner accommodating the offices, being exempt from the circuit, remains "unwrapped" with the bare floor and roof slab exposed. The two intersecting routes are, in turn, projected as an image onto the

41 Interview with the author, July 25, 2017.
42 Fuminori Hoshino/OMA. Fax to Cecil Balmond, December 12, 1988. OMAR 1538.
43 Lootsma and De Graaf, "In dienst van de ervaring," p. 34. Emmanuel Doutriaux in his review of the Kunsthal quotes Koolhaas explaining that the division was entailed by "urban necessities" (*nécessités urbaines*). Doutriaux, "Le Kunsthal de Rotterdam," in *L'Architecture d'Aujourd'hui*, 285 (1993), p. 7.
44 The department for urban development described the urban planning prerequisites for the Kunsthal in two separate documents that were probably both produced in the first half of 1988: "Randvoorwaarden Kunsthal," dated March 16, 1988, and "Stedebouwkundige randvoorwaarden." The latter document is undated, but it is likely to be from a later point in the same year as it refers to the document of March 16, 1988. OMAR 4509.
45 OMA, "Kunsthal Rotterdam." Site plans, September 7 and October 7, 1988. OMAR 1744. Stadsontwikkeling Rotterdam, "Museumpark," December 1987. OMAR 4477.
46 Jacques Lucan, "Processus et programme contre composition—Rem Koolhaas," in *Composition, Non-Composition: Architecture et Théories, XIXe-XXe siècles*, Lausanne: EPFL/PPUR, 2009, pp. 544–50.
47 Sketches: OMAR 1538, 1546. Covers: OMA, "Kunsthal Rotterdam," December 7, 1988. OMAR 1537. OMA, "Kunsthal Rotterdam," December 14, 1988. OMAR 3343.
48 Koolhaas reportedly referred to the circuit of the completed building as a Moebius loop. See Tracy Metz, "Show Piece: KunstHAL, Rotterdam, the Netherlands," in *Architectural Record*, 3 (1993), p. 68; Doutriaux, "Le Kunsthal de Rotterdam," p. 7.

OMA/Rem Koolhaas, Kunsthal II. Cover of the booklet dated December 14, 1988.

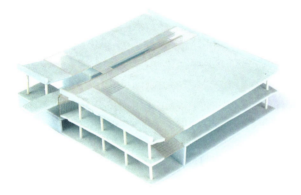

OMA/Rem Koolhaas, Kunsthal II, November 1988. Scale model.

levels of Hall 2 and the roof. In this regard, some of early December's working models are particularly telling: strips of translucent plastic reproduce the course of the two passageways, literally dividing the blue foam of the floor and roof into "four separate squares" (→ F 4.12).[49]

      That the first version of Kunsthal II approximates the diagram of its inner organization was not merely a consequence of the project not yet being worked out in more detail; the scheme of December 1988 was also an attempt to shape the architecture of the arts center by turning the representation of problem (cruciform division) and solution (spiraling circuit) into form. As an image of the program and its spatial organization, the scheme anticipates much of the notion of the diagram, as discussed by Anthony Vidler, Robort Somol, and Peter

Eisenman from the late 1990s onwards.[50] And yet there were limits to the concept, or diagram, as a source of form. The choice of the square as a point of departure, the proportions of the floorplan's three sections (2 to 1 to 4), the positioning and adjustment of the Skew Ramp do indicate concern for proportion, composition, and formal cohesion;[51] none of it could be deducted from the cruciform division and spiraling circuit of the arts center. Two later adjustments may serve as further examples. The first concerns the ramp ascending to the roof. On December 7, it was shifted slightly to the east, obviously with the aim of contributing to the cohesion and balance of the whole. Thanks to this shift, the two triangular openings between the margins of the rotated ramp and the roof were of exactly the same size. Furthermore, with the ramp more visibly penetrating the southwest corner of Hall 2, it interferes with both adjacent sections of the building to a comparable visual degree; just like the beginning of the ramp can be seen from the auditorium, its upper end "sticks out" into the southwest corner of Hall 2.[52]

The second example concerns the west facade. In a set of elevations dating from December 14, the diagonal wall in Hoshino's fax is replaced by a horizontal one covering the whole length of the facade (→ F 4.13).[53] Lifted to the height of Hall 3 and the offices, the displacement of the wall breaks with the logic of the Moebius loop, generating two loose ends: one next to the wall of the west facade itself, and

F 4.13

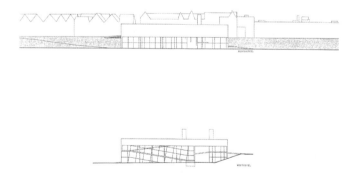

OMA/Rem Koolhaas, Kunsthal II, December 14, 1988. North and west elevation.

49 OMAR, MAQV 502.03.
50 See, for instance, Robert Somol, "The Diagrams of Matter," in ANY, 23 (1998), pp. 23–26; Anthony Vidler, "Diagramme der Utopie," in Daidalos, 74 (2000), pp. 6–13; Peter Eisenman, "Strategies of the Void: Rem Koolhaas, Jussieu Libraries, 1992–93," in Ten Canonical Buildings: 1950–2000, New York: Rizzoli, 2008, pp. 200–29.
51 The fact that Hoshino mentioned these proportions in a 1995 explanation of the project indicates that they were deemed important within the design team. Fuminori Hoshino, "Kunsthal," in Kenchiku Bunka, 579 (1995), p. 78.
52 OMA, "Kunsthal Rotterdam," December 7, 1988. OMAR 1537.
53 OMA, "Kunsthal Rotterdam," December 14, 1988. OMAR 3343.

the lower one along the service road. The remainder of the west elevation is glazed. Multiple reasons for this change are conceivable: in order to open the auditorium up towards the park; to have at least one exhibition space (Hall 3) without any openings for exhibits such as graphic works that are sensitive to daylight; for the sake of formal coherence; because only now did the binary division into a "full" half and an "empty" one become a unifying principle for all four facades.[54]

Seeds

While the spiraling circuit and the motif of the Moebius loop are agents of cohesion and unity, the same design contains the seeds of a counterforce, acting as agents of diversity and the autonomy of parts. An additional purpose of the layout of the facades was to diversify the different sections of the circuit, for instance. The motif of the two-faced ribbon wrapped twice around the building imposed a rigorous binary logic of opening and closure. All four facades of December 14 are divided into two horizontal strips, one "void" and the other solid. By consequence, vertically adjacent spaces open up in opposite directions. The proportions and dimensions of Halls 1 and 2 are much alike, but the inversion of the respective openings enhances the difference between the two spaces. The idea is captured by a freehand sketch in addition to Hoshino's December 2 axonometric view of the facades. It shows an S-shaped section, apparently of Hall 1, level with and open to the park, and Hall 2, level with and open to Maasboulevard. The double exposure of the Kunsthal to both the park and the highway, which Koolhaas later referred to in shorthand as a "dual situation," was now set to distinguish the character of the two main exhibition spaces while resonating with the diagrammatic logic of the scheme. Yet the ribbon-like envelope was an idea in its own right: an addition to and not simply a consequence of the "spiral in four separate squares," which apparently was meant to "spawn" other related concepts that nonetheless exceeded its factual reach. If proof were needed for the independence of the envelope, it is found in the aforementioned divergence between the actual circuit and its representation in the exterior.

The other agent of diversity was the hybrid structural system, which had already been introduced in the December 2 scheme (→ P 5.2–5.4). At the side of the auditorium, the columns are distributed on a square grid with a bay size of approximately 7 meters; at the side of the large exhibition halls the columns are aligned along the lateral walls in intervals of about 4 meters, flanking a space of about

30 meters. In the center of Hall 1 four additional cruciform columns are arranged in a square so as to bridge the large span of the ceiling. A sketch shows them tapering towards the top (→ F 4.9), recalling Mies' project for the Bacardi administration building in Cuba and the convention hall in Chicago.[55] Hall 2, for its part, was conceived as a free-span space, covered by open-web trusses. It seems that even at this early stage, the structure was supposed to combine some parts in steel frame and other parts in reinforced concrete. Since all columns were meant to be visible, it is obvious that the hybrid quality of the structural system, too, was meant to vary the character of the spaces, not unlike the "individualized" Vierendeel trusses of Kunsthal I. That the architects were fully conscious of these sketches' structural implications is beyond doubt: Cecil Balmond was deeply involved in the design of Kunsthal II from its very inception.[56]

A very fluid whole

Koolhaas apparently showed Van Krimpen a model of Kunsthal II during an unexpected visit to the latter's Amsterdam gallery. According to Van Krimpen's own account, he was immediately enthusiastic.[57] On December 14, the new scheme was first presented to the building committee. The circuit largely corresponds to the scheme of December 2, apart from the Skew Ramp; like Hellingstraat, it was divided into an interior half—ascending to the roof—and an exterior half, conceived as a sloping garden. Koolhaas introduced the design with a critique of Kunsthal I, explaining that the open space under the building had proven problematic, while the restricted budget did not allow for a better solution. With the new scheme, standing directly on the ground, the open connection between the park, the Kunsthal, and the dike would come into its own. His subsequent explications contained most of the key points of OMA's later project statements: the two routes dividing the building into four parts; the two ramps cleverly converging at a single point; the glass wall dividing Hellingstraat into "a museum part and a recreation part"; the circuit in the shape of a "continuous (square) spiral"; the autonomy of the spaces allowing for differing simultaneous uses—this last one being a request made by Van Krimpen, seemingly after his fax of November 15.[58]

54 In principle, the same applies to the south facade, even if only its upper half is visible from Maasboulevard.
55 OMAR 1548.
56 Conversation with the author, Rotterdam, February 15, 2023.
57 Interview with the author, July 28, 2020.
58 "Nieuwbouw Kunsthal/6e Bouwcommissie," December 14, 1988. OMAR 1436. The requirement comes up in a written comment on OMA's scheme. In OMA's files the comment is kept attached to the fax of November 15. Later on, Van Krimpen would insist on an option for using the main spaces independently, including a demand for separate entrances.

The minutes record that Van Krimpen welcomed OMA's new design as "a different/better scheme." According to a first estimate, the costs amounted to 26 million guilders, which was a million more than the budget provided. Based on the new scheme, a definitive version of the preliminary design (*Voorlopig Ontwerp*) was to be delivered within one month. The definitive design (*Definitief Ontwerp*) of the Kunsthal was to be completed by the middle of April 1989. The opening was envisaged for January 1992. The updated program of requirements—the minutes apparently refer to Van Krimpen's additional requests and preferences—would provide the basis for further planning.

An A3 booklet entitled "Kunsthal Rotterdam/14 December 1988" shows the scheme Koolhaas presented to the building committee (→ F 4.11).[59] Whereas the sketches and models of the past six weeks had been exclusively concerned with the design of the Kunsthal, the December 14 booklet includes a site plan that shows the arts center's immediate surroundings (→ F 4.14). The building had been shifted to the dike as close as regulations would permit, only just maintaining the required 23-meter minimum distance from the watershed. Nonetheless, there remained a gap of some 5 meters between the southern edge of the Kunsthal's perimeter and the sidewalk of Maasboulevard. It was meant to be bridged by a sloping, tongue-like extension of the floor that would be used as a driveway. Partly covered by the cantilevered roof, this platform would descend from the level of Hall 2 to the edge of Maasboulevard one meter below.

As with Kunsthal I, the low volume and largely transparent envelope of the December 1988 scheme contrasted with the built environment. Apart from the brick buildings surrounding the arts center, this applies to the tower of Erasmus University as the area's dominating building. The constellation of the flat square pavilion—freed from the vertical slab of Kunsthal I—and the tower of the hospital recalls the compositional principle of Mies van der Rohe's Federal Center in Chicago and his Dominion Center in Toronto. A further similarity with Kunsthal I is that, thanks to the ingenuity of its circuit, the scheme of December 1988 shows some kinship to the architecture of spectacle and wonder that is so characteristic of world expos. In fact, there is an expo pavilion among the structures that the Kunsthal has been likened to. Belgian architect and critic Paul Vermeulen has pointed to a series of striking parallels between the Kunsthal and Konstantin Melnikov's pavilion for the 1925 International Exhibition of Modern Decorative and Industrial Arts in Paris: "Melnikov's wooden pavilion can certainly serve as a rudimentary prototype of a building which is cut into pieces by

F 4.14

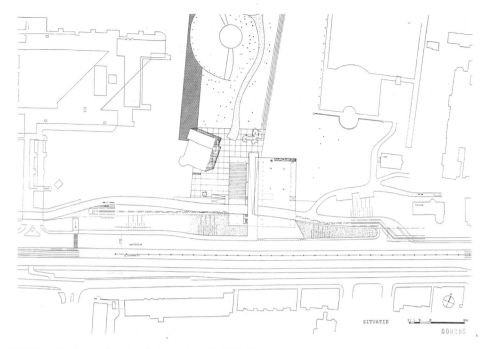

OMA/Rem Koolhaas, Kunsthal II, December 14, 1988. Site plan.

F 4.15

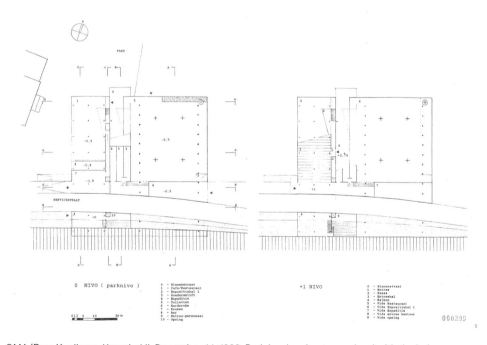

OMA/Rem Koolhaas, Kunsthal II, December 14, 1988. Park level and entrance level with the balcony projecting into the restaurant.

59   OMA, "Kunsthal Rotterdam," December 14,
     1988. OMAR 3343

a half-covered road, has its entrance on this self-generated road and despite the chopping up, forms a spatial unity."[60]

In the scheme of December 14, a straight flight of stairs has been introduced in order to connect the area around the main entrance with the restaurant below (→ F 4.15). The stair's upper landing is perfectly horizontal and protrudes as another balcony into the void above the restaurant. In section, the small space overlaps both with the auditorium and the restaurant, undermining the complete division between the two spaces. In plan, the balcony's triangular shape accurately reproduces the northwest corner of the Skew Ramp on top. Apparently, the intention was to release the restaurant from its spatial and visual isolation with regard to the rest of the building. Even if located outside the circuit, the restaurant was one of the building's major spaces and a likely destination for visitors. With the balcony as a reverberation of the Skew Ramp and its intrusive geometry, a central and inherently connective feature of the design is being "passed on" to the otherwise cut-off space. The floorplans do not yet distinguish between solid and glazed partitions. But the cross sections and elevations—even if rudimentary—suggest that the partitions between the different parts of the circuit, including those along Hellingstraat, were by and large intended to be transparent. Within the building perimeter, it seems, a maximum of transparency was envisaged. The arts center's interior as of December 1988 was devised as a single continuous space, organized on different levels that were mutually visible (→ F 4.16).

May '68 programming?

OMA would repeatedly seize on the nexus of ideas upon which the Kunsthal circuit is based. The Jussieu Libraries in Paris (1992), the Educatorium in Utrecht (1993–97), the Dutch embassy in Berlin (1997–2004), and the Casa da Musica in Porto (1999–2005) are obvious examples of this. In the case of the libraries, OMA reframed the theme of the circuit, thereby bringing themes and qualities to the fore that were already latent in the Kunsthal scheme of December 1988 (→ F 4.17). The eight floors of the building are connected by a series of straight and curved slopes so as to form a single continuous surface that makes it possible to ascend from the bottom to the roof in a spiraling movement without encountering any stairs or steps. For *New York Times* critic Herbert Muschamp, the libraries made "the most spectacular use of the spiral form since Frank Lloyd Wright's Guggenheim Museum."[61] Koolhaas himself used the term "trajectory" to

F 4.16

OMA/Rem Koolhaas, model showing the passage from Hellingstraat to the auditorium, and the garden ascending to the roof. Probably December 1988.

F 4.17

OMA/Rem Koolhaas, Jussieu Libraries, Paris (1992). Conceptual model illustrating the fluid relation between the different floors.

60 Paul Vermeulen, "Clad in Tonalities of Light," in *Architectuur in Nederland: Jaarboek 1992/1993*, eds. Matthijs de Boer et al., Rotterdam: NAi Publishers, 1993, p. 91.

61 Herbert Muschamp, "Some Unfinished Business on St. Germain," in *The New York Times* (February 14, 1993).

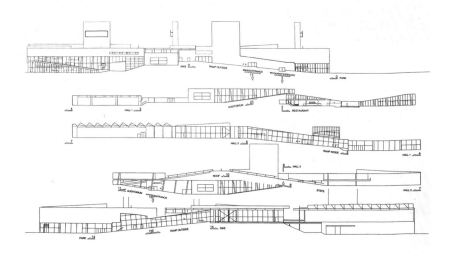

OMA/Rem Koolhaas, Kunsthal II. Exterior and interior elevations, assembled as continuous sequences.

denote the libraries' interlacing floors and, later on, the spiraling *rues intérieurs* like those of the Casa da Musica or the Dutch embassy.[62] Another idea, latent in the Kunsthal, is to treat the floor as a pliable surface—that is, as a floor which may diverge from the horizontal at any point in the requisite angle or curve. Like the "loop trick" of the Kunsthal's two reversed ramps, the "deformed" floor in the libraries is one of the "Universal Modernization Patent(s)" to which Koolhaas and his co-authors referred when staking OMA's "claim for eternity" in 2004.[63] In *S, M, L, XL*, in order to capture the way in which a moving visitor would sequentially experience the architecture, OMA proposed a continuous montage of cross sections and elevations showing the route in its entirety, and variations on this type of representation were used for the embassy in Berlin. Hoshino recalls that when inspecting the model of the Kunsthal, Koolhaas habitually used an endoscope to simulate the perspective at eye level while moving about.[64] After the building was completed in 1992, the architects produced several montages of multiple consecutive interior and exterior elevations;[65] published in an issue of *techniques & architecture* in June 1993, these elevations might have been OMA's first attempt at translating the episodical experience of architecture into drawing (→ F 4.18).

    Analogies between Le Corbusier and Koolhaas with respect to their ideas about the perception of architecture, on the one hand, and film and the technique of montage on the other have been repeatedly discussed, outlining a genealogy that begins with Auguste Choisy's analysis of the Acropolis and its subsequent adoption by Sergei Eisenstein and Le Corbusier.[66] Martino Stierli, in his recent book *Montage and the Metropolis*, explores in depth the relation between Choisy's notion of the picturesque, Eisenstein's concept of filmic montage, and Le Corbusier's architectural promenade in addition to the role of montage in Koolhaas' work in the 1970s.[67] Cynthia Davidson and Aarati Kanekar, in their essays on the Kunsthal of 1997 and 2015 respectively, point out the parallels between filmic montage and the arts center's formal heterogeneity—both authors refer to the completed building—as an experience of discontinuity, opposed to the continuity of movement that the circuit implies.

Conversely, the countercultural charge of the Kunsthal and its spiraling circuit has only rarely been discussed.[68] That Koolhaas wished his building to be seen in such terms is beyond doubt. In *S, M, L, XL*'s chapter on the Jussieu Libraries, he straightforwardly recalls the events of May 1968 in Paris. A picture from that month by French photographer Bruno Barbey shows cars scattered on a street in the Quartier Latin district, many of them turned over and burned out, perhaps after a confrontation between protesters and authorities.[69] The text running parallel to the illustrations for OMA's project insists that the interior of the libraries, featuring an ascending floor, is a "warped interior boulevard," "urbanized," "a social magic carpet." The metaphors link the concept for the interior to the street as the quintessential public realm. The libraries too, Koolhaas seems to say, might be appropriated for a revolutionary endeavor, with the building as a secret accomplice. The formal stress on "surface" takes on a metaphorical quality: the "trajectory" is to replicate the continuity of the public space outside the building. A sequence of photos illustrates this ambition; the images show the architect's hands producing a model of the libraries' stacked floors

62 Rem Koolhaas and Bruce Mau, *S, M, L, XL*, New York: The Monacelli Press, 1995, pp. 1320–21.
63 AMOMA/Rem Koolhaas, *Content*, Cologne: Taschen, 2004, pp. 73, 79.
64 Interview with the author, July 25, 2017.
65 OMAR 3336. Marie-Christine Loriers, "Culture Oblique: KunstHAL, Rotterdam," in *Techniques & Architecture*, 408 (1993), pp. 82–87.
66 Cynthia Davidson, "Koolhaas and the Kunsthal: History Lesions," *ANY*, 21 (1997), pp. 36–41; Aarati Kanekar, "Space of Montage: Movement, Assemblage, and Appropriation in Koolhaas' Kunsthal," in *Architecture's Pretext: Spaces of Translation*, London: Routledge, 2015, pp. 135–44; Ingrid Böck, *Six Canonical Projects: Essays on the History of Ideas*, Berlin: Jovis, 2015, pp. 214–17.
67 Martino Stierli, *Montage and the Metropolis: Architecture, Modernity, and the Representation of Space*, New Haven: Yale University Press, 2018, pp. 180–267.
68 Jeffrey Kipnis' 1996 essay "Recent Koolhaas" is something of an exception. Kipnis used the term "disestablishment" to denote what he saw as an antiauthoritarian quality to the Kunsthal and OMA's latest work in general, without, however, drawing a parallel to the 1960s. As for the Kunsthal, Kipnis refers mainly to the entrance sequence and the choice of finishes. "Recent Koolhaas," in *El Croquis*, 79 (1996), pp. 28–29.
69 Rem Koolhaas, "P.S. Unravelling," in *S, M, L, XL*, Koolhaas and Mau, p. 1306. The same chapter is also the source of the subsequent quotes.

Philippe Gras, barricades in Île-de-France/Paris, May 1968.

out of a single sheet of paper which, corresponding to the *parvis* of the campus, figures as the equivalent of the street (→ F 4.17). Muschamp commented in 1993: "the design converts to constructive form the explosive forces that erupted here twenty-five years ago."[70] For Muschamp, the work of OMA in general and the libraries project in particular remain "philosophically attuned" to the spirit of '68.[71] In the same year, Koolhaas, who according to his own account visited Paris as a journalist during the uprisings, interpreted the design for Jussieu as the result of " a horrible 'May '68 programming,'" but also, more positively, as "a very political project" that responds to the "thinking back then."[72] (→ F 4.19)

With the street photo of May 1968 among the pictures introducing the Jussieu Libraries in *S, M, L, XL*, Koolhaas establishes a direct connection between the Parisian project and the Kunsthal. In the chapter on the Rotterdam arts center, a picture of the same street, perhaps taken on the same day—and likewise by Bruno Barbey—interrupts the thirty-four-page photo spread simulating a guided tour through the building. While "visiting" the auditorium, the image of revolution intrudes, indicating the interior of the Kunsthal, too, as an extension of the street, a "warped boulevard" that is open to uncontrolled appropriation and escalation.

Koolhaas has laid other trails that point in a similar direction. *Ramp*—one of the fifteen volumes of *Elements of Architecture*, which was published in 2014 with Koolhaas as its editor in chief—draws attention to the work of Claude Parent. The drawings of this French architect, as well as his and Paul Virilio's writings, pivot around the concept of the *fonction oblique*, advocating and illustrating a built environment that mainly features inclined surfaces. Like Koolhaas with the Kunsthal, Parent and Virilio envisaged a space without walls: instead, the "walls" of their designs are tilted to the point of becoming walkable ramps. As with the Kunsthal, the oblique floor is designed not only with circulation in mind, but for any kind of use. The authors of *Ramp* explain: "Parent's ramps for living on would attempt to create hierarchy, destabilize relationships, change how we make love, read, eat."[73] In fact, the inhabitants of these structures were meant to move about freely as nomads engaging in any kind of activity. Virilio wrote in 1966: "To bring about change, it is necessary to devise an urbanism in which circulation becomes habitable—an architecture in which an animating oblique function supplants the neutralizing one of the fixed horizontal plane, an architecture in which mankind is propelled by the very profile of its habitat, in which the city becomes an enormous projector, or torrent of every kind of activity, every kind of fluidity."[74]

    Taken together, the texts, quotes, and illustrations compiled in *Ramp* contain catchwords and evoke ideas that have been critical for Koolhaas' thinking ever since *Delirious New York*: "a more intense form of interaction," a destabilization of human relationships, and, implicitly, the unpredictable encounter of activities.[75] In other words, the dynamism of the oblique floor, of free movement and unspecified use, appear to have implied for Koolhaas—at least in 2014—first and foremost a societal dimension. But to what extent, if at all, were Koolhaas' ideas becoming aligned with the antiauthoritarian agendas of the 1960s?

    Bart Lootsma, in his 1999 article "…Koolhaas, Constant, and the Dutch Culture in the 1960s" has pointed to a series of "obvious visual correspondences between some of the work of OMA and the models and drawings of New Babylon," referring to the visionary urban project by Dutch artist Constant Nieuwenhuys.[76] Among the correspondences listed are "the continuous folding floor-planes" along with "the use of [permeable] constructions instead of walls to define spaces"; while writing these words, Lootsma might have had the Jussieu Libraries and the Kunsthal in mind, as far as OMA is concerned.[77]

70 Herbert Muschamp, "Some Unfinished Business on St Germain."
71 Ibid.
72 Nikolaus Kuhnert, Philipp Oswalt, and Alejandro Zaera Polo, "Die Entfaltung der Architektur," in *Arch+*, 117 (1993), p. 22.
73 Rem Koolhaas and Irma Boom, eds., "Ramp," in *Elements of Architecture*, Rem Koolhaas et al., Cologne: Taschen, 2018, p. 2245. First published as a separate volume in 2014.
74 Paul Virilio, "Habitable Circulation," in *Architecture Principe*, 3 (April 1966). Quoted in *The Function of the Oblique*, ed. Pamela Johnston, London: Architectural Association, 1996, p. 68.
75 "[…] a more intense form of interaction." Koolhaas and Boom, "Ramp," p. 2305.
76 Bart Lootsma, "…Koolhaas, Constant, and the Dutch Culture in the 1960s," in *Hunch*, 1 (1999), p. 170.
77 Ibid.

F 4.20

Constant Nieuwenhuys, model of New Babylon. Combination of sectors.
Photo: Victor E. Nieuwenhuys.

To be sure, the comparison needs to be approached with caution, given the three decades separating the 1990s from the 1960s; but Lootsma's conclusion that "these parallels are superficial" appears somewhat premature.

At the turn of the 1960s, Constant was an active member of the Situationists, who were headed by French theorist Guy Debord. In his writings and lectures of this period, Constant envisaged the future city—New Babylon—as an entirely artificial environment of "mass culture" where "technology becomes nature," transferring the "social space" of what used to be the street to the interior platforms of immense structures with multiple levels (→ F 4.20).[78] Constant envisions a "complete freedom of action" and movement, a "movable interior structure," and a "frequent transformation of the interior," evoking the idea of spontaneous appropriation:[79] "Let's imagine, then, that at a given moment x number of individuals find themselves inside one of the sectors [of New Babylon]. That the sector is divided into many spaces of different size, form, and atmosphere. That each of these spaces is at the point of being transformed: being built, destroyed, mounted, dismounted. [...] That all the individuals present actively participate in this incessant activity. That each person can circulate freely from one space to another."[80] In more than one regard, the Jussieu Libraries and the Kunsthal qualify as bits, or sectors *en miniature*, of New Babylon. The "sprayed" typography used for the title of *Content*, a follow-up to *S, M, L, XL* published in 2004, curiously resembles Constant's signature, and the similarity appears to be more than a coincidence. The motto put forward in the editorial—"instability as a new source of freedom"—could easily have been his.[81]

So it seems that the very motif of the Moebius loop, as inscribed in the scheme for Kunsthal II, has been endowed with a countercultural charge. In his recent article "The Pliable Surface," Roberto Gargiani pointed to the close resemblance between this photo spread, showing Koolhaas' hands producing the model of the libraries on a sheet of paper, and another one, showing the hands of Brazilian artist Lygia Clark while cutting a ring of paper in the shape of a Moebius loop (→ F 4.21).[82] The pictures are part of Clark's participatory project *Caminhando*, which dates from 1963. The Moebius loop, Clark explained, "makes us live the experience of a time without limit and of a continuous space."[83] The sculpture series *O dentro è o fora* (The Inside Is the Outside) is likewise based on the Moebius loop, and also thematizes the unity of supposedly distinct spaces. According to his own account, Koolhaas had been familiar with Clark's work since the 1960s, and some of it was presented in *S, M, L, XL*. In a 2005 interview, Koolhaas explained: "For me, the work of artists like Hélio Oiticica or Lygia Clark has key importance."[84] If so, Koolhaas is likely to have been aware of Clark's notion of the Moebius loop while he was working on the scheme for the Kunsthal in December 1988.[85] In both cases there is a substantial kinship between Clark's understanding of the Moebius loop as a form that suspends division, on the one hand, and the emphatic openness of the scheme for the arts center on the other.[86] For one thing, the two routes crossing the building make it permeable for the public—a common *sujet* of 1980s museums that William Curtis has called the "'democratic' path." Curtis, in his review of Stirling's Staatsgalerie in

---

78 Constant Nieuwenhuys, "Unitary Urbanism," quoted in Wigley, *Constant's New Babylon*, pp. 132–35. Lecture held at the Stedelijk Museum, Amsterdam in December 1960.
79 Constant Nieuwenhuys, "New Babylon: Outline of a Culture," quoted in Wigley, *Constant's New Babylon*, pp. 162, 164. Chapter of an unpublished book manuscript that was written between 1960 and 1965.
80 Ibid., p. 164.
81 Brendan McGetrick "Editor's letter," in *Content*, AMOMA/Koolhaas, p. 16. The signature features prominently in the logo of the Constant Foundation: https://stichtingconstant.nl.
82 Roberto Gargiani, "The Pliable Surface," in *The Companions to the History of Architecture*, eds. David Leatherbarrow and Alexander Eisenschmidt, vol. IV of *Twentieth Century Architecture*, general ed. Harry Francis Mallgrave, Chichester: John Wiley and Sons, 2017, p. 658.
83 Cornelia H. Butler and Luis Pérez-Oramas, eds., *Lygia Clark: The Abandonment of Art, 1948–1988*, New York: Museum of Modern Art, 2014, p. 160.
84 Jean François Chevrier, "Changing Dimensions," in *L'Architecture Aujourd'hui*, 361 (2005), p. 98.
85 Koolhaas repeatedly compared the circuit of the Kunsthal to a Moebius loop. See note 48.
86 The intricate relation of interior and exterior at the Kunsthal is extensively discussed by Michel Moussette in "'Do We Need a Canopy for Rain?': Interior-Exterior Relationships in the Kunsthal," in *Architectural Research Quarterly*, 3/4 (2003), pp. 280–94.

Lygia Clark, *Caminhando*, 1963.

Stuttgart (1977–84), refers to the public footpath across the block as a "common demand in [West] German architectural competitions."[87] It has been suggested by Reinhold Martin that these "democratic paths" were supposed to signal the institutions' "openness" and "accessibility" in opposition to the supposed inaccessibility of governmental institutions in eastern countries during the Cold War.[88] The gesture of openness resonates in the concept of the Kunsthal circuit, which is devised as a seamless extension of Hellingstraat and, implicitly, the public realm, just like the trajectory of the Jussieu Libraries four years later.

The conspicuously irreverent treatment of the genre of the museum has its place here. The exterior of the Kunsthal, viewed from Maasboulevard, has been rightly compared to a "motorway service station."[89] The resemblance to Mies' gas station on Nun's Island (1967–68) is particularly compelling. A forecourt, a podium, a perron, a vestibule, a ceremonial stair, enfilades, and vaulted spaces lit by lanterns from above: all the "thresholds" of the traditional museum—borrowed from temples and palaces, popular among postmodern architects— are either missing at the Kunsthal or transformed beyond recognition. The entrance hall of the arts center is hardly recognizable as such. Half ramp, half auditorium, with no helpdesk or cloakroom in sight and, by consequence, somewhat abandoned, the space had little in common with the lobbies that late-twentieth-century visitors to museums were used to.

What are we to think of the overtones, insinuations, and affinities to the anarchic spirit of '68, which were partly supplied by Koolhaas' publications and partly implied by the design of the Kunsthal itself? Holger Schurk's recent book *Project ohne Form* includes some 200 stills from video recordings of OMA's Rotterdam office, captured between 1986 and 1989 by Dutch artist Claudi Cornaz.[90] Like photographer Hans Werlemann, who documented much of OMA's work during the 1980s and 1990s, Cornaz was part of the "Utopia" collective, a group of about twenty people from various professions who were squatting in an abandoned Rotterdam waterworks. Equipped with roller skates and a helmet camera and apparently without being obliged to follow any kind of script, Cornaz roamed and filmed the architects' premises during office hours. The Office for Metropolitan Architecture that Cornaz documented and that Schurk describes in his book was one of permeable borders, a fluid inner organization, and considerable freedom, somewhat reminiscent of Warhol's Factory in Manhattan. And Bruno Barbey's photo of the riots in Paris? Reverberations of '68, it seems, were among the countercultural adventures that Koolhaas' metropolis had to offer. This is perhaps the ultimate meaning of the spatial continuity of the Kunsthal, once described by Koolhaas as "a very fluid whole."[91]

An internalized park

When OMA settled on the new scheme for the Kunsthal in December 1988, Koolhaas might have regarded the circuit first and foremost as an answer to a specific site and a specific brief that had become vital to the project. But it must have soon become clear that the circuit and the ideas connected to it would make it possible to reframe a series of issues that had been central to his notion of architecture throughout the 1980s. If it is true that during the second half of the decade Koolhaas envisaged the "programmed surface" of open spaces like parks as an alternative to an "architecture of walls," the principle of the pliable floor, which was latent in the Kunsthal scheme, offered a "third way" between these two seemingly irreconcilable alternatives. Having

---

87 William Curtis, "Virtuosity Around a Void," in *Architectural Review*, 1054 (1984), p. 41.

88 Reinhold Martin, *Utopia's Ghost: Architecture and Postmodernism, Again*, Minneapolis: University of Minnesota Press, 2010, pp. 155–57.

89 Deyan Sudjic, in his 1993 review, would compare the Kunsthal to a "motorway service station." Deyan Sudjic, "The Museum as a Megastar," in *The Guardian* (January 25, 1993), p. A7.

90 Holger Schurk, *Projekt ohne Form: OMA, Rem Koolhaas und das Laboratorium von 1989*, Leipzig: Spector Books, 2020.

91 Mil De Kooning, "OMA in Nederland: Rem Koolhaas in gesprek," in *Vlees & Beton*, 12 (1989), n.p.

sloping regular floors (→ F 4.18), as in the entrance hall, allowed for the seamless expansion of the "programmed surface" to the third dimension.[92] Differently programmed sections could be traversed in a continuous movement without interruption like the parallel bands on the rectilinear promenade of OMA's scheme for Parc de la Villette. It is not by chance that Koolhaas called the Jussieu project a vertical landscape and its "trajectory" a boulevard, taking recourse to terms he had used ten years earlier to describe the central promenade of his design for the park in Paris.[93] In *Delirious New York*, Koolhaas advertises the spatial isolation of each floor as a seedbed of diversity in terms of program and use; but, as has been seen, the "schism" between the floors also prevents the very diversity it permits from being experienced and interacted with. The spiraling floor offered a solution to the dilemma, or at least a way in between. A high-rise version of Parc de la Villette was conceivable: the circle squared. In an interview with the author Koolhaas stated: "The true ambition of the building was to deny the relevance of individual floors. And therefore, it's basically work on the section, and trying to liberate the section."[94] Several faxes and drawings of the Kunsthal annotated by Koolhaas during the subsequent months betray an atmosphere of enthusiasm. Koolhaas explains: "I felt that it was a totally new thing. And for that reason there was an enormous animation. You don't have a feeling of actually inventing something in architecture, and this really felt like an invention."[95]

It was around this time, in the final years of the decade, that OMA's emphatic commitment to parks and parklike projects came to a halt. Museumpark would be the last of this kind. And it is the project for the Jussieu Libraries that—contrary to the logic of scale—concludes *S, M, L, XL*. The back cover of the book describes the project as a "novel," thereby granting it the status of an ending. Reconciling the continuity of the "programmed surface," or floor, with the discontinuous half of architecture, or wall, appears indeed to be the argument of a story that begins in Berlin and Manhattan, and goes on with Parc de la Villette. As far as the Kunsthal is concerned, this story ends here: with the consolidation of the spatial configuration of its circuit in December 1988.

92 Landscape architect Petra Blaisse, who also contributed to the interior design of the Kunsthal, has suggested that "the whole building is like a park, going up and then through and on the roof, and then back again." Interview with the author, September 24, 2018.
93 Koolhaas, "P.S. Unravelling," pp. 1316, 1320–21. In OMA's project statement for Parc de la Villette the straight central axis of the circulation is called "Boulevard," while the park as a whole is described as a *"designed landscape."* Jacques Lucan, ed., *OMA—Rem Koolhaas*, Princeton Architectural Press: New York, 1991, pp. 87–88, 91.
94 Conversation with the author, Rotterdam, February 15, 2023.
95 Ibid.

P 6.1 January 25, 1989. Basement.

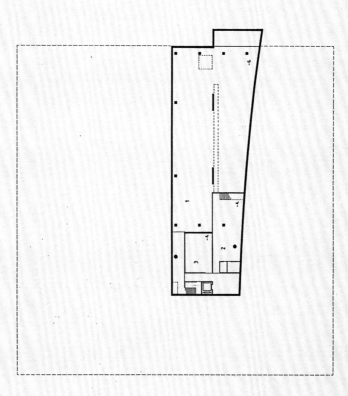

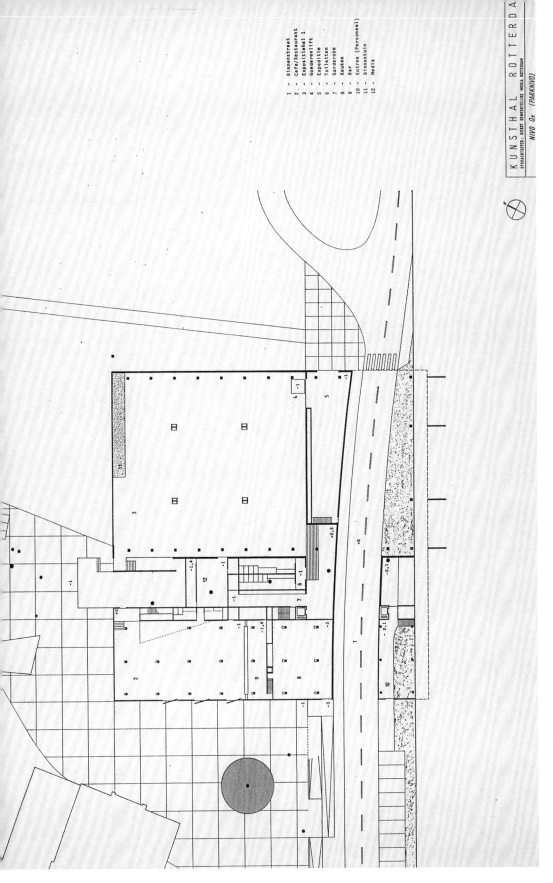

P 6.2   January 25, 1989. Park level.

P 6.3 January 25, 1989. Level of the main entrance.

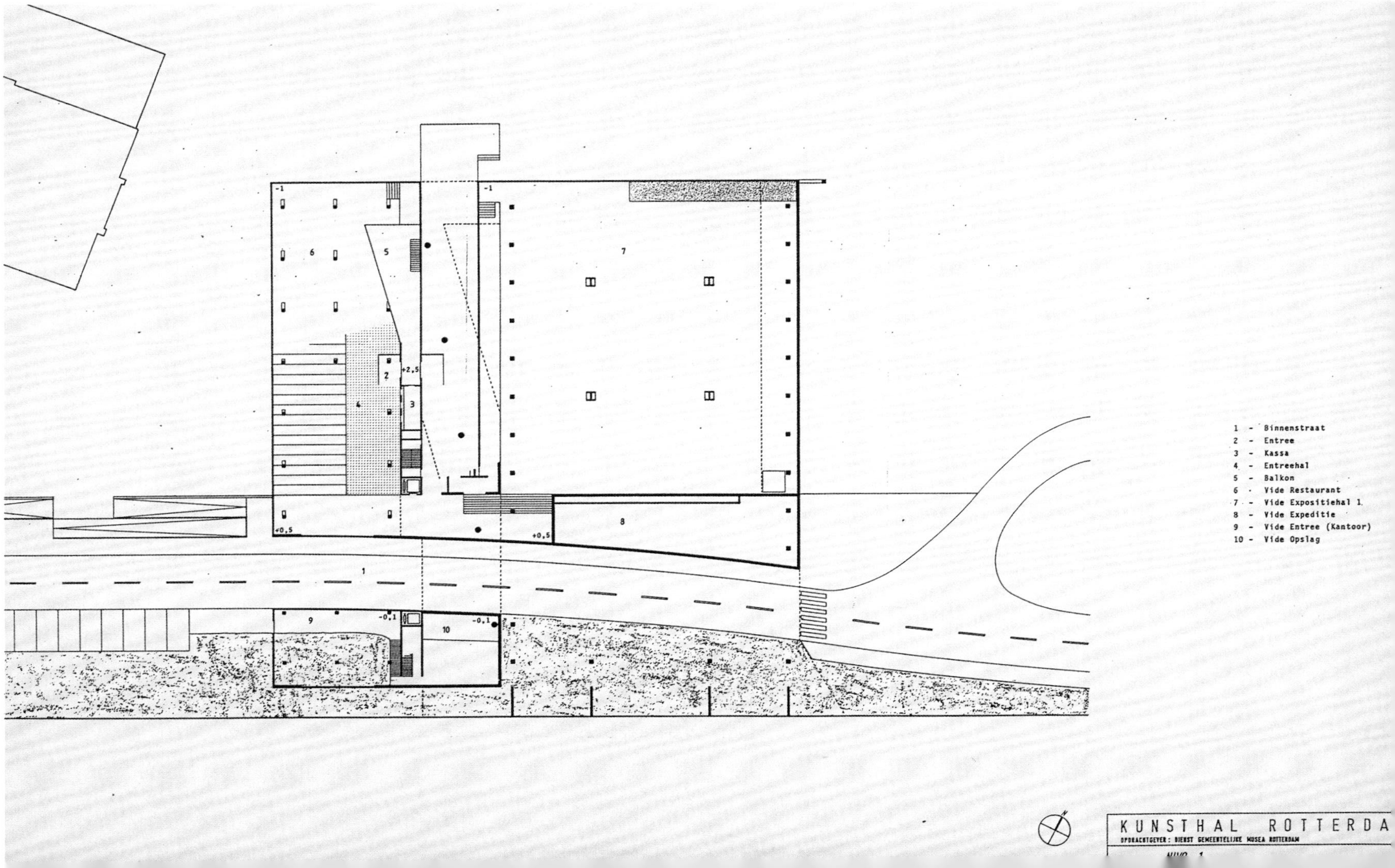

1 - Binnenstraat
2 - Entree
3 - Kassa
4 - Entreehal
5 - Balkon
6 - Vide Restaurant
7 - Vide Expositiehal 1
8 - Vide Expeditie
9 - Vide Entree (Kantoor)
10 - Vide Opslag
KUNSTHAL ROTTERDA
OPDRACHTGEVER: DIENST GEMEENTELIJKE MUSEA ROTTERDAM

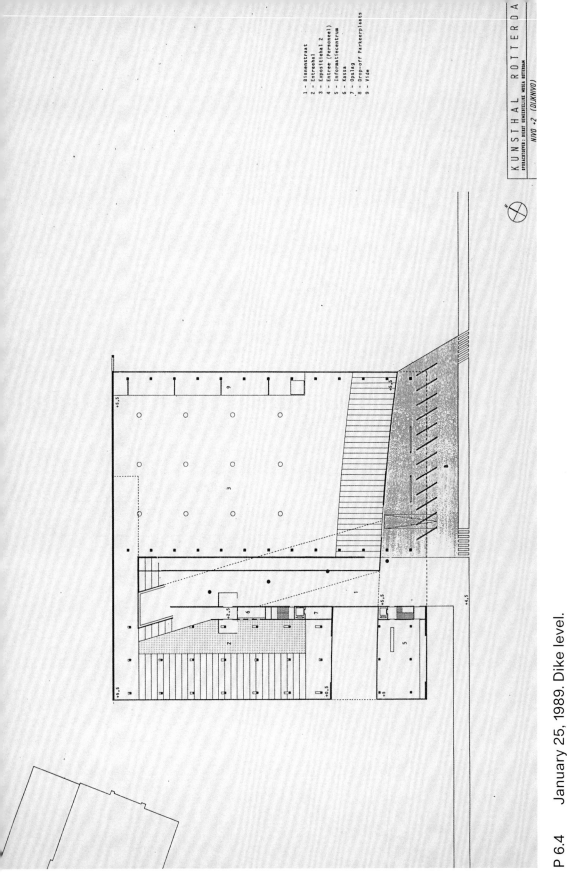

P 6.4   January 25, 1989. Dike level.

P 6.5 January 25, 1989. Third level.

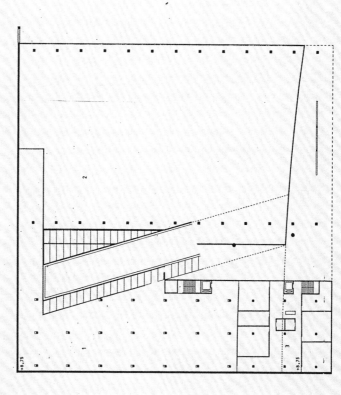

P 6.6   January 25, 1989. Roof.

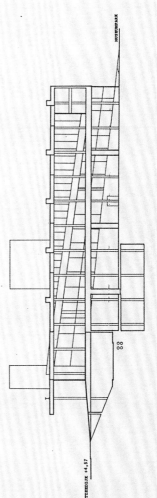

P 6.7 January 25, 1989. Cross sections (north to south). Above: restaurant, auditorium, Hall 3. Below: Halls 1–2.

P 6.8 January 25, 1989. Cross sections (north to south).

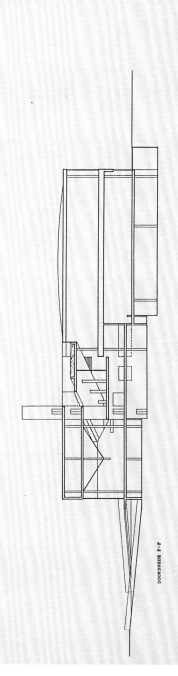

P 6.9 January 25, 1989. Cross sections (east to west).

P 6.10   January 25, 1989. South and east elevation.

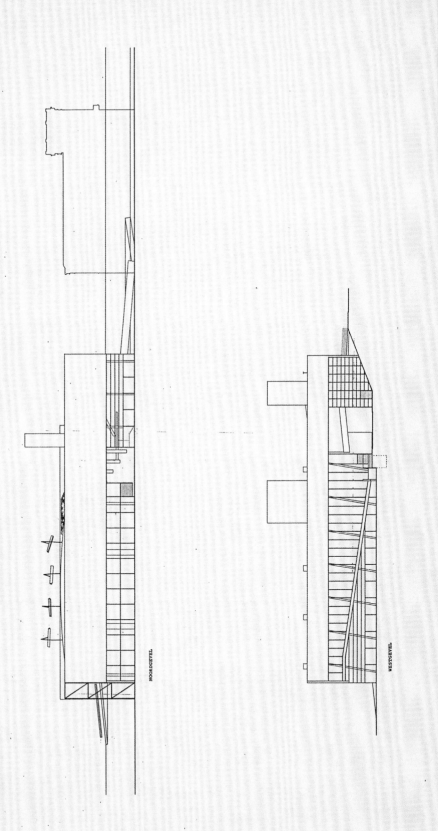

P 6.11 January 25, 1989. North and west elevation.

P 6.12   Picture of the model included in the booklet of February 25, 1989.

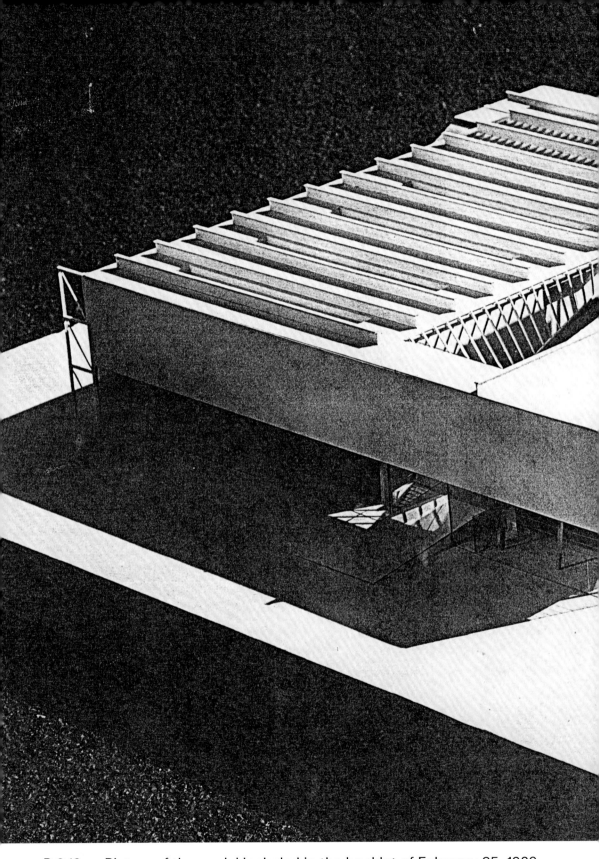

P 6.13   Picture of the model included in the booklet of February 25, 1989.

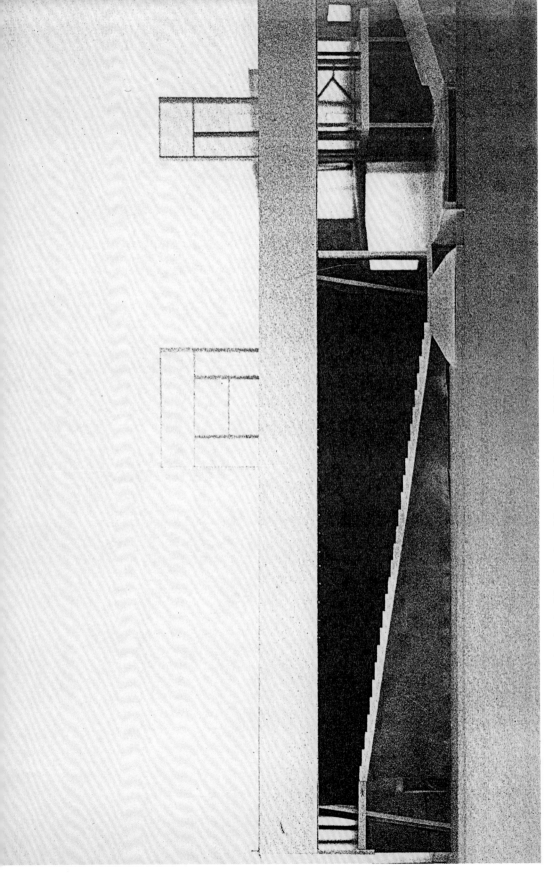

P 6.14   Picture of the model included in the booklet of February 25, 1989.

Modernism Obsolete

A New Approach for a New Europe

The triumph of the West,
of the Western idea ...

Francis Fukuyama, 1989

One of the topics Koolhaas commented on most intensively in 1989 was his penchant for the modernism of the 1920s, 1930s, 1950s, and 1960s—an issue which also recurred in the reviews of OMA's Netherlands Dance Theater in The Hague, IJplein in Amsterdam, and Patio House in Rotterdam. In several interviews Koolhaas confesses his unease about OMA's modernist image and the ubiquity of modernist references in Dutch architecture at the time. To Koos Bosma and Hans van Dijk he explains: "I've been trying for a good three years now to shake off that stigma of being modern, for the very reason that it is so casually bandied about in the Netherlands."[1] OMA's advocacy of modernist architecture was no doubt much less visible and distinct a position within the Dutch context than it had once been on an international level. When Aldo van Eyck railed against postmodernist and rationalist architecture for what he saw as a treacherous aberration vis-à-vis the modernist tradition, he did it with such vehemence that Koolhaas' contemporaneous criticisms appear subtle by comparison. In addition to Léon Krier, the primary target of his 1980 article "Rats, Posts, and other Pests" were Aldo Rossi, Ungers, and "the Americans" who were present at the Venice Biennale that year.[2] The model Van Eyck held up was what he called the "Great Gang"—artists, writers, and architects of the early twentieth-century avant-gardes, among them Rietveld, Duiker, Van der Vlugt, Aalto, and Le Corbusier. In a 1987 lecture he ridicules the "criminals" "Léon K.," "Robert V.," "Philip J.," "Robert S.," and "Richard M." with unmitigated malice.[3]

In a 1989 interview with Mil De Kooning, Koolhaas accused his Dutch colleagues of having been not so much immune to postmodernism as rather oblivious of it, while imitating OMA's work at large.[4] On several occasions in the 1990s, Hans van Dijk illustrated the adherence of architects in the Netherlands to its modernist legacy by referring to a series of articles that had been published in the Dutch weekly *Intermediair* in 1980, in which "almost all of the twenty-three invited architects admitted at the end of the day to feeling inspired by the moderns."[5] In his lecture "School Master Modernism," given at the conference "How Modern is Dutch Architecture?" in 1990, Van Dijk referred to the same event, recalling that "there is talk with evident emotion about buildings such as Van Nelle, Zonnestraal, House

1   Koos Bosma and Hans van Dijk, "Interview met Rem Koolhaas," in *Archis*, 3 (1989), p. 43. Quoted in *OMA/Rem Koolhaas: A Critical Reader*, ed. Christophe Van Gerrewey, Basel: Birkhäuser, 2019, p. 163.
2   Aldo van Eyck, "What Is and Isn't Architecture: à propos of Rats, Posts, and other Pests (RPP)," in *Lotus International*, 28 (1980), pp. 15–19.
3   International Design Seminar (Indesem), TU Delft, 1987. https://www.youtube.com/watch?v=Uf7RyqXIYmM (accessed August 4, 2022)
4   Mil De Kooning, "OMA in Nederland: Rem Koolhaas in gesprek," in *Vlees & Beton*, 12 (1989), n. p.
5   Hans van Dijk, *Twentieth-Century Architecture in the Netherlands*, Rotterdam: 010 Publishers, 1999, p. 144.

Schröder, and the orphanage in Amsterdam, and about teachers from Berlage to Van den Broek, from Duiker to Van Eyck."[6]

Like Van Dijk, Hans van der Heijden saw the Dutch adherence to the modernist tradition as being closely related to the way architects were trained at the University of Technology in Delft (known as TU Delft).[7] Van der Heijden pictured the situation during the 1970s and 1980s as trench warfare in a territory of modernist "masters," remote from the debates on postmodernist architecture: "The debate was colored, if not dominated by a paralyzing controversy in the setting of the Technical University Delft (the largest of the two architecture schools in the country). The players were divided into two distinct camps, one formed by architects like Aldo van Eyck and Herman Hertzberger and the other led by Carel Weeber. As former Team-X rebels, Van Eyck and Hertzberger claimed the humanist morals of the early modernist heroes Rietveld, Duiker, Van de[r] Vlugt and Bakema. [...] Weeber, by contrast, fitted into the rationalist line of architects like Berlage, Oud and Van den Broek, who had a much more institutional perception of the profession."[8]

The almost exclusively modernist frame of reference—as opposed to the classicist leanings that were generally attributed to postmodernist architecture—comes as no surprise given the leading figures of the Dutch architectural scene in the 1980s: in addition to Van Eyck, Hertzberger, and Blom, there were architects like Wim Quist, Carel Weeber, Jan Henket, Mecanoo, Joe Coenen, Benthem Crouwel, DKV architecten (Dolf Dobbelaar, Herman de Kovel, Paul de Vroom), and—just about to enter the stage—Wiel Arets, and Van Berkel & Bos (→ F 5.1–5.3). At a Delft conference in 1990, Herman de Kovel, cofounder of the Rotterdam architecture firm DKV and a former collaborator with OMA, observed a revival of the "heroic 'Nieuwe Bouwen'" movement in Dutch architecture of the 1980s, notably in terms of form—a quality that applied as much to his own practice's Agniesebuurt housing project in Rotterdam (1984–88) as to OMA's IJplein buildings (1979–89).[9] Christophe Van Gerrewey has observed that "during the '80s, the recuperation of modernist techniques that so defined the IJplein project had become omnipresent in Dutch architecture," suggesting that the fear of epigones had prompted Koolhaas' decision to quit his position at TU Delft, "where the cut-and-paste method of the IJplein project has indeed become omnipresent in studios and publications, and in the work of both professors and alumni."[10]

The 1990 conference at TU Delft was held to mark Koolhaas' departure, and it was Koolhaas himself who had chosen the topic. In his

F 5.1

Mecanoo, Kruisplein housing, Rotterdam, 1981–85.

F 5.2

Mecanoo, Hillekop housing, Rotterdam, 1985–89.

6 Hans van Dijk, "Het onderwijzersmodernisme," in *Hoe modern is de Nederlandse architectuur?* ed. Bernard Leupen at al., Rotterdam: 010 Publishers, 1990, p. 177 (author's translation).
7 Van Dijk, ibid., p. 147. Hans van der Heijden, "The Netherlands–Koolhaas and the Profession at Play," in *An Architect's Guide to Fame*, eds. Paul Davies and Paul Schmiedknecht, Oxford: Architectural Press, 2005, pp. 106–07.
8 Ibid.
9 Herman de Kovel, "Over de actualiteit van 'moderne architectuur,'" in *Hoe modern is de Nederlandse architectuur?* Leupen, p. 67.
10 Christophe Van Gerrewey, "A Weissenhofsiedlung for Amsterdam: OMA's IJplein," in *Log*, 44 (2018), pp. 89–90, 90–91.

F 5.3

DKV architecten, Agniesebuurt housing, Rotterdam, 1984–88.

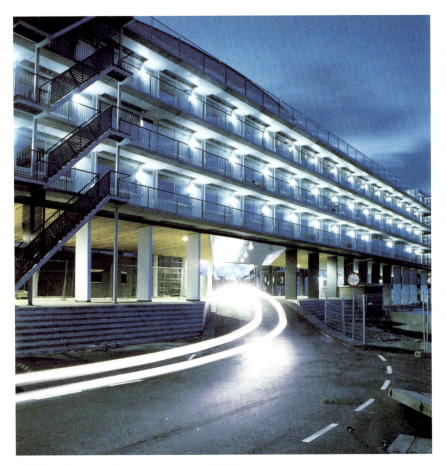

F 5.4

OMA/Rem Koolhaas, IJplein, Amsterdam, 1981–88.

own talk, he offered a self-critique of the IJplein project that was simultaneously a flagellation of his peers (→ F 5.4). Without addressing the issue of imitation directly, he observed: "This [the IJplein project] made explicit reference to pre-war modernism, though, updating or revising it in accordance with our own ideas [...]. At the same time that language had become so prevalent in Holland—a triumphalist and ubiquitous cliché, even—that we were beset with serious doubts on this matter."[11] In the often quoted outburst that followed, he suggested that the self-assurance of the latest Dutch modernist wave was based on a negligence that failed to reflect the ongoing transformations of society: "How is it possible for Christ's sake that in a century informed entirely by instability and change, in the art best equipped to reflect society, and in a language, that of architecture, celebrated especially for the capacity of transformation—that despite all this, buildings ranging over a hundred-year period still look so much alike?"[12] In his lecture, Koolhaas gave a sole example of recent architecture conveying the feeling of "a new condition": Aldo Rossi's Il Palazzo (1987) in Fukuoka—a building with a strictly symmetrical plan, a base, a front and columns in red travertine, green steel lintels, and a cornice of renaissance-like dimensions. To his peers, the architecture of Rossi's hotel must have seemed essentially postmodernist and—in 1990, two years after the *Deconstructivist Architecture* show—somewhat hard to comprehend as an outlook on things to come.[13]

With these forces rather than against

Another topic that recurs in the interviews Koolhaas gave in 1989 is *The Contemporary City*, a book about cities like Tokyo, Seoul, Atlanta, and the periphery of Paris that he was working on at the time.[14] The book has never been published as the study it was initially intended to be, but apparently the essays written for *S, M, L, XL* built on the research that had been accomplished for this project. In 1994, Koolhaas explained: "I had started researching *The Contemporary City*. As I progressed, I realized that you cannot write a profound book on that subject unless you concentrate on it for years. [...] The research, which

---

11 Rem Koolhaas, "How Modern is Dutch Architecture?" in *Mart Stam's Trousers: Stories from Behind the Scenes of Dutch Moral Modernism*, eds. Crimson, Michael Speaks, Gerard Hadders, Rotterdam 010 Publishers, 1999, p. 161. First published in 1990 under the title "Hoe modern is de Nederlandse architectuur?"
12 Ibid., p. 161.
13 Ibid., p. 166.

14 For instance, Herman Selier, "Voor een beter Nederland: De architectuur van Rem Koolhaas," in *NRC Handelsblad* (March 3, 1989). Cervelló, "I've always been anxious," p. 84.

in fact did not reach any real conclusion, also proved to affect our work at the office. [...] At the same time, pressure was being applied to publish a monograph. I didn't want to write a traditional monograph. So, since two books were impossible—a popular monograph and an academically sound book on the contemporary city—the combination of *S, M, L, XL* resulted."[15]

Koolhaas also held seminars on *The Contemporary City* with his students at TU Delft.[16] In April 1988, likewise at the university in Delft, he had initiated the symposium "Whether Europe" on the future development of European cities. Henri Ciriani, Nigel Coates, Wolfgang Schett, Fritz Neumeyer, Zaha Hadid, Bernard Tschumi, Hans Kollhoff, Carel Weeber, Kees Christiaanse, Jean Nouvel, and Stanislaus von Moos were invited to discuss a series of tendencies that were expected to emerge in European architecture and urbanism within the next fifteen years. Themes included on the agenda were the shifting relationship between center and periphery, open spaces like parks as a new type of project, "adventurous developers" and "ambitious municipalities" as a new type of client, and a new kind of public space.[17] Koolhaas was particularly interested in the dynamics underlying the transformation of the contemporary city—often simply referred to as "the forces"—and the way they affected the role of the architect. To Marta Cervelló he explained: "One of the most disturbing aspects [of contemporary architecture and city planning are] the persistent attempts to control large parts of the city by systems of architectural or architectonic composition—even if they are "deconstructed"—that clearly have absolutely nothing to do with the forces that now operate. I've been working to find elements that can be controlled, with these forces rather than against."[18] On another occasion he observed: "one must simply realize that forces in society have changed."[19] Regarding his notion of the term "forces"—so critical for his thinking in these years—a statement made in January 1991 is instructive: "Marshall Berman's book *All that Is Solid Melts into Air*," he explained during a discussion with students at Rice University, "describes modernization and modernism as a kind of maelstrom, which implies that in a way, you have no choice in terms of your fundamental alignment with the dominant forces. It is the kind of alignment that the surfer has to make with the wave."[20]

Perhaps the metaphor that Koolhaas famously came out with in 1985—"architecture is carried by the forces of the Groszstadt as a surfer is carried by the waves"—was inspired by Berman's book, which was first published in 1982.[21] Based on a rereading of writings by Karl

Marx and Friedrich Nietzsche—who has always been crucial for Koolhaas' thinking—Berman draws a picture of perpetual capitalist modernization which is full of themes and motifs that have marked Koolhaas' ideas ever since the 1970s: the inescapable subjection of modern societies to the forces of (capitalist) modernization; the condition of permanent instability, permanent danger, permanent need for renewal; the conviction that the only sensible way to deal with the governing forces is to surrender in such a manner that one may exploit their powers for oneself. "To be modern [...]," Berman writes, "is to experience personal and social life as a maelstrom, to find one's world and oneself in perpetual disintegration and renewal, trouble and anguish, ambiguity and contradiction [...]. To be a modernist is to make oneself somehow at home in the maelstrom, to make its rhythms one's own to move its currents in search of the forms of reality, of beauty, of freedom, of justice, that its fervid perilous flow allows."[22]

At the end of the 1980s, a new major "force" was the developer. In 1989, Koolhaas recalled the audacious spirit of Dutch housing corporations, entrepreneurs, and authorities in the 1920s; with regard to his own present, he observed: "But now no one has enough money and everything is eventually decided by developers, whether it's so-called left-leaning or right-leaning initiatives for the city. The developers have the final say."[23] Similarly, in 1992, while elaborating on OMA's strategy for Melun-Sénart of focusing on the unbuilt environment (the "void"), Koolhaas explained: "the rest of the city we would declare residual or surrender completely to the typical force, the developer's politics that now dictates so much of the generation of the city."[24]

---

15 Hans van Dijk, "De architect is verplicht om een respectabel mens te zijn," in *Archis*, 11 (1994), pp. 18–19. Quoted in Van Gerrewey, *A Critical Reader*, p. 335.

16 Tracy Metz, "Nederland mist respect voor de architect," in *Avenue*, 24 (January 1989), p. 64.

17 Bernhard Leupen, Preface, in *Whether Europe: Symposium Reader*, Delft: Technische Universiteit, 1988, pp. 5–6.

18 Marta Cervelló, "I've always been anxious with the standard typology of the average architect with a *successful* career," in *Quaderns*, 183 (1989), p. 84.

19 Bosma and Van Dijk, "Interview met Rem Koolhaas," p. 45 (author's translation).

20 Lynn Fitzpatrick and Doug Hofius, eds., *Rem Koolhaas: conversations with students. Architecture at Rice 1991*, Houston: Rice University, 1991, pp. 75–76.

21 Rem Koolhaas, "Elegy for the Vacant Lot," in *S, M, L, XL*, Koolhaas and Bruce Mau, New York: The Monacelli Press, 1995, p. 937. First published under the title "Éloge du terrain vague" in 1985.

22 Marshall Berman, *All That Is Solid Melts Into Air*, London: Verso, 2010, pp. 345–46. First published in 1982.

23 Bosma and Van Dijk, "Interview met Rem Koolhaas," p. 42 (author's translation).

24 Rem Koolhaas, "Urban Operations," in *Columbia Documents of Architecture and Theory*, vol. 3 (1993), p. 33. The lecture was held at Columbia University on October 19, 1992.

A future to be contemporary

In the last chapter of *All That Is Solid Melts Into Air*, Berman writes: "Many modernisms of the past have found themselves by forgetting; the modernists of the 1970s were forced to find themselves by remembering. Earlier modernists wiped away the past in order to reach a new departure; the new departures of the 1970s lay in attempts to recover past modes of life that were buried but not dead. [...] At a moment when modern society seemed to lose their capacity to create a brave new future, modernism was under intense pressure to discover new sources of life through imaginative encounters with the past."[25] Perhaps this very idea encouraged Koolhaas at the turn of the 1990s in the reverse sense: grasping the opportunity of a society that, after a pause of two decades, was ready to shape its own future.

Towards the end of the 1980s, Koolhaas started employing the terms "modern" and "contemporary" as ideological opposites. In an April 1989 interview, he stated: "I'm trying more and more not to be modern, but to be contemporary," betraying the programmatic character of his book project *The Contemporary City*.[26] The most important efforts in this context, however, were OMA's competition entries in 1989, notably the designs for the sea terminal in Zeebrugge (→ F 5.5), the ZKM center for art and media in Karlsruhe (→ F 5.6), and the National Library in Paris (→ F 5.7). Referring to the three 1989 projects he told Paul Vermeulen: "First we imposed on ourselves a series of obligations. One of them was that we needed to break with the vocabulary of modernism."[27] On another occasion, Koolhaas explained that OMA's scheme for Zeebrugge was to implicate "the smallest possible number of references."[28] In comparison with OMA's earlier work, the absence of borrowings from modernist architecture is indeed salient and bespeaks the wish to lessen the reliance of OMA's production on the modernist past. But for Koolhaas, at the time, being contemporary was also about size, because he saw the large building as architecture's prime task in the following decade.

Europe lagging behind

It was in 1989 that Koolhaas first announced his ambition of introducing a sense of large scale to European architecture, during an interview with Tracy Metz. When discussing OMA's competition entry for the City Hall in The Hague (1986), he explained: "That's such a mass of cubic meters, it's often a whole city that is being added. In Europe,

F 5.5

OMA/Rem Koolhaas, competition entry for the sea terminal in Zeebrugge, 1989.

F 5.6

OMA/Rem Koolhaas, competition entry for the ZKM arts and media center in Karlsruhe, 1989–92.

25 Berman, *All That Is Solid Melts Into Air*, p. 332.
26 Bruno Fortier, "La grande ville," in *L'Architecture d'Aujourd'hui*, 262 (April 1989), p. 93 (author's translation).
27 Paul Vermeulen, "Metropolitane architektuur," in *De Standaard* (April 28/29, 1990) (author's translation).
28 Cervelló, "I've always been anxious," p. 84.

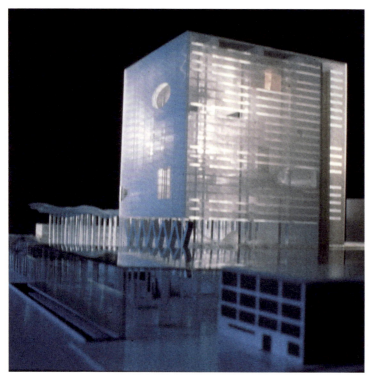

OMA/Rem Koolhaas, competition entry for the National Library in Paris, 1989.

a comparable large scale hardly exists. In America they have been struggling with this for much longer, and they've experienced the consequences of this kind of breakthrough. It heralds a new chapter in architecture, whether you like it or not. I want to introduce comparable mutations into European architecture."[29]

The scale of the project in The Hague was unprecedented in OMA's oeuvre. IJplein in Amsterdam had hitherto been OMA's largest project with a floor area of 17,575 square meters; the program for the City Hall, however, stipulated a surface area of 150,000 square meters.[30] In 1989, the size of the competitions varied between 25,000 and 250,000 square meters: 25,000 for the sea terminal in Zeebrugge;[31] 31,000 for the ZKM media center in Karlsruhe;[32] 220,000 for the business center at Frankfurt Airport;[33] and 250,000 for the National Library in Paris.[34] By far the largest project was the development of Euralille, a business center of 800,000 square meters attached to Lille's new TGV station (→ F 5.8). Like the Kunsthal—which had a total surface area of less than 8,000 square meters—the whole development was implemented within a time frame of six years by a total of seven different architects. In sheer figures, the projects for Paris, Lille, and Frankfurt in 1989 clearly surpassed the largest American developments presented seven years earlier at the conference in Charlottesville.[35] Apart from the scale, Koolhaas' description of the main actors involved in the Euralille project perfectly corresponded to the constellation predicted for the near future at the Delft symposium in April 1988: an "adventurous developer" and an "ambitious municipality" in a Europe of sociocultural change. In a project statement about the Zeebrugge sea terminal, Koolhaas introduced the scheme as a Tower of Babel "for the new ambition of Europe."[36] Ben van Berkel and Caroline Bos reported in a review of the same competition: "This too is typical for Koolhaas, in that he likes to comment on his current designs in the mass media. Nowadays, newspapers and talk shows focus on the consequences that the events of 1992 will have on Europe; and Koolhaas sees his design as an effortless and entertaining aggregation of the various European countries in a well-oiled machine."[37]

F 5.8

OMA/Rem Koolhaas, masterplan for Euralille and Congrexpo, Lille, 1989–94.

29 Metz, "Nederland mist respect voor de architect," p. 64 (author's translation).
30 Hajime Yatsuka, "'I combine Architectural with Specificity with Programmatic Instability,'" in *Telescope: The Printed City*, 4 (1989), p. 11.
31 Koolhaas and Mau, *S, M, L, XL*, p. 608.
32 See https://oma.eu/projects/zentrum-fur-kunst-und-medientechnologie (accessed May 24, 2020).
33 Koolhaas and Mau, *S, M, L, XL*, p. 476.
34 Ibid., p. 608.
35 The largest projects presented were Philip Johnson and John Burgee's International Palace in Boston (180,000 m^2) and Henry Cobb's Fountain Place in Dallas (175,000 m^2). See Chapter 1.
36 OMA/Rem Koolhaas, "Une tour de Babel pas comme les autres," in *Architecture Mouvement Continuité*, 4 (September 1989), p. 22.
37 Ben van Berkel and Caroline Bos, "Terminal als landmark: Vijf ontwerpen voor Sea Trade Center in Zeebrugge," in *Archis*, 8 (1989), p. 13 (author's translation).

Revising the agenda

Since the second half of the 1980s, the process of European integration had been visibly gaining momentum, and Koolhaas was highly perceptive to the implications for his profession. The impact of this process, the experience of Euralille, the competitions of 1989, and the revolutions in Eastern Europe between 1989 and 1991 all prompted him to come up with ways of overcoming OMA's dependence on the modernist past. Koolhaas took the prospect of implementing projects in Europe that were comparable in size to large American developments as an occasion to reframe the notion of the skyscraper he had outlined in *Delirious New York*. The process of reworking his ideas on Manhattan into an architectural agenda would evolve until the mid-1990s; it can be traced back to Koolhaas' 1988 lecture "Atlanta," then appears again a year later in the essay "The End of the Age of Innocence?" and once more in the 1991 talk "Precarious Entity," while receiving its most elaborate form in *S, M, L, XL*, namely in 1994's "Bigness" manifesto. At the turn of the 1990s, Koolhaas sought to outline a new paradigm for the cities and architecture of Europe, based on recent developments in the United States and a series of east Asian metropoles like Tokyo and Seoul. There are striking correspondences between the agenda of the forthcoming European Union and the revised approach taken by OMA, which took shape almost as a parallel development in the form of writings, interviews, lectures, and projects. The further evolution of the Kunsthal's design unfolded against this backdrop.

At the turning point of European integration

In 1983, French finance minister Jacques Delors convinced President Mitterrand to abandon his policy of national protectionism and seclusion in favor of driving forward the vision of a strong Europe governed by transnational institutions.[38] Delors' presidency of the European Commission that followed (1985–95) essentially coincides with what is generally considered the "turning point in the history of European integration" (→ F 5.9).[39] In June 1985, the Schengen Agreement was signed, in February 1986 the Single European Act, and in February 1992 the Treaty on European Union (more commonly known as the Maastricht Treaty). It was during these years that the most significant achievements were made in a process which by the turn of the century had transformed the European Community into the European Union with open internal borders, a single market, a single currency, a central

F 5.9

Jacques Delors, president of the European Commission, 1985–95.

bank, and a partial yet minimal transfer of national sovereignty to European institutions. Meanwhile, the community expanded: Spain and Portugal joined in 1986, followed by Austria, Sweden, and Finland in 1995. The increase in member states, markets, workforces, and production resources lent increasing weight internationally to the progress of European integration. For a number of years, the EU became "popular," and was closely monitored as a potential competitor in other parts of the world, above all in the United States.[40] In a July 1988 issue of the *New York Times*, Steven Greenhouse argues: "Individually, the nations of Europe find it hard to be seen as equals by the superpowers. It might be a different story with a united Europe of 320 million people."[41]

38 Mark Gilbert, *European Integration: A Concise History*, Plymouth: Rowman & Littlefield Publishers, 2012, pp. 118–19. See also Antonio Varsori, "The Relaunching of Europe in the Mid-1980s," in *European Integration and the Atlantic Community in the 1980s*, eds. Kiran Klaus Patel and Kenneth Weisbrode, Cambridge: Cambridge University Press, 2013, pp. 231–32, 234.
39 Gilbert, *European Integration*, p. 6.
40 "It was the new thrust towards integration after 1985 which refocused external attention on the EC. There were, for instance, not inconsiderable fears, expressed most notably in the United States, that the market would only be the CAP writ large, a protectionist 'Fortress' Europe. More significant for the Union were the EFTA states which, fearing the adverse effect the single market might have on their own economies, sought not only reassurance from the EC, but also involvement in the market." In *The Community of Europe: A History of European Integration since 1945*, Derek W. Urwin, London/New York: Longman, 1995, p. 245.
41 Gilbert, *European Integration*, p. 147.

At the root of these dynamics were profound structural changes of global dimensions. One of them was the collapse of the colonial system and its consequences, still felt by multinational companies in countries like the United Kingdom, France, and the Netherlands. In addition, since the 1970s European business had been struggling to compete with big corporations from the United States and Japan, which were "far ahead in technological research and development of the most modern high-tech industries" such as computer and communication technology.[42] The situation was further aggravated during Ronald Reagan's presidency (1981–89), marked by a policy of *laissez-faire* capitalism, privatization, deregulation of the financial sector, low taxes, and a belief in the self-regulation of markets,[43] which turned the United States into the first so-called "post-industrial" society, privileging finance over production.[44] As historian Ivan Berend puts it, "American influence and dominance in international organizations allowed the sweeping neo-liberal deregulatory regime adopted in the US to function as the cultural-ideological companion and driver of globalization."[45] Measured by the yardstick of the new regime, Europe's major deficits were "the *fragmentation* of markets, inadequate *size of firms*, and lack of significant state sponsorship," followed by low labor market mobility, rigid wage structures, and high social benefits.[46] What seemed deficient in the late 1980s at least partly coincided with what until then had been deemed achievements of the welfare state. It was under the acute pressure of American and Asian competition that a "joint venture" of European politicians and corporations—"sensing that the danger of marginalization was a real one"[47]—succeeded in overcoming Europe's "backwardness," and entered a new dimension of European integration, comprising such achievements as the introduction of the single market and the euro.

Synchronization

There are multiple parallels between these developments and Koolhaas' statements and OMA's projects in 1989: the notion of Europe lagging behind the United States and Japan; the notion of Europe in need of catching up; the emulation of American economic policies, and the emulation of the American city; the deregulation of financial markets and the deregulation of urbanism; the promotion of big corporations, and the promotion of big buildings, the larger the better. On a figurative level, the contraction of programs into huge compact volumes, which was characteristic of OMA's most recent work, echoed the need of

European corporations to overcome the fragmentation—of markets, legislation, standards, infrastructure—limiting their growth. The shift is remarkable, given that virtually all projects of the 1970s and 1980s were composed of multiple, often heterogeneous volumes. The Netherlands Dance Theater, Villa dall'Ava, and the Byzantium are but the most obvious examples. The 1988 scheme for the NAi is the first to propose a collage of solids that is largely enclosed by an exterior overall volume, but the notion of the exterior's volumetric unity is somewhat undermined by the cantilevered roof slab and the leaning tower that passes through it from inside. The volumetric unity of OMA's schemes for Zeebrugge, Karlsruhe, and Paris is more determined. Like the NAi, the design for Zeebrugge provides an "internalized" composite volume: a spiraling parking ramp at the bottom, and, on top, a semicircular hotel, a wedge-shaped void, a rectilinear office tower, and the steps of an auditorium. But unlike the scheme for the NAi, the integrity of the compact curved volume is preserved, and the same holds true for OMA's competition entry for the convention center in Agadir (1990), which provides a square prism of three "autonomous" layers. The project for Congrexpo (1990–94) varies the latter principle, its compact egg-shaped volume being composed of three heterogeneous segments.

      Strictly speaking, neither the National Library nor the ZKM media center in Karlsruhe are solitary prismatic volumes: the "cube" at the center of the library is surrounded by a series of low volumes, and the lower part of the media center's vertical prism connects to a volume of exactly the same width, the length depending on the version. But in both cases there is a pronounced hierarchy from the verticality and size of the main volume to the lower parts of the building that contrasts with the principle volumetric "anarchy" of previous projects like the extension of the Dutch parliament, the Netherlands Dance Theater, the Byzantium, Villa dall'Ava, and many others. The design for the National Library, like that for the media center, does convey the image of a solitary prismatic colossus, an image which has been reinforced by the fact that most of the pictures published focus on the main volume.

---

42 Ivan T. Berend, *The History of European Integration: A New Perspective*, London: Routledge, 2016, p. 112.
43 Ibid., p. 136.
44 Henk Overbeek and Kees van der Pijl, "Restructuring Capital and Restructuring Hegemony: Neo-Liberalism and the Unmaking of the Post-War Order," in *Restructuring Hegemony in the Global Political Economy: The Rise of Transnational Neo-Liberalism in the 1980s*, ed. Henk Overbeek, London: Routledge, 2005, pp. 19–20. First published 1993.
45 Berend, *The History of European Integration*, p. 112. See also Stephen R. Gill, "Neo-Liberalism and the Shift Towards a US-Centred Transnational Hegemony," in *Restructuring Hegemony in the Global Political Economy,* Overbeek, pp. 246–82.
46 Berend, *The History of European Integration*, pp. 108, 110.
47 Ibid., p. 149.

European giants

In 1990, Koolhaas declared the "Very Large Building" to be "the theme of the end of the century [...] a type that proliferates effortlessly in North America, Japan and South Korea," while still being a novelty in Europe.[48] The introduction of the large scale in Europe was now "about Europe's modernization," and no longer merely the personal ambition he had confessed a year previously to Tracy Metz.[49] In 1991, at the "Anyone" conference in Santa Monica, Koolhaas identified the shift of scale as "the strongest force in operation."[50] He did not claim, however, to have anticipated this shift: "I was sincerely convinced that the explosion of scale that had taken place in America and that was taking place in Japan and all over southeast Asia, would simply never make an appearance in Europe. But in the last three or four years certain modifications in European culture have forced me to revise some of these assumptions, especially the assumption that the issue of scale would never play a major role in Europe."[51]

This statement indicates that 1987/88 was the point at which he reframed his vision of Europe. By then, the Single European Act had been signed, and 1992—scheduled to be the year of the Treaty on European Union—held out the promise of a united Europe with a common currency and a single market. Meanwhile, the process was not limited to political agreements and the ratification of treaties. In Europe, it was paralleled by a wave of mergers: "Mergers [...] progressed rapidly in the late 1980s. Among the 1,000 larger firms, mergers in 1982–83 numbered 117, [...] in 1987–88, 383, in 1988–89, 492; in 1989–90, 662. Together these increased European companies to sizes comparable with the American giants. [...] The Single Market initiatives were working."[52]

The common market as a whole, too, was supposed to grow in order to become globally competitive. The fast expansion of the European Community during the 1980s and 1990s was deemed an economic necessity by some, if only to open up new pools of consumers and cheap labor.[53] Among the synchronizations required for the single market to function, the most consequential for OMA was probably that of Europe's physical infrastructure. The expansion of the high-speed railway system comprising the TGV, Thalys, and ICE involved large architectural developments. OMA's projects for Euralille, Frankfurt, and Zeebrugge, and to a lesser extent Karlsruhe, are projects of this kind. At the conference in Santa Monica, Koolhaas envisaged architecture (re-)gaining a political dimension: "Now I believe that one of the most important things to understand in terms of the present developments in Europe is that architecture has suddenly acquired a genuine, even political, importance, and that for the first time the powerlessness of the architect has been reversed: after two decades of deep unpopularity, there is now a very strong public, political expectation that the architect will be involved and will be able to articulate the self-inflicted, sometimes cosmic surgery that Europe is undergoing at this moment."[54]

A *fait accompli*

For as long as socialism had existed as a factual alternative to capitalism in eastern Europe, the two systems and their respective advocates had been competing with one another. It has often been argued that the successful institution of the welfare state during the postwar era in western Europe and in the United States was a consequence of the fact that decision makers on both sides of the Atlantic felt the need to prove the superiority of the Western model through the diffusion of a higher living standard.[55] A fundamental revision of the policy had already begun to take shape with the economic crises of the 1970s, and then, ever more visibly, during the tenures of Margaret Thatcher (1979–90) and Ronald Reagan (1981–89) (→ F 5.10). Berend describes the growing ideological estrangement of the political Left from its socialist origins: "The Keynesian economics that had dominated in postwar Western Europe, and the state intervention and regulation it had prescribed as solutions, were now declared a problem. New ideologies, rooted in the socio-economic sensibilities of post-industrial consumer middle-classes, successfully challenged the policies of Left-leaning parties, which had served the European postwar recovery so well. The Left parties lost their self-confidence, as well as their mass support, and subsequently they shifted their political platforms to the center. The 1970s and 1980s essentially incubated a new political culture and Zeitgeist, an amalgam of triumphant neoliberalism, neoconservatism, and postmodern culture and ideology."[56]

---

48 Koolhaas, "The End of the Age of Innocence," in *OMA–Rem Koolhaas*, ed. Jacques Lucan, Princeton Architectural Press: New York, 1991, p. 165.
49 Nikolaus Kuhnert and Philipp Oswald, "Die Inszenierung der Ungewissheit: Rem Koolhaas im Gespräch mit Nikolaus Kuhnert und Philipp Oswald," in *Arch+*, 105/106 (1990), p. 68.
50 Rem Koolhaas, "Precarious Entity," in *Anyone*, ed. Cynthia Davidson, New York: Rizzoli, 1991, p. 148.
51 Ibid., p. 149.
52 Berend, *The History of European Integration*, p. 164.
53 See ibid., pp. 3–4, 181.
54 Koolhaas, "Precarious Entity," p. 149.
55 Mark Swenarton, Tom Avermaete, and Dirk van den Heuvel, for instance, point out the significance of this competitive situation for the Western welfare state of the postwar era: "After the Second World War the need for reconstruction propelled economic growth and provided once again resources for welfare state expansion, while rivalry with the Communist block—the Cold War—proved imperative for a non-revolutionary route to social improvement." Swenarton, Avermaete, and Van den Heuvel, Introduction to *Architecture of the Welfare State*, London: Routledge, 2015, p. 7.

F 5.10

Left: Ronald Reagan, president of the US, 1981–89.
Right: Margaret Thatcher, British prime minister, 1979–90.

After the fall of the Berlin Wall in November 1989 and the dissolution of the Soviet Union in January 1991, the inferiority of socialism was generally considered a *fait accompli* (→ F 5.11).[57] Koolhaas was quick to draw conclusions. At the TU Delft symposium in April 1990, he said: "I think it's absolutely essential too—and I utterly fail to understand why it hasn't happened yet in some way or the other—that there should be an ideological response to the sudden disappearance of socialism, which in almost all cases has latently nourished and provided the justification for our modern architecture, whether we are open about it or not."[58]

Koolhaas does not say whether the "ideological response" to the disappearance of socialism should align to the ideology that prevailed, indicating Rossi's Il Palazzo hotel in Fukuoka as a "possible

F 5.11

The Berlin Wall at the Brandenburg Gate, November 9, 1989.

answer to such questions."[59] Three years later, in 1993, it is the very lack of ideological commitment that he advertises as the essential merit of Rossi's project: "Il Palazzo dominates its surroundings like a samurai castle. It looks cynical—deliciously fascist. [...] Rossi did not do the interiors or the nightclubs that invade the stoic exterior, but his envelope has a weird fascination. It is pure emblem, Rossi without ideological ballast: hyper-Rossi."[60] Koolhaas adds: "It is a gene splice: Rossi's poetry, first stripped of ideology, then boosted by Japanese ingenuity."[61] Globalization of architecture, Koolhaas suggests, implies the abandonment and principle insignificance of (obsolete) ideological content. A nod to *The Gay Science* at the end of the essay seems to propose a Nietzschean recovery from false scruples.

56 Berend, *The History of European Integration*, p. 165.
57 Ellen Dunham-Jones observed in 2014: "Ironically, if the Berlin Wall launched Koolhaas' critique of architecture, it was the Wall's demolition in 1989 that amplified the relevance of his ideas. Deng Xiaoping's subsequent opening up of the Chinese markets in 1992 with the exhortation 'Enrich yourselves!' was another accelerant. Not only had capitalism won, but the spirit of '68 had lost. Marxist critiques and labor unions were swatted away by the neoliberal consensus in favor of free markets. Notions of 'the public good' were challenged and increasingly replaced by privatization and emphasis on 'individual responsibility.'" Dunham-Jones, "Irrational Exuberance," in *Architecture and Capitalism: 1845 to the Present*, ed. Peggy Deamer, London: Routledge, 2014, p. 155.
58 Koolhaas, "How Modern is Dutch Architecture," p. 165.
59 Ibid.
60 Rem Koolhaas, "Globalization," (1993) in *S, M, L, XL*, Koolhaas and Mau, p. 364.
61 Ibid.

Manhattanism reframed

In 1990, based on the experience of Euralille and the 1989 competitions, Koolhaas began to synthesize the architectural and urban implications of the large scale in a series of theorems. In the essay "The End of the Age of Innocence?", he singles out four of them, referring explicitly to "Manhattan architecture" and implicitly to the principles of "Manhattanism" as outlined in *Delirious New York*: first, "the impossibility of organizing, with a single architectural gesture, a building disconnecting the autonomy of its parts"; second, "the liberating potential of the elevator (through its ability to establish connections more mechanical than architectural) which allows architects to step outside traditional categories of composition"; third, "the façade that can no longer divulge anything about the interior of the building, its center being too far removed from the skin. The idea of the interior and the exterior become two separate projects"; fourth, "these buildings enter—by moving beyond the good and the bad—a dangerous domain, by the single fact of their size: their impact is wholly independent of their quality."[62]

The first and third points refer to the relationship between the program and the exterior. Articulating the "extremely large, bizarrely composed programs" as form and negotiating the corresponding autonomy of parts with the formal unity of the exterior is perhaps the most important theme of the 1989 competitions.[63] The heterogeneity of the interior tends to oppose the notion of unity in terms of both program and form. That applies in varying degrees to the projects for Zeebrugge, Karlsruhe, and Paris. Each is marked by the tension between a single dominating volume and its inner complexity and variety. At the "Anyone" conference, Koolhaas pointed out the consequences of large-scale building for the city as a whole: "It is no longer a public realm but rather a series of privacies that are inflated to the scale of the public or in some cases to the semipublic."[64] In *Delirious New York*, this issue was addressed repeatedly and extensively.[65] The suggestion of conceiving the European city in such terms was new. Koolhaas proposed Atlanta—as a city without a center—and the periphery of Paris as alternative models. The proposition clearly opposed the notion of the historic urban center as the sole urban paradigm, following up on his criticism of the IBA or the "Reconstruction of the European City." While the European advocates of the planned city failed to see their limited range of influence with regard to the new urban dynamics, Koolhaas argued, America with its unplanned sprawls had discovered "a vast new area of possibilities and freedom."[66]

Glee and horror

Until the early 1990s at the very least, Koolhaas harbored ambiguous feelings towards the new urban paradigm and the freedom it provided, in a manner that was reminiscent of the early 1970s when he started his research on Manhattan.[67] In his 1988 lecture on Atlanta, he said: "It is intriguing how Portman's Architecture, and American Architecture in general, presents the unusual combination of hard-headed business sense with fantastic or imagined solutions; and how this reveals a major tragedy: in spite of its enormous architectural display, it has no architectural quality whatsoever."[68] When talking to Hajime Yatsuka in 1989 about the growth of the urban periphery and how architects had neglected it, Koolhaas explained: "it's very hard, say, when I drive around Atlanta, to actually find things beautiful or exciting—and the same goes for the *villes nouvelles* around Paris— you could go around saying everything is ridiculous there, or you could also surrender to the feeling that maybe it's a very unique landscape that is emerging there."[69]

When the topic was touched upon in 1992, his collocutor, Alejandro Zaera Polo, observed that Koolhaas seemed to accept "a certain cultural and productive condition" as a frame for his work, asking how he articulated this acceptance in his judgements. Koolhaas' reply betrays unease: "I have an interest in professional activity, I want to build: to a frightening extent that means basically accepting most of the time. [...] I'm certainly provoked in a deep sense by this acceptance. It engages me. In that sense, my interest in Atlanta, for example, is ambiguous. Basically I try to postpone the moment of judgement as long as possible to derive as many influences as possible from it."[70] Zaera Polo persists: "But how do you deal ideologically with this acceptance? We are talking about the possible end of [the] public realm,

62 Koolhaas, "The End of the Age of Innocence?" p. 165.
63 Rem Koolhaas in an interview with Paul Vermeulen. *De Standaard* (April 28/29, 1990) (author's translation).
64 Koolhaas, "Precarious Entity," p. 149.
65 For instance, in the paragraph on "Control," Koolhaas writes: "no longer does the city consist of a more or less homogeneous texture [...] but each block is now alone like an island, fundamentally on its own." Rem Koolhaas, *Delirious New York: A Retroactive Manifesto for Manhattan*, New York: The Monacelli Press, 1994, p. 97. See also the paragraph on "Venice," pp. 120–23.
66 Rem Koolhaas, "Atlanta," in *S, M, L, XL*, Koolhaas and Mau, p. 112.
67 In a 1973 letter to Adolfo Natalini of Superstudio, he wrote: "I am in the grip of a sudden, frenzied investigation and design of the particular, delirious public interiors, embarrassingly 'pathetique' [...] all 'hysterical architecture.' All these things are very enjoyable, but also very nerve-racking, because of the absence of reliable criticism and comment; it is hard to know whether all the interests which have insinuated themselves into my preoccupations, are good or stupid or both." Quoted in Roberto Gargiani, *Rem Koolhaas/OMA: The Construction of Merveilles*, Lausanne: EPFL/PPUR, 2008, p. 15.
68 Koolhaas, "Atlanta," p. 106.
69 Yatsuka, "'I combine Architectural with Specificity with Programmatic Instability,'" p. 11.
70 Alejandro Zaera Polo, "Finding Freedoms: Conversations with Rem Koolhaas," in *El Croquis*, 53 (1992), p. 22.

of civil society, of the humanist thought [...] Should this acceptance be considered as revolutionary or as complacent?" Koolhaas rejects both options, explaining: "We are seduced; we feel simultaneously glee and horror. [...] It's not complacency but fascination, and in fascination there is always an element of surrender."[71]

Surrender continues to be a recurring motif in Koolhaas' writings, right up to the most recent essays included in *S, M, L, XL*. "Beyond signature," he suggests, "Bigness means surrender to technologies; to engineers, contractors, manufacturers, to politics, to others."[72] In essence, it is the "surrender to the definitive instability of life in the Metropolis" advertised in *Delirious New York* and conflated later on in the metaphor of the surfer.[73] Surrender implies relinquishing control.[74] According to the "Bigness" manifesto, the loss of control that large buildings entail allows for subversion and freedom. Bigness, Koolhaas proclaims, "is the one architecture that engineers the unpredictable. Instead of enforcing coexistence, Bigness depends on regimes of freedoms, the assembly of maximum difference. Only Bigness can sustain a promiscuous proliferation of events in a single container."[75] In his lecture at the UIMP in 1988, Koolhaas qualifies the urban development of Atlanta as "extremely subconscious" and the "importance of abandoning the claim of control" as one of the lessons European architects may learn from.[76] Like *Delirious New York*, these and other statements from that period indicate the underlying paradigm of the surrealist concept of the unconscious as a liberating force.

Koolhaas posited "Bigness" and the "American skyscraper" in opposition to the European megastructures of the 1950s and 1960s, referring explicitly to "Yona Friedman's *urbanisme spatiale*" and, more implicitly, to the work of Constant and Archigram.[77] The very immensity of such propositions, Koolhaas argued, secured them the status of unrealized dreams, whereas the high-rise of the New World had been able to materialize the potential of the large scale long before that; like New Babylon or the Walking City, the skyscraper, as advocated by Koolhaas, internalizes urban life. Otherwise, the difference is plain. In "Bigness," Koolhaas was proposing neither perpetually growing, all-encompassing structures nor a distinction between modular systems of a supporting frame and flexible infills, but a discrete, compact building with a single unifying skin.[78] And yet even in "Bigness" there was a surviving remnant of the antiauthoritarian promise that many megastructures held: the promise of suspended control, of possible "difference," of freedom. Koolhaas has never been explicit about what is specifically to be expected of this liberation: whether it was supposed to provide a surrealist experience confined to people's hours of leisure, or whether it was ultimately expected to induce revolutionary dynamics of social change, as conjectured by the early surrealists. The repeated suggestion of a "social condenser" as a model for metropolitan culture (in *Delirious New York*, in the project statement for Park de la Villette, etc.); Koolhaas' criticism that Rowe had amputated the social agenda from modernism; the criticism from his Dutch peers of adhering to modernist forms without ideological content; and the same criticism leveled at deconstructivist architecture:[79] all this lends itself to the inference that Koolhaas felt obliged to some sort of Left-leaning agenda or ideology. In 1977, Kenneth Frampton exercised cautious precision in ascribing to the yet unbuilt oeuvre a "radical potential which is critical of communism in its ascendancy as it is of capitalism in its decline."[80] George Baird, in the same issue of *Architectural Design*, identified OMA's projects as "social condensers" that were "revolutionary" in their fusion of modernism and metropolitan ambitions.[81] Patrice Noviant, in 1981, read OMA's work "as an activation of modern architecture in its *dimension as a social project*," implying a "sign of the desire for social change."[82]

A parable of unbridled neoliberalism

S, M, L, XL was difficult to understand in such terms. Many reviews, attempting to guess what kind of society the book would suggest, diagnosed a general correspondence with the ideas of the political Right. Koos Bosma wrote: "If we trace the successive levels of scale of Typical Plan, Bigness and Generic City, we get a parable of unbridled neoliberalism—a consumer world without cultural ambitions."[83]

71 Ibid., pp. 22–23.
72 Koolhaas, "Bigness," in *S, M, L, XL*, Koolhaas and Mau, p. 514.
73 Koolhaas, *Delirious New York*, p. 157.
74 "[…] it [Bigness] can only be achieved at the price of giving up control." Koolhaas, "Bigness," p. 513.
75 Ibid., p. 511.
76 Koolhaas, "Atlanta," p. 112.
77 Koolhaas, "Bigness," p. 504.
78 According to Reyner Banham, it is precisely these qualities that distinguish enormous buildings like the Vertical Assembly Building at Cape Canaveral from the megastructure. Reyner Banham, *Megastructure: Urban Futures of the Recent Past*, New York: The Monacelli Press, 2020, p. 13. First published in 1976.
79 In 1985, Koolhaas explained: "The modernism of Colin Rowe—because in his own way he has been one of the messengers of modernism— has been completely amputated of its social program, the social for him being the pinnacle of the ridiculous." Patrice Goulet, "La deuxième chance de l'architecture moderne …," in *L'Architecture d'Aujourd'hui*, 238 (1985), p. 9 (author's translation).
80 Kenneth Frampton, "Two or Three Things I Know About Them: A Note on Manhattanism," in *Architectural Design*, 5 (1977), p. 317.
81 George Baird, "Les Extrêmes Qui se Touchent?" in *Architectural Design*, 5 (1977), pp. 326–27.
82 Patrice Noviant, "Rem Koolhaas: Un européen sans humour," in *Architecture Mouvement Continuité*, 54/55 (1981), p. 59.
83 Koos and Bosma, "S, M, L, XL," in *Planning Perspectives*, 12 (January 1997), p. 118.

The encouragements for a reading of this kind are varied. The propagation of the large scale itself emulated the neoliberal quest for maximum size—ever larger corporations, the expansion of budgets, markets, labor pools, and turnover—informing the process of European integration. The commitment is underlined by the dimensions of *S, M, L, XL* as a book, as well as its weight and bold typography. A gusto for diagrams and figures, large ones in particular, is accompanied by a tone of managerial fact-checking that is new in Koolhaas' writings. Ellen Dunham-Jones rightly observed in 2014: "Although literally referring to big buildings, Bigness also indirectly includes the big business, big government, big firms, and big money required to make them."[84] In the opening passages of "Bigness," Koolhaas observes: "It seems incredible that the size of a building alone embodies an ideological program."[85] Richard Sennett wrote in a review from 1996: "*S, M, L, XL*, Rem Koolhaas' new book, asks designers to think big. Although commercial architects don't need such encouragement, socially conscious architects do. The culture of the Left since the 1960s has emphasized smallness. Small is the dimensions of the *gemeinschaft*, of face-to-face relations in communities where people know each other. Small is also the dimension that least risks damaging others when designing their dreams."[86]

Koolhaas, who in the 1980s used to ridicule the small-scale policy of what was known as "Dutch structuralism," could scarcely fail to see this dimension of his argument.[87] The occasional references to Nietzsche and writings like *Beyond Good and Evil* and *The Gay Science* seem both a late retort to the humanism advocated by Van Eyck and Hertzberger and an alignment with a neoliberalist ideology that does away with "social thought." In accordance with both the latter and with Nietzsche's philosophy of strength, Koolhaas warns that deplorable yet inevitable social consequences of the new economic paradigm need to be embraced: for example, when identifying the idea of large-scale architecture as an "amoral domain" that breaks "with ethics,"[88] when suggesting that "we have to dare to be utterly uncritical,"[89] or when stating that the new architecture "excludes, limits, separates from the 'rest.'"[90] "Housing is not a problem," he states, obviously referring to contemporary slums, while declaring the modernist tradition of socially engaged mass housing to now be obsolete: "It has either been completely solved or totally left to chance; in the first case it's legal, in the second case 'illegal.'"[91] The role of this envisaged urbanism is not to reform and correct: "Redefined, urbanism will not only, or mostly, be a profession, but a way of thinking—an ideology: to accept what exists."[92]

In 2014, Dunham-Jones drew a parallel to the economic restructuring of the United States: "Instead of empowering communities to envision and administer their future, he [Koolhaas] calls for a 'Lite Urbanism,' the equivalent of deregulation. And much like Wall Street's arguments for the deregulation of banking at the time, Koolhaas bathes Lite Urbanism's promises in glowing, liberatory, progressive ambitions, while omitting reference to its risks of abuse by the interests of short-term capital."[93] For Jacques Lucan, the built version of the Euralille and OMA's Congrexpo showed that Koolhaas' writings, specifically the essay "Bigness," needed to be taken literally. His 1995 review concludes by reconsidering *Delirious New York* and the closing paragraph on the Downtown Athletic Club as a metaphor: "What did it announce? It announced, according to Koolhaas, the separation of mankind into two tribes: the tribe of those capable of utilizing all the equipment of modernity, i.e. the 'bachelors' of the club; and the tribe comprising the rest of the traditional human race, i.e. those who do not belong to the club."[94]

>I don't want to call it unity

The concept of "Bigness," Koolhaas explains in *S, M, L, XL*, is intended as a polemic, leveled against "contemporary doctrines that question the possibility of the Whole and the Real as variable categories and resign themselves to architecture's supposedly inevitable disassembly and dissolution."[95] The passage seizes on an often-quoted lament from 1993, in which Koolhaas addresses the influence of French theory on architecture: "There is Derrida who says that things cannot be whole

---

84 Dunham-Jones, "Irrational Exuberance," p. 157.
85 Koolhaas, "Bigness," p. 496.
86 Richard Sennett, "The Dialectics of Scale," in *Harvard GSD News* (Summer 1996), p. 45.
87 "Over the last 20 years, large sectors of the architectural world in Holland have been in the grip of the local doctrine of Dutch Structuralism. Claiming Aldo van Eyck's Orphanage and allied researches of the Dutch 'Forum' Group as their ancestors, the doctrine preaches that, in the name of humanism, all larger institutions can and should be broken up into smaller components which re-establish the human scale—as if each institution, whatever its nature, will become more transparent, less bureaucratic, more understandable, less rigid through the mere fact of subdivision." Rem Koolhaas, "Urban Intervention: Dutch Parliament Extension, The Hague," in *International Architect*, vol. 1 (1980), p. 50.
88 Koolhaas, "Bigness," p. 502.
89 Rem Koolhaas, "Whatever Happened to Urbanism?," in *S, M, L, XL*, Koolhaas and Mau, p. 971.
90 Ibid., p. 967.
91 Koolhaas, "The Generic City," in *S, M, L, XL*, Koolhaas and Mau, p. 1253.
92 Koolhaas, "Whatever Happened to Urbanism?" p. 971.
93 Dunham Jones, "Irrational Exuberance," p. 159.
94 Jacques Lucan, "The Voluntary Prisoner of Architecture," in *Domus*, 774 (September 1995), p. 26.
95 Koolhaas, "Bigness," p. 503.

anymore, there is Baudrillard who says that things cannot be real anymore, there is Virilio who says that things cannot exist anymore, and then there is chaos theory which also has a strong impact. I think—since 1989—there has been an onus on architecture to oppose these tendencies."[96]

The criticism clearly challenged the theoretical affiliations of close peers like Tschumi, Eisenman, and Nouvel. Its scope, however, was broader, and aimed at the whole current of deconstructivism along with the penchant of contemporary Japanese architecture towards chaos theory. In a 1990 interview, Koolhaas criticized approaches of this kind as nonsensical simulations of chaos and its aesthetics,[97] establishing—as he put it two years later—a "naive, banal analogy between a supposedly irregular geometry and a fragmented world, or a world where values are no longer anchored in a fixed way."[98] The formal inventions of constructivism, suprematism, and cubofuturism had been spurred on by the socialist, anti-bourgeois ideology of the 1920s. Apparently due to its lack of similar ideological underpinnings, Koolhaas dismissed deconstructivist architecture as "ultimately [...] decorative."[99] He was not alone in this view: the 1988 MoMA show, for example, was criticized for establishing a formalist relation between deconstructivist architecture and its constructivist precedents. Mary McLeod wrote in 1989: "Like postmodernism, this new tendency rejects the fundamental ideological premises of the modern movement: functionalism, structural rationalism, and faith in social regeneration. [...] Finally, deconstructivism, too, emphasizes the formal properties of architecture. (In this regard, it is ironic that Russian constructivism, with its political and social programs, is considered a primary source.)"[100]

Unlike McLeod, Koolhaas was not criticizing the predisposition of deconstructivist architecture to enter into the cycles of capitalist commodification and consumption, but rather—like the formal adherence to early modernism in the Netherlands—condemning its use of forms that lack any proper ideological basis. There is no direct mention in "Bigness" of either the theory of deconstruction or chaos theory, but phrases like "paroxysm of fragmentation," "phony disorder," and "orchestration of chaos" obviously stand for the architecture inspired by these schools of thought.[101] Koolhaas calls their approach a defense line of dismantlement, referring to the failure of (European) architects to cope with the large-scale building. He accuses these architects of making false promises by manufacturing "compositions of almost laughable pedantry and rigidity, behind apparent wildness."[102]

By contrast, it is the seeming inoffensiveness of the large-scale building, Koolhaas assures us, that allows for "programmatic hybridizations/proximities/frictions/overlaps/superpositions"—that is, in his terms, destabilization and subversion.[103]

Koolhaas' critique of deconstructivism was anticipated by a shift in OMA's work away from volumetric disintegration. In a 1990 interview, Koolhaas explained his commitment to the large scale as a means to "break with deconstructivism."[104] The statement shows that he did wish to distance his work from what was generally taken to be deconstructivist architecture, and, implicitly, that he did consider the architecture of OMA, too, as marked—at least partly—by deconstructivist characteristics. What did he mean by "deconstructivist"? His writings and statements from the mid-1990s indicate that Koolhaas saw fragmentation, denying the integrity of the (volumetric) whole, as *the* quintessential trait of deconstructivist architecture. In 1996 he explained: "The whole idea of Bigness rests on a debate centered around deconstructivism. I wanted to emphasize the possibility of creating whole things."[105] In "Bigness" the term "whole" appears five times, precisely in this sense. In that same year he clarified the matter to Zaera Polo: "I think Bigness is useful in terms of counteracting the obsession with traces and ghosts and in terms of overcoming the obsession with the fragmentary or the chaotic."[106]

Much of this was already implicit in Koolhaas' comments and essays from 1989–90. Taken together, these pronouncements make it possible to outline two opposing groups of issues, terms, and ideas that can be synthesized in two equations. The first equation groups deconstructivism and its emulation of chaos; the past of (and reference to) modernist architecture; and, in one way or another, the existence of socialism as a lost precondition:

> deconstructivism = chaos = modernist references = being modern = language of dead ideology

---

96 Kuhnert, Oswalt, and Zaera Polo, "Die Entfaltung der Architektur," p. 24 (author's translation).

97 Nikolaus Kuhnert and Philipp Oswalt, "Die Inszenierung der Ungewißheit," in *Arch+*, 105/106 (1990), p. 70.

98 Zaera Polo, "Finding Freedoms," p. 29.

99 Ibid.

100 Mary McLeod, "Architecture and Politics in the Reagan Era: From Postmodernism to Deconstructivism," quoted in *Architecture Theory Since 1968*, ed. K. Michael Hays, Cambridge, Massachusetts: The MIT Press, 2000, p. 691. The essay was first published in 1989.

101 Koolhaas, "Bigness," p. 506.

102 Ibid., pp. 505–07.

103 Ibid., pp. 506–07.

104 Chantal Béret, "Rem Koolhaas: La condition métropolitaine," in *Art Press*, 148 (1990), p. 19.

105 Isabelle Menu and Frank Vermandel, "Interview: Rem Koolhaas," in *Euralille: The Making of a New City Center*, ed. Espace Croisé, Basel: Birkhäuser, 1996, p. 62.

106 Alejandro Zaera Polo, "The Day After: A Conversation with Rem Koolhaas," in *El Croquis*, 79 (1996), p. 23.

The second equation groups the large scale as a means of reestablishing the integrity of the whole; a principle absence of references and precedents; the idea of contemporary architecture as an architecture that is not indebted to the past; and the ideology of surrender which is equivalent to embracing the "new" ideology embodied by the large scale:

> large scale = wholeness = no references = being contemporary = surrender to new ideology

The first group contains what Koolhaas wished to overcome, while the second is what he envisaged as a new agenda. The issue of fragmentation is implicit in both, either in terms of form (deconstructivist architecture) or in terms of program (large-scale building). Koolhaas considered the fragmentation of program to be an inevitable consequence of the large scale. The idea is already latent in 1990's "The End of the Age of Innocence," and Koolhaas is fully explicit about it in his lecture at the "Anyone" conference in 1991, referring to OMA's design of the National Library in Paris: "Perhaps the most profound statement of the building, and the one that gave me the most ideological satisfaction, occurred when all of the plans were superimposed in a single image because the image represented the coexistence of all these elements in a single building. I think that after all the dis's or ab's of the 1980s, it seemed to open the possibility that, in spite of the fragmentation, there could also be a legitimate and interesting attempt to assemble fragments in order to create a precarious entity—I don't want to call it a unity—to organize in a single building the coexistence of these autonomous elements without doing any injustice to their specificity or their programmatic delicacy" (→ F 5.12).[107] The overtones of societal analogy and metaphor are distinct. The cohesion of the whole is provided by the enclosure, within which no assimilation is enforced. This allows for diverse entities, which may develop freely, both in terms of program and form. The apparent ideological alignment of the large scale with the new economic paradigm, Koolhaas seems to be saying, is compatible with the principles of the Left: nonconformist freedom, the open society, pluralism, even subversion.

In "Bigness," Koolhaas insists on the difference between the autonomy of parts and fragmentation: "This impossibility [of controlling architecture with a single gesture] triggers the autonomy of its parts, but that is not the same as fragmentation: the parts remain committed to the whole."[108] Koolhaas does not explain what this commitment consists of. Perhaps he had OMA's two library projects for

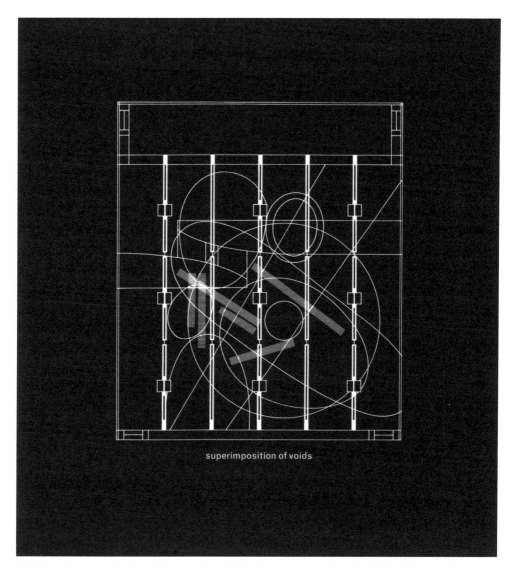

OMA/Rem Koolhaas, National Library in Paris, 1989. The superimposition of voids (public spaces).

Paris in mind. At the National Library, OMA's design articulates the functional diversity through the formal diversity of the voids. But the voids don't really read as fragments, appearing instead as variations of a common theme inscribed in an entirely homogeneous overall structure. As far as the Jussieu project is concerned, it is the formal unity of the "pliable surface" and the spatial continuity it permits that connects the two libraries housed by the building. For any large-scale project of this period, however, the primary agent of unity is the clear-cut outline of the exterior's volume. An exterior composed of multiple volumes virtually disappeared from the office's production for several years.

107 Koolhaas, "Precarious Entity," p. 155. On the fragmentation of the program, see also p. 151.

108 Koolhaas, "Bigness," p. 500.

P 7.1 Park level.

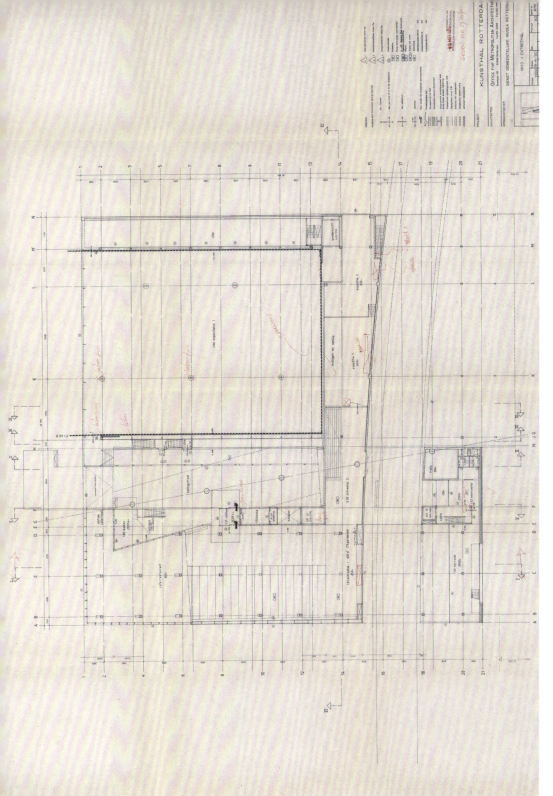

P 7.2 Level of the main entrance.

P 7.3   Dike level.

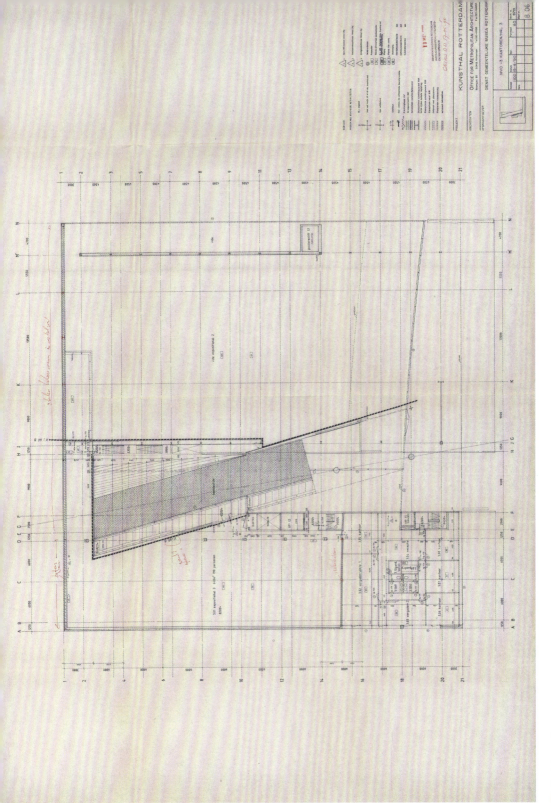

P 7.4 Third level.

P 7.5 Roof.

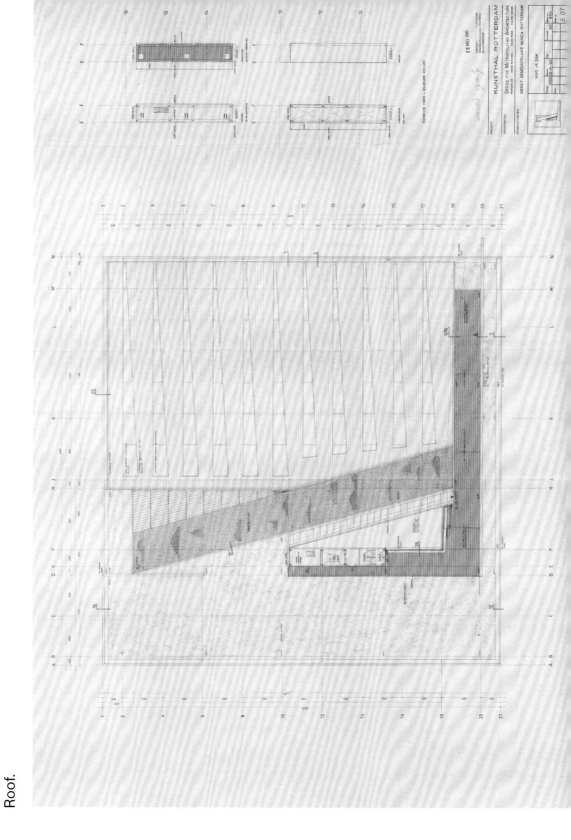

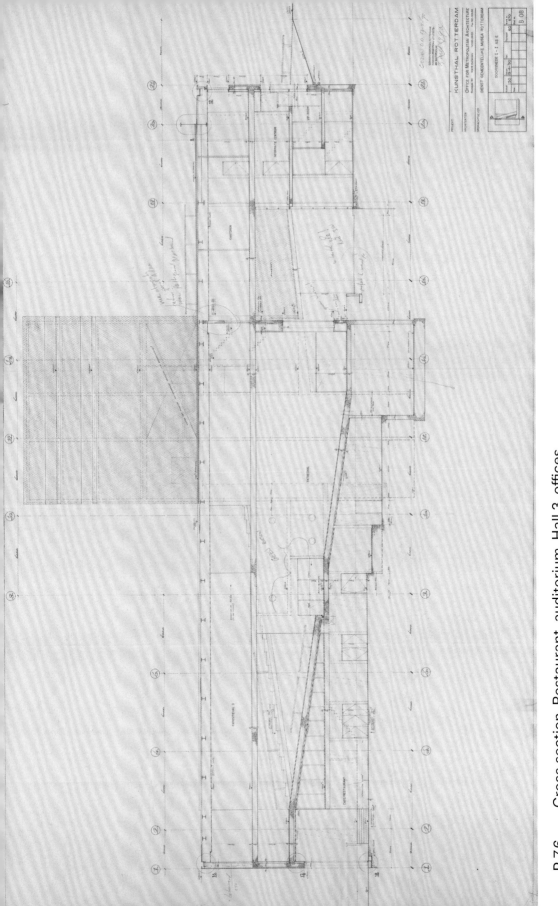

P 7.6　Cross section. Restaurant, auditorium, Hall 3, offices.

P 7.7 Cross section. Hellingstraat and service wall of Halls 1 and 2.

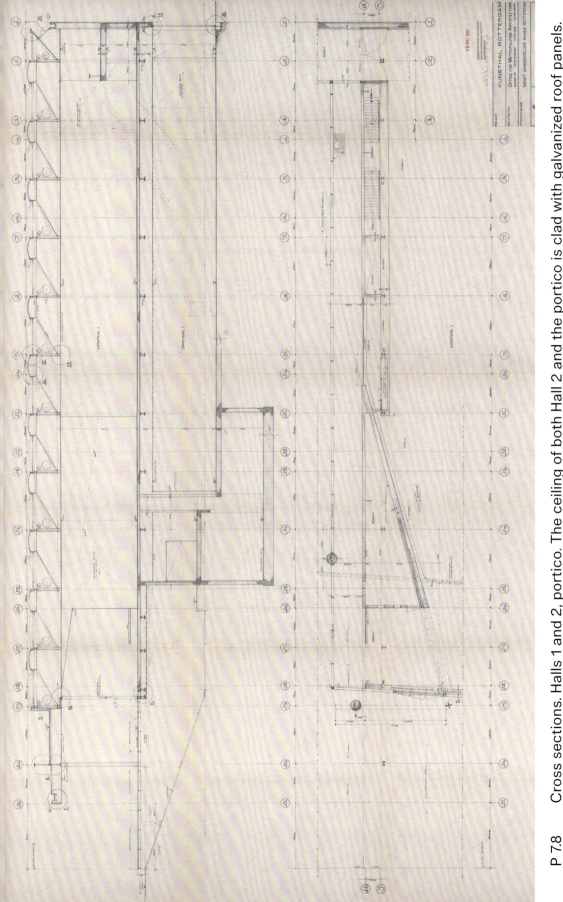

P 7.8   Cross sections. Halls 1 and 2, portico. The ceiling of both Hall 2 and the portico is clad with galvanized roof panels. The terrace of the portico is raised 60 cm above street level.

P 7.9   North elevation. Cross section along the service road, looking south.

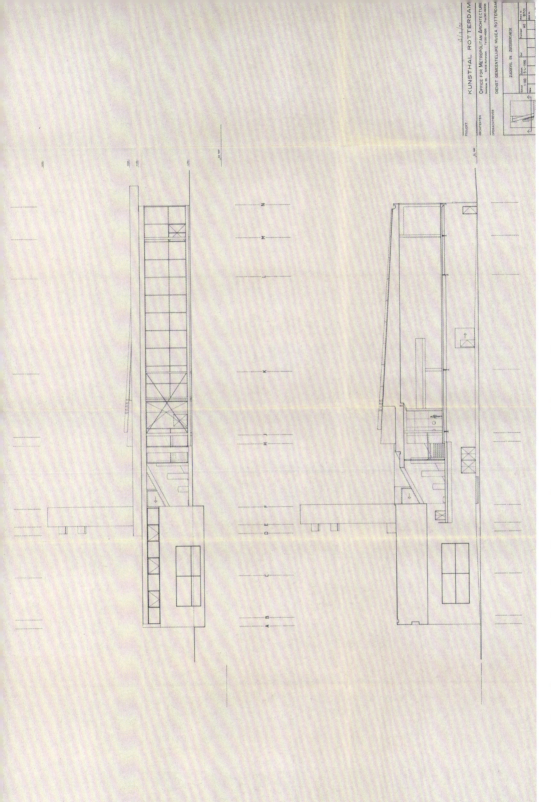

P 7.10　South elevation. Cross section along the service road, looking north.

P 7.11　East and west elevation.

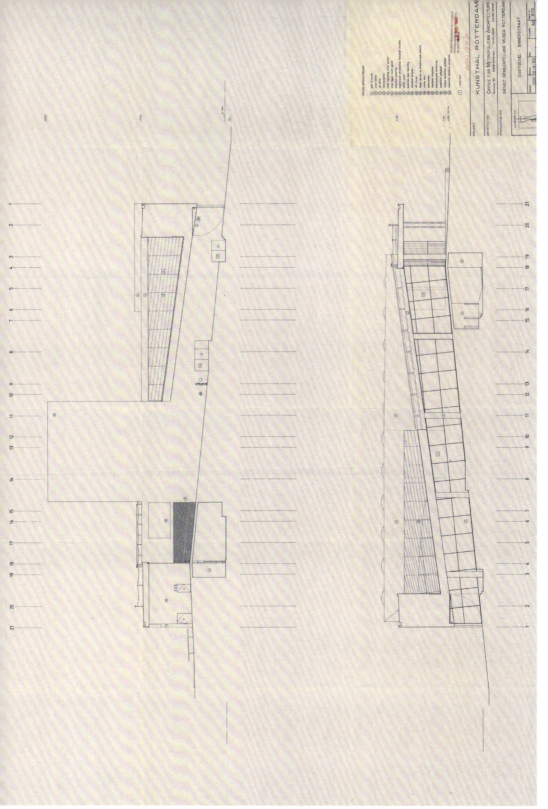

P 7.12 Elevations along Hellingstraat.

P 7.13 Finishes of Hall 2. The ceilings of both Hall 2 and the portico are clad with galvanized roof panels.

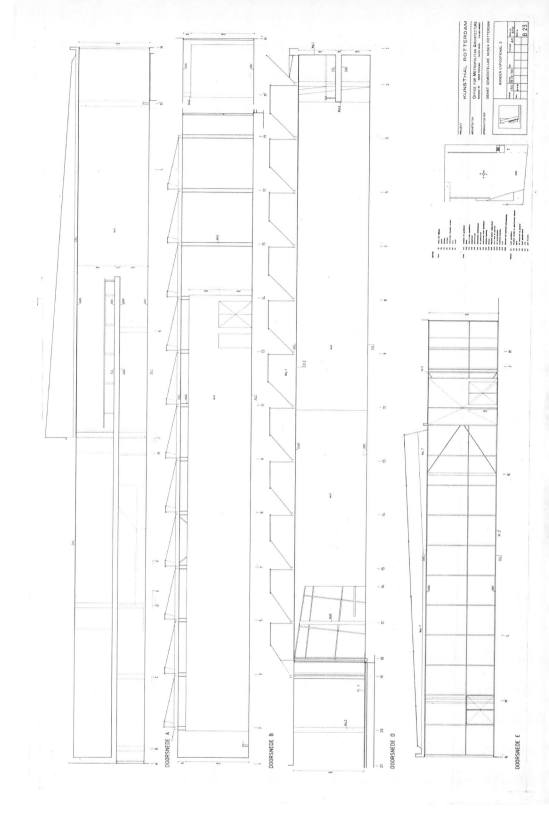

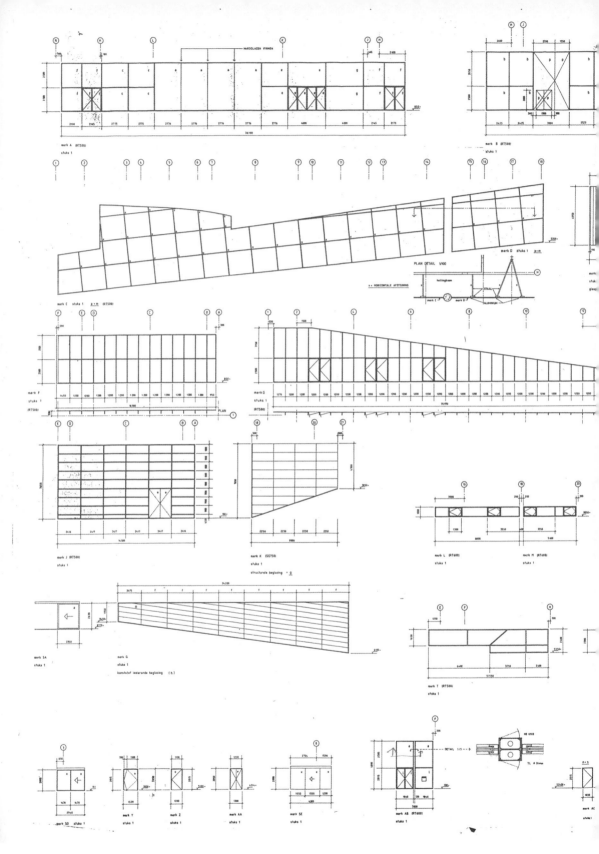

P 7.14 Overview of the fenestration.

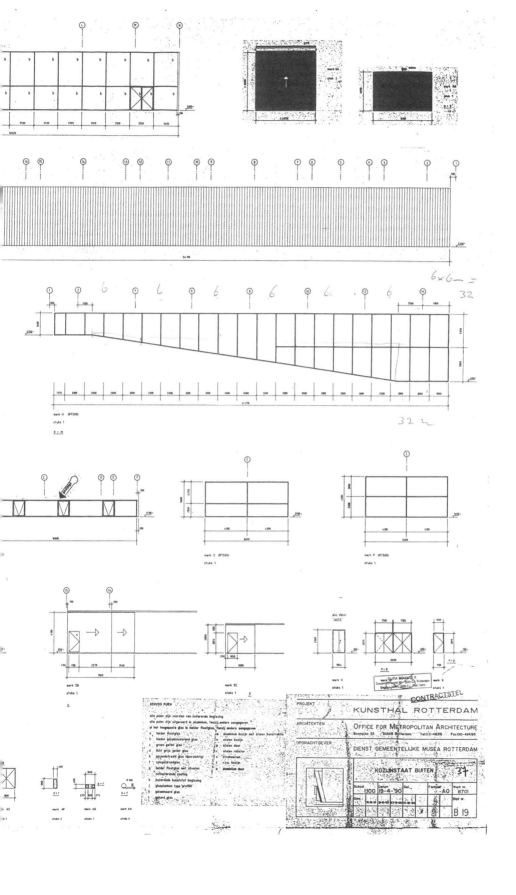

Fragmentations
The Development of the Design 1989–92

6

Suddenly—how am I to convey it?
Well, suddenly the darkness turned into water.

Joseph Conrad

To what extent did OMA's December 1988 scheme for the Kunsthal reflect Koolhaas' take on the rise of deconstructivist architecture and the recent turn towards European integration? Although not a large project in itself, the scheme contained three ideas that were at the core of how Koolhaas envisioned revising OMA's approach to architecture and urbanism at the time. First, creating architectural form on the basis of the program's spatial organization in order to exorcise the ghosts of the discipline's modernist past. In December 1988, this was plainly a dismissal of what Koolhaas saw as the deconstructivist dependence on early avant-garde architecture. It went hand in hand with OMA's sudden and emphatic embrace of the present, facilitated, for its part, by Europe's recent spirit of optimism. Second, organizing the circulation in the shape of a spiral, or loop, conceived as an internalized public space. This idea was of strategic importance for the large building in epitomizing Europe's "new ambition," because it compensated for the urban isolation that its insular autonomy entailed. Third, using the compact volume as an antidote to formal fragmentation, confining the articulation of programmatic complexity and diversity—which, according to Koolhaas, was a direct consequence of the "Very Large Building"—to the space contained by a single unifying volume.

In addition to the volumes themselves, the envelopes of OMA's sea terminal in Zeebrugge, the National Library and the Jussieu Libraries in Paris, the Nexus Housing project in Fukuoka, and the convention center in Agadir are marked by the concern for formal cohesion, and even more so—about one decade later—the largely homogeneous skins of buildings like the Dutch embassy in Berlin (1997–2003), the Central Library in Seattle (1999–2004), the Casa da Musica in Porto (1999–2005), the CCTV Headquarters in Beijing (2002–12), the Wyly Theatre in Dallas (2004–06), and the National Library in Qatar (2005–17). Conversely, the interior and exterior of the ZKM media center in Karlsruhe, the Congrexpo in Lille, and the Educatorium in Utrecht (1993–97) contest the sense of unity implied by the compact outlines of the overall volume, and emphatically so. As of 1989, the design for the Kunsthal took a similar turn. Between December 1988 and the completion of the arts center in October 1992, rather than tuning down the formal fragmentation of parts—initially limited to the hybrid structural system—Koolhaas and his collaborators increased it to an unprecedented extreme. There is no indication, however, that Koolhaas believed the Kunsthal, Congrexpo, and media center to be laggards that were failing to keep pace with OMA's new architectural agenda. In *S, M, L, XL*, all four projects feature prominently. Almost eighty pages are dedicated to the ZKM media center in Karlsruhe, which is more than to any other project, built or unbuilt. The picture of the bleeding corpse at the end of the chapter next to the sardonic obituary "Passion Play" bespeak bitter regret about the loss of the project in June 1992.[1] The retrospective view tends to underestimate how groundbreakingly new these designs felt at the time of their inception. There was a vast gulf both to OMA's composite volumes of the 1980s and to contemporary deconstructivist designs, the volumetric rigor of OMA's recent prisms and ellipsoids visibly contrasting with the "apparent wildness" of projects by Hadid, Coop Himmelb(l)au, Libeskind, Gehry, and Eisenman. Further, the schemes for the sea terminal, the media center, the Congrexpo, and the National Library had been entirely cured of the air of nostalgia. The accent was now on newness, eschewing familiar images of the modernist past.

Projects within the project

Throughout November and the first half of December 1988, the collaboration between Koolhaas and Hoshino was particularly close, and the outcome was achieved on the basis of self-imposed goals and the pursuit of genuinely architectural ideas. This was to change in the following year. Especially in the first half of 1989, a great deal of inspiration for significant developments came from outside: from Ove Arup, above all, but also from Wim van Krimpen, the Kunsthal building committee, and municipal authorities. Adjustments to the program, changes imposed by savings, and the specifications of the structural system and the building services all needed to be incorporated into the design. Given the increasing number of planners and third parties involved, the architects were flooded with ever new requirements, proposals, and "solutions." The various parts and facets of the project threatened to develop a dynamic of their own. In the case of the structural system, Koolhaas embraced these dynamics in principle, since the structure, or more precisely its visible parts, were meant to display their independence and relative "freedom" within the hybrid whole. Conversely, Koolhaas wished the building services to interfere with the interior as little as possible. Technical installations were generally kept out of sight, concealed in the voids of coffered ceilings and hollow walls.

Most of the changes and details added between January and October 1989 were a direct response to Arup's proposals and Van Krimpen's wishes. In February, Van Krimpen compiled a further list of requirements, which in all likelihood was included in the revised and definitive brief for the arts center.[2] Most of these stipulations regarded the building's technical infrastructure and equipment, entailing a significant cost overrun during the tendering stage. At a meeting of the Building Committee on April 7, Koolhaas dubbed Van Krimpen's revised program a "program of wishes," anticipating that the technical requirements would be irreconcilable with the agreed cost limit.[3] In order to allow for different events taking place parallel to each other, Van Krimpen stressed the need for the exhibition halls to function independently of one another in terms of lighting, darkening, heating, ventilation, and broadcasting facilities. For the same reason, each exhibition area was to be provided with a separate entrance and a cash desk as well as direct access to the bathrooms and cloakroom. In a set of plans dating from February 25, a triangular ticket booth has been introduced in Hall 2, providing an optional second entrance to the building. Most consequential for OMA's design, however, was Van Krimpen's persistent demand that permanent "closed walls" be provided and any nearby columns removed in order to facilitate the hanging of pictures. The latter wish ran counter not only to OMA's concept of varying the character of the main circuit on the basis of the visible structural parts, particularly the columns, but also to the idea of keeping the visual relation between the different levels and ramps as fluid as possible. Despite these concerns, OMA introduced two walls in Halls 1 and 2: one adjacent to the interior half of Hellingstraat and another adjacent to the void connecting the two spaces along the east facade, creating a narrow space of two stories that Koolhaas dubbed "Gallery Van Krimpen" (→ F 6.1).[4] The wall separating Halls 1 and 2 from Hellingstraat, for its part, absorbed ten out of a total of eleven columns aligned alongside the western perimeter of the two spaces. In Hall 3, two of the three rows of columns—at the center and along the western facade—were omitted (→ F 6.2).[5] In the auditorium, three columns in the central row were truncated to avoid blocking the view. Now that the column's lower part had been removed, cable trusses connected the bottom of the pendent "stump" to the tops of the lateral columns (→ F 6.3).[6]

    The riser shafts and suspended ceilings and ceiling voids of the main galleries required for the ducts of the mechanical services further increased the isolation of the circuit's different parts, notably along the building's central section parallel to Hellingstraat. To

1 Rem Koolhaas, "Passion Play," in S,M,X,L, Koolhaas and Bruce Mau, New York: The Monacelli Press, 1995, pp. 762–63.
2 "Re: Kunsthal, Rotterdam / List of requirements with regard to the optimum use of possibilities on the basis of the drawings already developed by OMA, dated 25 January 1989," February 18, 1989. OMAR 1436. The revised program of requirements had been announced at the building committee meeting on January 25.
3 Verslag van de 9e Bouwcommissie Nieuwbouw Kunsthal, April 7, 1989. OMAR 1518.
4 Wim van Krimpen in an interview with the author, July 28, 2020.
5 OMA, "Kunsthal Rotterdam, Nivo +3," February 25, 1989. OMAR 1749.
6 See axonometric view by Copro bv, 3-D CAD tekenburo. OMAR 1850.

F 6.1

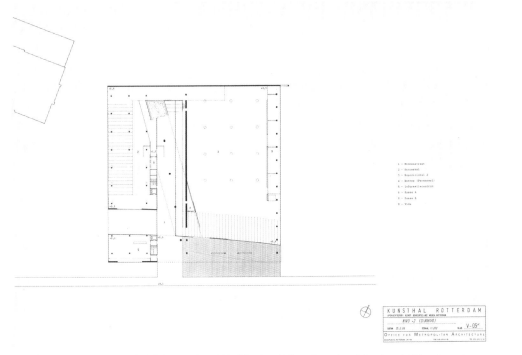

OMA/Rem Koolhaas, Kunsthal, February 25, 1989. Dike level. The triangular ticket booth (8) projects into Hall 2 (3). Two additional walls embrace the center of the space. Adjacent to Hall 2 is the void dubbed "Gallery Van Krimpen" (9).

F 6.2

OMA/Rem Koolhaas, Kunsthal, February 25, 1989. Third level. Hall 3 (1) with only one row of columns.

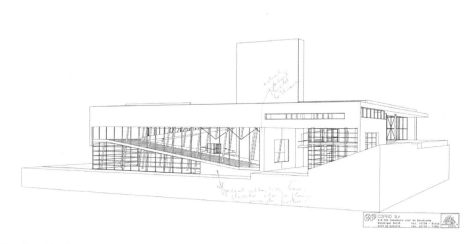

OMA/Rem Koolhaas, Kunsthal, January 1989. View from the southwest. Cable trusses support the truncated columns in the auditorium.

accommodate the main plants of the mechanical services, a basement of about 600 square meters was added to the north of the service road along the east to west axis of the building (→ P 6.1). From the mechanical room, both main sections of the building are served by vertical risers. To the east, a shaft at the back of Hall 1 connects to the ceiling of the exhibition space. Having crossed the ceiling of Hall 1, parts of the ducts enter a further riser shaft adjacent to Hellingstraat and then spread out in the ceiling of Hall 2. To the west, a vertical riser connects the basement to all the levels of the building. Two additional risers are located at each side of a large window to the rear of the auditorium's stage area. The two main risers are enclosed by continuous service walls flanking both sides of Hellingstraat (→ F 6.4). By mid-July 1989, the service wall for the eastern section accommodates not only the riser but also a fire escape, the pockets of sliding fire doors, and a large alcove to store a curtain. To the south, the wall adjacent to Hall 2 clads the diagonal edge of the Skew Ramp, cutting into the space, thereby forming the triangular ticket booth. The 2.5-meter-wide service wall for the western section stretches all along Hellingstraat and is filled with a host of secondary functions: in addition to a large riser shaft, a fire escape, the vertical circulation of the office block, an elevator, a control

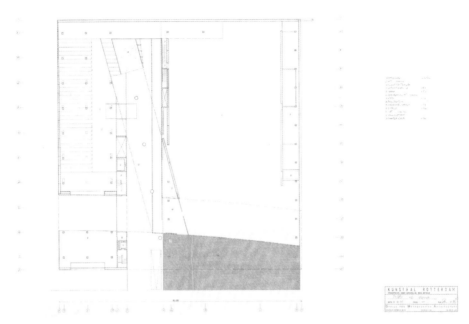

OMA/Rem Koolhaas, Kunsthal, October 10, 1989. Service walls on both sides of Hellingstraat. The alcove to store the curtain is above the ticket booth (5) of Hall 2 (4).

room overlooking the auditorium, and the ticket counter for the main entrance. The "Engineering Report" produced by Arup in July proposes to supply and extract humidified and filtered air from the ceiling in all three exhibition halls. In the remainder of the building, the services are limited to mechanical ventilation. In the auditorium, air is supplied directly from the service wall and through the front of the steps of the seating, the ducts running in a suspended ceiling above the restaurant, while being extracted at both sides of the window behind the stage.[7] Underfloor convectors—radiators in the offices—are distributed along the exterior walls to provide heating. Above the level of the roof, the main service wall is transformed into a service tower, an approximately 10-meter-tall and 13-meter-long steel frame construction to house air-cooled condensers, the extract plant for the kitchen and toilets, and the supply and extraction plant for Hall 3. At a meeting of the building committee in July, Koolhaas suggested using the two main sides of the tower as billboards.[8] Elevations that show the tower advertising a motor show and an exhibition on designer Isamu Noguchi illustrate the idea (→ F 6.5)[9]

Three systems for a start

The layout of the building services and the structural system was devised by Ove Arup's London office, essentially in the period from December 1988 to April 1990. Arup's team was headed by structural engineer Cecil Balmond. Between April 1989 and January 1990, Arup produced drawings in a scale of 1 to 100 of the structure and the building services along with a number of corollary reports, revising the concept of both the structure and the services repeatedly and substantially. During those years, Koolhaas commuted between Rotterdam and his private house in London. Koolhaas himself has pointed out that he regularly worked with Balmond on the project of the Kunsthal during these London stays, stressing the "intense interaction" with the structural engineer and its significance for the design.[10] In a conversation with the author, Koolhaas explained: "Cecil had a very strong architectural ambition. Therefore, the most fundamental discussions were with Fumi[nori Hoshino] and with him. About every issue. About how present the structure should be. How interesting the absence of structure

F 6.5

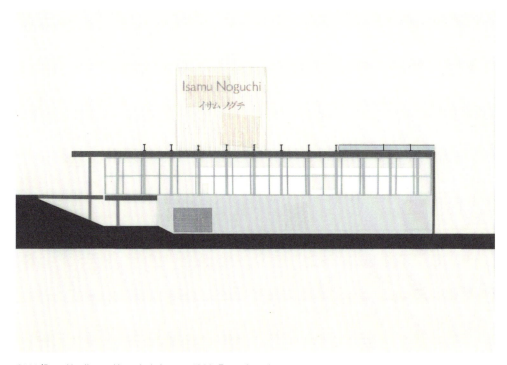

OMA/Rem Koolhaas, Kunsthal, August 1989. East elevation.

7   The ducts supplying the seating were eventually concealed in the void between the steps and the floor slab so as to avoid a coffered ceiling in the restaurant.
8   "Verslag van de 12e Bouwcommissie Nieuwbouw Kunsthal," July 20, 1989. OMAR 1519.
9   OMA, "Kunsthal Rotterdam, DO 14," July 19, 1989. OMAR 3276.
10 Conversation with the author over Zoom, February 8, 2023.

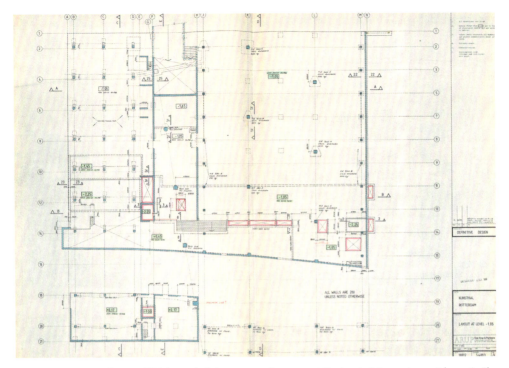

Ove Arup, Kunsthal, August 1989. Layout of the structural system at the level of the restaurant (axes A–E) and Hall 1 (axes J–N). 4.5 m grid between axes B and D. 6.0 m grid between axes J and M.

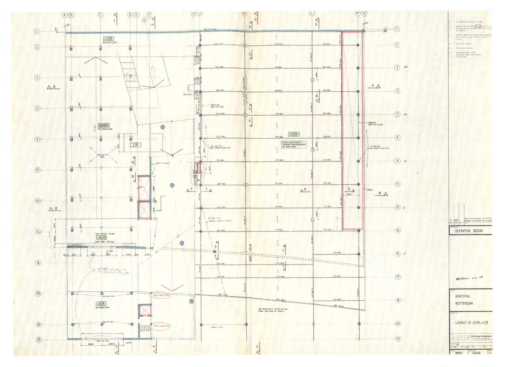

Ove Arup, Kunsthal, August 1989. Layout of the structural system at the level of the auditorium (axes A–E) and Hall 2 (axes J–N). The Skew Ramp on *pilotis* is framed by axes F and H.

F 6.8

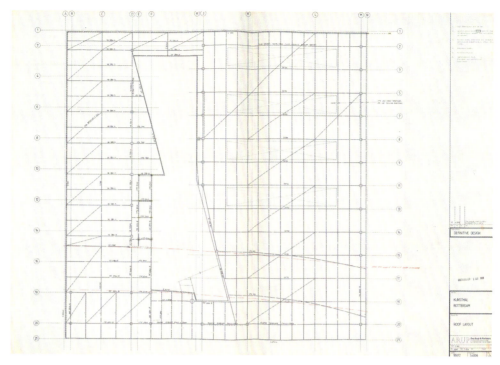

Ove Arup, Kunsthal, August 1989. Layout of the structural system. Roof.

was or not. So it was really fundamental in that sense."[11] The collaboration extended continuously from Kunsthal I to OMA's project for the NAi, to the design for Kunsthal II and its implementation. In principal accordance with OMA's December 1988 scheme, Arup's drawings provide a tripartite structural system: in the eastern section, based on a grid of 4.5 by 4.5 meters, there would be a steel frame construction; the western section, based on a grid of 6 by 6 meters, would feature a construction in reinforced concrete; in the central section, Hellingstraat and—carried by a single row of columns arranged diagonally—the Skew Ramp would likewise be in reinforced concrete (→ F 6.6–6.10).

    The engineering report produced by Arup in July 1988 specifies structures of cast-in-situ reinforced concrete for the western and central section: columns with square cross sections (400 by 400 mm) and—renouncing an intermediate layer of beams—flat slab floor plates of varying strength.[12] Whereas the columns of the office block are vertical, those of the auditorium are perpendicular to its slope, extending at this oblique angle to both the restaurant below and to Hall 3 above. In the central section, five columns with circular cross sections—

11 Conversation with the author, Rotterdam, February 15, 2023.
12 Ove Arup, "Engineering Report. Definitive design: Kunsthal Rotterdam," July 1989.

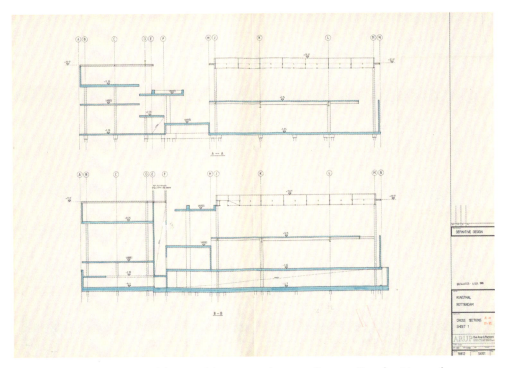

Ove Arup, Kunsthal, August 1989. Layout of the structural system. Cross sections (east to west). The Skew Ramp on *pilotis* is framed by axes F and H. The exoskeletal girder on top of Hall 3 (axis D) is on the roof.

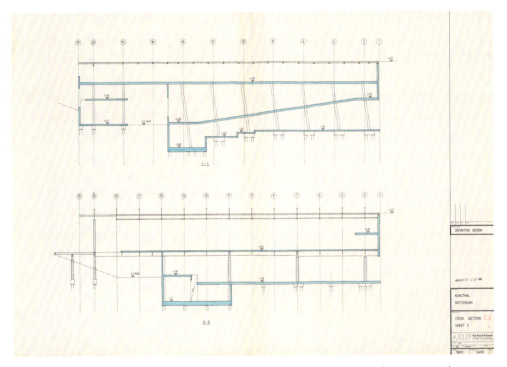

Ove Arup, Kunsthal, August 1989. Layout of the structural system. Cross sections (north to south). Above: the restaurant, auditorium, and Hall 3. Below: Hall 1 and the steel plate girders spanning Hall 2.

i.e. *pilotis*—support the Skew Ramp, which, in turn, is reinforced by upstand beams above the columns and along the edges of the roof garden (→ F 6.7, 6.9).

To the east, there are two rows of lateral columns with H-shaped cross sections, one aligning along Hellingstraat's interior half, the other flanking the eastern facade (→ F 6.6–6.7).[13] At the time, the intention was to encase the columns in concrete, clearly to satisfy the requisite fire safety measures. The same applies to the four columns at the center of Hall 1, which were initially envisaged as cruciform but by the end of January 1989 had been replaced by large steel columns, likewise with H-shaped cross sections (→ F 6.6). A system of primary trusses (800 to 1000 mm in height) running north to south and secondary beams (600 mm in height) running east to west spans the space (→ F 6.9–6.10). For the floor of Hall 2, the report specifies a "[c]omposite steel/concrete structure" consisting of a metal deck and a 160-millimeter in-situ lightweight concrete slab.[14] Both the principle of a lost shuttering combined with in-situ concrete and the minimal dimensions of the floor slab would eventually be implemented, allowing Hall 1 to achieve its maximum height.[15]

For a couple of months, a continuous roof plate in concrete was envisaged, but by July 1989 the planners had settled for a solution in steelwork, probably in order to save costs.[16] In August, a roof plan shows a continuous steel frame of common rolled I-beams (200 to 280 mm in height), partly supported by larger primary beams (450 mm in height) (→ F 6.8). Thirteen huge steel plate girders—partly exoskeletal, with I-shaped cross sections—free-span the 31.5-meter distance between the lateral columns of Hall 2 and the portico (→ F 6.10).[17] Above the exhibition hall, four of the intervals were intended to serve as skylights.

The construction Arup devised for reducing the loads of the two massive slabs of the north facade was a hybrid in its own right. The challenge was not to compromise the image of a "floating mass"

13 Ove Arup, "S002, P4, with comments to Arch 30/06/89"; "S4004, first issue to arch 29/7/89"; "S4005, issued to all parties 29/7/89." Arup London Archives. The columns would be encased in concrete, obviously to ensure the requisite fire protection. On this issue see Fuminori Hoshino/OMA, "Comments about technical drawings for Definitive Design of Kunsthal," dated August 8, 1989. Arup London Archives.

14 A report in January already specified a composite construction: "The slab between these elements is cast using a metal deck as a permanent shutter and for tensile strength." Ove Arup and Mirvat Bulbul, "Kunsthal: St. [Structural] Report and queries," January 30, 1989. OMAR 3267.

15 This is evident from the "as built" plans of Rotterdam's public works department. IUW, "Vloer 5.300+ STR H–N/1-19-20," August 28, 1993. Stadsarchief Rotterdam.

16 A switch from concrete to steel was one of the moneysaving options listed at the meeting of the building committee in June. "Verslag van de 11e Bouwcommissie Nieuwbouw Kunsthal," June 23, 1989. OMAR 1518.

17 Ove Arup, "Kunsthal Rotterdam: Roof Layout," August 1989. OMAR 1761.

and to avoid conventional columns as visible supports, which would make the wall look like a giant beam in a trilithic system. As of January, the eastern edge of the north facade was held in place by a freestanding open-web truss. The vertical truss looks like a willfully improvised amendment, somewhat reminiscent of the canopy of Stirling's Staatsgalerie in Stuttgart (→ P 6.11). Two further structural members with an improvised appearance echoed the motif: first, an exoskeletal plate girder—ultimately painted orange—protruding from the roof of the portico, whereby the length of the cantilever precisely matches the depth of the vertical truss (→ P 6.10);[18] second, another exoskeletal plate girder on top of Hall 3; like the vertical truss, the girder helps to hold the floating wall of the north facade in place; thanks to the girder from which the facade is suspended, it was possible to omit one— and at a later stage, two—of the columns of Hall 3 (→ F 6.9). In Hall 1, the western row of the central columns was shifted to the north by 4.5 meters, likewise in support of the massive exterior wall above; with the distance to the facade reduced to 3 meters, the cantilevered primary beam was able to carry part of the load (→ F 6.6, 6.10). The architects willingly embraced the spatial implications of the shifted columns. Hoshino recalls Koolhaas referring disapprovingly to the initial arrangement of four central columns as a "box in a box."[19] The new solution proposed six columns, arranged in two rows of three—five of them located in Hall 1 and one in the adjacent loading area; shifting one bay between the two rows permitted the latent division of the space into a central zone and a peripheral one to be suspended, or, in Koolhaas' own words: "I suggested asymmetry here. I really disliked these regular column grids because they create compartments."[20]

Due to the weakness of the ground and the shallow water table, the report suggests precast concrete piles for the foundations to be driven 4 meters into the sand. Concrete caps would be a meter deep, connecting the piles to the columns and loadbearing walls, except for the 0.8-meter-thick floor slab of the basement where no pile caps were needed. A foundation plan dating from August shows that the number of piles per cap varied between one and five according to the loads expected (→ F 6.11).[21] The plan betrays the extra loads of the "floating wall" carried (in the western section) by the column of Hall 3 supporting the exoskeletal girder (axes 2 and D) and (in the eastern section) by the central column of Hall 1 supporting the cantilevered beam (axes 2 and K). The difference in stress, however, was not meant to be visible. All the slanted columns of Hall 3 and the auditorium have identical cross sections, and so do the five columns of Hall 1, contrasting the

F 6.11

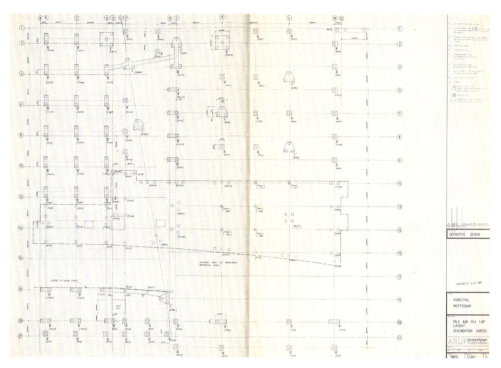

Ove Arup, Kunsthal, August 1989. Layout of the structural system. Piles and pile caps of the foundations.

constructive and formal autonomy of structural elements, such as the open-web truss of the north facade, the cantilevered steel plate girder of the portico, and the cable trusses of the auditorium.

The means of securing stability can vary according to the type of construction. Arup's July report specifies diagonal bracing for the steelwork of both the roof and the lateral columns. The composite steel and concrete structure of the floor of Hall 2 acts as a rigid body plate. The stability of the building's western section in concrete relies on a "combination of frame action and shear walls."[22] In his 2007 book *informal*, Balmond explains that the slanted columns and the floor slabs of the auditorium and restaurant act in tandem as moment frames.[23] The July report further mentions shear walls contributing to the stability of other areas of the building. Most of the walls that are

18 This is evident from the north elevation, which shows both elements projected onto one another to suggest a single structure. OMA, "Kunsthal Rotterdam: Aanzichten Noord & Westzijde," January 25, 1989. OMAR 4138. The same configuration appears in the elevations of February 25, 1989. OMAR 1749.
19 Interview with the author, July 25, 2017.
20 Conversation with the author, Rotterdam, February 15, 2023.
21 Ove Arup, "Kunsthal Rotterdam: Pile and Pile Cap Layout," August 1989. OMAR 1761.
22 Ove Arup, "Engineering Report. Definitive Design: Kunsthal Rotterdam," section 1.6.5, July 1989.
23 Cecil Balmond, in *informal*, Munich: Prestel, 2002, p. 81. Toni Adam recalls that the city's public works department initially opposed the solution: "They [the columns] are full of steel. So they could not put the concrete in the moulds, there was so much steel [...] That is why the construction engineers [of the public parks department] didn't want to do it." Interview with the author, September 25, 2018.

F 6.12

OMA/Rem Koolhaas, Kunsthal, August 1989. South elevation.

suitable for resisting shear forces are distributed along the building perimeter, notably the concrete walls adjacent to the service road and the lower half of the eastern facade. To be sure, the division of the structure into three parts was not and never would be consistent. The continuous wall along the north facade, that along the service road, and the continuous steel frame of the roof extend over all three sections of the building, while the Skew Ramp interferes with both neighboring structures. But these inconsistencies are neither sloppiness nor compromise. To generate a visible variety of form was the one and only purpose of the structure's conceptual tripartition, rather than a neat division into technically autonomous units.

 Like the structure

The Kunsthal II project was published in a series of articles in autumn 1989.[24] The illustrations shown at this point, along with a set of drawings by OMA dating from October 10, give an idea of how far the design had evolved (→ F 6.4–6.5, 6.12–6.15).[25] Details in a scale of 1 to 5 specify the layering of floors, ceilings, and walls throughout the building, providing a first comprehensive catalog of the materials selected for the construction.[26] For the three exhibition halls, suspended ceilings in plasterboard have been proposed. Walls would be clad in a wood-based material covered with cloth, as Van Krimpen wished. Parquet is listed for the floors of Halls 2 and 3, likewise in accordance with Van Krimpen's preferences; the floor of Hall 1 would be "epoxy," while "rubber" was planned for the slope of the auditorium and parquet for its seating area; Hellingstraat would be made of asphalt, and metal grating would be used for the platform of the portico.

Obviously, the floor was not supposed to stress the continuity and coherence of the circuit by dint of a single, homogenous surfacing, neither should it celebrate the autonomy of each space with a "singular" finish. Like some parts of the structure, each flooring tends to extend to more than just one space. As with the slanted columns extending from the restaurant to the auditorium to Hall 3, the epoxy extends from the auditorium to Hall 1, the asphalt of Hellingstraat continues beyond its transparent partition, and the parquet of Hall 2 reappears in Hall 3. The drawings show the main service wall clad with translucent plastic panels, visible on all three levels of the building's western section. In as much as this wall fosters the spatial diversity of the circuit, it resonates with the diversity implied by the binary pattern of the Moebius-looplike facades. And yet the service wall was implied neither by this motif nor by the "spiral in four separate squares." Like the structure with slanted columns, the service wall is a largely autonomous part of the design.

In a building like the Palazzo del Te in Mantua, too, spaces connect to continuous enfilades, although their shape and size varies, as does the treatment of the walls, ceilings, and floors. The Kunsthal is a different story, of course, among other things because its plan largely denies the autonomy of spatial units along the circuit. There are neither doors nor lintels nor thresholds. Exterior walls, both glazed and solid, extending from one space to the next without interruption consistently blur the transition between adjacent spaces—for instance, between Hall 2 and Hall 3, or between Hall 2 and the corridor leading to the auditorium—following the principle of *enjambement* as understood by Le Corbusier. Along the route, the opening between two adjacent spaces is always maximized, stressing the confluence of the spatial sequence. In the late 1980s, this combination of spatial continuity and diversity is likely to have appeared inconsistent. Many of the best-known more recently built museums have shared the essential "white

24 OMA/Rem Koolhaas, "Le Kunsthal de Rotterdam," in *Architecture Mouvement Continuité* (September 1989), pp. 30–33; OMA, "Three Projects for Rotterdam," in *Quaderns*, 183 (1989), pp. 85–93; John Welsh, "Double Dutch," in *Building Design* (December 1989), pp. 18–24.

25 OMA, "Kunsthal Rotterdam: DO," October 10, 1989. OMAR 1759.

26 OMA, "Kunsthal Rotterdam: Opbouw details," October 10, 1989. OMAR 1764.

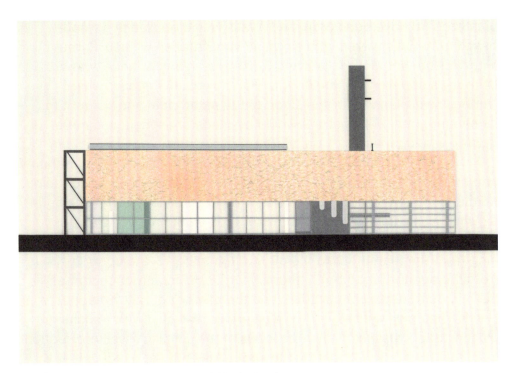

OMA/Rem Koolhaas, Kunsthal, August 1989. North elevation.

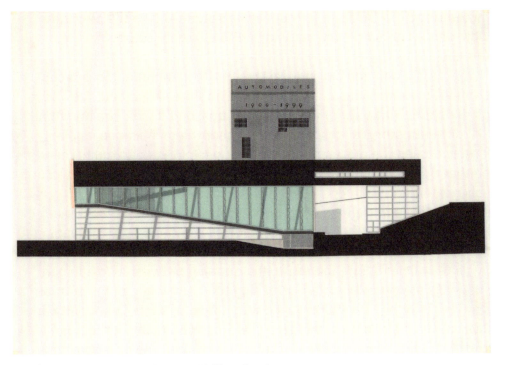

OMA/Rem Koolhaas, Kunsthal, August 1989. West elevation.

F 6.15

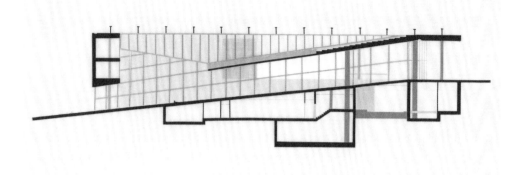

OMA/Rem Koolhaas, Kunsthal, August 1989. Cross section. Hellingstraat.

continuity" of the interior, examples being the museums by Hollein (Mönchengladbach, Frankfurt), Ungers (Frankfurt), Meier (Frankfurt, Atlanta, De Moines), Piano (Houston), Isozaki (Los Angeles), and Dissing+Weitling (Düsseldorf). In the Kunsthal, visitors would find the modernist vocabulary of spatial continuity and unity, but it would be "contradicted" by the diversity of materials.

The exterior of the Kunsthal, too, saw a pronounced "estrangement" of parts. The details listed in October specify exposed concrete as the material for the massive walls of the east and west facade, and "natural stone" for those of the north and south facade. The elevations in the September issue of *AMC* are collages (→ F 6.5, 6.12–6.15). Black cardboard represents the wall of the west facade, gray cardboard the wall of the east facade, and a yellowish, veined material the stone cladding of the north and south facades. The design of the large glass walls is based on two main aims: to distinguish between the building's eastern and western sections, in manifest correspondence to the hybrid structure; and to distinguish between areas belonging to the circuit and the remainder of the spaces with extensive fenestration, such as the restaurant and the office block. In the building's eastern section, the glass walls of Hall 1, Hellingstraat, and the south and east side of Hall 2 form a coherent sequence of a somewhat Miesian looking fenestration composed of huge square window units. But in the October plan, the fenestration of the east facade was replaced by a wall of channel glass planks, turning the glazed surface into yet another element of its own (→ P 8.16). The fenestrations of the western section, in turn, are based on a grid of approximately 0.9 meters (vertical intervals) by 2.25 meters (horizontal intervals). In the case of the west-facing glass wall of the office block, the grid is fully developed. Only horizontal mullions are provided for the restaurant, and for the auditorium they are solely vertical. As a consequence, the generous rhythm of 2.25 meters, combined with unrestricted height, contrasts with the 0.9-meter intervals present in the two other fenestrations. The contrast is further increased through the use of filigree open-web trusses and green tinted glass for the auditorium in contrast to the clear glass envisaged for both the offices and the restaurant. The large dimensions of the window units for the auditorium are akin instead to the fenestration of the building's eastern section, i.e. to spaces that belong to the circuit, just like the entrance hall.

The cantilevered steel plate girder of the portico rests on three (encased) steel columns and a concrete column hidden in the office block (→ F 6.12). The columns—until February there had been two of them at the center in analogy to the central columns of Hall 1—are aligned with the structural grid of the building's eastern section. The two columns at the western margin of Hall 2 are cross braced. Together with the first *pilotis* of the Skew Ramp nearby they form a group of three with no apparent connection to the solitary column at the other end of the portico.[27] The glass wall of Hall 2, overlooking the portico, is slightly curved (→ F 6.4). Like the "hidden" northern facade of the office block's lower stories, the curve aligns with the service road at the foot of the embankment, namely its southern edge. A curtain, which could be stored in the alcove of the service wall, would make it possible to divide Hall 2 along the northern edge of the road. Together with Hellingstraat, the space enclosed by the curved glass wall and curtain—and continued by the void between the office block and the auditorium—was to evoke the image of the two crossing routes.

An explanatory note dating from February states: "Any design for the Kunsthal needs to do justice to the duality of its location: *in* Museumpark and *at* the Westzeedijk. An urban face [*stedelijk gezicht*] symbolizes its orientation towards a 'mass,' the park side implies traditional museal contemplation."[28] However, there is no explanation about what makes the south facade an "urban face." It seems that the exterior of the Kunsthal responds to its surroundings with differing degrees of formal diversity. If one equates heterogeneity with urbanity and homogeneity with contemplation, the north facade is surely the building's most contemplative side, and the fragmented structure facing Maasboulevard its most urbane. Similarly, the collage-like diversity of the west facade does reflect the simultaneous proximity of Villa Dijkzigt and Erasmus University, whereas the "quiet" of the east facade is only disrupted by the proximity of the highway.

With the methodical multiplication of finishes, rhythms (fenestration), and the "individualization" of constructive elements, which were all too evident by October 1989, OMA transferred the principle of structural hybridity to the design of the Kunsthal as a whole. It goes without saying that the diversification of parts ran counter to the legibility of the binary structure and the motif of the Moebius loop underlying the layout of the facades. The glass planks do not read as the sequel of the mullioned glass wall to the south, neither does the cladding in natural stone read as a continuation of the black concrete wall to the west. Nonetheless, each facade continued to be divided into two horizontal halves, most of them treated as pairs of dichotomous, ribbonlike strips. As with the interior, the two concepts coexisted, the tension between them left unresolved.

OMA's team

In 1989, at least four OMA staff members collaborated on the project, in addition to Koolhaas and Hoshino. Jo Schippers, a civil engineer by training, became increasingly involved over the years.[29] As a general rule, it was either Koolhaas or Schippers who attended the meetings of the building committee in the company of one further member of OMA's staff, and it used to be Schippers who represented the office in meetings with the contractor, the Rotterdam firm Dura.[30] Schippers' key responsibility were costs, the time schedule, and organizational issues. As of July 1989, Italian–Dutch architect Toni Adam served as the project manager for the Kunsthal.[31] Adam had joined OMA in 1984.

27 OMA, "Kunsthal Rotterdam. DO 05," July 19, 1989 and October 10, 1989. OMAR 3276, 1759.
28 OMA, "Kunsthal," February 25, 1989. OMAR 1794 (author's translation).
29 In a catalog for an exhibition on OMA at deSingel in 1988, Schippers is listed as a technician. Carolina De Backer, ed., *Office for Metropolitan Architecture*, Antwerp: deSingel, 1988, p. 6.
30 His name appears in the project files from May 1989 onwards. From the very beginning, it was Schippers who represented OMA in the regular meetings with the contractor Dura and the municipality dedicated to the technical details of the planning process.
31 The minutes of a meeting with the municipality in April 1989 appear to be the first time his name was mentioned in the context of the Kunsthal. OMA, "Nieuwbouw Kunsthal Rotterdam," April 11, 1989. OMAR 1520.

By 1989 he had garnered considerable experience in building, having worked on several buildings in the IJplein development and the Frederiksstraat apartment block in Amsterdam, among other projects. Moreover, just before joining the Kunsthal team he had been active on a workspace for mentally disabled people in Amersfoort, called "de Stapsteen."[32] Adam was responsible for the collaboration with Arup and the local authorities, including those departments of the municipality that were in joint charge of the structural system and building services, along with Arup. He set up and supervised a team of draftsmen within OMA. According to Adam, the first technical drawings were prepared by the recent startup Bureau Bouwkunde, a firm that offered support for architectural planning. Adam recalls that Leo van Immerzeel was recruited from this office, a draftsman who subsequently went on to prepare a large number of the detail drawings. Van Immerzeel placed his drawing table next to Hoshino for the next couple of years, giving the latter plenty of occasion to supervise his work.[33] It is evident that Koolhaas' associate Ron Steiner was involved in some of the detailing too, and according to Hoshino he did some of the earlier drawings. Isaac Batenburg, who was later hired on an interim basis, seems to have played a significant role during the construction phase.[34] The number of OMA staff members who contributed to the project, however, is much larger, and even the list of names included in S, M, L, XL seems to be incomplete.[35] Yet not a single team member worked on the Kunsthal exclusively: Hoshino was involved in the Nexus project in Fukuoka (1988–91), as was Van Immerzeel, who was also associated with the Veerplein development in Vlaardingen, completed in 1989; Adam, who was also the Museumparkproject manager, recalls having worked on other projects parallel to the Kunsthal.[36]

Models, not faxes

All sorts of sketches and drawings were produced for the Kunsthal in large numbers. Nonetheless, it seems that the primary tool for the development of the design was not drawings but models. This is indicated less by the dozen surviving models and pictures of models scattered among the papers than by the accounts given by Hoshino and Adam. Hoshino recalls having struggled throughout the process to get a hold of the project by graphic means—be it floorplans, vertical sections, perspective or axonometric drawings. Accurate 3D drawings furnished by the firm Copro were apparently supposed to clarify certain "visibilities" from specific vantage points, some of them commented upon by Koolhaas (→ F 6.3). After the summer of 1989, however, no further 3D drawings were commissioned. The fax has repeatedly been described as a medium that used to be critical for the development of OMA's designs. In a 2008 interview with Koolhaas, Mark Wigley suggests that "the fax machine is the single most important design tool in your studio."[37] Koolhaas eventually agrees, praising the format it imposes, the need to focus on "essences," the case in point that the fax "liberates one from meetings," and the continuity of focused production it induces. Hoshino recalls: "Because Rem was often away from the office it was very difficult to talk to him in person. He often took off, saying that he was reachable at this number at this hotel in Miami or wherever. So many of my colleagues in the office sent him many faxes, sometimes out of despair. But I couldn't send him models which were crucial for this project. Somehow, he kept on coming to me and the models I had made, so that we could discuss about the Kunsthal. But I never really knew beforehand when he would come exactly. So I needed to be ready all the time to discuss with him whenever he showed up. Whatever the issue was, I got used to finding two or three at-least-reasonable solutions, paying attention to the consequences for the rest of the design, and keeping the dossier in a pile. Whenever Rem came, I grabbed the whole pile and went through it with him."[38] The faxes exchanged on behalf of the Kunsthal are legion, but the number of those exchanged with Koolhaas on design issues appears to be relatively small. As it seems, the model was the favored tool for testing ideas and taking major decisions. Hoshino recalls: "we looked at it [the model], we talked about it, and at that moment we took the decisions. Of course, some of the issues we could solve in 2D; we couldn't make models all the time, and we didn't have 3D on the computer. Then, of course, we could make a sketch and based on the sketch we could make decisions. But the crucial issues we checked on the model."[39]

32 Interview with the author, September 25, 2018. Adam recalls that the building was visited by Van Krimpen, who was particularly fond of its interior due to the closed walls and skylights.
33 Interviews with the author, July 25, 2017 and September 25, 2018.
34 Hoshino in an interview with the author, July 25, 2017. Batenburg's name recurs in the OMAR files.
35 Koolhaas and Mau, *S, M, L, XL*, p. 1275. Missing on the list are, for instance, Maartje Lammers and Alexa Hartig, who were mentioned by Hoshino and Adam, and Jan Verwijnen, who is listed in the minutes as the Kunsthal's project manager between February and May 1989.
36 Interview with the author, September 25, 2018.
37 Mark Wigley, "Rem Koolhaas and Mark Wigley in Discussion," in *OMA: Office for Metropolitan Architecture, Rem Koolhaas. Casa da Música*, ed. Fundacão Casa da Música, Porto: Fundacão Casa da Música, 2008, p. 169.
38 Interview with the author, July 25, 2017. The interview is also the source of the subsequent comments by Hoshino.
39 Ibid.

Back to full force

Between January and October 1989, virtually all significant changes to the design were reactions to proposals by Arup, the authorities, and the client. Areas untouched by external interference—such as the fenestration—saw few changes over a period of nine months, and those that did occur were relatively cautious. The absence of initiative on the part of the architects is obvious if compared to the somewhat radical redevelopment of the design between November 1989 and April 1990, which was almost exclusively driven by the initiative and architectural ambitions shown by OMA. One possible explanation is that much of Koolhaas and Hoshino's attention had been absorbed by other projects from the spring to the winter of 1989: Hoshino was taken up with the Nexus Housing project in Fukuoka, completed in 1991; Koolhaas—Fukuoka aside—was focused on developing Euralille and the 1989 competitions, notably Zeebrugge, Karlsruhe, and Paris, with deadlines set between the beginning of April and mid-August.[40] But a number of other projects are also likely to have consumed a certain amount of Koolhaas' energy and time; two competitions for an office complex at Frankfurt Airport and a school for civil engineers in Paris, as well as an urban study for Antwerp called "Stad aan de strom," were all submitted in 1989, and the Parisian villa was completed in 1991.[41]

In November 1989, the municipality set March 1, 1990 as the deadline for delivering specifications regarding the tendering procedure for the Kunsthal.[42] This meant for OMA that the design needed to be as advanced and "buildable" as possible by that point. Once the drawings and specifications for the tendering were submitted, major changes would be less likely to get approved. Over the following two months or so, Koolhaas and his collaborators not only worked out the construction of the Kunsthal in more detail, they also substantially redesigned many parts of the project. The intensity of the endeavor, its often experimental character, and the partly unexpected outcome have much in common with the "feverish" rush for a new scheme in November/December 1988. OMA submitted the drawings for the tendering and building application with a delay of six weeks.[43] The drawings that were eventually issued, dated April 19, 1990, comprise floorplans, sections, and elevations in a scale of 1 to 100, elevations of the interiors in a scale of 1 to 50, as well as twenty-four details in a scale of 1 to 5 (→ P 7.1–7.14).[44] The plans specify much of the construction of the envelope along with the finishes for the interior. Ove Arup delivered the definitive design of the structural system and the services in January.

The completion of the definitive design marked the end of the most intense collaboration between Arup and OMA. Arup and the planning section of Rotterdam's public works department then switched roles, as had been agreed one year previously by the municipality and OMA. By May 1990 at the latest, all the technical drawings of both the structural system and the building services, including the specifications for the bidding process, had been furnished by municipal engineers, and Arup's task was limited to assessing their propositions as consultants.[45] The first pile was driven into the ground on June 8.[46]

Much of the project's development between summer 1990 and fall 1992 dealt with the "hidden" depths of its construction and technical equipment. And yet the construction, for its part, was—and was meant to be—largely visible and thus an integral part of the design to be worked out in all its spatial, material, and technical complexity. The ubiquitous intersections between the interior and exterior, the numerous nonorthogonal intersections, the extreme diversity of materials and constructive systems: all this required an unusual amount of detailing. Exceptions were the rule. But the work was not limited to routine problem-solving that would bring the project of April 1990 "under control," not even during the two years and five months while the Kunsthal was under construction. To some extent, the increase in detail went hand in hand with a further increase in diversity that would strain the relative autonomy of the various parts in terms of their construction and form.

The development of the project from 1990 onwards may seem inconsistent with Koolhaas' critique of deconstructivist architecture as far as the issue of fragmentation was concerned, all the more so as his idea of creating a new whole was already discernible in some of OMA's competition entries in 1989. In the case of the Kunsthal, rather than disappearing, fragmentation was—once more—being transformed.

---

40 The three deadlines were April 1 (Zeebrugge), July 7 (Paris), and August 20 (Karlsruhe). See Holger Schurk, *Projekt ohne Form: OMA, Rem Koolhaas und das Laboratorium von 1989*, Leipzig: Spector Books, 2020, p. 136.

41 Koolhaas mentions the two lesser known competitions in a 1989 interview with Marta Cervelló. Marta Cervelló, "I've always been anxious with the standard typology of the average architect with a *successful* career," in *Quaderns*, 183 (1989), p. 80.

42 Minutes of the fifteenth meeting of "Bouwcommissie Nieuwbouw." OMAR 1519. The meeting took place on November 21, 1989.

43 See the minutes of "Bouwcommissie Nieuwbouw" meetings on November 21, 1989 (OMAR 1519), March 16, 1990 (OMAR 1521), and April 6, 1990 (OMAR 1521).

44 OMAR 1784, 1786, 2847. Details by Stadsarchief Rotterdam (box 4).

45 The first structural drawings by the Rotterdam public works department date from May 1990. The drawings were carried out by the ingenieursbureau utiliteitsbouw- en waterbouw (IUW, Office for Utility and Hydraulic Engineering) and the ingenieursbureau staal- en werktuigbow (ISW, Engineering Office for Steel Construction and Toolmaking). OMAR 1583, 1785.

46 Hélène Damen, "Bouw Kunsthal gestart," in *De Architect* (July/August 1990), p. 9.

The assemblage of "fragmented" volumes was being translated into collages of essentially two-dimensional planes. In a brief but astute review of the Kunsthal, Terence Riley wrote in 1992: "The intention seems to have been to diminish the significance of the building's form to magnify the importance of the facades as screens. In a sense, the figure of the building is transferred to the facades."[47] "Figure" here refers to the outlines of volumetrically complex designs like the Netherlands Dance Theater or Villa dall'Ava. In retrospect, OMA's elevations of the NAi seem to anticipate this kind of transfer: the inner assembly of volumes with heterogeneous skins is projected onto the transparent screen of the facades, turning them into images of collages. The facades of the ZKM media center in Karlsruhe are likewise based on this idea, with respect to the extent to which they display the inner prism, its openings, and structural components. At the Kunsthal the constellation is different, as there is no dichotomy between a containing and contained volume. In principle, each main space touches the facades directly with two or three of its sides. The layout and detailing of the facades appear to adopt and transfigure the projected image of inner complexity of the NAi or the media center, while the degree of formal fragmentation matches the most disintegrated composite volumes of OMA's earlier work, as if to deny all claims of unity that the singleness of the prismatic volume seems to imply.

Inventory of problems

A note by Koolhaas, dated January 6, 1990, reads: "To all collaborators of the Kunsthal project: Since we are involved in a very intense effort to complete the design issues before 25th January, it is crucial that we are in the office together during these hours. It is therefore crucial that the work starts at 9.30 AM each day. There will be at least three meetings a week at 18.00 PM. Best regards, Rem K."[48]

Notes made by Hoshino during a meeting that appears to have taken place on the previous day indicate how the work was organized.[49] Apart from Hoshino himself, Rem Koolhaas, Ron Steiner, and Toni Adam were also present at the meeting. Among other things, the notes announce the construction of a model in a scale of 1 to 50, in all probability the one published two years later in *El Croquis*, which is likely to have been built by Steiner for the most part (→ F 6.16).[50] Adam would be in charge of technical issues, costs, and coordinating external parties, while Van Immerzeel would take care of the detailing. Among the tasks Hoshino listed for himself were to "see every drawing" and

F 6.16

OMA/Rem Koolhaas, Kunsthal, approx. 1990–92. Model in a scale of 1 to 50.

F 6.17

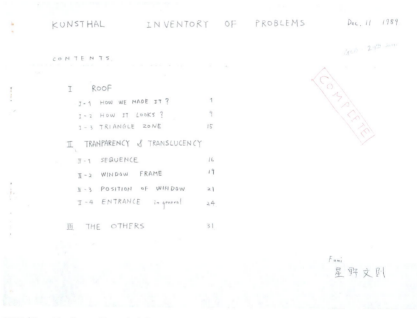

OMA/Rem Koolhaas, Kunsthal, December 1989. Cover of Fuminori Hoshino's "Inventory of Problems."

47 Terence Riley, "Rem Koolhaas/OMA: Urban Constructions," in *Newsline Columbia University*, vol. 5 (September 1992), p. 2.
48 OMAR 1160–63.
49 "Meeting," January 5. No year is given, but the issues discussed strongly indicate that the meeting took place in 1990. OMAR 1524.
50 *El Croquis*, 53 (1992) and 79 (1996). According to modelmaker Frans Parthesius, who frequently collaborated with OMA during this period, the model is likely to have been built by OMA's own staff. Email to the author, June 10, 2020. Toni Adam has suggested that the model was built by Ron Steiner. Email to the author, June 11, 2020. The model is held by the HNI: MAQV 494.

"continue to sketch." Hoshino did produce countless sketches and drawings. The archives hold hundreds of them, their size ranging from A4 to large formats of various dimensions: these included quick freehand sketches; loose dossiers with annotated sketches or carefully composed booklets of sketches, outlining ideas and principles for the development of the design; and axonometric drawings in pencil on tracing paper, often in a scale of 1 to 50, visualizing how parts of the construction would connect. The sheer number of sketches indicates that they provided an important means of steering the planning process. Apart from being easily sent as faxes, they had the advantage of being produced very quickly. Speed must have been a vital issue, because only a medium as fast as this would allow Hoshino to cover— and to some extent control—virtually every detail of the design in close collaboration with Koolhaas.

In November/December 1989, Hoshino compiled a booklet entitled "Inventory of Problems," consisting of thirty-nine A3 pages with annotated sketches (→ F 6.17).[51] The booklet gives an idea of the issues at stake at that point: a new roof for Hall 2, the detailing of various transparent and translucent surfaces, the organization of entrances (main, secondary, staff), and a series of miscellaneous details. The existence of several copies indicates that Hoshino's "Inventory" circulated among team members as a set of guidelines. According to Hoshino's own account, it served a double purpose: first, to provide a basis for discussions with Koolhaas as well as with consultants, manufacturers, and other parties involved; and second, to avoid a loss of control over the design and the increasing diversity of its parts.[52] In fact, a significant share of the booklet seems to be aimed at compiling a catalog of principles for detailing the materials and constructive systems for the exterior. Many of the principles and ideas outlined in the inventory were pursued further as the project was implemented. Some of these will be traced below through this process of concretization, adjustment, and transformation, paying considerable attention to OMA's efforts to tame the unruly dynamics of constructive diversification and counteract the structure's implied monolithic volume and mass.

Miter joints

By April 1990, OMA had settled on a travertine cladding of the walls for both the north and south facades of the office block; fair-faced concrete was specified for the remaining three exterior walls. The principles defined in the inventory for the detailing of the corners were

F 6.18

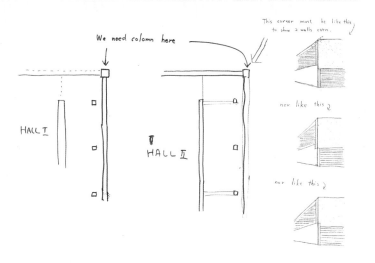

OMA/Rem Koolhaas, Kunsthal, December 1989. Fuminori Hoshino's "Inventory of Problems." Principles for the detailing of the corners of the facades.

F 6.19

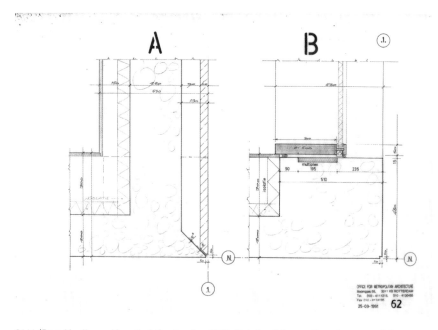

OMA/Rem Koolhaas, Kunsthal, September 1991. Details of the northeast corner of the facade. Left: miter joint between concrete wall and travertine cladding.

51 Fuminori Hoshino/OMA, "Kunsthal: Inventory of Problems," December 11, 1989. OMAR 3276.
52 Interview with the author, July 25, 2017.

implemented almost literally (→ F 6.18). Where opaque and transparent or translucent surfaces meet, "priority" is given to the former: the wall shows its depth at the edge. The final details provide visible edges which are about 50 centimeters wide, suggesting a massive wall of the same depth. It was probably impossible to reduce the edge at the northeast corner of Hall 1 any further. The vertical open-web truss supporting the "floating" concrete wall of the north facade had been removed by February 1990.[53] Instead, the edge of the eastern wall in exposed concrete was reinforced to serve as a column in disguise, and would look as if it were the actual strength of the wall.[54] At the northwest and southwest corners a depth of 50 centimeters was adopted, apparently for the sole purpose of establishing a "standard" width for three details that vary on a common formal theme.[55] But the notion of massiveness and depth, implicated by the 50 centimeters of material strength, is contested wherever a travertine clad wall connects to a wall in concrete (→ F 6.19).[56] A miter joint separates the two sides of the corner, making both the travertine cladding and the exposed concrete look like implausibly thin surfaces, capable of meeting along an imaginary line like two sheets of veneer. The miter joint and its implicit denial of depth reappears on a smaller scale at the exposed edges of the travertine clad walls.

The service wall between Hellingstraat and the auditorium is clad on both its main sides with corrugated plastic panels—an option already listed in the inventory—as if to evoke the idea of a solid translucent slab. But the structure that eventually materialized "disclaims" this notion in multiple ways. Where the service wall emerges from the roof and turns into a service tower, three sides of the slab are covered with expanded metal grating, and the fourth with corrugated sheathing, its flimsy edges left exposed. If this is too subtle to be noticed consciously, the porch at the main entrance reveals the truth—of secondary space enclosed by two thin layers—to any visitor at the very moment they enter the building. Moreover, the semi-transparency of the material is contrary to the illusion of monolithic solidity, or mass. Parts of the substructure shine through, and in the dark the illuminated openings onto the passageway become plainly visible (→ P 8.12). On the side of the auditorium, large parts are illuminated by fluorescent lights behind the corrugated sheathing (→ P 8.13). Not only are the light tubes themselves visible, but also the grid of the substructure, the floor plates, and transverse walls, as well as a window frame inserted into the layer of wired glazing, cable routes, and junction boxes, suggesting a hollow technical apparatus of machinelike complexity.

F 6.20

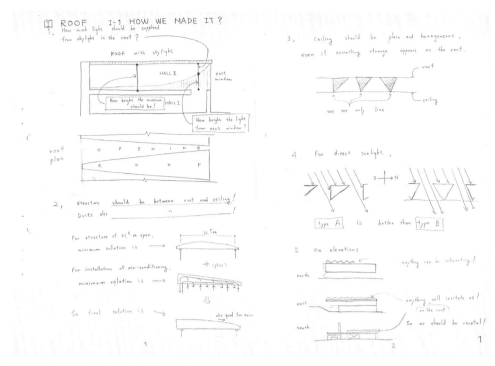

OMA/Rem Koolhaas, Kunsthal, December 1989. Fuminori Hoshino's "Inventory of Problems." Concept for the new roof of Hall 2.

The roof and Hall 2

In November 1989, OMA began to design an entirely new roof for Hall 2, which had far-reaching consequences for the eastern section of the building.[57] The first twelve pages of Hoshino's inventory are entirely dedicated to this subject, half of them focused on how the structure might accommodate the bulky ducts of the mechanical services (→ F 6.20). Like the service wall in corrugated plastic, much of the redesign of the roof and ceiling for Hall 2 is an episode of "contested" volume. Along the east to west axis the new roof is triangular in section. Its edge along the Skew Ramp descends from a height of 2.5 meters to 80 centimeters along the eastern facade. The thick edge of the wedge-shaped volume only becomes visible from the roof terrace. Conversely, looking from the east, the same roof appears flat and

53 A revised set of drawings in February seems to be the first without the truss. OMA, "Kunsthal Rotterdam," February 16, 1990. OMAR 1780.
54 In his "Inventory of Problems" Hoshino mentions a requisite column at the northeast corner. Hoshino/OMA, "Kunsthal: Inventory of Problems," p. 33.
55 The loadbearing part of all three walls is 20 centimeters wide. See details by OMA nos. 41 and 57, dated October 11, 1991; and no. 62, dated September 25, 1991. OMAR 1812.
56 The ambiguity has already been observed by Ed Melet in The Architectural Detail: Dutch Architects Visualize Their Concepts, Rotterdam: NAi Publishers, 2002, p. 117.
57 Hoshino's "Inventory of Problems" includes twelve sketches of the new roof, dated November 20, 1989.

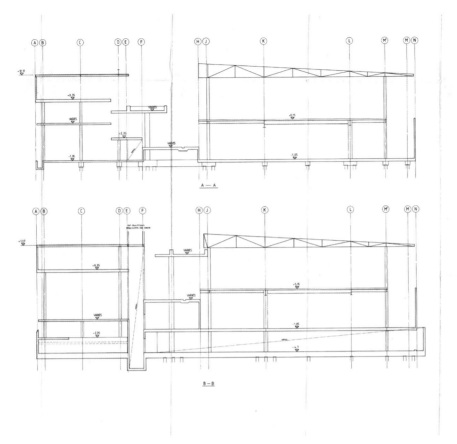

Ove Arup, Kunsthal, January 1990. Cross sections of the structural system (east to west).
Right: the new roof of Hall 2.

confluent with the roof of the portico. In order to keep the edge of the roof as thin as possible, the columns alongside the east facade are shifted several meters to the west (axis M), incorporating them into the partition that separates the void from the two stacked exhibition halls (→ F 6.21). In turn, the void has been "filled" with a metal grating floor, creating a second corridorlike gallery space that is level with Hall 2 (→ P 7.3). The advantages were numerous: first, the eastern ends of the girders would be turned into cantilevers, which requires the least height along the facade, thereby reducing the main span from 31.5 to 28 meters; second, Van Krimpen's year-long wish for column-free walls was now consistently met, both in Hall 1 and in Hall 2; third, sixteen out of the twenty-two lateral columns were located within walls, and those uncovered no longer needed to be encased in concrete.[58] Fourth, the roof's triangular section approximated the space required for the mechanical services; as the central riser shaft is located at the western margin of Hall 2, the dimensions of the ducts decrease, just like the height of the trusses, from west to east. Fifth, just like the trusses in section, the skylights are triangular in plan, widening from almost zero at the east side of Hall 2 to roughly 2 meters at its western edge. The amount of zenithal light decreases from west to east, while the amount of light entering through the facade increases, approximating constant luminosity throughout the space (→ F 6.20).[59]

In collaboration with Arup, OMA developed a structure of triangular open-web trusses to generate the roof's wedge-shaped cross section.[60] On the western side of Hall 2, thirteen single trusses cantilever 1.25 meters from the columns supporting them (axis J), before connecting to a Vierendeel truss (axis H) with a constant height of 2.5 meters (→ F 6.21). The short span between the row of columns and the cantilever coincides with the depth of the service wall adjacent to Hall 2. To the south, where the Skew Ramp cuts diagonally into the roof, the Vierendeel truss of relatively slender cross sections transforms into a heavy primary truss with diagonal bracings (→ P 8.9). This latter truss free-spans all along the cut-out section of Hall 2 from axis 11 to axis 19, carrying the load of four trusses spanning Hall 2. To the south, the primary truss is supported by a single cruciform column; its position on axis 19 running from east to west is defined not by the structural grid but by the junction of the Skew Ramp, the roof of Hall 2, and the roof of the portico (→ P 7.3).[61]

Arup's plans from January 1990 and those completed by OMA in April anticipate much of the solution that was eventually implemented.[62] The latter propose an aluminum covering for the exposed surfaces of the roof of Hall 2 and ribbed roof panels in metal both for the ceiling and the portico (→ P 7.8, 7.13).[63] The triangular skylights are covered with conically vaulted polycarbonate panels, with a perforation in the ceiling allowing the light to filter through. The ducts of the ventilation are fastened to the triangular trusses and separated from the skylights by vertical and sloped panels, probably serving as reflectors

58 OMA, "Kunsthal Rotterdam," April 19, 1990, B 03-06. OMAR 1784. By October 1989 all the freestanding columns—nine out of sixteen in Hall 1 and sixteen out of twenty-two in Hall 2—had been encased in concrete. OMA, "Kunsthal Rotterdam," DO 03-06, October 10, 1989. OMAR 1773, 1759.

59 Hoshino illustrated the idea in his "Inventory of Problems." OMA/Hoshino, "Inventory of Problems," pp. 1, 9

60 Most of Arup's final plans for the definitive design are dated January 1990. For the roof of Hall 2, see S 4106, "East Roof Details" and S 4106, "Cross Sections: Sheet 1." Arup London Archives.

61 In Arup's plan of January 1990 the column is slightly shifted with regard to axis 19. Ove Arup, "East Roof Layout," S4011. Arup London Archives. The position, however, would be corrected by April 1990.

62 OMA, "Kunsthal Rotterdam," April 19, 1990, drawings B05, B07, B10, B11, B15. OMAR 1784. The first drawings by OMA corresponding to the new roof layout date of February 16. OMAR 1772.

63 OMA, "Kunsthal Rotterdam: Principe details," details nos. 10 and 23, April 19, 1990. Stadsarchief Rotterdam (box 4).

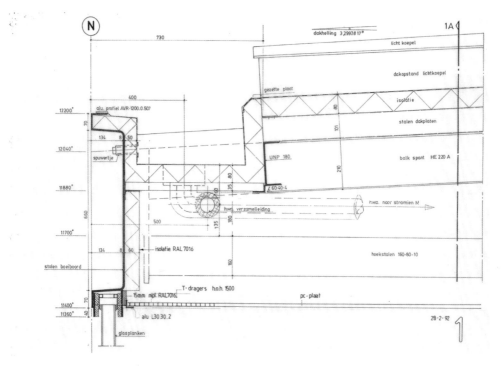

OMA/Rem Koolhaas, Kunsthal, February 1992. Detail of the cornice along the east facade.

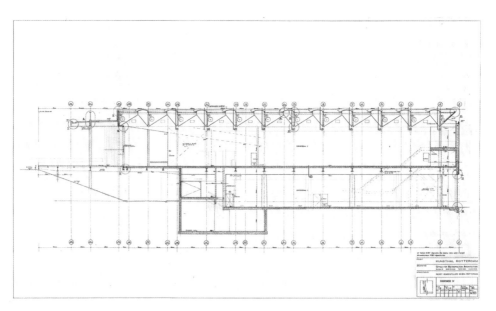

OMA/Rem Koolhaas, Kunsthal, March 1992. Cross section. The portico and Halls 1 and 2 with the new roof structure.

for the daylight. The bottom chord of the trusses is split into two steel angles in order to supply the space with air through the gap in between. The air extracts are aligned along the western wall of the exhibition space, likewise concealed in the voids of the ceiling. The details dating from April 1990 show the eastern ends of the triangular trusses stepped back in such a manner that the entire construction from the gutter to the ceiling and covering would not exceed the height of 80 centimeters.[64] The edge of the roof, topping the glass planks of the facade, is clad with sheet metal, approximating the contours of a Miesian double T-cornice (→ F 6.22).[65]

In late 1991, the idea of giving Hall 2 a flat suspended ceiling of galvanized roof panels was abandoned.[66] Left uncovered, the plasterboard-clad voids containing the ventilation ducts—right triangles in cross section—were exposed to view (→ F 6.23–6.24). As a consequence, the curtain rail, reiterating the inner curve of the service road, was omitted as well. However, the recess of the service wall that would store the curtain was preserved, and consequently the large alcove overlooking Hellingstraat became an erratic residue of an otherwise abandoned idea. In the new layout of the ceiling, the sloping sides of the plasterboard triangles were retained as they were, whereas their vertical sides were replaced by translucent polycarbonate panels to filter daylight.[67] In section, the revised ceiling resembles an inward-turned sawtooth roof. The character of the space changed profoundly. Only now did the implicit dynamism of the roof structure become visible: the triangular trusses, the slope of the roof, and the triangular skylights were translated into a series of "triangular cones"—half translucent, half opaque— with distinct sculptural qualities (→ P 8.15). Their pointed cross sections, ever changing dimensions, and slightly bent surfaces resonate with the spatial dynamism of the ramps, sloping floors, slanted columns, and angled walls, extending the building's partly "oblique condition" to Hall 2 in its entirety. At the same time, the materials used for the ceiling, as well as the exposed edges of the plasterboard and polycarbonate panels, unmistakably show the enclosure of the roof as an assembly of thin, heterogeneous surfaces. And like the service wall in corrugated plastic, the flat polycarbonate panels of the ceiling show almost everything they conceal.

64 Ibid., detail no. 2.
65 Ibid., detail no. 1.
66 See, for instance, OMA, detail no. 1, November 22, 1991. OMAR 1831. See also OMA, "Kunsthal Rotterdam: Plafond Expositiehal 2" W601A. October 30, 1991. OMAR 1817. The new ceiling details had been worked out by the beginning of 1992. See OMA, details nos. 23, 24, 24A, 24B, 25, 400, 401, 417, and 418. February 28, 1992. OMAR 1807.
67 The use of polycarbonate is mentioned in the minutes of a building committee meeting in August 1992. "Verslag Bouwcomissie Nieuwbouw Kunsthal," August 24, 1992. OMAR 3266.

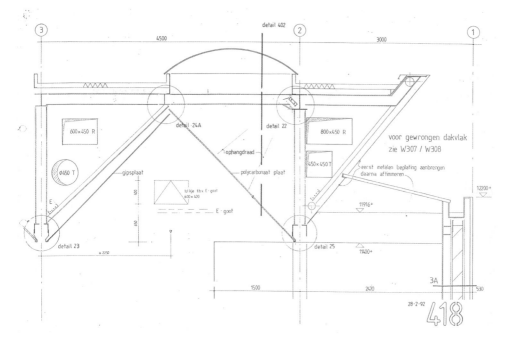

OMA/Rem Koolhaas, Kunsthal, December 1989. Detail of the roof of Hall 2. The triangular voids containing the ducts of the mechanical services are clad by panels in plasterboard (tilted to the right) and panels in polycarbonate (tilted to the left). Air is supplied through the split bottom chord.

Another consequence of the new solution is the exposure of the horizontal bracing, which is composed of 108-millimeter-wide steel tubes that connect to the bottom chord of the open-web trusses spanning Hall 2. Most of the tubes add up to a parabola crisscrossed by four diagonals, extending from the northeast corner of the ceiling (the column at the intersection of axes M and 2) to the east corner of the portico's ceiling (the column at the intersection of axes M and 20) (→ F 6.25). Both the ends of the parabola and the diagonals connect to a straight line of bracing (axis M), which in turn connects to an H-beam set into the wall of the northern facade.[68] The distinct figurative quality of the parabola dissociates the bracing from the system of the trusses, turning it into an element of its own. At the same time the ceiling of the portico, now clad with corrugated polycarbonate panels, has become more independent from its counterpart in Hall 2. The same holds true for the former void, or "Gallery Van Krimpen," where the ceiling of the oblong space has been covered with flat translucent polycarbonate panels.[69]

F 6.25

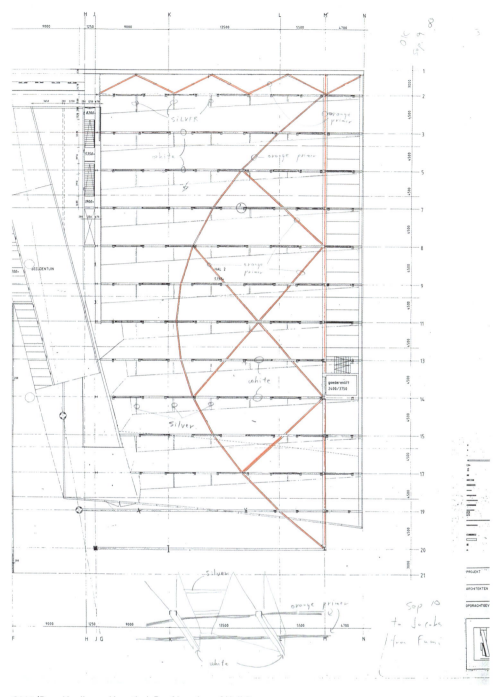

OMA/Rem Koolhaas, Kunsthal. Roof bracing of Hall 2.

68 OMA, detail no. 25, February 28, 1992. OMAR 1807.

69 Changes to three ceilings were announced at a building committee meeting in February 1992. They were accepted under the condition that the changes would entail no extra costs. "Verslag Bouwcomissie Nieuwbouw Kunsthal," February 4, 1992. OMAR 1523.

Remainders

The collages completed in autumn 1989 depict the twelve exoskeletal plate girders spanning Hall 2, the one on the portico, and the one on the roof of Hall 3 as being identical. Conversely, with the roof structure implemented, the plate girders on the portico and Hall 3 were the two sole remainders of what used to be a larger system of girders. A couple of sketches that were included in the inventory indicate that Hoshino considered replacing the plate girder of the portico with an open-web truss that would match the trusses spanning Hall 2.[70] After all, Hall 2 and the portico belonged to the same section of the structural system. The plate girder, however, was retained, as was its 3-meter cantilever to the east, which had initially aligned precisely with the depth of the vertical open-web truss at the northeast corner but then had been omitted altogether by February 1990 (→ F 6.16). Moreover, the idea of reproducing the curved service road along the dike by means of glazed "inlays" in the two ceilings was largely abandoned. In the July 1989 version, the transparent reproduction of the road's curve had already disappeared from both the floorplan of Hall 2 and the roof plan of the western section, and by April 1990 it had been removed from the roof altogether. But the curved facade of Hall 2 was retained, as was the curved void undercutting the offices.

From this moment on, the "remainders"—the cantilevered plate girder, the plate girder on top of Hall 3, the curve of the glass wall, the void below the offices—were difficult to "read," in the sense that the concepts and ideas from which these forms emerged were almost impossible to reenact. As parts of a whole that has been lost, they are fragments in a literal sense. The surviving drawings and models in no way indicate any attempts to tone down the impact of apparent wantonness. On the contrary, there is something methodical about progressively assembling inconsistencies like these. The outcome is not without parallels to the surrealist *cadavre exquis*: its ambiguous unity, its resistance to rational intelligibility, its inclination to baffle, its mysteriousness—or, in terms of its approach: the methodical embrace of inconsistency.

Principles

A note written by Hoshino in March 1991 reads: "One of the most interesting thing[s] about [the] Kunsthal is that it has many contrasts, or ambi[guous] or even contradictor[y] aspects at the same time; simple but various, big but small, bright but dark, wild but delicate, etc. So for [the] detailing, we know that it's not so easy, because we don't like most of the conventional detail and because [the] Kunsthal is too complicated to solve every detail problem with 1 nice detail. But we also don't want to invent 100's of different details for 100's of different situations. So I want to suggest to make a few principles and to try to apply them as much as possible; from [the] big window to [the] small window, steel door, internal wooden door, sliding door, etc."[71]

Hoshino's note, which merited the comment "Ok by Rem," was obviously addressed to his colleagues. It introduces four pages with annotated sketches on the detailing of the fenestration (→ F 6.26–6.28). The note indicates that Koolhaas and Hoshino discussed the heterogeneity of the design as a quality that implied the risk of arbitrary multiplicity. This risk had already become latent by April 1990, when OMA issued the drawings for the building application and the bidding process. The layout and detailing of the fenestration differed not only between the building's eastern and western section, but also from facade to facade, and within each facade from fenestration to fenestration, as shown by a synopsis of the glazed surfaces (→ P 7.14).[72] The only remainders of motivic continuity from one surface to the next are the two sides of the restaurant and the glass wall alongside Hellingstraat "passing on" its tilted squares to the southern side of Hall 2, where they fuse into an image of Miesian serenity. The glass wall of Hall 1, although containing some approximate squares, was turned into a Mondrianesque composition of partly vertical proportions with tinted glass in green and gray, sanded glass, clear glass, and aluminum doors (→ P 7.9). More clearly than in earlier versions, the west facade "admits" to the affinity between the restaurant and the auditorium, but "insists" on the priority of the circuit and the spaces that belong to it, whereas the structural glazing and mirror glass of the office block bespeaks its functional discreteness and inaccessibility by the public (→ P 7.11). Every fifth bay, a mullion in the restaurant and auditorium aligns with another one, loosely resonating with the 6-meter rhythm of the structural grid.

But the image of relative continuity conveyed by the elevations of April 1990 is deceptive, given the inevitable abstraction entailed by drawings in a scale of 1 to 100. In April 1990, OMA's project foresaw eight different principles of detailing for the fenestration

---

70 OMA/Hoshino, "Inventory of Problems," p. 11.
71 "Principle of Window," March 17, 1991.
    OMAR 1629.
72 OMA, "Kunsthal Rotterdam," April 19, 1990. B19.
    OMAR 1786.

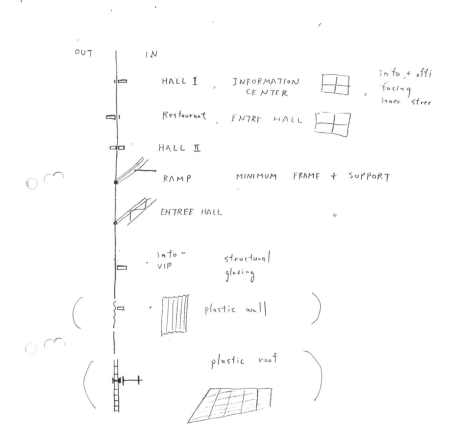

OMA/Rem Koolhaas, Kunsthal, March 1991. Page from a note by Hoshino listing different types of mullions used for the Kunsthal.

alone:[73] There would be aluminum mullions on the inner side of the glazing (Hall 1, offices along the service road); aluminum mullions on the inner side of the glazing supported by steel tubes (Hellingstraat); aluminum mullions on both sides of the glazing (Hall 2); aluminum mullions on the outer side of the glazing (restaurant); aluminum mullions combined with open-web trusses, encased between two discrete layers of glazing (auditorium);[74] aluminum mullions supported by

F 6.27

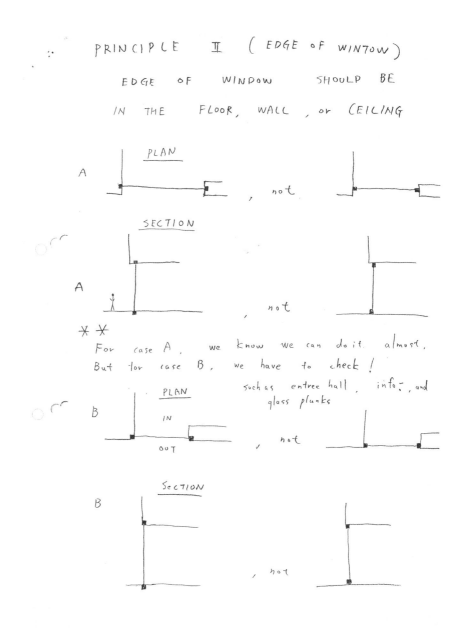

OMA/Rem Koolhaas, Kunsthal, March 1991. Page from a note by Hoshino listing the solutions for the detailing of window frames used for the Kunsthal.

glass fins (Hall 1); mullions combined with structural glazing (west facade of office block); and mullions combined with flat polycarbonate panels (stepped ramp leading to Hall 3) (→ F 6.26). In the auditorium, the depth of the open-web trusses increases from bay to bay as the

73   The argument made in the following two paragraphs draws on multiple sources. Overview glazing: OMA, "Kunsthal Rotterdam," B19, April 19, 1990. OMAR 1786. Floorplans, cross sections, elevations: OMA, "Kunsthal Rotterdam," B 02-17, April 19, 1990. OMAR 1784. Details: OMA, "Kunsthal Rotterdam: Principle details," April 19, 1990. Stadsarchief Rotterdam.

74   OMA, "Kunsthal Rotterdam," B19, April 19, 1990.

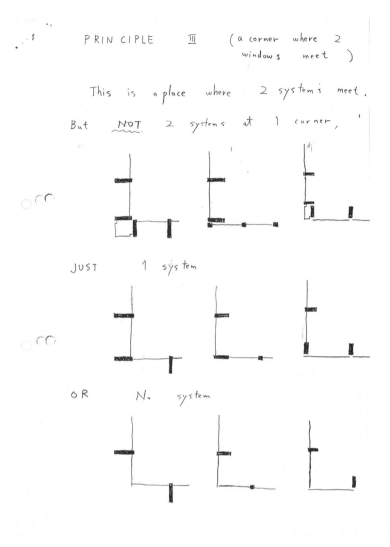

OMA/Rem Koolhaas, Kunsthal, March 1991. Page from a note by Hoshino listing the solutions for the detailing of the corners of the fenestration envisaged for the Kunsthal.

floor of the auditorium descends, apparently in order to secure sufficient bracing (→ P 7.3). The same principle is applied to the "massive" mullions of the restaurant below (→ P 7.1). Next to the plastic sheathing—flat along the roof garden, corrugated along Hellingstraat—seven types of glass are listed in total: clear glass, green and gray tinted glass, glass with a reflecting silvery coating, sandblasted glass, wire glass, and channel glass.[75] The mullion's width of about 50 millimeters and aluminum as the material selected for most of them are the sole visual bonds tying the fenestration together.

F 6.29

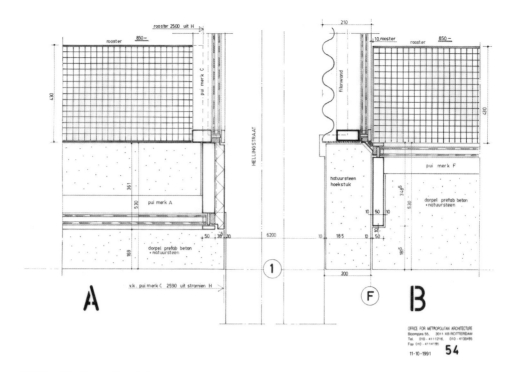

OMA/Rem Koolhaas, Kunsthal, October 1991. North facade. Details of the corners between the glass walls along Hellingstraat.

F 6.30

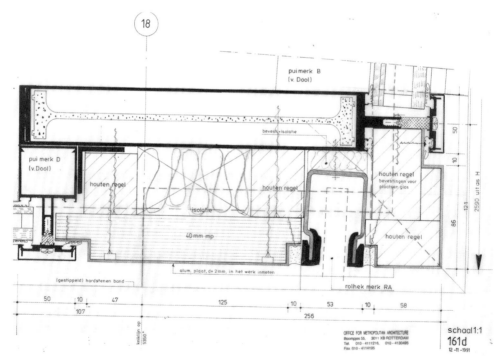

OMA/Rem Koolhaas, Kunsthal, November 1991. Detail of the corner between the southern facade of Hall 2 and the glass wall bisecting Hellingstraat.

75 OMA, "Kunsthal Rotterdam," B20, April 19, 1990. OMAR 1786.

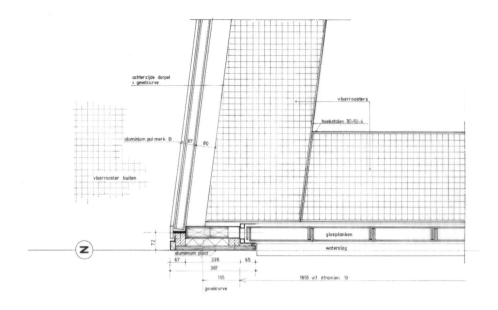

OMA/Rem Koolhaas, Kunsthal, September 1991. Detail of the corner between the southern and eastern facades of Hall 2.

According to Koolhaas the persistent diversification of the construction and materials was much about the relation of the building and its surroundings, but also about conditioning the visitors' spatial experience. With regard to the particularly varied fenestration of Hall 1 he recalls: "I can remember very clearly that it was the kind of view outside that sometimes can be really green and sometimes be almost colorless. So, it's more about perception."[76] In the same conversation, however, he mentioned an entirely different aspect, a radical questioning, rather, of established building practices. For OMA, he explained, the Kunsthal "was the first kind of major building on a really serious scale, so it also meant a kind of surprise that every building has the same kind of glass. Why is that? There was the really fundamental question of how the majority of my colleagues operated."[77]

    The layout of the fenestration, the mullions, the types of glass, and the translucent panels were largely implemented as specified in April 1990. Most of the fenestration is based on a system of uninsulated mullions in aluminum with sharp-edged rectangular cross sections by manufacturer Van Dool. Whereas the depth varies between 300 and 80 millimeters, the width of 50 millimeters remains constant in complete accordance with the wishes of the architects. However, the

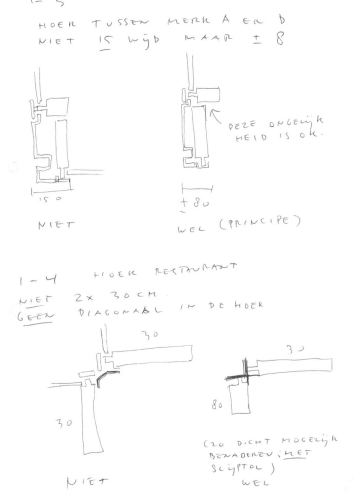

OMA/Rem Koolhaas, Kunsthal, August 1991. Fax to Herman Jacobs in which Koolhaas instructs him to change the corner details of the fenestration.

implementation of the detailing, as defined by Hoshino's note of March 1991, was less consistent (→ F 6.26–6.27). Many window frames that are fully visible today were meant to be hidden; that is, set into the adjacent walls, floors, ceilings, and lintels. Similarly, most of the corners between glass walls that join at right angles also diverge significantly from what the note had suggested. At both corners of the restaurant facing north, a pair of two mullions forms a Miesian open corner, with the structural part of the mullions located outside the glazing; the diagonal aluminum plate of 60 millimeters in width that

76 Conversation with the author, Rotterdam, February 15, 2023.
77 Ibid.

F 6.33

OMA/Rem Koolhaas, Kunsthal. Note by Fuminori Hoshino on options for shuttering and tie bolts of the exterior walls in fair-faced concrete.

bridges the joint is a "third element" the architects tried to eliminate repeatedly, but apparently no better solution was found for avoiding a thermal bridge.

In the eastern section, the mullions' structural part is located on the inner side of the glazing, and single mullions are supposed to form the corners between two adjacent walls of glass. The architects eventually conceded the use of two mullions, forming what from the outside would appear to be a single mullion of 80 millimeters in width (→ F 6.29–6.31). The widths of the corners as implemented measure 89, 97, and 146 millimeters respectively; although based on the same principle, the three corners were "individualized"—contrary to the architects' intentions—due to the differing technical requirements at each corner. For Koolhaas, the visibility of the frames as much as the detailing of the corners were major issues. In August 1991 and again two months later he sent a lengthy fax to construction supervisor Herman Jacobs, complaining that the detailing did not correspond to what had previously been agreed upon (→ F 6.32).[78] In both faxes, Koolhaas referred to OMA's technical drawings—which were then apparently being supervised by Jacobs on the construction site—in contradiction to the instructions given by Hoshino.[79] OMA completed the technical drawings of the facades by mid-November, incorporating only a few of the changes demanded by Koolhaas.[80] The corners were implemented in accordance with the drawings.

F 6.34

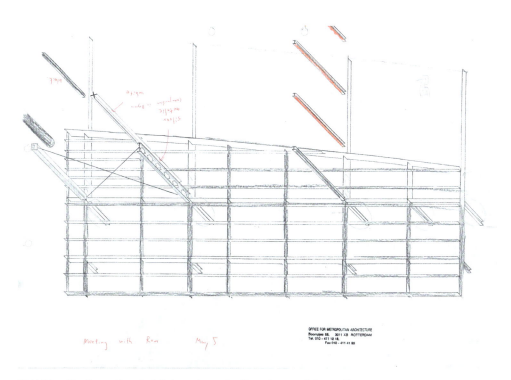

OMA/Rem Koolhaas, Kunsthal. Color scheme for the columns of the portico.

78 Rem Koolhaas, fax of August 12, 1991. OMAR 1462.
79 Fuminori Hoshino in an interview with the author, July 25, 2017. OMA's final drawings of October 10, 1989 and the drawings of April 19, 1990.
80 OMA, "Kunsthal: Details," details nos. 54, 75, and 161d. OMAR 1812.

Sameness

The April 1990 plans propose two different materials for the massive walls: 4-centimeter-thick cladding in travertine of the north and south facades, and walls of 20 to 25 centimeters width in fair-faced concrete for the east and west facades as well as for the lower half of the south facade. The plans specify a different color for each of the three concrete walls: white (east facade), black (west facade), and gray (south facade) (→ F 6.33). An annotated sketch by Hoshino outlines three options for the pattern of the shuttering and tie bolts, two of the propositions suggesting that the patterns be varied from facade to facade.[81] But the idea had apparently been abandoned by the beginning of 1991. A number of elevations produced in January and March approximate the version eventually implemented.[82] The same system of shuttering is used for all three concrete walls, with the panels measuring 1.5 by 3 meters. Even though the pattern of the tie bolts, arranged in horizontal rows, varies slightly from facade to facade, the color—black, white, gray—is the only distinct feature to distinguish the three concrete walls. The two walls clad in Spanish travertine are each divided into rows of about 43 centimeters in height, which are in turn composed of tiles of three different lengths.[83] In both cases the irregular pattern of the tiles and the relatively minimal joints (8 millimeters) pull the surface together, approximating the literally monolithic quality of the concrete walls. In all probability, the relative uniformity of the solid walls was partly based on a compositional idea of providing a homogeneous backdrop against which the variety of the glazed surfaces could unfold. The essential absence of variation within the opaque surfaces thus reinforces the compositional principle on which the facades' coherence depends most: the binary division into two opposites.

A podium, a perron, a ceremonial staircase

In 1990 and 1991, the portico facing Maasboulevard was subject to a series of changes that helped to both unfold and compromise the structure's ennobling connotations. What used to be a sloping driveway until February 1989 was turned into a horizontal terrace, level with Hall 2 and raised 60 centimeters above the sidewalk of the boulevard (→ P 7.8).[84] Security concerns are likely to have been the reason for this shift. The need to prevent cars from breaking through the glass wall of Hall 2 was discussed by the building committee in December 1989.[85]

F 6.35

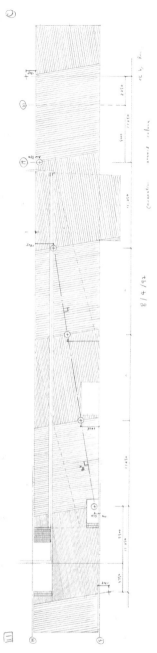

OMA/Rem Koolhaas, Kunsthal. Hellingstraat. Pattern proposed for raking the concrete flooring. The pattern extends seamlessly from the exterior to the interior part of the ramp.

81 A "concrete wall," December 11, no year. OMAR 1621.
82 OMA, "Kunsthal Rotterdam," W300 (March 5, 1991), W302 (January 23, 1991), W305 (March 5, 1991). OMAR 1817.
83 OMA, "Kunsthal Rotterdam: Noordgevel/Travertin," March 26, 1992. OMAR 2842. Drawings by the manufacturer Stone & Cladding, "Kunsthallen Rotterdam," Gevel 1–4, July 16, 1992. OMAR 1596, 1598.
84 In absolute terms, the floor was raised only 10 centimeters while the sidewalk of Maasboulevard was lowered 50 centimeters. This is evident from the respective elevation labels in OMA's final drawings of October 10, 1989 and the drawings of April 19, 1990.
85 "Verslag van de 16e Bouwcommissie Nieuwbouw Kunsthal," December 20, 1989. OMAR 1519.

As an elevated terrace, the open platform bears some resemblance to a podium or plinth, even if the detailing undermines this notion: the platform "floats," visibly detached from the ground, and the galvanized metal grating of the decking forestalls any notion of massiveness or nobility while also allowing daylight to enter the service road below.[86] Of the three columns supporting the cantilevered plate girder, the H-column to the east is the only regular one, in the sense that its shape is identical with the lateral columns inside the building (→ F 6.16, 6.34). Its counterpart at the western end of the portico continued to be encased in concrete as yet another remainder of an obsolete stage of the design. The support in concrete and the adjacent column in steel—castellated with hexagonal openings—frame a cross of tensile bracing rods. Together with the first *pilotis* and the cruciform column supporting the Skew Ramp, the portico thus unites five differently shaped columns that are made of either steel or concrete. Further, as a potential "spare" support, the handrail on the east side of the terrace—a tree trunk, mounted on two steel supports—may represent the sixth column, removed from the center of the portico in summer 1989. The "irony" of the handrail as much as the asymmetry and heterogeneity of the columns no doubt run counter to the ennobling impact of columns arrayed in front of a building. And yet the columns gained in stature. Instead of being interchangeable parts of a steel frame they became "individuated," possessing something of the self-contained character of the classical column.

Similarly, Hellingstraat acts much like a perron and a ceremonial flight of stairs—and as with both of those, the two bisected parts of the central ramp are architectural elements of transition, suspense, preparation, and theatrical exposure. But, as in the case of the portico, the finishes eschew familiar images of architectural "nobility." The drawings of April 1990 foresee black asphalt for the surfacing of the public passage, fair-faced concrete for the *pilotis* and the bottom of the Skew Ramp, and corrugated polycarbonate all along the side of the main entrance. Later on, the colors of the floor and the columns were switched: the *pilotis* were painted black and the ramp received a raked finish in concrete. If the white wall behind the glazed partition announces the "museum," the flimsy and raw materials of the other side flirt with the image of a public underpass.

No doors

With the introduction of the two service walls on both sides of Hellingstraat, much of the visual unity of the interior was reduced to a series of occasional glimpses from one level to the next between spaces that are essentially self-contained. Still, the glass wall bisecting Hellingstraat and the one between Hall 2 and the portico do preserve something of the interior's lost visual unity. In both cases, the floor transcends the glazed barrier between the interior and exterior, making the partition appear as if it were an arbitrary, technically unavoidable membrane. The concrete finish of Hellingstraat extends up to the service wall alongside the ramp's interior section, and the metal grating of the portico terrace "intrudes" into Hall 2, covering the underfloor convectors all along the curved fenestration (→ F 6.35).[87] Further, the last of the lateral H-columns to the east stands on the portico, corroborating the sense of continuity between the space outdoors and Hall 2.

No barrier needs to be overcome to access the portico and Hellingstraat.[88] Only at night is the latter closed for security reasons, and the architects took great care to make the two gates disappear during daytime. A roller grille descends from a cavity in the portico facing Maasboulevard, and a gate of expanded metal grating is lowered from the ceiling of the passage next to the park.[89] If the perimeter marks its threshold, the Kunsthal is a building "without doors." The portico and Hellingstraat signal its accessibility. The bold, spacious, and spectacular gesture contrasts with the inconspicuous character of what used to be the actual entrance to the arts center before the building was transformed in 2013/2014: a horizontal landing, branching off from Hellingstraat; two porthole windows for ticket sales; and a pair of sliding doors—in aluminum, like a dozen further doors, including fire and service doors.[90] Perhaps the architects feared that a more articulate entrance would have compromised the primacy and openness of Hellingstraat and the portico.

---

86 OMA, "Kunsthal Rotterdam," B23, April 19, 1990. OMAR 2847.
87 On this issue, see Michel Moussette, "'Do we Need a Canopy for Rain?': Interior–Exterior Relationships in the Kunsthal," in *Architectural Research Quarterly*, 3/4 (2003), pp. 280–94.
88 According to Moussette, the invisibility of the entrance and the narrow passage between Hellingstraat and the auditorium undermine the (seeming) openness of the building. Moussette, "'Do we Need a Canopy for Rain?'" p. 287. Everything depends on what one considers the actual entrance of the building to be: the "inevitable" doors, or the open portico and Hellingstraat.
89 OMA, "Kunsthal Rotterdam," B12, April 19, 1990. OMAR 1784.
90 The large orange arrows pointing to the entrance were added later on, apparently in response to many visitors' difficulty in finding the entrance.
91 Anna Klingmann, "Architektur als kollektiver Erlebnisraum," in *Tain*, 5 (1998), p. 52 (author's translation).

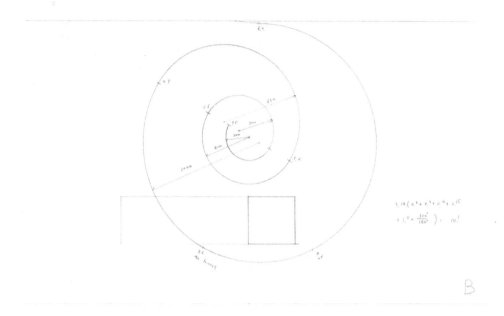

OMA/Rem Koolhaas, Kunsthal. Study by Fuminori Hoshino for the spiral where the curtain rail would be stored. The stored curtain would wrap around one of the lateral columns in the auditorium.

No finish

In 1998, in an interview with Anna Klingmann, Koolhaas explained: "If you look at most public buildings, you will realize that they demand rather dry inventories of requirements, and that there is no superordinate territory that goes beyond the specification of single activities. For this reason, we treat circulation surfaces as one of the last domains open to a whole series of uses."[91] When he was asked who the supposed user of the circulation areas would be, Koolhaas replied: "There is no supposed user and no supposed use. So, for instance, the current use of the Kunsthal really is a very limited version of what was originally intended. The Kunsthal was actually planned as a multifunctional building in which a whole series of different events would be organized. The only part of the program that could be employed for that purpose was something that you might interpret either as a circulation surface or as a marked space within an urban field, allowing for an intensification of the urban experience."[92]

A "marked space within an urban field" are words suggesting something less than a building, a minimalism of means, open boundaries—the ideal of an architecture that is all floor and no walls.

The Museumpark podium is this kind of space: a square composed of black asphalted "streets." With its asphalt flooring, the Kunsthal's Hellingstraat was meant to pick up on this motif, an idea that was not abandoned until the end of 1990, perhaps even as late as October 1991.[93] Visitors crossing the podium would recognize the Kunsthal as its continuation, or vice versa. The reappearance of the "black tarmac" was to announce what the Kunsthal was about, or rather what the Kunsthal ought to be. As implied by the photo of the Parisian street in May '68 that interrupted the spread on the Kunsthal in *S, M, L, XL*, Koolhaas saw the areas of circulation as the built counterpart of the street in a straightforward, matter-of-fact sense: as the last resort for potentially unplanned appropriation, endowed with the key quality he used to ascribe to the *terrain vague*, urban void, or park in the 1980s.

The transparency of the building's central section, which was initially planned with no or only few visual barriers, would have instantly revealed the seamless continuity of Hellingstraat and the circuit, indicating the various slopes and floors as an expansion of the "public space" outside in a similar manner to OMA's project for the Jussieu Libraries. After the introduction of the service walls, little of this visual continuity was left. Indeed, much of it was translated into a symbolic form of continuity. The detailing of the interior as worked out between 1990 and 1992 appears to have been largely about inspiring a sense of rawness. As Michel Moussette has rightly suggested, the "without-finish" quality of much of the interior recalls the exterior of an urban space.[94] It is not the image of the street being evoked, but rather that of an unfinished construction site, notably thanks to the spaces that are first encountered. Once the asphalt of Hellingstraat had been replaced by a finish in raked concrete, the passageway was sandwiched between two seemingly raw floor slabs (→ P 8.12). The auditorium on the other side of the service wall is detailed as a sequel if not a twin space of Hellingstraat. The sloping floor of the entrance hall, specified in OMA's definitive plans as a "cement decking with a wear-resistant quartz finish," approximates the appearance of concrete. Along with the square columns set back from the enclosure and the flat ceiling without downstand beams, both in exposed concrete, the space recalls Maison Dom-Ino just as Le Corbusier's 1914 rendering shows it: as the bare skeleton of a structure without loadbearing walls (→ P 8.13).

92 Ibid. (author's translation). A shorter version of this quotation can be found in Chapter 3.
93 OMA/Fuminori Hoshino, fax to Rem Koolhaas, October 11, no year. In the fax Hoshino mentions a possible switch from asphalt to concrete. Other issues discussed indicate that the year was 1991.
94 Moussette, "'Do we Need a Canopy for Rain?'" p. 289.

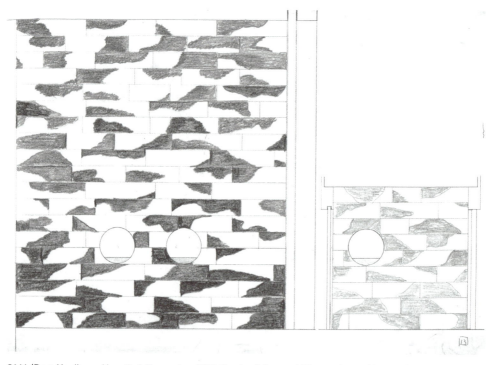

OMA/Rem Koolhaas, Kunsthal, December 1989. Study of the cowhides envisaged for the front of the ticket booth in Hall 2.

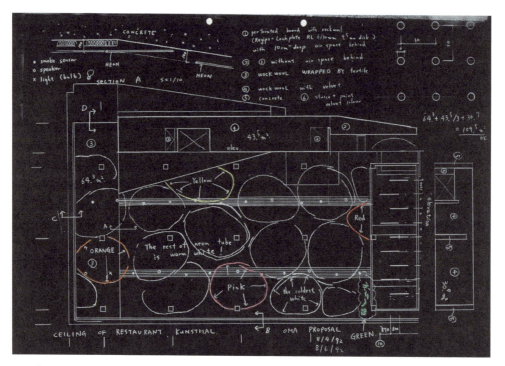

OMA/Rem Koolhaas, Kunsthal, June 1992. Study for the neon circles illuminating the restaurant.

Fragmentations   The Development of the Design 1989–1992

Tilted bundles of uncovered fluorescent light tubes have taken the place of the three truncated columns, while preserving the latter's dimensions and angle precisely. The service wall and its translucent sheathing of corrugated plastic, shared with Hellingstraat, comes across as an improvised fitting rather than an actual finish; the sense of improvisation is reinforced by the irregular-looking pattern of the vertical fluorescent light tubes illuminating the wall from within. The cladding of the wall at the back of the stage and the floor of the seating area strike a similar chord, and are tellingly specified as "underlayment panels," i.e. plywood.[95] The actual seating consists of stackable chairs in a dozen different colors, randomly arranged in an analogy to a field of flowers.[96]

A curtain serves both as blackout fabric and as a flexible partition, apparently taking recourse to OMA's scheme for the NAi. It was designed by Petra Blaisse, who was also responsible for the curtains in OMA's Netherlands Dance Theater and Villa dall'Ava. The ovoid rail is poured in place into the concrete ceiling. At the lower landing of the ramp a spiraling track branches off. The spiraling track winds around one of the columns and serves to store the curtain (→ F 6.36). The cloth blocks the light and absorbs sound, while also integrating speakers for high frequencies; the speakers for low frequencies are incorporated into the steps of the seating.[97] The cloth is double layered, with black cotton velvet on the outside and gray glass fiber on the inside. When fully drawn, the curtain is suggestive of a temporary theater stage. At the same time, it makes the reference to Maison Dom-Ino more explicit in recalling Le Corbusier's concept of the *plan libre* and the curvilinear partitions that often appear in his projects.

A gray "cement decking" that was reminiscent of concrete and similar to the flooring of the auditorium was also used for Hall 1 and the corridor in between.[98] The lack of finish is a motif further echoed by the five central columns in steel. In his 1993 review of the Kunsthal, Ed Melet reports that Koolhaas would have preferred to use massive timber columns instead. Melet explains: "But since the budget would

---

95 OMA, "Kunsthal Rotterdam," B27, April 19, 1990. OMAR 1786. The key reads "underlayment plaatmateriaal."

96 Petra Blaisse in an interview with the author, September 24, 2018.

97 Inside Outside/Petra Blaisse, "Kunsthal Rotterdam, 1991–1993, 'Noise Dress, Flower Field,'" in *Inside Outside / Petra Blaisse: A Retrospective*, October 9–19, 2018, ETH Zürich, Zurich: gta exhibitions, 2018, n. p.

98 That is indicated by the floorplans and the pictures of the opening exhibition "Het koninklijk paleis" (November 1, 1992–January 24, 1992) and the subsequent exhibition "Autodesign in Nederland" (January 30, 1993–March 28, 1991). In 200 in *2000: Acht jaar Kunsthal Rotterdam, Kunsthal Rotterdam*, Zwolle: Waanders Uitgevers, 2000, n. p. Floorplan: OMA, "Kunsthal Rotterdam," W902 B, March 3, 1992. OMAR 1840. The flooring of Hall 1 and the adjacent gallery has not survived to the present day.

not stretch to solving the structural and detailing problems posed by yet another material, he settled for steel profiles, which he chose to clad in hollow tree trunks."[99] According to Hoshino, the cladding provides the requisite fireproof covering for the steel structure (→ P 8.14).[100] In either case, the debarked trunks evoke an implausible, stagelike image of primordial rawness, while also echoing Museumpark and its trees. Overhead, the trunks fade away in the dark void of the black suspended ceiling made of plasterboard. About 200 uncovered fluorescent light tubes are spread all over the black surface at irregular distances, recalling a dark spangled sky into which the "treetops" disappear.[101] Like the sculptural covering of Hall 2 and the ceilings in metal grating and polycarbonate of "Gallery Van Krimpen," the ceiling of Hall 1 helps to "redeem" the space from the universal whiteness that has been so characteristic of museum interiors over the past two decades. Like the columns and other visible parts of the structure, the ceilings of the Kunsthal "individualize" the spaces, and the diversity of their materials, finishes, colors, and shapes contrasts with the uniformity of the white walls.

Due to the new layout of the roof, which had been worked out between November 1989 and the beginning of 1992, Hall 2 changed significantly, as has been seen.[102] The first pictures show a gray shiny plastic flooring—instead of the parquet specified in 1990—matching the industrial connotations of the new ceiling and the channel glass planks, metal grating, and polycarbonate panels used for the adjacent spaces.[103] The front of the ticket booth at the entrance to Hall 2, which was ultimately painted black, was initially conceived as a membrane of cowhides pierced by two loophole windows (→ F 6.37).[104] Unlike the solution implemented—a solid wall painted white—the cowhides would have dismantled the triangular volume at the southern end of the service wall into a succession of autonomous screens.

Apart from the five leaning columns in exposed concrete, all the features of Hall 3 correspond to the conventional gallery space of a museum: the floor received a parquet finish, the suspended ceiling in white plasterboard was equipped with halogen spotlights, and all the walls were covered with multiplex panels, likewise to be painted in white. Semi-concealed fluorescent tubes along the slightly raised edges of the suspended ceiling light up the walls. However ordinary, the museal character of Hall 3 which, for once, fully accords with the wishes of Van Krimpen, adds to the spatial variety of the circuit. Although not an exhibition space, the same can be said about the roof garden. Before ascending to Hall 3, a ribbon window on the corridor between

Hall 2 and the auditorium opens onto the green slope of the Skew Ramp's exterior half. Like the curtain in the auditorium, the garden was designed by Petra Blaisse. A more recent project statement explains: "Seven ancient pear trees, with their irregular shapes, stand spread over a carpet of ivy. Underneath the carpet 6200 bulbs of varied types are planted to introduce seasonal change and color affects from spring through winter."[105] Just as the asphalt originally specified for Hellingstraat was intended to echo the podium of Museumpark, the pear trees would echo the orchard at its entrance.[106]

Limiting the palette

The interior design of the restaurant was completed in 1992, emulating the auditorium in its display of rough-looking materials, and similarly leaving the raw concrete structure of columns and ceiling unfinished. The floor was covered with rough, second-hand wooden planks. The front of the bar was clad with rough plywood, similar to that used in the auditorium. The character of the space changed significantly when the Kunsthal was partially transformed and renovated in 2013/2014, and this affected the restaurant more than any other part of the building. The eighteen neon circles "scribbled" onto the ceiling in six different colors were designed by Günther Förg (→ F 6.38), who had been invited to work on the interior by Van Krimpen, seemingly on an informal basis.[107]

Between 1991 and 1992, the architects often took recourse to materials and products that were already being employed: the travertine covering "spread" from the facades to the entrances; the plywood cladding from the auditorium to the bar of the restaurant; the flat polycarbonate panels from the covering of Hellingstraat to the ceiling of Hall 2 and the ceiling of the adjacent gallery space; the corrugated sheathing from Hellingstraat to the ceiling of the portico; the galvanized metal grating from the terrace of the portico to the coverings over the underfloor convectors in the auditorium, Halls 1 and 2, and to

---

99 Ed Melet, "Perfect Disorder: Detailing and Construction," in *OMA/Rem Koolhaas: A Critical Reader*, ed. Christophe Van Gerrewey, Basel: Birkhäuser, 2019, p. 287.
100 Interview with the author, July 25, 2017.
101 OMA, "Kunsthal Rotterdam," W600, April 22, 1992. OMAR 2855.
102 See notes 60–62.
103 The floorplan specifies "kunstofvloer." OMA, "Kunsthal Rotterdam," W905 A, February 3, 1992. OMAR 1840. In a set of undated floorplans with annotations by Hoshino the surfacing is dubbed "industrial floor." OMAR 1632.
104 OMA, "Kunsthal Rotterdam," B24, April 19, 1990. OMAR 2847. Sketch: OMAR 3348. The cowhides are still visible in the model in a scale of 1 to 50, held by the HNI.
105 Inside Outside/Petra Blaisse, "Kunsthal Rotterdam, 1991–1993, 'Noise Dress, Flower Field,'" n. p.
106 Several drawings dating from November 1991 specify asphalt as the surface for Hellingstraat. See OMA, "Kunsthal: Details," nos. 164, 164a, and 165, November 12, 1992; nos. 167 and 168, November 21, 1992. OMAR 1812.
107 Wim van Krimpen, interview with the author, July 28, 2020.

the floor, stairs, and banisters of "Gallery Van Krimpen." The Kunsthal's otherwise ostentatious heterogeneity was methodically counterbalanced by repetitions and variations of the same permeating all parts of the building, the exterior included. To be sure, these recurrences foster the impact of formal cohesion. But they do so in a subtle, inconspicuous manner that is felt rather than consciously noticed. The ubiquitous use of fluorescent light tubes is a good example: they are plainly visible in Hall 1 (→ P 8.14), in the adjacent gallery space (under the beams), and as hanging light columns in the auditorium (→ P 8.10); they are covered but visible behind the corrugated sheathing in the auditorium, along the floor of Hellingstraat (→ P 8.12), and above the ceiling of the gallery next to Hall 2 (one long straight line) (→ P 8.16); and they are largely concealed but still discernible in the ceiling of Hall 2,[108] at the stepped edges of the ceiling in Hall 3, and under the seating of the auditorium. The light tubes are omnipresent, but the degree of recognizability varies, often allowing for a rather unconscious kind of recognition. The sense of fragmentation prevailed.

A postmodern gloss

Probably in autumn 1991, some of the colors specified for varnishing the steelwork were redefined.[109] In the case of the cruciform column next to the black *pilotis* at the edge of the portico, the architects settled on white. Silver metallic was chosen for the castellated column connected by cross bracing to its encased neighbor in fair-faced concrete, black for the H-column at the opposite end of the portico and, ultimately, for those in Halls 1 and 2. The most conspicuous modification is the introduction of orange for the bracing of the roof in Hall 2, the exoskeletal girder on top of the portico, and its counterpart on the roof of Hall 3 (→ P 8.1, 8.3). On the one hand, the orange color is reminiscent of a primer, making the protruding plate girder look all the more unfinished, as if still in need of trimming. On the other hand, bright and jaunty colors used to be a typical feature of postmodern architecture. Examples include postmodern "icons" such as Charles Moore's Piazza d'Italia in New Orleans (1976–79), many of the facades in Strada Novissima at the 1980 Venice Biennale, and James Stirling's Staatsgalerie in Stuttgart (1977–83). In Stuttgart, bright red orange was used for the revolving doors, with pink and blue for the "improvised" steel structure of the canopy. Combined with the no less improvised-looking plate girders of the Kunsthal, the orange color "activates" the building's otherwise latent affinities to postmodern architecture. Apart from the formal fragmentation, the use of bright colors and their alleged appeal to popular taste, irony, classical references, "quotes," and a taste for stagelike theatrical qualities are essential characteristics of what was and is widely regarded as postmodern architecture. All of them are present at the Kunsthal, albeit to varying degrees.

The illumination, as in much of OMA's work, betrays a taste for "effect." Spotlights set in the basalt finish of the embankment flood the portico through the terrace's metal grating from below, while spotlights hidden in the *pilotis* cast cones of light in "all" directions,[110] and the steps of the auditorium are illuminated like a TV stage (→ P 8.10–8.12). In a 1994 essay by Richard Ingersoll, the Kunsthal figures as a prime example of the ironic quality of OMA's work. The tree-trunk columns in Hall 1, the tilted columns in the auditorium, the note of "consumerism" struck by the service tower's billboard are among the "jokes" and ironic ambiguities that Ingersoll refers to.[111] A chapter of Emmanuel Petit's book *Irony* is dedicated to Koolhaas' work in the 1970s and 1980s.[112] As Petit points out, Koolhaas uses the parodic distortion of canonical works of architecture or the juxtaposition of seemingly irreconcilable positions to articulate covert motivations of modernist architecture, the historical dialectics within modernist architecture and urbanism, and the transient nature of ideological legitimacy. The Kunsthal, even though it is not discussed in Petit's essay, is particularly rich in such distortions and juxtapositions. The plan is divided into a Corbusian half in concrete and a Miesian half in steel (→ P 7.3). If the western half combines a Maison Dom-Ino and the *plan libre* with the *pilotis* of the ramp system, Hall 2 approximates the "neutral plan" and clear span structure of the late Mies. The visible part of the columns makes the latter reference explicit: H-columns in steel, painted black. It has often been observed that the portico resembles Mies' National Gallery in Berlin. The "cornice" detail along with the fascia of the east facade was modified in 1991/1992, apparently to resemble the Miesian double-T more closely; the sheathing of bent metal plates dating from April 1990 was replaced by a single C-shaped element in steel that was painted black like the original version and all of one

---

108 In the opening under the bottom chord of the trusses, single, fully visible tubes were added to the pairs of light tubes at the top chord of the trusses. They can be seen in a picture accompanying a 1994 review in *A+U*. *A+U*, 287 (1994), pp. 134–35.

109 Colored and annotated drawings. May 5/September 9, no year. OMAR 1732. The visibility of the bracing in Hall 2 indicates that 1991 was the year of origin. The colors largely correspond to the building as it was in 1992.

110 The columns are diagonally pierced by cylindrical voids. Two spotlights are fixed within each void, pointing in opposite directions. A perspective sketch by Hoshino illustrates the impact. OMAR 1727.

111 Richard Ingersoll, "Rem Koolhaas e l'ironia," in *Casabella*, 610 (Mar 1994), p. 17.

112 Emmanuel Petit, "Rem Koolhaas," in *Irony: Or, The Self-Critical Opacity of Postmodern Architecture*, New Haven: Yale University Press, 2013, pp. 178–211.

piece (→ F 6.22).[113] Below the roofline, the five different columns of the portico parody the postmodern taste for quotation, while the Miesian neutrality inside is but one "hue" along a colorful *promenade architecturale*. The travertine cladding, in turn, recalls the classicist tendencies of recent museum architecture as well as postmodern leanings towards the discipline's classical tradition. No other building by OMA can match the abundance of explicit references. That is not to say that Koolhaas, while designing the Kunsthal, ceded to a similar penchant; but apparently he chose—at some point—to indulge in proverbial "penchants" of postmodern architecture in order to make them thematic. The "excessive" use of quotes indicates this purpose. "Excess," Tafuri wrote in the mid-1970s, "is always a bearer of consciousness."[114]

---

113 Compare detail no. 1, dating from April 19, 1990 (Stadsarchief Rotterdam, box 4) with facade detail no. 1 dating from February 28, 1992 (OMAR 1812).

114 Manfredo Tafuri, "The Ashes of Jefferson," in *The Sphere and the Labyrinth: Avant-Gardes and Architecture from Piranesi to the 1970s*, Cambridge, Massachusetts: The MIT Press, 1990, p. 297. First published in Italian in 1980.

P 8.1   View from Westzeedijk.

P 8.2 Portico.

P 8.3 View from the service road. Hall 2 and portico.

P 8.4 View from Museumpark. North and west facade.

P 8.5 West facade.

P 8.6   Auditorium, Hellingstraat, and Skew Ramp.

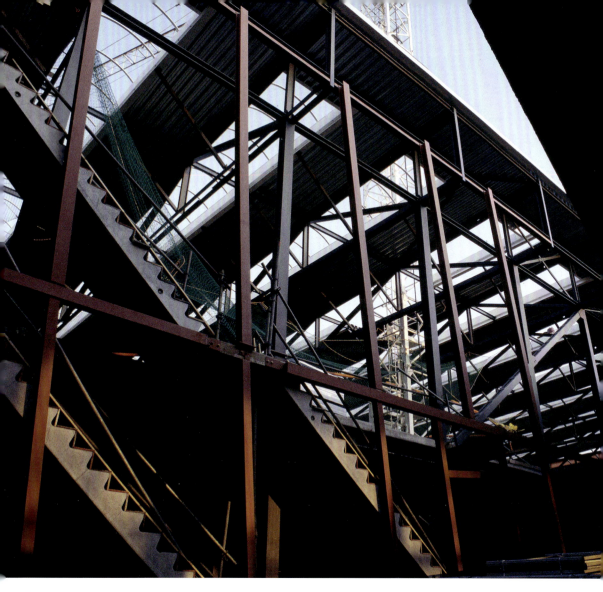

P 8.7   View from Hellingstraat towards Halls 1 and 2.

P 8.8   Hall 2.

P 8.9　　Skew Ramp. Left: Vierendeel truss along Hall 2, after the bend reinforced by diagonal bracings.

P 8.10   West facade. Inside the auditorium (left) are the illuminated steps of the seating.

P 8.11 Portico.

P 8.12 Hellingstraat.

P 8.13   Auditorium and service wall.

P 8.14   Hall 1. Left margin and behind the car: steel columns clad with hollowed-out tree trunks.

P 8.15 Hall 2.

P 8.16 Hall 2. The channel glass planks of the gallery along the east facade are behind the partition.

P 8.17 Balcony projecting into Hall 2. The tilted columns of the auditorium in the background.

P 8.18 Left: stepped ramp ascending to the roof. Right: auditorium.

Excess Is Always a Bearer of Consciousness

The Building of October 1992

When they thought that they were at length
prepared for this undertaking, they set fire
to all their towns ...

Julius Caesar

The opening of Kunsthal II was repeatedly postponed. In December 1988 it was scheduled for February 1992.[1] On August 3, 1990, the *Rotterdams Nieuwsblad* ran the headline: "Project costs five million more. Construction of Kunsthal will be stopped."[2] The missing sum was provided three weeks later by the Dutch minister of welfare, health and culture, Elco Brinkman, with the budget now totaling 25 million guilders.[3] In November 1992, the municipality announced a further cost overrun of 5 million guilders.[4] By then, the major construction work had been completed. The Kunsthal opened to the public on November 1, after its inauguration by Queen Beatrix on October 31, 1992. The building committee continued to meet once a month until April 1993, but the issues at stake were of little consequence in terms of design, perhaps with one exception. In 1990, an art competition was held, funded by the contractor Dura. The jury—Koolhaas among its members—met in fall 1990 and unanimously selected the proposal by Henk Visch from four submissions.[5] Visch proposed a sculpture representing a camel and its guide placed on a blue "desert" of concrete between the Kunsthal and Villa Dijkzigt. Only in June 1992, when it became clear that the budget of 200,000 guilders would cover camel and guide but not the "desert," did Visch suggest locating the figures on top of the orange exoskeletal girder protruding from the Kunsthal's portico.[6] In December, the camel and guide were set on the plate girder for a test.[7] Koolhaas and Dura, who had agreed to the experiment, wanted to see "the camel" removed, but in January 1993 it was still on the girder, where it has remained to this day (→ P 1.3).[8]

Why?

Between 1992 and 1994 about twenty reviews of the Kunsthal appeared in European, American, and Japanese journals and newspapers. The reception was largely enthusiastic. Terence Riley held that "the Kunsthal is surely OMA's most important built work to date," while Kenneth Frampton deemed it "the most rigorous and exhilarating civic work that Koolhaas has produced to date," and Belgian architect and critic Paul

1 "Nieuwbouw Kunsthal/6e Bouwcommissie," December 14, 1988. OMAR 1436.
2 "Project vijf miljoen duurder," in *Rotterdams Nieuwsblad* (August 3, 1990) (author's translation).
3 "Brinkman geeft vijf miljoenen voor kunsthal," in *Rotterdams Nieuwsblad* (August 28, 1989).
4 "Bouwcommissie: Nieuwbouw Kunsthal," November 30, 1992. OMAR 3266. The costs increased incrementally over the years for a variety of reasons. It seems that OMA was only marginally responsible for this occurrence.
5 The other participants were Günther Förg, Martha Schwartz, and Borek Sipek. "Henk Visch wint prijsvraag KunstHAL," in *De Architect* (December 1990), p. 27.
6 "Verslag van de 32e Bouwcommissie Nieuwbouw Kunsthal," February 11, 1991. OMAR 1522. Verslag Bouwcommissie: Nieuwbouw Kunsthal," June 18, 1992. OMAR 3266.
7 "Bouwcommissie: Nieuwbouw Kunsthal," December 17, 1992. OMAR 3266.
8 "Bouwcommissie: Nieuwbouw Kunsthal," January 14, 1993. OMAR 3266.

Vermeulen thought that the Kunsthal provided "the most stimulating experience produced in years by Dutch architecture."[9] The fragmented quality of the building, for its part, did not go unnoticed. Marie-Christine Loriers saw it as an echo of the complex juxtaposition of the two crossing routes and spiraling circuit; Sabine Schneider as a surrealist quality; the editors of ARCH+ as an approximation of the successive stage sets of theater plays; Emmanuel Doutriaux as an unresolved tension between control and instability reminiscent of Michelangelo; Lootsma and De Graaf as a response to the heterogeneity of the surroundings and an architectural experience akin to the "dynamic experience of art"; and Deyan Sudjic as a—deconstructivist—analogy to an "uncertain, fragmented world."[10] In her 1997 essay on the Kunsthal, Cynthia Davidson interpreted the fluidity of the circuit and the fragmented character of the architecture as two complementary features.[11] Davidson compared the juxtaposition of the continuity of the spectator's movement and the formal discontinuity of both exterior and interior to Jean-Luc Godard's use of the jump cut in film and, ultimately, to the discontinuous notion of time described by Gilles Deleuze in his writings on cinema. Aarati Kanekar, in her 2015 essay, picks up on Davidson's argument. Kanekar elucidates the parallels between the Kunsthal's design and the principle of filmic montage, taking recourse to Sergei Eisenstein and Le Corbusier in their receptions of Auguste Choisy's analysis of the Acropolis in Athens. She compares the Kunsthal's formal and constructive diversity to Eisenstein's concept of cut and disclosure.[12] The latter, Kanekar argues, concerns "commentaries within the architectural discourse"—but which commentaries, or which discourse, she does not say.[13] It is true, however, that there is something distinctly communicative and commentary-like about the Kunsthal, which has everything to do with the formal fragmentation to which Kanekar, like all the above authors, is referring. Indeed, it appears that the relation of the whole and its parts is particularly apt for exploring the intellectual reach and ideological charge of this piece of architecture. There is a question implied here that is rather overdue: How was it possible to work out the formal and constructive fragmentation of the design with passion, and even add to it, at a moment—from 1989 onwards—when Koolhaas was setting out for the conquest of a new whole, notably in opposition to the idea that architectural form should "picture" the fragmented condition of the present? Doesn't the formal fragmentation of the Kunsthal imply a similar "banal analogy" of world and form, even if the kind of fragmentation differs from that of the deconstructivists? Furthermore, and no less significant: How was it possible to endow the design of the Kunsthal with a host of modernist "memories," while wishing "not to be modern, but to be contemporary," and to "shake off that stigma of being modern"? This wish was expressed clearly and repeatedly in 1989, i.e. *prior* to working out much of the detailing in line with modernist precedents. As has been shown, this happened only at the turn of 1990 and during the two years or so that followed.

Some sort of pluralism at play

The final chapter of Martino Stierli's *Montage and the Metropolis* is dedicated to *Delirious New York* and related urbanist ideas of the 1970s and 1980s. Stierli points to the analogy between the vision of the modern city advocated in Koolhaas' book and a pluralist model of society. "In the late twentieth century," Stierli writes, "metropolitan montage becomes an increasingly encyclopedic medium of pluralism."[14] In addition to *Delirious New York*, Ungers and Koolhaas' 1976 project for Berlin—envisioning Berlin as a city archipelago—figures here as an example. Stierli does not claim that Koolhaas adopted the term pluralism itself, seemingly aware of the fact that Koolhaas rejected the word and consciously avoided its use.[15] But Stierli is right in suggesting that the thing itself—pluralism as the notion of multiple ideologies, political persuasions, religions, and ways of life coexisting within a single society—is manifest in much of Koolhaas' work from the 1970s and 1980s.

9 Terence Riley, "Rem Koolhaas/OMA: Urban Constructions," in *Newsline Columbia University*, vol. 5 (September 1992), p. 2; Kenneth Frampton, "Kunsthal a Rotterdam," in *Domus*, 747 (1993), p. 43; Paul Vermeulen, "Clad in Tonalities of Light," in *Architectuur in Nederland: Jaarboek 1992/1993*, eds. Matthijs de Boer et al., Rotterdam: NAi Publishers, 1993, p. 91.

10 Marie-Christine Loriers, "Culture oblique: KunstHAL, Rotterdam," in *Techniques & Architecture*, p. 408 (1993), pp. 82–87; Sabine Schneider, "Kunsthalle in Rotterdam: Trügerische Transparenz," in *Baumeister*, 11 (1992), pp. 41–44; Editorial staff, "Kunsthalle Rotterdam,"in *ARCH+*, 117 (1993), pp. 50–53; "Le Kunsthal de Rotterdam," in *L'Architecture d'Aujourd'hui*, 285 (1993), pp. 7–8; Bart Lootsma and Jan de Graaf, "In dienst van de ervaring: KunstHAL van OMA in Rotterdam," in *De Architect*, 1 (1993), pp. 20–25; Deyan Sudjic, "The Museum as a Megastar," in *The Guardian* (January 25, 1993), p. A7.

11 Cynthia Davidson, "Koolhaas and the Kunsthal: History Lesions," in *ANY*, 21 (1997), pp. 36–41.

12 Aarati Kanekar, "Space of Montage: Movement, Assemblage, and Appropriation in Koolhaas' Kunsthal," in *Architecture's Pretext: Spaces of Translation*, London: Routledge, 2015, p. 143.

13 Ibid., p. 144.

14 Martino Stierli, *Montage and the Metropolis: Architecture, Modernity, and the Representation of Space*, New Haven: Yale University Press, 2018, p. 26.

15 In 2015, Koolhaas stated "'Pluralistic' is a word I never would use." Florian Hertweck and Sébastien Marot, eds., *Die Stadt in der Stadt–Berlin: ein grünes Archipel*, Zurich: Lars Müller Publishers, 2013, pp. 137 (author's translation). Also published in English as *The City in the City–Berlin: A Green Archipelago*. In the same interview he explains: "I don't say that from a sense of intolerance, but for me any Anglo-Saxon word about politics is completely useless. I don't know what to make of 'pluralistic.' I think it is a very reduced notion of diversity," ibid., p. 139 (author's translation).

The dismissal of the uniform city as a model for urban planning is indeed an obvious parallel, not only between the city archipelago and *Delirious New York*, but also between both of these and *Collage City* by Rowe and Koetter. In the revised version of the publication accompanying the Berlin project, *The City in the City*, Ungers linked the project explicitly to the pluralist model of society: "Also from a political and societal vantage point," he explained, "it is a pluralistic concept in which several ideologically diverging ideas coexist."[16] Rowe and Koetter suggested the principle of collage as an urban approach in analogy to Karl Popper's "open society," which started off as a rejection of the totalitarian claim to absolute truth. Referring to Rowe's notion of contextualism, Stierli writes: "the integration of architectural object and urban space was meant not to produce homogeneity, but rather difference and contrast, indicative of a pluralist and heterogeneous urbanism of the present."[17]

With his 1987 masterplan for Melun-Sénart, Koolhaas, as Stierli puts it, "dismisses modernist totalitarian, all-encompassing planning for a piecemeal, insular development of the region."[18] Koolhaas' own explanation of the project was indeed not without overtones of societal allegory. Referring to the linear unbuilt areas called "islands," he asserted: "Each island can be developed almost completely independently from the others; the archipelago model ensures that the islands' unlimited freedom ultimately reinforces the coherence of the whole."[19] The figure of thought resembles Koolhaas' 1972 allegory of Manhattan entitled "The City of the Captive Globe"—an "ideological skyline" that rises from the "islands" of the uniform street blocks.[20] "The more each 'Island' celebrates different values," Koolhaas wrote, "the more the unity of the archipelago as system is reinforced."[21] Both assertions flirt with the option of being "overinterpreted," evoking the image of a society that prides itself on being essentially heterogeneous, and that considers the individual freedom it allows for—and, ultimately, its belief in individual freedom—a strength.

A farewell to the welfare state

When Charles Jencks, who had always advertised the ideological flexibility of postmodern architecture, visited the Kunsthal in 1993, he commented: "It [the building] is certainly going in the post-modern direction with lots of color, lots of humor, lots of tactility, lots of mystery, lots of surprise." During Jencks' subsequent visit to OMA's Rotterdam office, Koolhaas remarked, as if to counter the ideas of his friend:

"The definition of modernism without dogma is for me one of the most shocking non-sequiturs and the most repulsive concepts I know."[22] *Modernism Without Dogma*, however, was the title of the Dutch exhibition at the 1991 Venice Biennale featuring the work of young architects from the Netherlands such as Wiel Arets, Ben van Berkel, Willem Jan Neutelings, and Mecanoo. Hans Ibelings, who curated the exhibition, was referring specifically to the disentanglement of the modernist tradition of form from its socialist ideological roots. In the exhibition catalog, Ibelings wrote: "there is a renewed interest among younger architects in the intellectual tradition of modernism, an interest legible in their attempt to uphold certain principles. No-one, however, harbors the illusion that it is possible or even desirable to revitalize the societal program to which these were originally linked."[23]

Koolhaas has always insisted on architecture's ideological commitment, when criticizing his peers, while remaining largely silent about the ideological implications of his own projects, notably about the ideological implications of their form. Neither has he commented on the ideological connotations of the heterogeneity that is characteristic of much of OMA's work in the 1980s. And yet such connotations can hardly be denied, least of all in the case of the Kunsthal. The heterogeneity of the Rotterdam arts center lends itself very well to a built image of the society from which the project emerged, in a manner that was not all that different from Ungers' pluralist notion of the city. The essentially composite, contradictory, nonhierarchical order of the architecture, the relative autonomy of its parts, and the more subtle commitment of these parts to the whole appear charged with overtones of the societal agendas of Western welfare states in the postwar era.

Dirk van den Heuvel describes the huge impact that Alison and Peter Smithson's reception of *Open Society and Its Enemies* by Karl Popper had on Dutch architecture of that era, and on the Forum Group in particular.[24] Written during World War II, Popper's book was an answer to the immediate threat of fascism and totalitarianism in those

16 Quoted in ibid., pp. 95–96 (author's translation).
17 Stierli, *Montage and the Metropolis*, p. 239.
18 Ibid., p. 241.
19 OMA/Rem Koolhaas, "Urban Planning Competition: New Town of Melun-Sénart 1987," in *OMA—Rem Koolhaas*, ed. Jacques Lucan, Princeton Architectural Press: New York, 1991, p. 114.
20 Rem Koolhaas, *Delirious New York: A Retroactive Manifesto for Manhattan*, New York: The Monacelli Press, 1994, p. 294. First published by Oxford University Press, New York, in 1978.
21 Ibid., p. 296.
22 Charles Jencks, appearing on the TV program *PRIMA VISTA!* Jenny Borger et al. (May 23, 1993), VPRO.
23 Hans Ibelings, *Modernism Without Dogma: Architects of a Younger Generation in the Netherlands*, Rotterdam: Nederlands Architectuurinstituut, 1991, p. 5. Published to mark the Venice Architecture Biennale in 1991.
24 Dirk van den Heuvel, "The Open Society and Its Experiments: The Case of the Netherlands and Piet Blom," in *Architecture of the Welfare State*, eds. Mark Swenarton, Tom Avermaete, and Dirk van den Heuvel, London: Routledge, 2015, pp. 132–52.

years, but the ideological contest between the Western model of an open democratic society and the more or less totalitarian states behind the Iron Curtain continued throughout the Cold War. Van den Heuvel shows how Popper's advocacy of an open, egalitarian, democratic society based on individual freedom reverberates in the Kasbah housing project in Hengelo (1969–74) by Aldo van Eyck's protégé Piet Blom. Commenting in 1970, Blom drew a picture of the residents' future that clearly embraced the idea of the multicultural, pluralist society: "[E]very house its own situation; houses for singles, houses for the many, for the working-class and migrant workers, students and civil servants, academics and artists, for adventurers, priests, a junk dealer, any trouble maker; for big and small families, for complete and broken marriages; for big and small children, for orderly, noisy, Christian, left-wing, right-wing, socialist, brown, green, yellow, white and black people."[25]

The kind of activity that Blom envisioned unfolding is not so different from Koolhaas' concept of the Kunsthal as a "marked space within an urban field," which ideally would be open to any kind of user and any kind of use. All 184 houses in the carpetlike development are raised on columns, providing the entire open space below for collective use (→ F 7.1–7.2). Van den Heuvel explains: "In its original conception the undercroft was meant as a Situationist *terrain vague*, an open landscape to be appropriated by that favorite of the post-war Dutch avant-garde, Johan Huizinga's playing man, or *Homo Ludens*."[26] Looking back, Constant's New Babylon in all its radicalism appears similarly indebted to the idea of a welfare state, anticipating how a state of this kind may ideally evolve, before *The Limits to Growth* became apparent during the economic crises of the 1970s: universal, all-encompassing structures that provide for all the material needs of society, with the organization of leisure and the intensification of experience as the last problems to be resolved. Van den Heuvel reports that the actual construction of experimental projects like those by Piet Blom—along with Van Eyck's Mothers' House in Amsterdam (1973–78), Hertzberger's Muziekcentrum Vredenburg in Utrecht (1973–79), and Van Klingeren's 't Karregat in Eindhoven (1970–73) as further examples—were facilitated by the representatives of the Dutch government, both at a national and communal level:[27] "The Netherlands provided some of the most radical experiments in architecture, all under the banner of the welfare state. They were sanctioned by would-be enlightened officials, who supported experiment and innovation as an alternative to the technocratic tendencies that were also part of the welfare state system."[28]

F 7.1

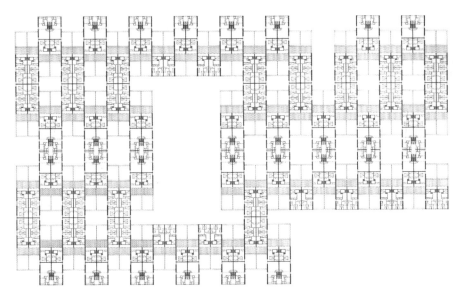

Piet Blom, Kasbah, Hengelo, 1969–74. Overall floorplan.

F 7.2

Piet Blom, Kasbah, Hengelo, 1969–74. Model.

25 Quoted in Van den Heuvel, "The Open Society and Its Experiments," p. 140.

26 Van den Heuvel, "The Open Society and Its Experiments," p. 141.

27 Ibid., p. 140.

Just like the NAi, the Kunsthal emerged from a partnership between the Dutch government and Rotterdam's municipality. The Kunsthal is the product of a welfare state that planned, built, and subsidized cultural institutions as much as public housing. And yet the Kunsthal was designed and built in a period marking the end of the Dutch welfare state in the form it had taken over previous decades. As Bart Lootsma points out, the Netherlands were particularly sensitive to the economic restructuring of Western economies and the neoliberal turn of European integration in particular: "As a small trading nation, the Netherlands is perhaps more susceptible to these developments than other countries and therefore forced to anticipate the developing situation, among other things, at a political level. The unification of Europe has played an important part in this because of policies committed to developing open markets. The required process of deregulation has obliged the Dutch government to abolish, privatize or otherwise change countless public agencies, subsidies and laws. An important byproduct of this process that has significantly affected architecture occurred when the official subsidies for social housing construction were terminated in 1994. The housing corporations that formerly commissioned projects on a non-profit basis all had their debts annulled, and have been obliged to operate as independent property developers on the free market ever since."[29] A more recent study on this subject suggests a causal link between the "grossing and balancing operation" to which Lootsma is referring and the process of European integration: "the post-1995 disengagement of government from their activities represents a form of privatization. It was partially motivated by the government's wish to limit its recorded budget deficits, as these were a part of the Maastricht Treaty's convergence criteria for membership of the new European single currency."[30]

The Kunsthal, as architecture, has little in common with the aforementioned examples of welfare state architecture. Within the boundaries of modular variation, Blom's Kasbah—as well as Dutch structuralism in general—is repetitive to the point of uniformity, implying the idea of an egalitarian society and a state that provides a neutral, homogeneous framework in which the diversity of an individualistic society may unfold. If, on a metaphorical level, structuralist architecture represents the state securing individual freedom, the architecture of the Kunsthal approximates the society *within* the state, whose actions may transcend the freedom granted. There is no universal order to "govern" the divergent parts of the building. It does not need much imagination to translate the formal and constructive autonomy of parts—from the single column to entire sections of the structure or the facades—into the image of individual and collective freedom within a pluralist and profoundly heterogeneous society (→ F 7.3). In this sense, the Kunsthal allowed for identification with the client—the city of Rotterdam, then governed by the social democratic PvdA—in advocating an open, pluralist society, and to the Rotterdamers who were in support of this kind of agenda. In 2013, Rotterdam historian Wouter Vanstiphout recalled his first encounter with the Kunsthal: "Seeing the building from the inside out, resembling an impossibly raw concrete mess in mid-collapse, was mesmerizing. [...] You felt vindicated and understood as one of Rotterdam's voluntary inmates. As so much great art, it is a merciless portrait of the city as well as its manifesto, and it feels like it has been made just for you."[31]

Unlike the structuralist buildings by Van Eyck, Hertzberger, Blom, and others, the structure of the Kunsthal does not provide a homogeneous framework. On the contrary, it is the structure that is

F 7.3

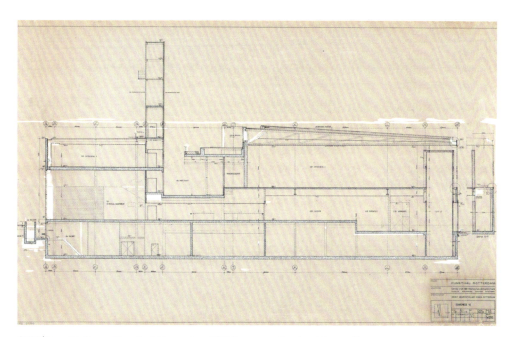

OMA/Rem Koolhaas, Kunsthal, November 1991. Cross section (east to west).

28 Ibid., p. 136.
29 Bart Lootsma, *Superdutch: New Architecture in the Netherlands*, London, Thames and Hudson, 2000, p. 21. Christophe Van Gerrewey mentions that during the 1980s "120,000 housing units are produced per year by the Dutch Ministry, only ten percent free market." See Christophe Van Gerrewey, "A Weissenhofsiedlung for Amsterdam: OMA's IJplein," in *Log*, 44 (2018), p. 87.
30 Marja Elsinga, Mark Stephens, and Thomas Knorr-Siedow, "The Privatisation of Social Housing: Three Different Pathways," in *Social Housing in Europe*, eds. Kathleen Scanlon, Christine Whitehead et al., p. 397.
31 Wouter Vanstiphout, in *Blueprint*, 331 (2013), p. 27.

distorted, oblique, out of line, and in conflict with other parts of the building, conveying images of instability and collision. The system itself seems out of joint, if not at the point of collapse or at the moment of its overthrow: as if the acts of spontaneous appropriation—"anticipated" by much of the detailing—afflicted the order from which they originated (→ F 7.4–7.7). Perhaps the rage is directed against a Foucauldian system of institutions, invisibly disciplining the purported freedom of a society that unknowingly complies to an inescapable weave of internalized rules. It is through such overtones that the Kunsthal appears faithful to Koolhaas' metropolitan agenda, for which subversion—understood as an impact on the existing order that is at the very least temporarily destabilizing—has always been essential. But in Koolhaasian theory, it is the task of program rather than form to induce instability. "In architecture," he explained in 1983, "you have a series of programs and so on, for example you can have an oyster bar, a gym, and a theater foyer, and you have to combine them in a way that is like the trigger making certain events explode."[32] At the Kunsthal, however, it is the architecture that does the job.

It has been mentioned above that Reinhold Martin has interpreted the "democratic path"—referring to public passages like the one traversing Stirling's Staatsgalerie in Stuttgart—as a *sujet* characteristic of the West German museum in the postwar era (→ F 3.1).[33] Hellingstraat crossing the Kunsthal and the overall transparency of the building continue this tradition. The connotations of egalitarian "openness" are implicit. It appears by no means unlikely that the idea of dividing the building into "four separate squares" was inspired by a contemporary building such as Richard Meier's Museum Angewandte Kunst (Museum of Applied Arts) in Frankfurt (1979–85), likewise composed of four "squares" at the junction of two intersecting routes (→ F 3.2). The "democratic path," however, also occurred in museum designs in other Western countries of that period, for example in Arata Isozaki's Museum of Contemporary Art in Los Angeles (1982–86), and as a bridged passage dividing the extension of the National Gallery in London (1985–91) by Venturi and Scott Brown from the existing building. As for Hellingstraat, Peter Eisenman's Wexner Center for Visual Arts in Ohio (1983–89), crossed by a fully glazed ramp, might have served as a model.

F 7.4

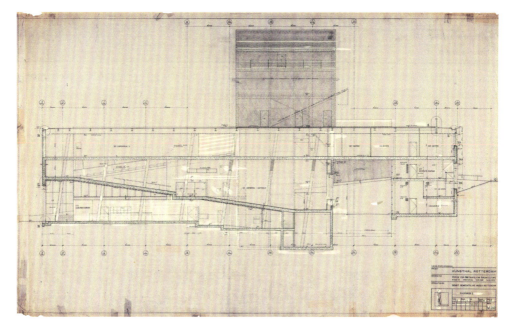

OMA/Rem Koolhaas, Kunsthal, November 1991. Cross section (north to south).

F 7.5

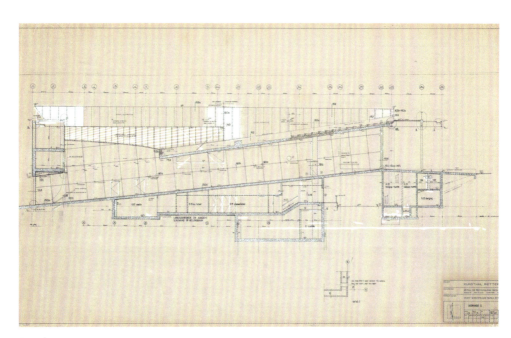

OMA/Rem Koolhaas, Kunsthal, July 1992. Hellingstraat. Cross section, looking east.

32 Franco Raggi, "Edonista-puritano," in *Modo*, 58 (1983), p. 26 (author's translation).

33 William Curtis, "Virtuosity Around a Void," in *Architectural Review*, 1054 (1984), p. 41.

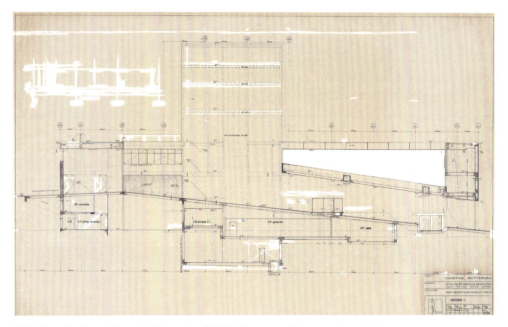

OMA/Rem Koolhaas, Kunsthal, November 1991. Hellingstraat. Cross section, looking west.

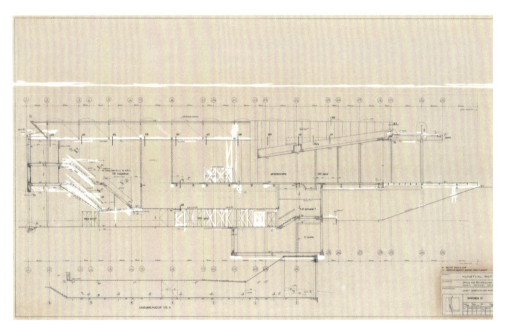

OMA/Rem Koolhaas, Kunsthal, March 1992. Cross section through the service wall of Halls 1 and 2.

The pull of the analogy

David Harvey in *The Condition of Postmodernity* and Fredric Jameson in *Postmodernism, or, the Cultural Logic of Late Capitalism* explain the fragmentation of form in postmodernist culture as an increasing fragmentation of experience. Harvey uses the term "time–space compression," denoting both a changed experience of time and space and the economic, political, and technological shift during the 1970s and 1980s that this experience reflects.[34] For Jameson, the contemporary experience of fragmentation is akin to the incapacity of "temporal unification" experienced by schizophrenics which dissolves the continuity of past, present, and future in "a series of pure and unrelated presents in time."[35] As the actual cause of the fragmented perception, both authors identify the emergence of new technologies and fundamental changes to the global economic system: the "emergence of more flexible modes of capital accumulation"[36] (Harvey) and "late capitalism"[37] (Jameson), entailing among other things a "new international division of labor, a vertiginous new dynamic in international banking and the stock exchanges [...] new form of media interrelationship [...] computers and automation."[38] If that is the case, it was merely a matter of perspective whether the thrust of European integration and the globalization of markets meant more fragmentation, or less. The individual was likely to experience those changes as a bewildering fragmentation of their environment in space and time, while the transnational corporation welcomed them as the unification of isolated economic domains. Harvey touches upon this ambiguity: "We thus approach the central paradox: the less important the spatial barriers, the greater the sensitivity of capital to the variations of place within space, and the greater the incentive for places to be differentiated in ways attractive to capital. The result has been the production of fragmentation, insecurity, and ephemeral uneven development within a highly unified global space economy of capital flows."[39]

---

34 In the chapter "Time–Space Compression in the Postmodern Condition," Harvey writes: "I want to suggest that we have been experiencing, these last two decades, an intense phase of time–space compression that has had a disorienting and disruptive impact upon political-economic practices, the balance of class power, as well as upon cultural and social life." David Harvey, *The Condition of Postmodernity*, Oxford: Blackwell Publishing, 2015, p. 284. First published in 1990.

35 Fredric Jameson, *Postmodernism, or, The Cultural Logic of Late Capitalism*, London/New York: Verso, 1992, p. 27.
36 Harvey, *The Condition of Postmodernity*, p. xii.
37 Jameson, *Postmodernism*, p. xix.
38 Ibid.
39 Ibid., p. 296.

Woody Allen's 1983 movie *Zelig* and Cindy Sherman metamorphizing beyond recognition in her staged self-portraits seem to be good ways of illustrating the perspective of the individual and the unceasing transformational gymnastics that it is compelled to perform in the changeable world of late capitalism. Harvey, who mentions Sherman's work repeatedly, interprets her photography of "masks" precisely in this sense of personal discontinuity.[40] Allen's fictional character Leonard Zelig, dubbed "the human chameleon," adopts the appearances and ways of any given social milieu, turning into a rabbi among rabbis as readily as he becomes a Nazi officer among Nazi officers, or a psychiatrist among psychiatrists, and so forth. Under hypnosis, Zelig wearily confesses two major motives for doing so: to be safe, to be liked. His restless metamorphosis is essentially a technique for survival. Jameson suggests that the socioeconomic discontinuity experienced by the individual may translate into formal fragmentation, referring to the music of John Cage and Bob Perelman's 1981 poem "China."[41] Jameson thus establishes a ("banal") analogy between world and form, quite similar to the one Koolhaas identified and dismissed as the conceptual core of deconstructivist architecture. Considering the eminent role of fragmentation and heterogeneity in OMA's work, one wonders about the extent to which Koolhaas himself succumbed to the pull of a similar analogy. It is of some significance, in this context, that Koolhaas studied and taught at American universities and at the AA School of Architecture in London. His studies at Cornell and his research in New York in the 1970s, as well as the fact that he taught and lived in London during the Thatcher era (1979–90) must have provided plenty of occasion to observe the "late capitalist" (the term "neoliberalism," with its negative connotations, only came into common use in the 1990s) restructuring of Anglo–American society at close range, long before it reached the European continent with full force in the wake of European integration.[42] As much as Koolhaas did believe in the necessity of an analogy between world and form in architecture, it appears likely that he considered some sort of renunciation of unity to be a matter of artistic credibility, if not truth. If so, only a different world or worldview could redeem architecture from the spell of fragmentation. And as has been seen, the "highly unified global space economy of capital flows" did offer a perspective of this kind.[43]

A style directed at the present, understood primarily in relation to the past

To this day, the obvious deconstructivist leanings of the Kunsthal play a marginal role in its reception. In the 1990s, Sudjic alluded to them in one of the few critical reviews of the building, while Bernard Hulsman identified with caution "some features that might be regarded as deconstructivist."[44] Perhaps the critique of deconstructivist architecture that Koolhaas voiced in a growing number of interviews prevented other reviewers from addressing the issue altogether. Needless to say, the "distortion" of the Skew Ramp, its rupture with the orthogonal order of the structural system, and its spatial interference with both adjacent sections of the building do have strong deconstructivist connotations. No less "deconstructivist" is the image of instability and collapse conveyed by the tapered columns of the restaurant, the auditorium, and Hall 3. In the Kunsthal, stereotypical deconstructivist traits coexist with those mentioned above that necessarily bring postmodern architecture to mind—parts of the building that provoke the notion of quoting something, or of being ironic, theatrical, or even classicist. This simultaneous exposure of deconstructivist and postmodernist features contradicted Koolhaas' declared rejection of either architectural current. At the same time, it questions the alleged opposition of deconstructivist and postmodern architecture, disclosing the common ground of their shared reliance on both formal fragmentation and past forms of architecture. If deconstructivist architecture implies the ongoing disintegration of a whole, notably the deconstructivism targeted by Koolhaas' critique, the postmodern quotation alone creates a sense of fragmentation. Being extracted from its original context, the citation is a fragment in a literal sense, just like the remainders of the project's previous stages.[45] The two attitudes converge in the Kunsthal's auditorium and in Hellingstraat, which are both deconstructivist distortions and postmodern quotes of Maison Dom-Ino and the *pilotis*. Just as Hadid's early projects rely on Malevich's suprematism, or Tschumi's follies at Parc de la Villette on the work of Chernikhov, the auditorium and Hellingstraat rely on Le Corbusier—although with the difference that the latter dependence is made thematic.

40 Ibid., p. 7.
41 Jameson, *Postmodernism*, pp. 28–29.
42 The issue appears crucial for understanding the enthusiasm with which Koolhaas devised OMA's new agenda at the turn of the 1990s. Back then, the alignment with Europe's economic restructuring must have appeared significantly less "inaccurate" than today, or even than the second half of the 1990s.
43 Harvey, *The Condition of Postmodernity*, p. 296.
44 Bernard Hulsman, "Kunsthal lijkt wel een overdoos," in *NRC Handelsblad* (October 31, 1992) (author's translation).
45 See Peter Bürger, *Theorie der Avantgarde*, Göttingen: Wallstein Verlag, 2017, p. 91. First published in 1974.

Victor Buchli, in a 2011 article, connects the propensity of postmodernist design and architecture to utilize fragmentation, quotation, parody, and pastiche to Lévi-Strauss' notion of bricolage, as outlined in the latter's book *The Savage Mind*. What Buchli has in mind is not the amateur's arbitrary range of means but rather a cultural condition that imposes an essential indebtedness to the past, because the new and whole is no longer attainable historically. This postmodern bricoleur, "accepts the world as it is and reconfigures it, rather than anticipating a new world and inventing it. In this respect the bricoleur has a different concept of time compared to the modernist: one that is retrospective, based on the continuous reworking of the received elements of the world, as opposed to prospective and filled with imagined new conditions and possibilities."[46] At the root of this attitude, Buchli discerns the violent backlash against political movements in 1968 and the subsequent retreat of utopian projections in Western countries.[47] Buchli writes: "Bricoleurs are avowedly non-utopian in the sense that they do not imagine a new language or set of material circumstances that would remake the world. It is no accident that postmodernism should have emerged in the wake of the collective disillusionment with progressive movements such as communism, following the Prague Spring of 1968. Any hopes still held by the European left for the project of Soviet socialism were brutally dashed. What some might call a nihilistic impulse, which postmodern design groups such as Studio Alchymia [sic] embodied, can be understood more as an acknowledgment that the utopian promise of Western rationality was doomed. All that could be done was to work with the ready-at-hand, the structures of capitalist industry and consumerism within which postmodern output emerged."

Not only the progressive Left was disillusioned; with the economic crises of the 1970s, Western societies seem to have lost confidence in the "feasibility" of their future on a much broader basis. In a 1983 interview with Franco Raggi, Koolhaas compares the general situation of architecture at the time to the morning after a party: "You know, when you're surrounded by a big mess, and everybody has a hangover headache." Asked what party he had in mind, Koolhaas replies: "The party of an architecture that is socially and aesthetically legitimate, of a 'powerful' design"—apparently referring to the socially and politically engaged modernist projects of the early twentieth century.[48] In Rowe and Koetter's concept of the Collage City—which does avowedly draw on Lévi-Strauss' notion of the bricoleur— utopia survives in the form of the politically neutralized fragment.[49]

Hadrian's commemorative villa at Tivoli, understood as "an accumulation of disparate ideal fragments," figures here as a model.[50]

From all that has been stated above, it should be clear that the formal fragmentation of OMA's early work is also closely related to borrowings from the past, namely modernist architectures of the 1920s, 1930s, 1950s, and 1960s. Much of what T. J. Clark says about Picasso, cubist painting, and the bohemia of the nineteenth century does apply to the relation between Koolhaas, modernist architecture, and OMA's work of the 1980s, the Kunsthal included: "Cubism […] is a style directed to a present primarily understood in relation to the past: it is a modest, decent, and touching appraisal of one moment in history, as opposed to a whirling glimpse into a world-historical present-becoming-future. It is commemorative. Its true power derives not from its modernity, that is, if we mean by this a reaching toward an otherness ahead in time, but from its profound belonging to a modernity that was passing away."[51]

Painted collage

For Koolhaas, the true power, to use Clark's words, of his work in the 1970s and 1980s appears to be a profound belonging to the short, fading modernity of the 1920s and 1930s. It allowed for a reflectivity that indeed recalls Picasso's collages and painted collages of the 1910s and 1920s to which the above quote partly refers. Of course, the comparison is limited to a twofold analogy: an analogy in terms of technique, i.e. collage, and the analogy of using collage to thematize one's own artistic tradition.[52] "Collage," Clark writes elsewhere, having in mind exactly this body of work, "entertained the idea that art's main forms and compelling figures could be generated, now, out of nothing but internal, differential play between any old elements. A patch of pure color, a piece of banal illusionism; a pattern of dots, a fragment of newsprint, a calling card, a key signature: what mattered was the energy of the sign's coexistence."[53]

46 Victor Buchli, "On Bricolage," in *Postmodernism: Style and Subversion 1970–1990*, eds. Glenn Adamson and Jane Pavitt, London: V & A Publishing, 2011, p. 113.
47 Ibid., p. 115.
48 Raggi, "Edonista-puritano," p. 28 (author's translation).
49 The technique of collage "might be a means of permitting us the enjoyment of utopian poetics without being obliged to suffer the embarrassment of utopian politics." Colin Rowe and Fred Koetter, *Collage City*, Cambridge, Massachusetts: The MIT Press, 1978, p. 149.
50 Ibid., p. 90.
51 T. J. Clark, *Picasso and Truth: From Cubism to Guernica*, Princeton: Princeton University Press, 2013, p. 74.
52 As with the recurring comparisons between Eisenstein and Koolhaas in their use of montage, the analogies discussed here are by no means intended to indicate the comparability of the broader historical context.
53 Ibid., p. 136.

In 1983, Koolhaas gave a rare comment on his own use of fragmentation, explaining: "I think that fragmentation is a natural condition that allows you to observe things as separate episodes which can be connected, or simply coexist by dint of vicinity so that meaning is ultimately generated through the presence of differences."[54] Russian director Sergei Eisenstein, when outlining his notion of the "dramatic principle" of montage in the 1920s, seems to spell out what Koolhaas has in mind: "*in my view montage is not an idea composed of successive shots stuck together but an idea that* DERIVES *from the collision between two shots that are independent from one another* [...]. As in Japanese hieroglyphics in which two independent ideographic characters ('shots') are juxtaposed and *explode* into a concept. THUS:

>   Eye + Water = Crying
>   Door + Ear = Eavesdropping
>   Child + Mouth = Screaming
>   Mouth + Dog = Barking [...]"[55]

In the final scene at the end of his 1925 film *Strike*, Eisenstein conveys the sense of carnage by combining pictures showing czarist soldiers that persecute and shoot the crowd of strikers with images showing the slaughter of cattle. In 1931, John Heartfield mounted the photo of a tiger's head onto a portrait of a "capitalist" with a swastika in his tie, ridiculing the social democrat's idea of supporting capitalism in order to tame it.[56] Picasso's 1912 collage *Feuille de musique et guitar* evokes the idea of music being played by combining fragments of a musical score with a "guitar" composed of differently cut and colored pieces of paper. There is, evidently, a basic operation common to all three works of art and their respective techniques of filmic montage, photomontage, and collage: to create meaning by combining at least two distinctly different images. Similarly, Fredric Jameson saw the principle of "differentiation" at the core of postmodern art: "I would like to characterize the postmodernist experience of form with what will seem, I hope, a paradoxical slogan: namely, the proposition that 'difference relates.' Our own recent criticism [...] has been concerned to stress the heterogeneity and profound discontinuities of the work of art, no longer united or organic, but now a virtual grab bag or lumber room of disjoined subsystems and random raw materials and impulses of all kinds. The former work of art, in other words, has now turned out to be a text, whose reading proceeds by differentiation rather than by unification."[57]

Jameson takes Nam June Paik's simultaneous display of television screens as an example. Paik confronts the beholder with the "impossible imperative" to read, Jameson explains, conjuring up the epiphany of a world governed by the incomprehensible flows of multinational capital. But apart from conveying such experiences of what Jameson identifies as the postmodern sublime, the message of the "text" is unlikely to be tangible and clear. Later in the book, Jameson points out what distinguishes Eisenstein's pedagogical use of montage from the montage in Godard's films: "It is no longer certain, for instance, that the heavily charged monitory juxtaposition in a Godard film—an advertising image, a printed slogan, newsreels, an interview with a philosopher, and the gestus of this or that fictive character—will be put back together by the spectator in the form of a message, let alone the right message."[58]

Asked in 1993 by Cynthia Davison whether "architecture itself is something one can read literally as text," Koolhaas replied: "I think some of the best works can be read as text."[59] Read as "text," OMA's early work is about many things, modernist architecture and urbanism, for instance, as well as modernization, mass society, surrealism, popular culture, and pessimism. In the Kunsthal, the historic reflection is extended to the present: to postmodernism, deconstructivism, and, implicitly, to OMA's own work of the past decade. This vast scope of diverse and at times contradictory positions would have been impossible to "address" with such explicitness if not through the "differential play between any old elements" (Clark) and the fragmentation of form it entails. The Kunsthal as a "text," however, is no more pedagogical or didactic than the films by Godard that Jameson refers to. It is barely possible to pin down a message, "let alone the right message." That the Kunsthal is about architecture, just as Picasso's pictures from the 1910s and 1920s are about painting, is relatively clear, but what it actually "says" about architecture much less so, as 1990s reviews of the arts center and their divergent "readings" demonstrate.

In the 1980s, the medium of collage played a significant role for OMA's architectural production.[60] Kunsthal aside, collages representing the facades were produced for the Netherlands Dance Theater, the Byzantium, Patio Villa and the NAi in Rotterdam, Villa dall'Ava, and

54 Raggi, "Edonista-puritano," p. 26 (author's translation).
55 Sergei Eisenstein, "Dramaturgy of Film Form," in *S. M. Eisenstein: Selected Works*, vol. I, *Writings 1922–34*, ed. Richard Taylor, London: BFI Publishing, 1988, pp. 163–64. Italics in the original.
56 John Heartfield, "Zum Krisen-Parteitag der SPD," in *Arbeiter Illustrierte Zeitung* (June 15, 1931).
57 Jameson, *Postmodernism*, p. 31.
58 Ibid., p. 191.
59 Cynthia Davidson, "Rem Koolhaas: 'Why I Wrote Delirious New York and Other Textual Strategies,'" in *ANY*, 0 (May/June 1993), p. 42.
60 On this issue, see Mathieu Berteloot and Véronique Patteeuw, "OMA's Collages," in *OMA: The First Decade*, pp. 66–74.

Pablo Picasso, *Portrait of a Young Girl*, 1914.

the ZKM media center in Karlsruhe.⁶¹ Strictly speaking, however, neither the Kunsthal nor its facades are collages or montages, at least not more so than any other building of its time. Each of the Kunsthal's surfaces—however distinct and different from the adjacent ones—is a construction in itself. Unlike a strip of wallpaper or a frame of a film, it is not "of one piece," and physically it does not coincide with what it relates to. The cruciform column of the portico was not retrieved from Mies' dissembled Barcelona pavilion. Rather, the Kunsthal resembles one of those paintings by Picasso that *imitate* collages (→ F 7.8). Like the collage, its painted imitation makes it possible to epitomize a multitude of antagonistic realities without truly committing to any of them. The Kunsthal, like Picasso's painted collages, evinces a taste for incompatibilities, using the formal and referential structure of the collage as a means to recall, to oppose, to reflect, to question, to undermine. The comparison is not intended to suggest any sort of reference to Picasso's art or the latter's influence on the work of OMA, but it may help to clarify the affinity of the Kunsthal's architecture to collage and its limits, purely in terms of technique.

Gallic wars

Koolhaas has repeatedly described his design strategies as well as those of other architects in military terms—as a military campaign, a blitzkrieg, a carpet bombardment, a stealth, a strategic weapon, a battle, a war.⁶² The impulse to prevail, in the field of architecture—to prevail through distinction in a Bourdieuian sense—might be one of the strongest and most persistent influences on Koolhaas' strategic choices. His often observed and avowed obsession with opposing has its place here. Studying these dynamics of distinction has been one of the guiding themes of this book, and a consideration of this kind may have the "last word" in the exegesis of the Kunsthal and the issue of fragmentation.

61 The collaged facades of Villa dall'Ava are held by the architecture collection of Centre Pompidou. Three facades of the Byzantium, featured on OMA's website, are apparently collages: https://oma.eu/projects/byzantium (accessed December 31, 2019).

62 Allusions to architecture and urbanism include: "military campaign" in an interview with Marta Cervelló, "I've always been anxious with the standard typology of the average architect with a *successful* career," in *Quaderns*, 183 (1989), p. 80; "bombardments of speculation," in Rem Koolhaas, "The Terrifying Beauty of the Twentieth Century," in *OMA—Rem Koolhaas*, ed. Jacques Lucan, Princeton Architectural Press: New York, 1991, p. 155; "Blitzkrieg" in an interview with Hans van Dijk, "De architect is verplicht om een respectabel mens te zijn," in *Archis*, 11 (1994), p. 18; "theoretical carpet bombardment" in Rem Koolhaas, "Atlanta," in *S, M, L, XL*, Koolhaas and Bruce Lau, New York: The Monacelli Press, 1995, p. 850; "strijd" (battle) in an interview with Mil De Kooning, "De economie van de verbeelding," in *Vlees & Beton*, 4 (1985), n.p.; "War" in Rem Koolhaas, "Singapore Songlines," in *S, M, L, XL*, Koolhaas and Lau, p. 1035; "stealth," in Koolhaas, "The Generic City," ibid., p. 1262; "strategic weapon" in Koolhaas, "The Generic City," ibid., p. 1264.

In his *Gallic Wars*, Julius Caesar reports that the Helvetic tribes, when preparing to conquer the territory of the Gauls, set fire to all their towns and villages so that "after destroying the hope of a return home, they might be the more ready for undergoing all dangers."[63] With the Kunsthal, Koolhaas similarly set a smoldering fire to the ground on which OMA was standing and which had nourished the best of its work for more than a decade: advocating modernism as a position; the modernist tradition as a frame of reference made thematic; formal fragmentation as a way of breathing life into its odds and ends, of creating built visions of metropolitan activity, suffusing OMA's work with irony, criticality, and subversion, and, ultimately, underlining architecture's potential to dispose of an intellectual dimension. The architecture of the Kunsthal, in all its kaleidoscopic ambiguity, exposes what Koolhaas identified as the moribund core of not only postmodern and deconstructivist architecture but also OMA's own: the perpetual dependence on the past and reproduction of a fragmented world—as if to mobilize the forces of denial for OMA's exodus to the realm of the large scale and the whole.

According to his own account, Koolhaas began to write *S, M, L, XL* in December 1992, a month after the Kunsthal had opened, after "thinking about it long before."[64] Only in the years that followed did it become fully apparent that Koolhaas and OMA were leaving their supposed homelands. The Kunsthal "knew" of the departure, and this knowledge is inscribed in its architecture. It is the knowledge of the form's ideological basis being eroded, of depending on forms borrowed from the past, of sharing this dependence both with postmodernist and deconstructivist architecture, and of self-critically exposing this dependence, of such a position being obsolete and eventually untenable. The obliqueness (and fragmentation) of the Kunsthal has nothing to do with the surplus of forces and the optimistic dynamism of constructivist architecture; rather it suggests collapse. In this sense, the Kunsthal appears as a work of destruction. Its actual "concern" is not to judge past failures or achievements, be they of modernist architecture, of postmodernist or deconstructivist architecture, or the work so far accomplished by OMA; its actual concern is the architectural production of tomorrow. The Kunsthal, as a work of destruction, is about the dependence *of the present* on a bygone era of modernist architecture and its ideological foundations. It demands departure.

In the work subsequently undertaken by OMA, the issue of nostalgia—nostalgia of the 1920s, 1930s, 1950s, and 1960s—would scarcely be raised again. Even the two projects closest to the Kunsthal, the ZKM media center in Karlsruhe and the Congrexpo in Lille, do not stress their dependence on modernist precedents. Despite their adherence to formal fragmentation, both projects bespeak the search for the new, eschewing the postmodern feel of quotation and pastiche as much as the deconstructivist gestures of collision and collapse. Perhaps Koolhaas had a presentiment while the Kunsthal was underway that the project would be something like the "last of its kind," an architecture marked by the reflection of its own modernist past, and so he pushed this sort of reflectivity to the extreme, accumulating and interweaving more quotes, pastiches, transformations, and violations of modernist precedents than ever before. More importantly, an "excess"—of pastness, of fragmentation—was necessary to make his argument heard.

Caesar reports that not a single enemy took flight during the fierce battle lasting an entire day, and according to Plutarch even the women and children fought back to the death. But the Helvetic tribes were defeated by the Roman troops all the same, and Caesar forced them to return to their devastated homelands. By contrast, the "exodus" of OMA would be lasting. Sanford Kwinter wrote in 1996: "Among architects [...] Koolhaas is the true American, for he is the only one to have attempted to engage the absolute and pure future."[65] During the 1990s, OMA *did* conquer the new territory marked out by the revised agenda of "metropolitan congestion," while retaining a set of essential themes and ideas: the reinvention of internalized collective space; the methodical exploitation of heterogeneous programs in the service of dense and intense experience; the interest in the (surrealist) creativity of the unconscious and the destabilizing loss of control; and the creation of hybrid structures and heterogeneous interiors that inspire the envisioned dynamics of program and use.

"In more than thirty years of writing about architecture," Herbert Muschamp wrote about OMA's Seattle Library in 2004, "this is the most exciting new building it has been my honor to review."[66] For Roberto Gargiani, the CCTV Headquarters, alongside a series of other projects from this period, represent the apotheosis of what Koolhaas had been striving for throughout his career as an architect: *merveilles*, namely projects that stun and surprise, taking recourse

---

63 Julius Caesar, *The Gallic Wars*, Merchant Books, 2012, p. 7.

64 Arie Graafland and Jasper de Haan, "A Conversation with Rem Koolhaas," in *The Critical Landscape*, eds. Michael Speaks, Arie Graafland, and Jasper de Haan, Rotterdam: 010 Publishers, 1996, pp. 220–21.

65 Sanford Kwinter, "Flying the Bullet, or When Did the Future Begin?" in *Rem Koolhaas: Conversations with Students*, New York: Princeton Architectural Press, 1996, p. 75.

66 Herbert Muschamp, "The Library That Puts on Fishnets and Hits the Disco," in *The New York Times* (May 16, 2004).

to a repertoire of surrealist techniques and imagery.[67] To be sure, OMA's projects of the 2000s and 2010s have been largely identified—often dismissively, in part approvingly—with phenomena that seemed to belong to the present as much as the future: globalization, consumerism, recent capitalism, postcriticality, managerial pragmatism, research-based design, iconic architecture. One can only speculate what Adorno, whose notion of Right Consciousness inspired this book, would have thought of these buildings. It is beyond doubt that he believed true art—and true architecture, in as much as it means participating in the sphere of aesthetics—would, by definition, oppose the rule of capitalism and consumerist culture. Neither does it appear likely that the "defeat" of socialism would have changed his mind. But it might have met Adorno's idea of Right Consciousness in going beyond the "certainties" of fragmentation, the quote, the pastiche, and the display of modernist references after the experiences of postmodernist and deconstructivist architecture. Adorno contested the idea that the wholesale rejection of affirmation was something art could blindly rely on. Against Herbert Marcuse's criticism of the affirmative character of culture, he objected: "Affirmation does not glorify what exists; it opposes death, the telos of all rule, in sympathy with what is."[68] Affirmation pays tribute to the "*faits sociaux*" in which, according to Adorno, all art is rooted due to its partly mimetic nature. Only the other, autonomous half of art critically transcends the status quo.[69]

In Rem Koolhaas' architectural oeuvre, an essential means of such transcendence appears to be some kind of formal fragmentation—manifest at the Kunsthal, internalized at the Seattle Library, subtle at the CCTV Headquarters, confined to the loose, "dangling" ends of its exoskeletal structure. The European flag proposed by AMO in 2001 is another example. Merging the colors of the single nations into a "barcode," the proposal seems to curry favor with the logic of universal commodification, as if to signal the recent rapprochement between Europe and the American and Asian models of capitalism: the multicolored barcode resembles a flag in fragments. In *Content*, Koolhaas and Reinier de Graaf explain: "Instead of suggesting an unwanted homogeneity, Europe should insist on the richness of its persistent diversity […]."[70] The idea was more than a whim. Reproposed in 2005 and 2006, OMA's current website classifies the work on Europe's corporate identity—"The [barcoded] Image of Europe"—as an ongoing project.[71]

Does the Kunsthal inaugurate this new Europe? Koolhaas seems to think so.[72] During a masterclass on November 2, 2017, he explained: "it really is extremely important to understand this building [the Kunsthal] as a manifesto for a new Europe. And in that sense, I really was tangibly and physically inspired, almost, to try to find an architecture, also a new architecture, that would do justice to a new Europe." The internalized street and compactness of the building do indeed anticipate two strategies that were key to OMA's work from the 1990s onwards. But the almost violent emphasis on openness, the self-assured display of fragmentation, the air of improvisation, spontaneity, imperfection, unruliness: all this seems much closer in spirit to the pleasures of a 1980s cross-cultural dystopia than to the rather obliging appearances of OMA's more recent icons. If, however, the Kunsthal does offer a *fin de siècle* image of what Adorno called Right Consciousness, its mimetic critical accuracy and scope—driven both by *dégoût* and a desire for distinction—may have no equal in the recent history of architecture.

67 Roberto Gargiani, *Rem Koolhaas/OMA: The Construction of Merveilles*, Lausanne: EPFL/PPUR, 2008, pp. 309–20.
68 Theodor W. Adorno, *Ästhetische Theorie*, Frankfurt am Main: Suhrkamp, 2000, p. 374. First published in 1970. Published in English as *Aesthetic Theory*, ed. and trans. Robert Hullot-Kentor, Minneapolis: University of Minnesota Press, 1998.
69 Adorno refers to the "dual character" of art to denote its limited autonomy. "The dual character of art: that of autonomy and *fait social* always betrays itself anew in the substantial dependencies and conflicts of both spheres." Ibid., p. 340 (author's translation).
70 Rem Koolhaas and Reinier de Graaf, "€-conography: How to Undo Europe's Iconographic Deficit?" in *Content*, eds. AMOMA/Rem Koolhaas et al., Cologne: Taschen, 2004, p. 383.
71 https://oma.eu/projects/the-image-of-europe (accessed July 9, 2020).
72 Kunsthal Rotterdam, "Masterclass Rem Koolhaas," November 2, 2017. The masterclass was held in the Kunsthal to mark the building's 25th anniversary. https://www.youtube.com/watch?v=CvJBqgGvq9c (accessed July 11, 2020).

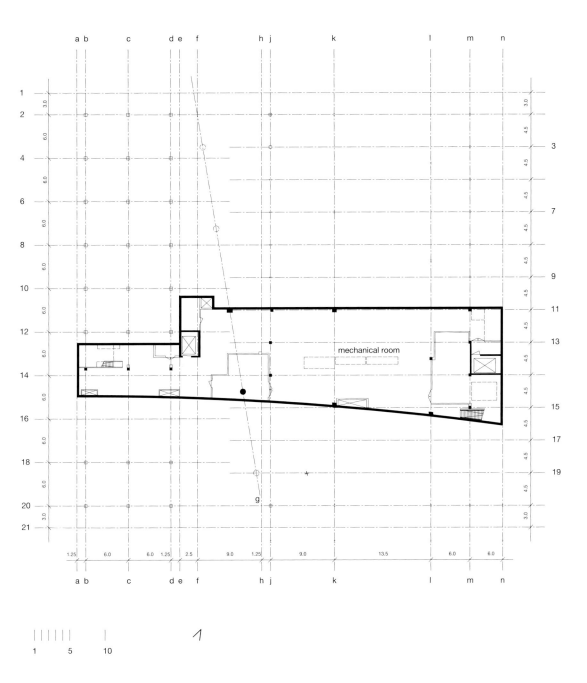

P 9.1 Basement and structural grid.

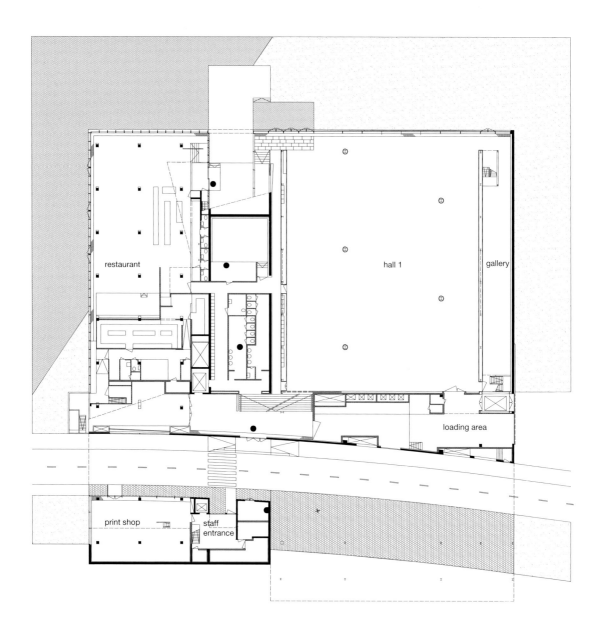

P 9.2   Park level.

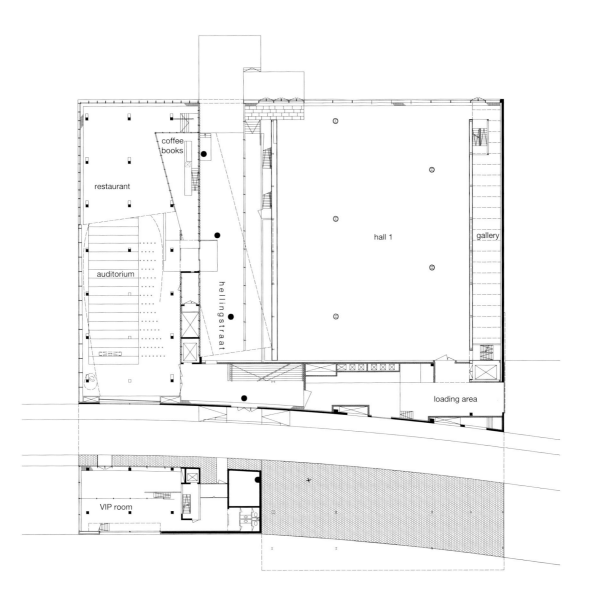

P 9.3   Level of the main entrance.

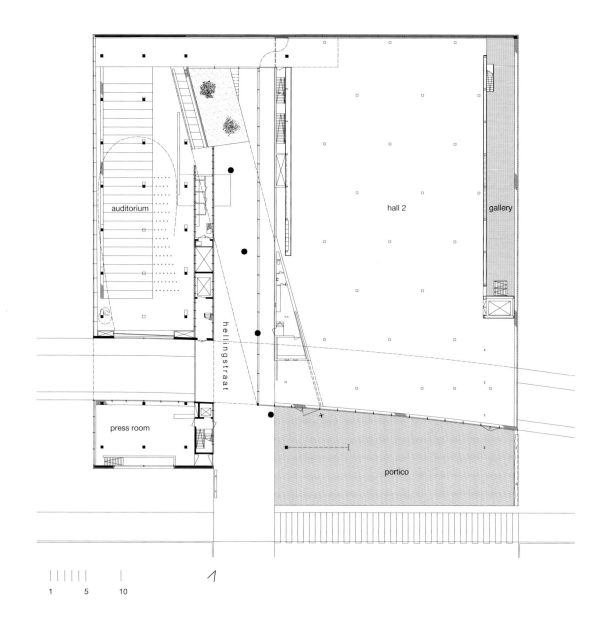

P 9.4 Dike level.

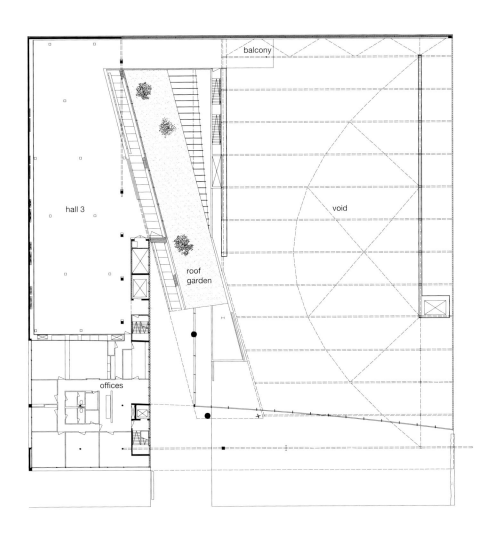

P 9.5   Level of Hall 3.

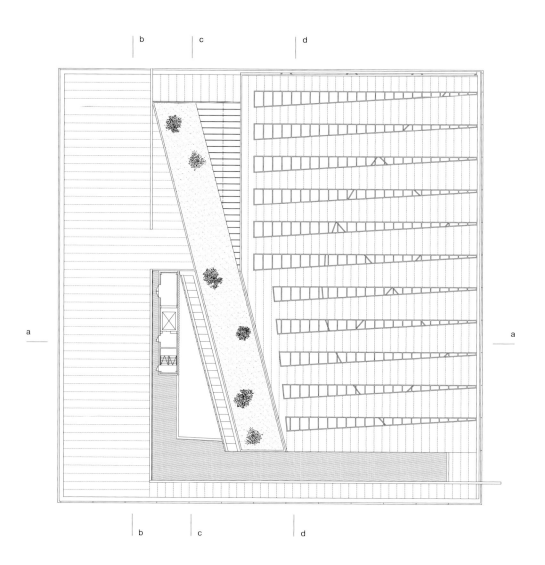

P 9.6   Roof.

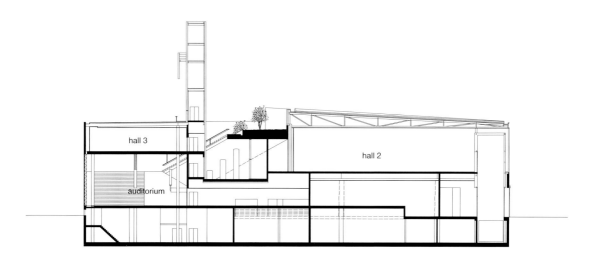

P 9.7   Cross section a.

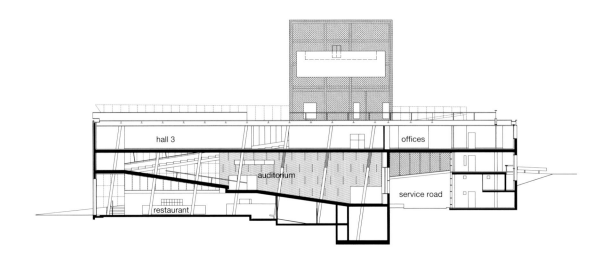

P 9.8   Cross section b.

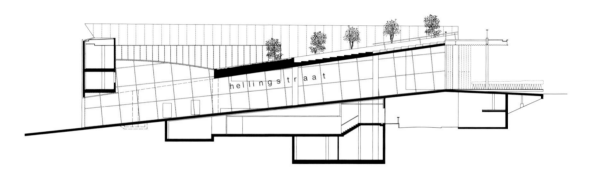

P 9.9 Cross section c.

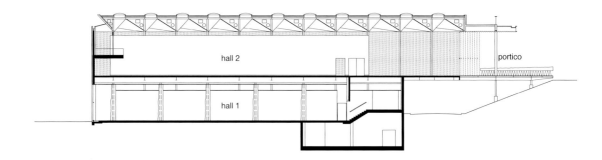

P 9.10   Cross section d.

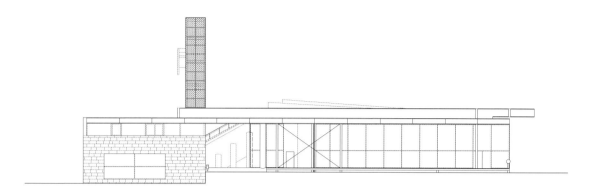

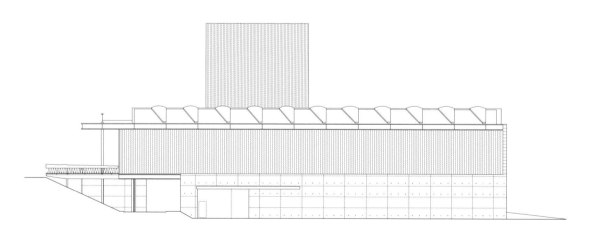

P 9.11 South elevation.
P 9.12 East elevation.

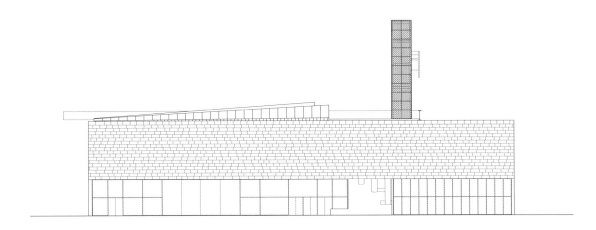

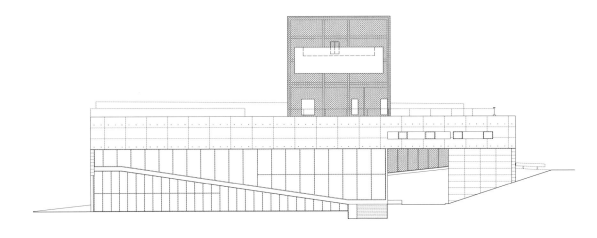

P 9.13　　North elevation.
P 9.14　　West elevation.

Appendix

	1985	1986	1987	1988
Kunsthal, Museumpark, NAi	– Rotterdam's municipality introduces the Inner City Plan ("Binnen-stadplan"), devised for a period of ten years	– Rotterdam's department for urban development ("Stadsontwikkeling Rotterdam") presents a first project for the Museumpark. – Rotterdam's alderman Joop Linthorst proposes creating the first Dutch arts center in Rotterdam	– Commission for the Kunsthal and the Museumpark	– April–October: Kunsthal I – June–October: NAi competition – October: Wim van Krimpen is announced as the Kunsthal's interim director – December: The building commitee adopts the scheme of Kunsthal II
OMA/ Rem Koolhaas: projects	– Police Station (1982-85), Almere	– City Hall, The Hague	– Dance Theater (1981–87), The Hague – Bus Terminal (1985–87), Rotterdam – Ville Nouvelle, Melun-Sénart, masterplan	– IJplein (1981–88), Amsterdam – Patio Houses (1984–88), Rotterdam – Marne-la-Vallée, Eurodisney
Rem Koolhaas: essays, talks	– "La splendeur terrifiante du XXe siècle," "Imaginer le néant," "Eloge du terrain vague," "Architecture: pour qui? Pourqoi?", essays published in L'Architecture d'Aujourd'hui	– "De wereld is rijp voor de architect als visionair," talk given at the ceremony for the Maaskantprijs, a Dutch architectural award		– "16 Years of OMA," essay published in A+U
Exhibitions, symposia, conferences	– Les immatériaux, Centre Pompidou, Paris	– Conference at the University of Illinois, Chicago. Transcripts published under the title Chicago Tapes in 1987	– Opening of the International Building Exhibition (IBA), Berlin	– Symposium Whether Europe, TU Delft – Deconstructivist Architecture, Museum of Modern Art (MoMA), New York
Political events	– Jacques Delors is appointed president of the European Commission (1985–95) – The member states of the EEC sign the Schengen Agreement	– Spain and Portugal join the EEC	– The Single European Act comes into effect	

1989	1990	1991	1992	1993
– Ove Arup devises the layout of the structural system and building services – November–December: Fuminori Hoshino's "Inventory of Problems" introduces substantial revisions and refinements to the Kunsthal project	– April: OMA finalizes the plans for the bidding process and the building application – June: The first pile of the Kunsthal is driven into the ground.	– Detailing and construction of the Kunsthal	– October: Opening of the Kunsthal	– September: Opening of the Museumpark
– Zeebrugge, Sea Terminal – Karlsruhe, Media Center – Paris, National Library – Frankfurt Airport, masterplan – Commission for Euralille (1989–94)	– Agadir, Convention Center	– Villa dall'Ava (1984–91), Paris – Nexus Housing (1988–91), Fukuoka	– Jussieu Libraries, Paris – Commission for the Educatorium (1992–97) in Utrecht	
	– April: "Hoe modern is de Nederlandse architectuur" (How Modern is Dutch Architecture), farewell lecture given at TU Delft – March–June: "OMA—fin de siècle innocente." Essay published in the catalog of the IFA exhibition, *OMA—fin de siècle. OMA à l'IFA*, Paris	– May: "Precarious Entity," talk given at the *Anyone* conference in Santa Monica		
		– *Modernism Without Dogma—A Younger Generation of Architects in the Netherlands*, Dutch exhibition at the Venice Biennale		
– January: George H. W. Bush (1989–93) succeeds Ronald Reagan (1981–89) as the president of the US – November: Fall of the Berlin Wall. The event inspires Francis Fukuyama's *The End of History and the Last Man*, published in 1992	– October: Reunification of Germany – November: The British prime minister Margaret Thatcher (1979–90) resigns	– June: Dissolution of the Warsaw Pact – December: Dissolution of the Soviet Union	– February: The member states of the European Communities sign the Treaty on European Union in Maastricht	– January: The EEC single market comes into effect – November: The Treaty of Maastricht comes into effect

IMAGE CREDITS

FIGURES

1.1: © OMA AMO/2023, ProLitteris, Zurich; Derick Snare; Richard Perlmutter; digital image © 2023, The Museum of Modern Art/Scala, Florence
1.2: © Embassy International Pictures
1.3: Photo: © Dan Grogan
1.4–1.5; 1.7–1.8; 2.10; 3.14; 3.18; 4.17; 5.4–5.7: © OMA AMO/2023, ProLitteris, Zurich; Photo: © Hans Werlemann/Hectic Pictures
1.6: © OMA AMO/2023, ProLitteris, Zurich; Paolo Portoghesi; Photo: © Paolo Portoghesi
2.1: Rotterdam Municipal Archives Collection, NL-RtSA_4001_I-215-15A
2.2: Rotterdam Municipal Archives Collection, NL-RtSA_4001_II-81
2.3–2.5; 7.1–7.2: Courtesy of Collection Het Nieuwe Instituut, Rotterdam
2.6–2.7; 2.9; 2.11–2.12; 2.15–2.16; 3.1–3.7; 3.10–3.13; 4.4–4.11; 4.13–4.16; 4.18; 5.8; 5.12–6.2; 6.4–6.5; 6.12–6.15; 6.17–6.20; 6.22–6.38; 7.3–7.7: © OMA AMO/2023, ProLitteris, Zurich
2.8: © Archiv Kleihues
2.13–2.14: By Yves Brunier © OMA AMO/2023, ProLitteris, Zurich
3.8: © Karl Schwanzer; Photographer unknown
3.9; 4.1–4.3; 4.12; 6.16: © OMA AMO/2023, ProLitteris, Zurich; Photo: Courtesy of Collection Het Nieuwe Instituut, Rotterdam
3.15: © Frank O. Gehry. Getty Research Institute, Los Angeles (2017.M.66), Frank Gehry Papers; Photo: © Tim Street-Porter
3.16: © Zaha Hadid Foundation; Photo: Edward Woodman © 2023, ProLitteris, Zurich
3.17: © 2023 Peter Eisenman; Photo: © Dick Frank Studio, Inc.
3.19: © Coop Himmelb(l)au; Photo: © Gerald Zugmann
4.19: Philippe Gras/Alamy stock photo
4.20: Constant Nieuwenhuys © 2023, ProLitteris, Zurich; Photo: © Victor E. Nieuwenhuys
4.21: Courtesy Associação Cultural Lygia Clark
5.1–5.2: Photo: © Mecanoo
5.3: Photo: © Hans Werlemann
5.9: © Communautés européennes 1985
5.10: AP Photo/Ron Edmonds
5.11: INTERFOTO/Alamy stock photo
6.3: © CP Copro bv
6.6–6.11; 6.21: Reproduced courtesy Arup
7.8: Pablo Picasso © Succession Picasso/2023, ProLitteris, Zurich

PLATES

1.1–1.18: © OMA AMO/2023, ProLitteris, Zurich; Photo: © Marco Cappelletti with DSL Studio
2.1: Rotterdam Municipal Archives Collection, NL-RtSA_4232_IX-3373-01-1
2.2: Rotterdam Municipal Archives Collection, NL-RtSA_4100_2005-5372
2.3: Collection Het Nieuwe Instituut, Rotterdam, OMAR f36 20a
2.4: Collection Het Nieuwe Instituut, Rotterdam, OMAR f36 26a
2.5: Collection Het Nieuwe Instituut, Rotterdam, OMAR f36 34a
2.6: Collection Het Nieuwe Instituut, Rotterdam, OMAR f36 37a
2.7: Collection Het Nieuwe Instituut, Rotterdam, OMAR f36 39a
2.8: Collection Het Nieuwe Instituut, Rotterdam, OMAR f36 42a
3.1–3.6: By Yves Brunier © OMA AMO/2023, ProLitteris, Zurich
4.1–7.14: © OMA AMO/2023, ProLitteris, Zurich
8.1–8.18: © OMA AMO/2023, ProLitteris, Zurich; Photo: © Hans Werlemann/Hectic Pictures
9.1–9.14: © Tibor Pataky

Front cover: © OMA AMO/2023, ProLitteris, Zurich; Photo: © Hans Werlemann/Hectic Pictures
Back cover: © OMA AMO/2023, ProLitteris, Zurich; Photo: © Marco Cappelletti with DSL Studio
Flaps: © OMA AMO/2023, ProLitteris, Zurich

THE AUTHOR

Tibor Pataky is a Zurich-based architect, architectural historian, and fiction author. In the 1990s, he experienced first-hand Rem Koolhaas' towering influence on architecture and the excitement of the newly united Europe while studying architecture at RWTH Aachen and IUAV in Venice. After practicing as an architect with the Swiss architecture studios Giuliani Hönger and Diener & Diener, he taught at ETH Zurich and EPFL Lausanne, where he completed a dissertation at the Laboratory for Architecture, Critique, History, and Theory in 2021. His writings include the novel *Fruchtmann* (2015) about a student of Joseph Beuys as well as various articles on the work of OMA published in *arq, archimaera*, and *werk, bauen + wohnen*.

IMPRINT

Editor, conception:
Tibor Pataky

Copy editing:
Nicola Morris

Proofreading:
Colette Forder

Design:
Bureau Sandra Doeller
(Sandra Doeller, Merle Petsch)

Image processing, printing, and binding:
gugler* Drucksinn, Melk/Donau, Austria

© 2023 Park Books AG, Zurich

© for the texts: Tibor Pataky
© for the images: see image credits

Despite best efforts, we have not been able to identify the holders of copyright and printing rights for all the illustrations. Copyright holders not mentioned in the credits are asked to substantiate their claims, and recompense will be made according to standard practice.

Park Books
Niederdorfstrasse 54
8001 Zurich
Switzerland
www.park-books.com

Park Books is being supported by the Federal Office of Culture with a general subsidy for the years 2021–2024.

All rights reserved; no part of this publication may be reproduced, stored in a retrieval system or transmitted in any form or by any means, electronic, mechanical, photocopying, recording, or otherwise, without the prior written consent of the publisher.

ISBN 978-3-03860-321-4 (print)
ISBN 978-3-03860-331-3 (open access publication)

DOI 10.58893/PA0001
https://doi.org/10.58893/PA0001

This work is licensed under a Creative CommonsAttribution-NonCommericial-NoDerivatives 4.0 International License (CC-BY-NC-ND).

The open access version of this publication was published with the support of the Swiss National Science Foundation.